Classroom
Group Behavior

Mary A. Bany

Division of Education
California State College at Los Angeles

Lois V. Johnson

Division of Education
California State College at Los Angeles

CLASSROOM
GROUP BEHAVIOR

GROUP DYNAMICS IN EDUCATION

The Macmillan Company, New York

Collier-Macmillan Limited, London

Library of Congress catalog card number: 63–20420

The Macmillan Company, New York
Collier-Macmillan Canada, Ltd., Toronto, Ontario

Printed in the United States of America

Preface

RAPID developments have taken place in the last twenty years in understanding, predicting, controlling, and guiding the behavior of persons who are members of small groups. This new area of investigation is contributing to a slow but gradual change in educational theory. Although the individual child and methods of individualized instruction are still major emphases in education, some recognition is being given to the fact that the classroom group setting and the class group interaction have an important influence upon individual learning and behavior. Educators discuss in theoretical terms the importance to the individual of providing a good group climate and they stress the values of group participation in planning and in problem solving. However, few attempts are made to close the gap between educational theory and actual classroom practice.

The focus of attention in teacher education programs for some years has been upon the individual child and how he learns and behaves, and teachers have concentrated upon *the individual and how he relates to the group* and have given little consideration to *the group and its influence upon the individual.* In most instances, training programs have overlooked the importance of developing teacher understanding of class group behavior. Because many teachers do not understand why groups behave as they do or how constructively to handle group behavior problems, they are forced into using power instead of skill as a means of controlling behavior. Since the use of power changes surface behavior only, or creates other and sometimes more difficult problems, teachers may be troubled by recurring classroom behavior problems.

This book was written to bring to teachers a basic understanding of the many dynamic forces that affect the class as a group. It is hoped that increased understanding of the various factors that influence group behavior will enable teachers to prevent many behavior problems. It is also hoped that the book will aid teachers in developing more effective teaching methods and employing more constructive practices when classroom group problems do occur.

In no way is the material presented here intended to minimize the importance of studying the individual child or to convey the idea that caring for individual differences is not an effective and desirable procedure. The thesis is that a study of the class as a group and its influence upon individual behavior will place in the hands of teachers significant insights as to how their effectiveness and productivity as directors of learning can be increased. It is believed that an understanding of group forces will aid teachers in preventing or solving many group behavior problems, and thereby enable them to better care for individual differences in behavior and learning.

From time to time psychologists have indicated important findings about group dynamics that have significance for teaching, but these findings have not been related to actual classroom situations or to actual teaching practices. An attempt is made in this book to define operationally the contributions of group research to education. To make an application of what is known concerning the psychology of groups, actual incidents of classroom group behavior are reported. These descriptions of specific classroom group situations are then analyzed according to what has been discovered concerning groups. It is recognized that it is ambitious for educators to attempt to identify group characteristics and analyze classroom behaviors. However, it is equally difficult for social psychologists to make practical, operational applications to classroom situations.

This book may be used in a number of ways. It may be employed as a basic text in classes designed especially for developing an understanding of classroom group behavior. Since the described behavior situations are accounts of actual incidents that occurred in classrooms, inexperienced teachers are given a realistic picture of the type and range of these problems. Supplemented by lecture, discussion, and observation, students can be given both theoretical and practical knowledge concerning ways such problems may be handled or prevented.

Classes established for experienced teachers who are continuing their professional training may use the book as basic reading. The references following each chapter are primarily reports of research studies. The listed references are purposely extensive to supplement the study of graduate students.

In institutions where separate courses in classroom group behavior are not offered, instructors of various education courses may use the book to supplement basic texts. Since the material relates to teaching in all subject areas of the curriculum, and to a range of grade levels, it is adaptable to many courses, seminars, and practicums in the areas of curriculum and method.

Classroom Group Behavior offers assistance to school districts that wish to establish in-service study groups. Not only can the participants' general understandings be increased, but by making cooperative studies of class groups, valuable information can be obtained and the quality of group living in the school and classroom can be enhanced. More can be discovered concerning the forces involved in the relationships among pupils, as well as the relationship between groups and teachers. Chapter 13 was designed to encourage and to aid such study groups.

Finally, this book offers an opportunity for independent investigation and independent study. Teachers who are no longer taking formal courses, but who are seeking to improve their professional understanding, may find the material helpful. The suggestions for ways to study group behavior contained in Chapter 13 may appeal to those teachers who are continually investigating and experimenting in their classrooms. Such studies by individual teachers, if reported, could make a valuable contribution toward further understanding of classroom groups.

A great debt is owed to the more than 300 teachers who were willing to give their efforts to describe group behaviors that created problems in their classrooms and to the many teachers who tried using participatory techniques with their classes. The majority of these teachers' reports were so clearly written that the only changes made were those to eliminate identifying data.

We are also indebted to Miss Marion Arzt, of the Alhambra, California, City Schools, who gave the first draft of the manuscript a critical reading and who spent many hours helping with the editing.

Los Angeles, California   Mary A. Bany
                                                              Lois V. Johnson

Contents

Part III   *The Teacher and the Group Behavior*   195

    Group Cohesiveness   197
    Interaction & Structure   225
    Transition   262

Part IV   *Techniques for Changing*
    Group Behavior   283

    Group Decision-making   284
    Members of the Learning Group   330
    Index to Classroom and Group   387

		PAGE
Part I	Introduction	*1*
1	Approach and Overview	*3*
2	Group Dynamics in Education	*11*
3	The Nature of Groups	*29*
Part II	Characteristics of Classroom Groups	*49*
4	Group Cohesiveness	*51*
5	Interaction and Structure	*76*
6	Group Norms	*116*
7	Group Goals	*157*

PAGE

Part III   Factors Influencing Group Behavior
in the Classroom 193

8   Group Composition 195
9   Instructional Leadership 218
10   Frustration 252

Part IV   Techniques for Changing
Group Behavior 283

11   Group Decision Techniques 285
12   Methods of Solving Group Problems 330
13   Study of Classroom Groups 363
     Index 403

Illustrations

Figure

1   Diagram of interaction as the center of group functioning
    with related group characteristics and factors *35*
2   Structure of a classroom committee engaged in preparing a
    report—showing roles, functions, and ascribed statuses
    (hierarchy) *82*
3   A standards chart from a primary grade *142*
4   An upper-grade standards chart *142*
5   The appearance and disappearance of group responses to
    frustration *261*
6   Communication pattern showing differential, completeness
    and accessibility of information *383*

7   An interactiongram showing speakers, receivers, and directions of oral speech *384*

8   Group composition: tendencies in groups *393*

Classroom
Group Behavior

Part I   **Introduction**

Chapter 1

Approach and Overview

CLASSROOM group behavior is an important study for teachers, whether they teach younger children in elementary schools or older children in secondary schools. Understanding how classroom groups behave and why they behave as they do is increasingly recognized as part of the teacher's needed professional knowledge. The teacher's ability to apply this knowledge and to develop class groups that are cohesive, have good morale, and work cooperatively toward socially desirable goals is essential for progress toward curricular learning and other educational aims. In some cases, the development of such group feeling must precede as well as accompany the usual school curriculum. Without it, little or nothing can be accomplished.

At times, almost all teachers face situations when the majority of children in the classroom seem bent on talking, moving around, or generally doing a number of things except what they are expected to do.

3

Although teachers plan well, some days are puzzling and frustrating because the class group as a whole reacts with undesirable behavior. When class group members waste time, become quarrelsome, refuse to cooperate, or otherwise behave in ways that impede the teaching-learning process, teachers often do not understand why their groups behave as they do or why the children do not respond in an acceptable manner. Conversely, on days when classes respond willingly and happily to suggestions, teachers seldom can explain why this behavior occurs.

Because most teaching today is done in a group situation and because most teachers, at some time or other, have problems with classroom group management, the aim of this book is to broaden the teacher's understanding of groups and group behavior. The group as it reacts *as a whole* is emphasized. The focus is upon actual group behavior problems that teachers in classrooms face. Consideration is given to group characteristics, factors influencing group behavior, the effect of the group upon individual behavior, and procedures designed to improve or change the behavior of a class. Essentially, a major concern is with increasing the effectiveness and productivity of teachers in all areas of the curriculum by extending their knowledge of groups and group influence.

Two decades of intensive scientific study of small group behavior have revealed many dimensions of groups and group influence that can, if made available to teachers, be usefully applied. For example, a knowledge of properties or conditions that may affect group behavior in an undesirable manner enables teachers to prevent many problems from arising, and such knowledge improves techniques in effecting desirable behavioral changes in groups and individuals. A more comprehensive view of group influence upon individual behavior increases understanding of the learning processes through which children's attitudes and characteristic behavior patterns are modified. In short, increased understanding of factors that underlie the behavior of classroom groups promises a new outlook on some of the more difficult aspects of the teaching job.

A Major Problem of Teaching

When teachers state the nature of their most difficult task, they often say that it is the problem of helping children to develop and accept desirable standards of conduct. Generally they call this part of their job the "development of discipline," or "maintaining order," or "establishing classroom control." Preservice teachers worry most about this aspect of teaching, and many experienced teachers say this is the most difficult and often the most frustrating part of the teaching job. When discussing teaching performance, school administrators are apt to mention first the degree of success the teachers have attained either in establishing order or in developing procedures that contribute to desirable classroom behavior.

Results of Investigations

Studies concerned with determining what teachers believe is their most difficult task have generally found that teachers say it is maintaining class order or class control. A study made in Ohio found that beginning teachers rated the maintaining of order or discipline as their primary problem. The same study found that school administrators considered the keeping of discipline to be the greatest problem of teachers.[1]

An extensive study of pupil behavior involving 10,000 classroom teachers found, among other things, that confusion resulting from the misbehavior of children made effective teaching very difficult in some schools. One facet of the study showed that approximately 60 per cent of the teachers indicated that the overall behavior of their class groups was difficult to handle on occasion. About one out of every 100 teachers said his class group members frequently misbehaved and were very difficult to handle.[2]

An investigation into teacher reactions to problem behavior found that problem behavior in classrooms was a cause for teachers leaving the profession. The study showed, also, that beginning teachers had the most difficulty with handling the behavior of class groups. The responding teachers indicated that they believed they were not getting enough help in understanding and coping with difficult classroom behavior. That they desired additional help was shown by the fact that a large number asked specifically for in-service training in the area of understanding and handling behavior problems.[3]

The problem of helping children acquire behavior patterns that contribute to the maintenance of order in the classroom is not new to teachers, as histories of education testify. The difficulty of "developing

[1] W. R. Flesher, "The Beginning Teacher," *Educational Research Bulletin*, 24:12–18, January 1954.

[2] National Education Research Division, "Teacher Opinion on Pupil Behavior," *Research Bulletin No. 2*, 34:51–107, April 1956.

[3] Merrill T. Eaton, Garret Weathers, and Beeman N. Phillips, "Some Reactions of Classroom Teachers to Problem Behavior in School," *Educational Administration and Supervision*, 43:129–139, March 1957.

discipline" or "keeping discipline" has existed ever since groups of children were organized for instructional purposes. For instance, Horace Mann told how discipline was kept in his time. He described a school of about 250 students where an average of 65 floggings were made each day.[4] As recently as 1928 an article appeared that classified school offenses into 17 types and recommended specific punishments for each type. These punishments included such things as assignment of extra work, public acknowledgment of fault, remarks to put offender in place, and other punishments.[5]

Present Status of "Discipline" in the Classroom

Newer points of view have theoretically outmoded these earlier procedures as disciplinary measures, even though the older procedures are still practiced in some places. The idea of "keeping discipline" has changed to "development of self-discipline." Yet all the while the need for developing self-discipline is talked about, little concrete help in accomplishing this is given teachers. Articles appearing in professional journals continue to discuss effective disciplinary practices. A recent publication devoted to ways of developing constructive control practices gives some suggestions for securing classroom control. Some of the suggestions made are: be alert and active; exhibit enthusiasm; be courteous; give clear, concise directions; make good use of voice tone to control a class; use common sense; and appear to be happy.[6]

An understanding of groups, their nature and characteristics, provides teachers with a more encompassing and rational basis from which to guide and direct their classes.

Clarification of the Problem

There is much confusion over the part of the teaching job called by such terms as *class control, class management, class order,* and *class discipline.* A variety of concepts is attached to these terms. The word "discipline" is an example of how the concept may vary and how its meaning depends on the user's basic orientation toward children and the teaching process.

[4] Pickens E. Harris, *Changing Conceptions of School Discipline,* New York: The Macmillan Company, 1928.

[5] H. W. James, "Punishments Recommended for School Offenses," *Elementary School Journal,* 29:129–131, October 1928.

[6] Irwin O. Addicott, *Constructive Classroom Control,* San Francisco: Howard Chandler, 1958, pp. 18–43.

"Discipline" may apply to the degree of order established in the class, or it may apply to the procedures used to achieve a certain order. It is often used in reference to individuals rather than to class groups as a whole. Since the word often carries with it a connotation of punishment, it is considered here to be an unsuitable and indefinite way of describing the general overall behavior of a class group. The term is even more ambiguous when applied to the practices by which desirable classroom behavior is attained.

The terms *class management, class order,* and *class control* may be misinterpreted in the same way as the word "discipline." These terms may be used to mean the degree of order, the kind of order or atmosphere, or the methods by which certain degrees of order are achieved. To increase the confusion, remarks such as "This teacher maintains good order," raise the question of the meaning of "good order." In what way does a class group behave so that it may be said, "The order in this room is good"?

Many misunderstandings arise because of the variety of concepts associated with the above-mentioned terms. What is involved, but not sufficiently appreciated, is the process of dealing with the class as a group. The problems that teachers have labeled class management, class order, and class control are, for the most part, problems of *classroom group behavior.*

Plan of the Book

The following chapters outline a set of interrelated concepts that develop or point out the characteristics or properties of groups. The forces that influence group behavior are discussed, and actual incidents of class group behavior problems are described to make the concepts more meaningful. Emphasis is placed not only upon the development of an understanding of group behavior, but upon ways this behavior may be guided or changed. In the last section, suggestions are made for developing techniques of group study.

Research studies in the area of group dynamics are devoted to the discernment and discovery of lawful relationships between the properties or characteristics and the forces or conditions that influence the group as a whole, and the process by which individual behavior in a group is modified by the group experience. Primarily, studies relating to cause and effect relationships that explain the behavior of groups similar to classroom groups are considered in this book.

Using examples drawn from teachers' classroom experiences, an effort is made to show that certain problems can take on new meanings in the light of findings from group research studies. This approach attempts to make the knowledge both practical and functional, but it is undertaken with recognition that not all that is presented here has been verified by experiments in school situations. To gain most from this presentation, teachers need to give it honest and disciplined thinking and they should attempt to make for themselves some studies of their own classroom groups. The material presented should be studied with the idea in mind that it is probably only teachers themselves who can discover many of the psychological principles that underlie the group behavior of children. This book is not about discipline, but it does attempt to develop some basic concepts about groups to enable teachers to deal with some of the familiar problems of classroom teaching without resorting to "disciplining" individuals or to threatening class groups. It is not primarily concerned with an analysis of what is meant by a "good" class or "good" behavior, but it is concerned with developing an understanding of why some groups are considered to be "good" and why some are so difficult to handle. It does attempt to show positive leadership practices that are effective in teaching children to respect others and to develop common norms of acceptable behavior. It does not advocate the imposition of one uniform set of attitudes, but it does attempt to show how desired attitudes may be developed.

A focus of the book is upon classroom group behavior problems and upon ways of preventing problems from occurring or guiding these problems when they do occur. The idea underlying this presentation is that children should be taught by experience to reason and to decide themselves what is right and what is acceptable behavior. Also underlying this presentation is the thought that children should be taught to defend what they believe is right, but to do so according to acceptable standards of behavior. In other words, class groups are not denied the right to challenge rules set for them, but instead are shown how they may challenge what they do not like in ways that are provided by a society of free people.

A greater understanding of group behavior can increase the likelihood that teachers will be more able to make life better, both now and in the future, for the children in their classes, and obtain for themselves a greater personal satisfaction from the hours they spend teaching.

Questions for Study and Discussion

1. Write your beliefs about the importance of the individual learner and the group in the public schools. Be prepared to explain or defend your position if questioned.

2. What constitutes good citizenship in school situations? Is it conforming to certain standards of behavior expected by the teacher? Is it primarily compliance to explicit or implicit rules? Is it conforming to behavior patterns expected by parents and the community?

3. Is it possible to teach children to conform to certain patterns of behavior and at the same time to develop individuality and independence? Is freedom of action necessary for the development of independent individuals?

4. Describe the kind of classroom behavior whose promotion is the specific responsibility of the school. What position must be taken by the school if the behavior learned at home or in the neighborhood is incompatible with the behavior that the school attempts to develop?

5. Is the teacher ever justified in imposing certain value premises upon children? Specify some attitudes or values, if any, that all teachers should attempt to develop with elementary children. What may be done if these attitudes or values are in conflict with those instilled in the home? Is the problem the same in the elementary and secondary schools?

Suggestions for Further Reading

Ambrose, Edna and Alice Miel. *Children's Social Learning: Implications of Research and Expert Study*. Washington, D.C.: Association for Supervision and Curriculum Development, National Education Association, 1958.

Battrick, Delmer H. "A Principal Looks at Discipline," *National Education Journal,* 47:375–376, September 1958.

Bradford, Leland P. "Developing Potentialities through Class Groups," *Teachers' College Record,* 61:443–450, May 1960.

Jenkins, David. "Interdependence in the Classroom," *Journal of Educational Research,* 45:137–144, October 1951.

Jennings, Helen Hall. "Using Children's Social Relations for Learning," *Journal of Educational Sociology,* 21:543–552, May 1948.

Lindgren, Henry C. "The Effect of the Group on the Behavior of the Individual," *Education,* 73:383–387, February 1953.

Maas, Henry S. "Applying Group Therapy to Classroom Practice," *Mental Hygiene,* 35:250–259, April 1951.

Martin, William E. and Celia Burns Stendler. *Child Behavior and Development.* New York: Harcourt, 1959, Pt. II.

Massoglia, Elinor Tripato. "How Children Learn and Live Together," *NEA Journal,* 51:61–62, March 1962.

Ojemann, Ralph H. "We Can Teach Human Relations," *Journal of Health, Physical Education, Recreation,* 26:20–21, 36, February 1955.

Passow, A. Harry and Gordon N. Mackenzie. "Research in Group Behavior Shows Need for New Teaching Skills," *The Nation's Schools,* 49:71–73, April 1953.

Willcockson, May. "Why Children Do or Do Not Accept Responsibility," *Social Education*, 24:25–27, 40, January 1960.

Young, Kimball. *Social Psychology*. New York: Appleton-Century, 1956.

Zander, Alvin. "Group Membership and Individual Security," *Human Relations*, 11:99–111, 1958.

Zeleny, Leslie D. "Experimental Appraisal of a Group Learning Plan," *Journal of Educational Research*, 34:37–42, 1940.

Chapter 2 # Group Dynamics in Education

KNOWING that teachers have been plagued for years by problems of classroom behavior, it is difficult to understand why educators have been so slow to apply significant findings from group research to classroom practice. A misunderstanding seems to exist among educators concerning the nature of group dynamics and what it seeks to achieve. This chapter attempts to clarify the relationship of this field of study to education, and to offer some explanations of why pertinent findings from group research have not been usefully applied to teaching methodology. Various emphases and interpretations given to group dynamics in education are examined. Because questions are asked and criticisms are made whenever group dynamics is mentioned in relation to education, some of these questions and criticisms are discussed in the final section of the chapter.

11

Historical Development of Group Dynamics in Education

Two pioneer books of the early 1940's—L. Thomas Hopkins's *Interaction: The Democratic Process*[1] and Baxter's and Cassidy's *Group Experience: The Democratic Way*[2]—focused directly upon the class group and its intraaction in the classroom. They were followed by a number of similar works and general articles in professional education journals.

During the late forties and fifties the importance to educators of viewing the class as a group was pressed with renewed vigor. Bradford, Benne, and Lippitt[3] called attention to the fact that a study of group dynamics could open the door to a greater understanding of the many complex forces operating in groups, and they pointed out that such study could bring about a greater understanding of the many problems of group behavior occurring in classroom situations. Trow and associates[4] presented a number of conclusions derived from research in group dynamics, conclusions that had relevance and held promise for improving teaching practice. They carefully synthesized certain findings in an effort to show their implications for teaching practice. For example, they stated that the conduct and beliefs of pupils were regulated to a large extent by the small cohesive groups within the classroom, and that these groups demanded that their members conform to certain group standards. The more cohesive the group, the more power it had over individual members. About the same time, the Association for Supervision and Curriculum Development[5] devoted a section of its yearbook to defining groups in the classroom and to discussion of the group process. The following year, Ruth Cunningham and associates published their action-research study, *Understanding Group Behavior of Boys and Girls*,[6] which directed the attention of teachers and educators toward

[1] L. Thomas Hopkins, *Interaction: The Democratic Process*, Boston: D. C. Heath & Company, 1941.

[2] Bernice Baxter and Rosalind Cassidy, *Group Experience: The Democratic Way*, New York: Harper & Brothers, 1943.

[3] Leland P. Bradford and others, "Promise of Group Dynamics for Education," *N.E.A. Journal*, 37:350–352, September 1948.

[4] William Clark Trow, Alvin E. Zander, William C. Morse, and David H. Jenkins, "Psychology of Group Behavior: The Class as a Group," *The Journal of Educational Psychology*, 41:322–338, 1950.

[5] Association for Supervision and Curriculum Development, *Fostering Mental Health in Our Schools*, Washington, D.C.: National Education Association, 1950.

[6] Ruth Cunningham and associates, *Understanding Group Behavior of Boys and Girls*, New York: Bureau of Publications, Teachers College, Columbia University, 1951.

viewing the class as a group. However, it did not make the necessary applications of group psychological theory to specific classroom situations,
and therefore little change in either teacher training practices or teaching methodology resulted from the study.

In the early fifties, Symonds [7] called attention of educators to there
having been an inadequate discussion of classroom relationships up to
that time, and he said that what had been written was of a very general
nature and had failed to elaborate any of the psychological principles
involved. He stated that the influence of the group on the development
of the individual and the consequent reactions had not been properly
emphasized or demonstrated. He asserted that the individual had suffered because of the tendency to ignore the influence of group dynamics.
His article introduced a special issue of the Journal of Educational Research, which was devoted to the dynamics of classroom groups.

Passow and Mackenzie [8] reviewed important group-research findings
that had significance for teaching methods at all levels. They commented
that some of the classroom difficulties, such as discipline problems, failure
in well-planned projects, and resistance of the class group to change,
could stem from a misunderstanding of the group processes in the classroom. The authors summarized by stating that children were taught in
groups, and those concerned with teaching methods needed to recognize
this fact.

Recent Emphases in Educational Literature

The advent of Sputnik turned educators' efforts toward speeding up
the educational process and toward improving teaching practices. In the
face of all the controversy about education and what should be taught
and how it should be taught, the National Society for the Study of Education chose to present a discussion of the dynamics of instructional
groups in Part II of its Fifty-Ninth Yearbook.[9] The yearbook committee
attempted to provide an exposition of the socio-psychological knowledge
of human groups that has significance for the operation of classroom
groups. The committee also attempted to develop the connections between this knowledge and some of the problems that face teachers in
their instructional practices. This focus upon group psychology once

[7] Percival M. Symonds, "Introduction to the Special Issue on Classroom Dynamics,"
Journal of Educational Research, 45:81–87, October 1951.

[8] A. Harry Passow and Gordon N. Mackenzie, "Research in Group Behavior,"
Nation's Schools, 49:71–73, April 1952.

[9] National Society for the Study of Education, "The Dynamics of Instructional
Groups," *The Fifty-Ninth Yearbook, Part II*, distributed by the University of Chicago
Press, Chicago, 1960.

again turned educators toward the consideration of classes as groups and what this implies for teaching practice.

Although a large number of group behavior studies were conducted during the period from 1953–1959, not much effort was made to apply the findings to school classroom groups until the N. S. S. E. Yearbook called attention to the group forces operating in classrooms. A recent copy of *The Review of Educational Research* [10] summarized a number of group studies that were important to education. Bradford [11] reviewed the group forces that affect learning and concluded that forces resulting from class group acceptance of the common task of encouraging learning for all members can be as influential in increasing individual member learning as such group forces are in improving individual production in industry.

Existing Educational Practice

The slow progress of education in translating new psychological knowledge into educational practice has been influenced by the following factors:

1. The tendency in educational practice to emphasize the individual and to individualize teaching methods.
2. The stress placed by group-minded educators upon the philosophy guiding the use of group techniques with little attention paid to the psychological principles underlying groups.
3. The use of imprecise and vague terms in methods texts, which hinders concept development relating to groups and their behavior.
4. The philosophical issues raised and the criticisms directed toward the use of group techniques in education.
5. The lack of a precise exposition of relevant psychological knowledge of groups and how such knowledge relates to actual classroom methodology.

This section of Chapter 2 discusses each of these five factors in more detail in an effort to clarify the foggy situation that now surrounds group dynamics and education.

Emphasis upon the Individual

From the time of Wickman's study of behavior problems of children,

[10] American Educational Research Association, "Human Relations in Education," *Review of Educational Research,* **XXIX,** No. 4, October 19, 1959.

[11] Leland P. Bradford, "Developing Potentialities Through Class Groups," *Teachers College Record,* **61:**443–450, May 1960.

published in 1928,[12] teacher education programs have devoted considerable time to developing an understanding of individual child behavior. Although this early study indicated that teachers lacked sufficient understanding of child behavior to recognize serious behavior problems, more recent studies indicate that teachers' attitudes, knowledge, and beliefs in this area have grown considerably. Stouffer [13] repeated Wickman's study to ascertain whether the passage of 25 years had been accompanied by any measurable change, and his study indicated improvement in teachers' recognition, understanding, and practice when faced with problems of individual child behavior. Another study, published in 1953,[14] also indicated that teachers' attitudes and knowledge concerning the personality and emotional adjustment of the individual child had changed over the years. This increased understanding of teachers in relation to child behavior was attributed to changes in teacher training programs, which over the years have increasingly given more and more attention to the topic of how the child grows, how his personality traits are developed, and what may be done when emotional or other difficulties interfere with his development.

Stendler [15] found that when teachers were asked what they considered to be the best way to handle certain problems of individual child behavior, the teachers for the most part, recognized and advocated constructive measures for dealing with the child. For the child who never finishes work on time, who cheats, who talks back to the teacher, who loses his temper when he does not get his way, the teachers favored such procedures as adjusting work, praising or encouraging, or studying the child to find causes for the behavior.

CHILD-CENTERED APPROACH TO GROUPS. The evidence indicates that teachers have increased their understanding of the individual over the past 30 years because of the emphasis given to individual learning and individual behavior in the training of teachers; however, modern educational theory has neither denied nor ignored the importance of the group in the learning situation. In recent years more and more attention has been given to the importance of individuals' learning to participate effectively in groups. However, educational methodology, for the most

[12] E. K. Wickman, *Children's Behavior and Teachers' Attitudes,* New York, The Commonwealth Fund, 1928.

[13] George A. W. Stouffer, Jr., "Behavior Problems of Children as Viewed by Teachers and Mental Hygienists," *Mental Hygiene,* 36:271–285, April 1952.

[14] Manfred Schrupp and Clayton M. Gjerde, "Teacher Growth in Attitudes Toward Behavior Problems of Children," *The Journal of Educational Psychology,* 44:203–214, April 1953.

[15] Celia Burns Stendler, "How Well Do Elementary School Teachers Understand Child Behavior?" *The Journal of Educational Psychology,* 40:289–498, December 1949.

part, is approached from a child-oriented point of view. The importance of the group is recognized, but the emphasis is upon individual development and ways the individual may be helped to relate positively to the group.

GROUP-ORIENTED APPROACH. Although some educators, and particularly elementary school educators, expound the values of employing group processes in certain instances, by far the majority of educators are child-oriented in their approach to methods of teaching. The proponents of group-oriented classrooms espouse group-centered techniques in classroom instruction, and stress the inseparability of the individual and the group. They believe that individuality and originality in individuals are developed through group participation. They place great emphasis upon individuals working together, and they particularly stress what can be achieved by having individuals working collectively upon problems.

A major goal of group-centered educators is the production of democratic citizens who can not only effectively participate in collective action, but also initiate the collective action necessary for the perpetuation of a democratic society. Because of their adherence to this value premise, great stress is placed upon collective group action. Both child-oriented and group-oriented educators approach teaching practice with the objective of educating individuals for effective living in a society of free men. Both stress the importance of the individual. Both emphasize the necessity for individuals to learn group process skills, and both strongly advocate the use of democratic teaching procedures. The differences, when analyzed in relation to methods of instruction, are found in the kind of instructional techniques advocated. Child-oriented educators propose practices designed to provide for individual differences, and they hope to develop each child to his maximum potential. Group-oriented educators propose practices designed to involve the whole class group. They suggest such techniques as socialized recitation and collective problem-solving.

DIFFERENCES IN VIEWPOINT. All true educators hold to the democratic ethic that is the central concern of group-centered educators, but all do not agree upon how democratic concepts are developed.

On the one hand, child-centered exponents have injected group process techniques into their practices, and claim this process develops social values important to individuals living in a democracy. These educators hold to the ideology of group-centered educators, but they emphasize the psychology of individual learning and do not stress the psychology of groups and the ways groups influence individuals. Group-centered educators, on the other hand, often exaggerate group techniques for learning out of proportion to their known value. They inflate the importance of collective action and fail to set limits upon when and where collective action by groups is pertinent.

Both individual-oriented educators and group-oriented educators stress the importance of developing effective group members to the extent that a false belief is often held by teachers regarding what is appropriate behavior for a "good" group member. Many teachers reveal by their statements that they believe a good group member must agree and conform to what appears to be accepted by the majority. Either blind conformity is expected or outward agreement is demanded. For an individual to take an opposite stand from the group, creative though this stand may be, is to brand this individual as a "poor" group member. A belief is held by some that a good group member tries at all times to agree and reach a concensus, for a good group participant does not obstruct the smooth flow of group processes or place barriers in the path of group progress even though he is firmly convinced the group is wrong.

It must be made clear at this point that no criticism is directed toward the value premise of educating children for living in a democracy. Rather, any stated or implied criticism is directed toward the confusion concerning ways that desired educational objectives may be achieved.

Vague and Imprecise Use of Terminology

What do educators mean when they use terms such as *group dynamics, group processes,* and *group relations?* Such phrases are often the topics for discussion in textbooks and lectures, but unfortunately the meanings attached to them are frequently imprecise. If an understanding of group behavior is to be developed, it is imperative to distinguish among things that are quite different. Also, clarity in communication is enhanced when terms are limited to the most explicit meanings possible.

GROUP DYNAMICS. The student of group dynamics is concerned with investigating the formation of and changes in the structures and functions of groups, and with discovering and formulating the principles that underlie the behavior of groups. The study of group dynamics attempts to explain the changes that occur within groups as results of forces or conditions that influence groups as a whole. It is also concerned with investigating the processes by which individual behavior is modified by group experience, and it attempts to make clear why certain things happen in groups, why groups behave as they do, and why members of groups react as they do. It endeavors to show what changes occur in groups over periods of time when numbers of persons interact in group situations.

Some of the distinguishing characteristics of group dynamics as a branch of knowledge have been identified by Cartwright and Zander.[16] One characteristic is a basic reliance on careful observation, quantification, measurement, and experimentation; another is that of constructing theories. Group dynamics not only describes group properties and the events associated with groups, it is concerned with how the observed phenomena are dependent on other phenomena or it seeks to discover principles regarding what conditions produce what effects. It is concerned with all of the disciplines in social science, and with improving functioning of groups of every kind by providing a firm knowledge of the laws governing group life.

Group dynamics has been described by Sargent and Williamson [17] as a movement that has developed out of Gestalt psychology and that stresses the social-psychological forces within the group. In education, the term is frequently used to describe a movement devoted to developing democratic ideals and to safeguarding the democratic way of life.

In education, the term often includes the democratic ideology as well as ways groups can be organized and managed in order to achieve certain objectives. Used in this sense, the term not only espouses a philosophy based on the democratic ideal, it covers the gains that can be obtained, both for society and the individual, through cooperative activities in groups. This broad use of the term does not limit its meaning to a field or inquiry dedicated to advancing knowledge about group life, but rather it refers to a set of value premises, a set of educational objectives, and a set of ways groups may be managed in order to achieve these objectives.

Another usage of the term in education refers to all the various techniques used by the group in problem-solving situations. These include such devices as buzz sessions, role-playing, group observation, and the like. Sometimes the term refers to the kind of leadership practices employed in helping groups improve their processes.

DYNAMIC GROUP. The term *dynamic group* refers to the process of restructuring—the adjusting and readjusting of members to one another. Webster's dictionary defines dynamics as " (1) the branch of mechanics treating of the motion of bodies and the action of forces in producing or changing their motion; (2) the moving, moral as well as physical, forces of any kind, or the laws relating to them." Thus, the interrelated parts of a group are never static or rigid, but rather they are constantly

---

[16] Dorwin Cartwright and Alvin Zander, *Group Dynamics: Research and Theory*, Evanston, Ill.: Row, Peterson and Company, 1960, pp. 5–9.

[17] S. Stansfield Sargent and Robert C. Williamson, *Social Psychology*, New York: The Ronald Press Company, 1958, pp. 541–557.

in motion or in the process of some change. A group, then, is dynamic because forces or conditions continually influence the group as a whole and create changes within the group.

Bonner [18] explains the dynamic character of the group as a condition that exists because members are continually changing their relationships with reference to one another. The changes occur because interacting individuals are in a state of tension and seek to resolve their tensions and return to equilibrium. Changes also occur because of changes in membership, internal and external pressures for change, and because the group proceeds through various levels of organization.

GROUP PROCESSES. The term *group processes* is frequently used interchangeably with the term *group dynamics*. When used in this manner, the term refers to the changes that take place in a group over a period of time, or it may refer to the use of the group to achieve desired democratic behaviors or understandings. A more precise, exact use of the term limits the meaning to the steps or methods followed by the group when it is engaged in exploring, investigating, and planning in problem-solving situations. This meaning includes not only the procedural devices used and the discussion techniques employed, but includes as well a consideration of the roles played by members and the practices used by leaders.

Education has placed a great emphasis upon the procedures followed in group planning, and upon the roles played by members. Particular stress has been given to how the individual members in the group may be helped to become "good" group members, and the skills that must be acquired in order to work well in a group situation. The efforts of education have been mainly focused upon developing an understanding of group processes that lead to group problem-solving and group consensus.

At times, this concern for developing skill in working in group situations has been emphasized to the extent that concern for the process has taken precedence over consideration of the particular problem on which a group has been working. Many times there has been a failure to recognize that groups do not function well on problems that are not truly of concern to the group as a whole. In methods-of-education classes, for example, students are sometimes grouped for the purpose of developing a unit. Such a problem may be a true group problem to a number of teachers working in a school system who have need for such a unit. To students in college classes, however, such a problem is more likely to be one of concern only to individuals. There are many reasons why this is true. College students in class situations are motivated by individual goals. The grading system creates competition among members. There

[18] Hubert Bonner, *Group Dynamics, Principles and Applications,* New York: The Ronald Press Company, 1959, pp. 4–6.

is no immediate reward or need for the assigned group to develop a unit except to satisfy the course requirements. In other words, there is no true group need and no true group problem.

GROUP RELATIONS. The term *group relations* refers to the manner in which individuals in the group react or relate to one another—whether members are attracted to or repelled by one another. In education, the term is often used to refer to an ideal situation. Group relations means, in this sense, "good" group relations. Members perceive the needs of other members. They have consideration for these needs, and they have skill in expressing their understanding. In other words, group relations is often used to mean a harmonious group situation where members interact constructively, where personal development is furthered, and where the group as a whole has very little difficulty in moving toward its goals.

Controversies and Criticisms

The previous section suggested that education focuses its attention on group processes and neglects the problems, with the result that an artificial kind of group interaction occurs. It was suggested too that the aim of the artificial group situations was to secure consensus. Students who do not concur with the group majority are sometimes labeled "poor" group members. Discussed also was the practice in education of inadequately defining terminology in this field.

Both educators and laymen have voiced similar criticisms. When these criticisms are aimed directly at something called group dynamics, as they often have been, then the situation becomes cloudy, for what do the critics mean by group dynamics? Usually it is only some particular aspect of groups that is placed under fire. An article written by Whyte in 1952 [19] criticizes what he calls social engineering. The discussion really centers around a philosophy underlying group dynamics, which the author sees as an "advocacy of conformity made scientific." He derides the overriding importance given to being a "good" or expert group member, and cites evidences gathered from college graduates to prove his point. He believes there is a worship of group harmony and group integration and that this smothers the individual and makes for planned mediocrity. Whyte does not criticize the efforts made by social psychologists and others to learn more about group behavior, nor does he deny the need for improved human relations, but rather he strikes out at the applications made of this new science in colleges and other places that

[19] William H. Whyte, Jr., "The Social Engineers," *Fortune*, 45:88–91, 108, January 1952.

turn out individuals who passively conform to "groupthink." However, Whyte does not criticize group dynamics as such. In fact, he states there is need for more understanding of social relationships, and he criticizes the overemphasis of a value premise that stresses, he believes, conformity of individuals.

There are others who have voiced skepticism about group dynamics. Some state that the basic assumptions underlying the use of group dynamics are open to serious challenge.[20]

The emphasis given to group processes in the public schools is ridiculed in another instance.[21] The author states that friendly mental midgets are created by an overemphasis upon the group process. This stress in schools upon creating a warm, friendly group causes individuals to sacrifice self-reliance for security. The class group becomes a refuge for intellectual softies, for in it they find shelter and they develop no initiative or individuality.

Educators themselves have issued warnings relating to the use of groups in school situations. Goodlad,[22] in a discussion of issues in education, warns that he believes the decision-making process is frequently conducted in a spirit of compromise instead of in a climate of vigorous intellectual inquiry, and that group processes must permit movement away from an atmosphere of acceptance. Real differences must be brought to the fore and examined.

Only a few of the criticisms that have been made of group dynamics in education are mentioned. However, such criticisms may contribute to the fact that educators have been slow to incorporate significant findings from group research into teaching practice. As a whole, they have been loathe to defend group dynamics unless it is cloaked by the democratic ethic. It may be that educators have ignored some of the psychological findings from group research because further emphasis upon groups might lead to additional criticism of educational theories and practices.

Lack of a Clear Exposition of Group Psychological Knowledge

Although a number of educational psychologists have analyzed group studies in a search for findings that have implications for teaching method,

[20] Robert Gray Gunderson, "Group Dynamics, A Symposium: Dangers in Group Dynamics," *Religious Education*, 46:344, November–December, 1951.

[21] John B. Barnes, "Do You Hide Behind Group Process," *School Executive*, 77:42–44, July 1958.

[22] John I. Goodlad, "Criticism, Skepticism, and Controversy," *Educational Leadership*, 14:398–399, April 1957.

a clear exposition of the psychology of class group behavior has not been available. The principal reason for this lack may be that there has been very little research conducted in classroom situations, and some doubt may exist about whether the results from studies of groups other than those in classroom situations are applicable.

Another reason for the lack of a clear description of group behavior is the extensiveness of the research and the fact that different investigators have concentrated their studies on numerous kinds of groups and on a great array of problems. Consequently, attempts to organize the results of studies are exceedingly difficult. The task becomes more complicated because the studies do not always supplement one another, and because all group aspects are interrelated. It is difficult to discuss cohesiveness without first having an understanding of how group norms operate. Interaction is hard to explain to someone who has no knowledge of cohesiveness. A point of beginning in group dynamics is difficult to establish.

Then, too, there is the question of when is a group a group in the general sense. Do certain findings apply to the total class groups, or only to the small subgroup structures?

Finally, the researchers in group dynamics, in summarizing their findings, have employed their own individual terminologies in many instances. The disparities in use of terms have made understanding especially difficult for those outside the field. Only recently has there been any standardization of terms. This semantic problem has placed a barrier before persons outside the field who wish to make applications of the findings from research to specific group situations.

Group Dynamics and Teaching Practice

Change is demanded of education today. The world situation has brought about a need for change in purpose, in concepts, and in teaching methods. To meet the critical needs of our society and to aid the classroom teacher who is under great pressure to reach increasingly higher standards, persons involved in teacher training must explore every possibility to help teachers improve their teaching practices. The place to start is at the point where teachers say they feel the least secure. This is the area of classroom control or class "discipline."

Increasing Teaching Effectiveness

If teaching practice is to be improved and if teachers are to be given the help they need, teacher-training institutions and in-service education programs must move forward and offer aid in areas where teachers say they need assistance. If teachers know how to direct group forces so they work *for* learning instead of *against* it, and if teachers are able to direct group forces so that few problems of group behavior or "discipline" occur, then the teaching–learning process can be vitalized. The class group can be a support to individual learning when it can develop appropriate standards of behavior that are conducive to learning. Such a group can create for itself that abstract condition known for so long a time as "the climate for learning." Learning in all areas cannot help but be facilitated if incidents that interrupt the learning process occur infrequently.

Ethical Problems

If teachers can be taught techniques for setting up conditions in their classrooms that will permit them to use other techniques for predicting, controlling, or changing behavior, questions such as the following must be faced and examined:

1. What moral right do teachers have to change the attitudes, beliefs, and behaviors of children?

2. Is it justifiable for teachers in a democratic society to employ psychological techniques to change attitudes and behaviors?

3. Will not the use of such practices tend to produce conforming and dependent personalities?

Undoubtedly many other questions could be raised relative to the thesis that teachers should be taught to provide conditions that will promote certain behaviors, to use the force of the group to change or develop attitudes, to use practices that will bring about desired behaviors. The discussion that follows concerning the preceding questions does not attempt to provide final answers. However, each question is examined to provide a frame of reference so such queries, or similar ones, do not continually arise when various practices and procedures are proposed in succeeding chapters.

What moral right do teachers have to change the attitudes and behaviors of the children in elementary classrooms? In this instance, we are talking about the attitudes children have toward learning and the behaviors that are necessary and conducive to learning in the classroom. Developing behavior conducive to learning involves either changing already-existing attitudes or developing attitudes where none previously existed. In either case, teachers must make value judgments as to what is "good" or "bad" behavior. Because of their training and background, some teachers believe learning takes place when the room is quiet and still. Therefore "good" behavior is quiet behavior. Others believe "good" behavior means immediate compliance to teacher requests and demands. The surface behavior exhibited by the class determines, then, whether the behavior of the class group is "good" or "bad." There are many teachers, the majority it is hoped, who view "good" behavior as that which is evidenced by children who are eager to learn, who question and discuss, and who are not easily distracted. These children can, within the limits determined by their stage of development, decide themselves how they will work, and what behavior standards they will follow. "Good" behavior to these latter teachers means that the class group members as a whole learn to take some measure of responsibility for their own behavior and do not need policing, but need only guidance and direction.

The question has been raised whether teachers have the right, ethically and morally, to impose their own—generally middle class values —upon the children in the classroom. Certainly some segments of American culture live with very different values than those held by most teachers, and there are some values held by teachers that they do not have the right to impose on children. For example, a teacher in the public schools has no right to instill the belief in the minds of children that the teacher's religion is the key to all good living. However, there are certain values that must be accepted by children if they are to work together in classroom situations on the common tasks of mastering skills, developing concepts, and learning content. For instance, class members must share certain common values regarding the rights of others or little learning takes place. When the question of the moral and ethical right of teachers to impose or develop values is limited to those values that relate directly to learning, few persons would argue that teachers are not justified in developing such values.

The question does not seem to be whether a teacher has the right to impose values or change attitudes and beliefs, but rather of defining the limits. What core values are to be instilled in pupils? What socially acceptable behaviors can we expect of first grade children as compared to those in the sixth grade? As for attitude change, good teachers have been doing this for a long time. In the course of teaching arithmetic, spelling, writing, and other skills, good teachers have made children want to learn, for they have known for a long time that unless receptive attitudes toward learning are developed very little learning occurs.

Some educators hold to the belief that children must be allowed freedom to develop appropriate attitudes and acceptable behaviors. They contend that if children are provided with a good climate for learning and are given the necessary facts, and if they are guided by appropriate procedures to examine the facts, desired attitudes and behaviors will be acquired. Since research has established that a great many attitudes are developed in early childhood, many before the children reach school, and since it has been determined that established attitudes and the predisposition to behave in one way rather than another is exceedingly difficult to change, educators who hold to the belief that exploring facts will change established attitudes are ignoring some important psychological principles. Living in a "democratic climate" or experiencing "democratic leadership practices" does not in itself change attitudes and behavior. The techniques used must be directed toward definite desired changes.

To the question of whether it is dangerous in a free society for teachers to be able to use psychological knowledge to change attitudes, beliefs, and behavior, and whether such practices are undemocratic, one may counter by asking another question. Is it not dangerous to any society if the teachers of the young are not able to guide, direct, or change undesirable behavior upon occasion? Some children arrive at school displaying behavior patterns that are not conducive to learning, and that make it difficult for others to learn. In other words, they do not respect the rights of individuals. Some children appear to believe that the way of life is to take what they want and destroy what they do not want. They base their behavior upon a code of every-person-for-himself. In such situations, is it not the function of education, as one agency, at least, to change the attitudes of such individuals?

Present educational procedures have been deplored on numerous occasions because of the claim that the practices employed in schools promote conformity and that nonconformity is penalized. Some persons state that conformity has become the approved habit, and dissenting is the unpopular practice.[23] Although there are answers to these criticisms, there is enough truth in them to merit thoughtful consideration. However, the problem of whether influencing and altering behavior by means of group forces produces conforming and dependent personalities must be considered within various frameworks. The word conformity needs to be defined. If conformity is the term used to describe individuals who behave in socially approved ways—that is, according to generally accepted customs, regulations, and laws, and with regard for the rights of others— then teaching or helping children learn to conform is one of the major objectives of education. It is another term for socialization, and is an aim of education in all societies. Often this is not what is meant by the

---

[23] Marguerite Hall Albjerg, "Blessed Is the Nonconformist," *College and University,* 36:14–19, Fall 1960.

term, for it is used in various ways. It has been pointed out that the word "conformity" has become burdened with too many meanings such as: standardized tastes; unreflective thinking; absence of social innovation; presence of conservative ideology; passive acceptance of norms of various groups; and a great regard for group approval.[24] The word is most commonly employed to describe individuals who tend to acquiesce and agree without giving due consideration or engaging in reflective thinking.

When conformity is regarded as the behaviors that are generally in accord with the customs and regulations of society and that reflect a concern for the society, then it does not necessarily follow that individuals who learn to conform are apathetic and quiescent. On the contrary, such individuals may dissent and strive for various social innovations, only they do so within the framework of the laws and regulations of the society. In other words, they do not dissent by organizing a gang and using destructive techniques, nor do they become beatniks or other kinds of social parasite.

The question then, whether the use of group forces to change behavior will produce conforming behavior, may be answered when the meaning of conformity is clarified. Certainly few people wish to develop a society of people who have a "mass mind." On the other hand, the rise of juvenile delinquency has aroused all civic-minded individuals, and has created intense concern and much study as to ways to develop attitudes in the young that will lead to constructive behavior and consideration for the rights of others. If psychological knowledge can be employed to promote socially desired behavior and conformity to the generally accepted rules and regulations of society, few will voice objections to such use.

Critics who claim that education is responsible for promoting conformity, and use the term in another sense impede understanding of the problem to which they refer. They are questioning whether educational practices are conducive to the development of individuals who question, who challenge, and who voice their dissent when they disagree. Group forces can be used to turn out uncritical, unthinking, passive followers, if that is the objective desired. On the other hand, the same forces can be used to turn out individuals who are self-directing, who have inquiring minds, and who form their own judgments as to truth. Use of psychological techniques will not produce individuals who go along with the undigested observations of the group unless that is the goal.

Knowledge now exists that can facilitate the development in individuals of attitudes that will predispose them to think, to question, and

[24] Walter P. Metzger, "On Youth and Conformity," *American Association of University Professors Bulletin,* **46:**357–360, December 1960.

to reflect. Society and educators need but choose the direction in which they will go.

To conclude, there are conflicting traditions and conflicting philosophies operating within the schools. On one hand, there is a conviction held by many that the purpose of education is to mold minds rather than import a discipline that will enable young people to form their own judgments and become the architects of their own fortunes. On the other hand, there are many who believe that education should develop free intelligence—that is, equip students with the habits of mind and the characters requisite for effective living in a free society. It must be emphasized that education for the free intelligence as against education for conformity in no way precludes instruction in skills and content such as reading, writing, arithmetic, social studies, and other areas of knowledge that are commonly accepted as necessary to transmit to the young. However, it is obvious that different philosophies of education dictate different uses of procedures and techniques. Use of group forces may be employed to mold minds, indoctrinate, and to produce conformity and passive acceptance. The same forces may be applied to increase learning in skills and content, to develop loyalty to ethical principles of a democratic culture, and to create thinking, independent individuals.

Questions for Study and Discussion

1. The emphasis upon use of group dynamics in classrooms has been criticized by a number of people. What are the dangers of overemphasizing group techniques?

2. In what ways are you influenced by your class group or your work group? Can you give examples of group influence upon individual behavior that you have noted among your friends?

3. Does a "good" group member block group progress when the group is working toward a goal? How might a good group member be described?

4. Are there times when an individual may best work alone on a problem even though the final solution affects the lives of many persons? Should group action always be taken when a problem of concern to all the group needs solving?

5. What kinds of problem situation might arise in the school room that would be best solved by group action?

Suggestions for Further Reading

Bonner, Hubert. *Group Dynamics: Principles and Applications.* New York: Ronald, 1959, Chapter 8, "Group Dynamics in Education."

Bradford, Leland P., Kenneth Benne, and Ronald Lippitt. "The Promise of Group Dynamics for Education," *N.E.A. Journal,* 37:350–51, September 1948.

Gunderson, Robert Gray. "Group Dynamics, A Symposium: Dangers in Group Dynamics," *Religious Education,* 46:344, November–December 1951.

Jenkins, David H. "Interdependence in the Classroom," *Journal of Educational Research,* 45:137–144, October 1951.

Maas, Henry S. "Understanding Group Processes," in *Fostering Mental Health in Our Schools.* Washington, D.C.: Association for Supervision and Curriculum Development, National Education Association, 1950.

McCaslin, Nellie. "A Critical Look at Group Dynamics," *School and Society,* 82:168–169, November 1955.

National Society for the Study of Education. *The Dynamics of Instructional Groups.* Chicago: U. of Chicago, 1960, Chapters I–II, pp. 3–29.

Slavson, S. R. *Creative Group Education.* New York: Assn. Pr., 1938.

Chapter 3   The Nature of Groups

THIS chapter examines the general nature of small groups to formulate an overall conception of the factors involved in the group phenomenon. All small groups have certain common properties and characteristics which interrelate in many ways. Groups may be studied profitably only if the parameters or properties that are applicable to all groups are established, described, and understood.

All small groups, including of course the class group, have common properties by which they can be described. However, the class group has some features that are more or less peculiar to it, and such a group can be described according to certain common group properties and according to its own specific characteristics. These common group properties and specific group characteristics provide a framework within which the functioning of class groups can be analyzed.

This chapter is concerned with defining and clarifying the term *group*. The properties of groups in general and the specific features and characteristics of the classroom group are examined, and a comparison is made between classroom groups and work groups in general. Following this overall picture of the nature of groups, subsequent chapters enlarge and develop many of the concepts discussed.

Development of the Group Concept

A small group has certain properties, characteristics, and behavior patterns that can be observed, studied, and described. At the mention of "group behavior," the question is sometimes raised, "Is the group an entity? Is there such a thing as group behavior?" To some persons who have concentrated upon the study of individual behavior, a group is no more than the sum of traits and actions that exist in separate individuals. Teachers often view their class groups in this manner. They see the class group as a number of individual parts, and it is difficult for them to view their classes as organized wholes, or to note that the group itself has characteristics of its own and behavior of its own. Viewing the class as a group of individuals overlooks the fact that when individual parts become organized into wholes, new characteristics, actions, and ways of behaving emerge that are not observable in the separate parts alone. This point may be illustrated by a baseball team whose interactions cannot be explained by observing the individual players separately, for the members are joined in a structure of relations, and from this structure the teamwork emerges. It may be noted that when one watches a baseball game, he may observe one member of the team or several members or the team as a whole, and although the group factor of teamwork varies with the quality of individual players, the team continues to function with substitutions of individual players. A team then, like many organized groups, has duration and continuation beyond that of any of its members, and it cannot be considered a simple sum of behaviors of individual members.

To answer questions about why class groups are on occasions difficult to control or manage, why they behave in certain ways, or what may be done to prevent certain behaviors from occurring, the action of the *whole* group must be observed, and when questions are raised about social situations, whether they involve clubs, classes, work groups, or play groups, the behavior of the whole must be taken into account at some point. Group behavior consists of an observable pattern of interaction, the structure that emerges, the cohesiveness or spirit of friendliness that pervades the group, the norms or rules for behavior that govern individual members, and the motives or goals of the group. Careful observation of these factors facilitates understanding and prediction of group behavior.

Definition of the Group

The group may be described in many ways, but there is no single clear-cut definition that adequately and quickly encompasses the concept of the small group. In brief, a group may be said to exist when two or more persons have as one quality of their relationship some interdependence and possess some recognizable unity. The members meet in face-to-face situations and form distinct impressions of each other. There is interaction—that is, each member reacts to the behavior of each other member. The individuals comprising the group not only interact, but they often act together in a unitary manner toward their environment.

At times the group has been defined as a social unit consisting of individuals who vary in this status-and-role relationship and that possesses a set of values or norms that regulates the behavior of individual members.[1]

Sometimes a group is defined in simple terms. Bonner,[2] for example, states that a group exists when two or more persons are aware of one another and when they interrelate in some important way.

Since the presence of persons together does not in itself guarantee the existence of a group, Stodgill[3] regards the group as an open interaction system. The system (group) is determined solely by the actions of the members and, further, he sees the group's identity as dependent upon the interactions taking place rather than upon the presence within the structure of any particular member.

Often persons interested in describing groups emphasize that a group must have a common interest or goal or some reason for being a group. In the case of a classroom group, for example, the question is sometimes raised as to whether a class can be a group in this respect, since children in a poorly conducted classroom might not have a common interest or aim, except that they might hold in common the desire to get out of the classroom as soon as possible.[4] A number of educators have questioned whether a classroom of children can be called a group, since

[1] Muzafer Sherif and Carolyn Sherif, *An Outline of Social Psychology,* New York: Harper & Brothers, 1956, p. 144.

[2] Hubert Bonner, *Group Dynamics: Principles and Applications,* New York: The Ronald Press Company, 1959.

[3] Ralph M. Stodgill, *Individual Behavior and Group Achievement,* New York: Oxford University Press, 1959, p. 18.

[4] Dugald S. Arbuckle, *Guidance and Counseling in the Classroom,* Boston: Allyn and Bacon, 1959, p. 326.

it is difficult to establish that children have a common aim or goal or that there is always a product or some accomplishment as a result of their being together.

As will be developed more fully later, the wish of a number of children to be a group, or the desire of members for groupness, may be the goal of a class group, so the foregoing definition does not exclude a class from being a group. Another way of saying this is that a class group provides an opportunity to satisfy the conscious and unconscious needs of the individual children to belong. This desire, to obtain satisfaction by forming an interacting group, becomes, in fact, the unstated or hidden desire of children gathered together in a classroom situation.

For the purposes of this book, a class group is described as several persons in a state of social interaction. It is not a number of individuals such as are enumerated on a roll sheet or class register, but is, instead, an association of persons with some degree of give-and-take. It may involve gross muscular movements, as when a number of individuals join together to play crack the whip or to engage in work such as piling up magazines and stacks of paper. It may involve communication through words and gestures. Or, again, it may involve both gross overt action and communication. The members may, and usually do, share some group goals, and they usually get some personal gratification out of joint activity, although this is not necessarily true.[5]

The basis for classifying human behavior into group behavior is interaction, for this is the property that all small groups have in common. In all definitions of small groups it is either implied or specifically stated that for a group to be a group interaction must take place. Mere physical closeness, if there is no mutual influence, does not make a group. This implies that persons in the group influence each other reciprocally, but does not mean that the members of a group influence each other equally. Interaction is what all groups have in common, and even though interaction is curtailed in some classrooms, the fact is that during the school day children meet and interact on the playground and other places. The effects are carried over into the classroom. Therefore, even though some class groups have little opportunity within the classroom to interact, have few aims in common, develop few norms, and are lacking in unity, they may be considered groups. If there is little opportunity in the classroom for interaction, if the group develops few common aims, norms, and has little unity, these characteristics typify the pattern or configuration of group properties that this particular class group possesses.

[5] For a brief discussion of some of the various definitions of "group," see Cecil A. Gibb, "Leadership," in Gardner Lindzey (ed.), *Handbook of Social Psychology,* Cambridge: Addison-Wesley, 1954, Chapter 24.

Characteristics of Groups

All groups have certain general properties in common. All groups, for example, have participants who are joined together for some reason. Each of the participants relates to the other participants in some way, and status-and-role relationships form. The participants usually develop degrees of liking for the group and/or for certain members of the group. In varying degrees, groups acquire or develop norms and values of their own, and these influence and regulate the behavior of the members, particularly in matters of importance to the group. The members interact, a structure forms, and norms and goals develop. However, groups vary in size and in their degrees of stability. The purposes for which they exist vary. They differ in organization, in leadership practices, in their degrees of independence, and in their relations to other groups. In fact, groups vary in a number of ways. Thus, in addition to the general properties, each group has certain characteristics of its own that distinguish it from all other groups. These variations provide each separate group with its own unique character. All classroom groups, for example, are like other groups in many respects, but they differ in their participants, purposes, organizations, and in other ways. Other causes of difference from group to group are that the varying properties of different groups interrelate in different ways in different groups, and that each group develops its own culture.

Properties of Groups

The *properties of groups* consist of those elements common to all groups. They are those qualities that describe the essential nature of groups and include such aspects as communication, structure, cohesiveness, norms, and goals. These properties have dimensions—that is, they vary in extent, degree, and in various other ways. The concern of much group research is with measurement of various group properties in the effort to determine various group dimensions. Since group properties are interrelated, the degree, extent, or size of one element influences all other elements.

Although certain minimum properties may be singled out when developing a general concept of groups, each group differs from every other group in some respect. Adequate description of any one group must be done in relation to the properties common to all small groups. The interrelatedness of the properties must also be considered, for these properties are not static, fixed quantities. They vary in degree, direction, and dimension.

Interaction

A number of people become a group when a condition exists in which each individual is affected by every other individual in the group. Individuals react one to another. This process involving the reactions of a number of persons to one another is called *interaction*. Although individual A reacts to individual B, and, in turn, B reacts to A, these reactions are not necessarily the same. By way of illustration, Susan responds to John and John to Susan, but each in a different way. Susan may run after John in an attempt to get his attention. John, on the other hand, may run away from Susan and make every effort to avoid her.

The concept of interaction, however, refers to more than mere member-to-member actions and reactions. It includes a range of social relationships wherein there is reciprocal stimulation and response between human beings. The concept of interaction includes ways in which individuals relate to one another and carry out the tasks essential for the development, maintenance, and growth of the group or social system. Interaction may occur between a group and another group, a group and the teacher, or between subgroups within the group. A study of interaction will direct attention not only to member-member relationships, but to the ways groups, subgroups, and teachers exert positive, neutral, and negative influences on one another. In the diagram in Figure 1, interaction is shown as the center of group functioning.

Interaction refers, then, to the modification of behavior that occurs when two or more persons come in contact for a period of time. Individuals influence one another through use of language, symbols, gestures, and other forms of communication. The term "interaction processes" refers to the recurrent patterns of interstimulation and response among individuals and groups that result in the development of cohesiveness, structure, norms, and mutual goals, or conversely, that may lead to conflict and disorganization.

The many situations in which persons and groups interact are so numerous that it would be impossible to catalog them all. The following reported incident is one random sample of the many situations in which members of the class group interact.

INTERACTION IN THE CLASSROOM

Jay, from the next classroom, punched several boys from this room for no apparent reason. He was hiding and punched the boys as they passed in line going to their room. Jay has had a reputation for being quite a "troublemaker" for two years. The girls saw the incident occur. When the class returned from noon recess (at which time the incident occurred), the girls in the class were very vociferous in backing up the

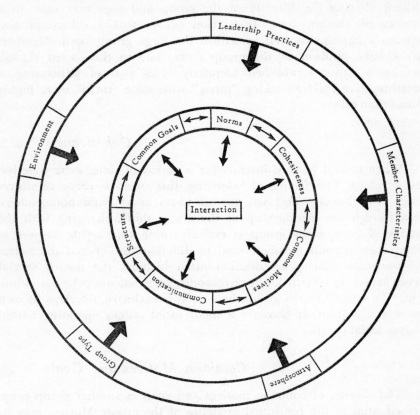

Fig. 1. Diagram of interaction as the center of group functioning with related group characteristics and factors.

statements made when the members of the class reported this affair to the teacher. After listening to what had happened, the members of the class acted as one body and voiced opinions that Jay was wrong and that he should be called in to answer for his actions. The class demanded that he give a reason for hitting our boys and indicated he should be made to answer for his actions.

Structure

To understand group behavior it is necessary to have a knowledge of the structural characteristics of the group. The structure of any group is complex. It involves a system of social stratification or a hierarchy in which various individuals stand high or low. The size of a group influences structure. When a group reaches a certain size, there may be a tendency for it to split into subgroups. These subgroups may form without altering the identity of the group and they may exist in a number of combinations. Interaction occurs within subgroups and between subgroups as well as within the large group itself. Members may change position in the group from time to time, even though there is a strong established hierarchy. This part of structuring is something like children taking "turns," with some "turns" more highly valued than others.

Cohesiveness

When several persons interact for a period of time, some cohesiveness develops. This feeling of belonging, this *esprit de corps,* reinforces bonds of fellowship and sets the members apart from nonmembers. Even though the membership of the group shifts, changing with the passage of time, every group is exclusive and has varying degrees of cohesiveness. Group members tend to differentiate between themselves and outsiders. This differentiation often includes the use of special names as well as certain forms of recondite or ritualistic behavior. Thus, it may be said that each group, because it is exclusive, develops its own mores and culture. It becomes a small social system operating within a larger social system.

Common Motives and Goals

The sharing of common motives and goals is another group property essential to the continued existence of the group. Motives may be conceived as predispositions toward certain kinds of behavior in an attempt to satisfy needs. They direct behavior toward a goal. A group continues to exist because through interaction, individuals can better satisfy their own needs, desires, interests, and aspirations. The needs of individual members differ and the group does not satisfy identical needs nor does it satisfy them in the same way for all persons. There are many ways by which a group satisfies the various needs of individual members.

Many persons desire to belong to a group because satisfaction is derived from "belongingness" as such. For youngsters especially, and for those older, as well, belonging satisfies needs for security, for approval, and for establishing a personal identity. Some individuals desire not only to belong, but they need to direct and influence others. Sometimes individuals are motivated to belong to a group because the activities of the group give satisfaction. Others find the group provides an opportunity to gain recognition and some sort of status. Whether the need is for power, security, friendship, or the like, groups function because these common motives may be satisfied through interaction.

Besides motives that direct behavior toward goals, the group as an entity has goals. The goals of the group direct its activity in certain directions. Sometimes the goals of a group are clearly formulated and openly agreed upon by members. Other times the goals are extremely vague and "hidden." The motives of each individual member influence the choice of a goal for a group, for the group goal must provide some satisfaction for each member or it will not be accepted. It is influenced by the nature of the members' motives, and then, in turn, the goal influences individual member behavior.

Standardization of Behavior or Norms

Studies of group behavior have found that individuals behave differently in groups than they do when they are alone. Groups have psychological influences that affect individual behavior, and groups have properties unlike those present in single individuals. The contact with other people elicits behavior from individuals that is different from the behavior that would be found in the same individuals if they were isolated.

All groups possess a power to influence attitudes and to standardize the behavior of members to a certain degree. This power exists in groups in varying amounts, but all groups tend to make members conform to the aims and values approved by the group. Both overt and subtle pressures operate to influence individual behavior. Conformity may be achieved because an individual desires to be approved and accepted by others. This kind of pressure is so subtle that most individuals are unaware that it is operating, and they do not recognize the changes that are made in their behaviors. Other pressures may be more obvious and are applied in a more direct fashion. They may range all the way from mild teasing to strong ridicule and, eventually, ostracism if the group member fails to conform. Overt or subtle as the method of applying pressure may be, the result is a certain amount of conformity to group standards and values. Individuals within the group modify to some degree their own personal value systems. They tend to approve what the group sanctions and discard what it condemns.

The following example reveals how group members sometimes attempt to achieve conformity to group standards.

OSTRACISM

During a volley ball game one of the girls became angry because she felt her teammates were not playing well and that as a consequence the side she was on was losing the game. She became so angry she began to call her teammates by a variety of abusive terms. She was stopped but not before she had hurled a number of invectives toward those who were antagonizing her.

The next period was devoted to organizing committees for a project the class had planned. She was completely rejected by her classmates, and no one would choose her to work on his committee. Nothing was said about her behavior on the playground, but in the days that followed, if it appeared she might break a room standard almost all of her classmates were quick to denounce her. From all appearances it seemed this group was ostracising a member who failed to conform to their ideas of good behavior.

Group Personality or "Syntality"

When all of the properties and characteristics of a group are viewed compositely they distinguish the group in much the same way that the personality of an individual makes him different from every other individual. As the analogy implies, groups, like individuals, may be described by patterns or peculiar configurations of characteristics. It is this difference in patterning and combining that makes each group unique. The personality of a group represents what the group is like as a *whole* and how it acts as a *whole*. For example, all groups have some degree of structure, but each group is identifiable by the peculiar nature of its inner organization. This involves the leadership pattern, the status system, the number of subgroups, and all the various factors that relate to the group's internal system. The final outcome or total performance of the group that comes about because of the group's own particular patterning of properties and characteristics and that gives it a unique identity has been labeled by Cattell as "syntality." [6]

The values endorsed by groups vary in the extreme. They range from the altruistic to the immoral. Both group norms and group personality reflect the values cherished by the group. A group may display intolerance to other groups or individuals on the grounds of race, social status, religion, nationality, family background, political beliefs, and

[6] Raymond B. Cattell, "Concepts and Methods in the Measurement of Group Syntality," *Psychological Review*, 55:48–63, 1948.

the like. Thus, prejudice may comprise one aspect of a certain group's personality pattern.

Certainly another quality comprising group personality is the degree of fraternal spirit. A group may display an atmosphere in which the members feel free because of a prevailing kindliness and friendliness. In another group, the converse may be true. An atmosphere of suspicion, jealousy, or high competitiveness may exist, and the personality of the group could be characterized as having a low level of cohesiveness and a small degree of internal freedom of interaction.

All of the various properties and characteristics in their various relationships when viewed collectively make a composite picture of the specific nature of the group and endow it with qualities that make up its personality and make it unique.

It must be emphasized that all groups have certain general properties and these properties vary in dimensions. A general description of a group is not dependent upon why the group came into existence, nor is it dependent upon whether the association of members is voluntary or involuntary. Furthermore, any general description of a group is not affected by the fact that members may be removed from or placed into the group by an external agent. A group may split into a number of subparts, but as long as the parts interact the group may be described by the same common properties. In brief, groups are of certain types and kinds and vary greatly in size, membership, and reasons for existence, but these differences do not change their general nature or their general properties.

Classroom Groups

One of the most important groups to the life of a child is the classroom group. If it fulfills his developing needs, he becomes an active, satisfied, contributing learner. If the child's needs are not satisfied to some extent by the class group and its activities, very little learning occurs.

The Nature of Classroom Groups

A class group is a social organization and by nature it is also a psychological grouping. It is a social group in that it is formally organized. There is a differentiation of role and responsibility regarding the aims, tasks, and goals of the group. Therefore, the group has distinctive action patterns because of the nature of its formal organization and because this organization has preset ways for the group members to act.

Although the aims and tasks and the relationship of participating members to each other are set down in the formal structuring of the group, additional types of expectancies develop in the interrelationships of individuals to one another. This is the psychological aspect of the classroom group. Within the formal organization, informal groupings arise. Members are in dynamic interaction with one another. This informal association of members provides many member satisfactions and dissatisfactions. The psychological member relationships affect morale, work operations, and member participation in the group. Just as the formal organization sets certain boundaries or limits by providing a framework in which the members work, so does the informal grouping of members set standards and expectancies for member behavior. Because of its social and psychological characteristics a classroom group has been referred to as a "socio-psychological" structure.[7]

PRIMARY GROUP. A classroom group, in the elementary school at least, is primary in nature in that members are together for long periods of time in intimate face-to-face relationships. Even though a warm, emotional tone does not pervade the group as a whole, usually congeniality and friendliness characterize a number of subgroupings within the larger group. Some of the children in the group, because they are thrown together, discover a bond of common interest and affection and enjoy doing things together. While the family is paramount in influencing the child's emotional and social development, these school groups also make their marks on the child. These relationships affect motivation, because children are sensitive to the favorable judgments of intimate friends and the opinions and responses of comrades. Thus, if some group members are enthusiastic about spelling, others will be influenced by their enthusiasm, and the same is true for other social behaviors. The significance of viewing the class as a primary group is that a primary group has the ability to bring about effective social control. A primary group is a structure of mutual liking that generates spontaneous friendly acts for the most part, although a primary group may ridicule or ostracize a member who does not behave according to group norms. Seen positively, the primary group becomes a value in itself, and not merely the means to another goal. It is friendship not made for an advantage, but rather it is personal and sentimental.

Human society relies heavily on such relations for its maintenance, and when the expectancies of the group are positive, such relation-

---

[7] Gale Jensen, "The Socio-psychological Structure of the Instructional Group," in Nelson B. Henry (ed.), *The Dynamics of Instructional Groups*, N.S.S.E. Yearbook, Chicago: University of Chicago Press, 1960.

ships contribute much to maintaining positive classroom atmospheres.

WORK GROUP. Groups are distinguished not only by their organizations and structures but also by the functions they perform. The class group is a *work* group. As in the case of other work groups, it is established as an organized group to achieve definite goals. Although goals of work groups differ, and they differ in characteristics, the *problems* that arise in organized work groups in regard to production and achievement are similar. For example, the extent to which a work group achieves its goals depends upon the productive efficiency of the group. Thus, a problem common to all work groups is one related to determining the type of group structure that will be most conducive to effective operation and to goal achievement. What patterns of interrelationships will enable the participants in a group to attain the objectives pleasantly and efficiently? This question is of concern to school groups and industrial groups alike.

The formal and informal structures present another problem common to all work groups. The formal organization is committed to prescribed goals and tasks and the leaders in the organization may make decisions related to task performance. These decisions, of course, affect member behavior, but informal structures may also have a great influence upon the member behavior because certain behavioral norms develop within these informal structures. A united informal group may make it difficult for leaders to impose their dictates upon the group. Leaders in the informal group may arise and express the wills or the sentiments of fellow group members. The informal groupings within a formally organized group may develop expectancies or "goals" that conflict with the prescribed goals and group tasks. Thus, determining the areas for group decision when there are certain prescribed tasks that must be accomplished if groups are to achieve their end-purpose is a difficult problem. A certain amount of "dealing" goes on between labor and management and between teachers and class groups, and these dealings psychologically affect production and achievement.

All work groups have a common problem regarding leader–follower relationships. Many of the significant relationships in work groups are of the superior-to-subordinate sort. The nature of these relationships can best be understood by comparing them to the relationship of the teacher and the children in the class group, although the same types of relationships exist between "boss" and worker or management and labor. An example is the prototype of the stern teacher who maintains discipline by relying largely on punishment. He is comparable to the executive in business who uses threats to force employees to obey his decrees. In either case, whether it is a child or employee, the individual is likely to react by resenting his position and by using some means to resist. This may be done by idling on the job, through sabotage, or by resisting in some way. A second comparison may be made of the teacher who believes he discharges his responsibility when he makes the assignments, explains the lessons, and sees to it that each child performs the assigned tasks. All teachers are aware of the importance of children feeling accepted and successful. There is a similarity here between the teacher and a leader in a work group who believes that seeing the job gets done is all that is necessary to successfully carry out his job. Members of any type of work group lose their zest for the job because the leader does not manifest a personal interest in each worker and fails to show regard for the feelings of the workers.

The psychological condition prevailing in the group is another problem that is common to all work groups. A healthy work atmosphere is necessary for maintaining successful working conditions whether the group is a school work group or an industrial work group. Both executives and teachers are apt to indulge in wishful thinking with respect to the psychological atmospheres or climates prevailing in their group organizations. They are inclined to believe that if they are pleasant and friendly and have the interests of the workers in mind, all will be well. In many cases, superiors and workers alike need help in improving the group relations. Usually there is need for a constant check to reveal the need for modifying existing arrangements and revamping policies. The problem of group morale is common to all work groups, and social psychologists have experimented widely to discover appropriate positive techniques and to show by actual results that certain kinds of techniques pay dividends in terms of production and greater member satisfaction with the job and with the work group.

Whether the group is a class group or another kind of work group, the persons engaged in leading such a group must have some understanding of the meaning of a group member's behavior. In other words, work groups of all types have problems with individual behavior and all face certain typical problems. For example, is the member really unhappy over wages (or grades), or is his real problem related to pressures at home or something else that irritates him? To what extent should the administrators and supervisors concern themselves with conditions outside the organization that affect a member's efficiency adversely? (School leaders have long been concerned with outside factors affecting children in the classroom. Their principal problem is one of finding the best ways to create changes in the environment that will improve a child's efficiency in his school job.) How should the leader of the work group handle individual behavior problems? What qualities or skills must a leader of a work group have in order to handle problems in social relations?

A work group, whether it is a school work group or an industrial work group, is a social system. The term "system" connotes a whole in which each part bears a relation of interdependence to every other part. Considering the school group as a "social system" is a useful concept for interpreting the activities of individuals who are members of work groups. For many years educators have been aware that a child's productive efficiency in the classroom is affected by his relations with his classmates, by the recognition he receives for his efforts, and by the psychological atmosphere prevailing in his work group. However, educational leaders have devoted more attention to improving methods of "efficient production" (methods of teaching) than to developing techniques for securing cooperation and developing a good "climate" for working. Although not oblivious to the fact that "getting children to work together effectively and with personal satisfaction" affects the achievement of school goals, educators have nevertheless been content to merely discuss the importance of "good" group relations rather than to develop actual workable techniques. Only recently have they turned to social psychology for answers to the complex problems involved in group interaction.

A class group may be classified as a formally organized work group. Formally organized work groups of all kinds have similar problems, but these problems must be considered in relation to the specific characteristics of a particular group, for work groups differ widely in their goals, member compositions, sizes, and many other factors.

General Characteristics of Classroom Groups

It is not unusual for class groups to be considered unique from all other types of work group. The distinctive nature of class groups is described in a number of ways. In one instance, the features considered distinctive of classroom groups are given as follows: (1) learning is the goal, or the purpose for which the group is brought together; (2) participation in the group is mandatory, and so are the goals; (3) the members of the group have no control over the selection of the leader, and no recourse from his leadership; and (4) other individuals and groups exert pressures and influences that are felt by the participants in the class group. In other words, classroom groups differ from all other work groups because of the distinctive natures of classroom goals, participants, leaderships, and relationships to other groups.[8]

[8] Jacob W. Getzels and Herbert A. Thelen, "The Classroom Group as a Unique Social System," in Nelson B. Henry (ed.), *The Dynamics of Instructional Groups*, Chicago: University of Chicago Press, 1960, pp. 53–82.

It seems that the broad principles of group action have major implications for classroom groups, even though some of the research into these principles is based on groups that seem unlike those found in school situations. Conceiving of a class group as having a nature quite distinct from other work groups makes it exceedingly difficult to explain class-group behavior in the light of known socio-psychological knowledge. It appears more useful to consider the classroom group as being *like* other formal work groups in many respects. Of course, as with all work groups, the specific characteristics of one type of work group will form a pattern peculiar to the group. Thus, classroom groups can be distinguished from other work groups, but also every other kind of work group can be so distinguished. There are certain general parameters that are applicable to all work groups including classroom groups.

The classroom group has been classified as a formal work group. It is an organized work group that can be described by the same broad descriptive terms as any other work group. Since it is a formal group, the expectations about the functions of members are defined and described by persons outside the group rather than by the group members themselves. Also, the organizational structure of roles and responsibilities regarding the aims, tasks, and goals of the group is not a matter of group decision. The responsibilities or duties are set down in the formal structuring of the group. However, additional types of expectations develop from the interaction of members themselves. This is to say that the formal structuring of a group does not completely determine in advance the many interpersonal relationships that occur. Many informal groupings arise from within the formal structure. The informal groupings perform functions also, not only in producing efficiency or inefficiency, but also in producing differences in group morale. For example, one function of the informal groupings of children in the class group is to protect the class by working with the teacher when his practices seem promising to their welfare or against the teacher when his practices are interpreted as a threat. Thus, informal groupings within the class group may be more powerful at times than the formal organization, but this is equally true of informal groupings in other work groups.

As a formally organized work group, the class group is like other formal work groups in many other respects. For example, it is a part of a larger organization—the school. It is only one group among many similar ones, for there are other grades and classes within the larger organization.

The class group is established by the community to accomplish certain changes. Other kinds of formal work groups are established to accomplish certain changes. In many instances, a formal work group is established to produce some material object (a refrigerator, a car, or the like), and there are many instances where the end purpose is something less tangible than a material product. In other words, like other work groups, the class group is organized for some end purpose, and many of its basic goals and activities are set by outside forces. This is true of most formally organized work groups. By way of simple illustration, a company may be formed to produce lead pencils. The group that is formed to actually shape the wood and insert the lead is only one group in a more complex organization, since other groups may be organized to box the pencils, sell them, and so forth. The individuals in the production group do not determine what article is to be manufactured, or how the product is to be shaped or made. The end purpose of the group is determined before the group is organized. The same condition exists with regard to classroom groups. The group is organized to accomplish certain purposes that are determined before the group is organized, and the members have little to say about the goals or aims or the kinds of tasks that must be performed to accomplish the end-purpose for which the group was organized.

The class group is like other formal work groups in other ways also. An outside force assigns a leader to the group and gives this leader responsibility and authority for seeing that the group accomplishes the goals set for it. Whether the leader is a teacher or a shop foreman or supervisor, his status imposes a structure on the group and defines some of the role relationships. With class groups and other kinds of work groups, the members expect the leader's behavior to fit their broad concept of what a leader should do and what he should be like.

Specific Nature of the Classroom Group

Determination of the specific nature of any work group requires an examination of its purpose, organization, tasks, type of leadership, and member characteristics. A class group differs from other work groups in only three major areas. First, its purpose is quite different from that of most work groups; second, the tasks necessary for the group to achieve its goals are distinctive from those of other work groups; and third, the member composition is unlike the compositions of most work groups.

Work groups are organized for different purposes, but always for the purpose of creating some change that a single individual could not bring about by his efforts alone. As we have already stated, the end purpose of some work groups is the production of nonmaterial products, and the end purpose of other work groups as the production of material product. One work group may be organized to promote a candidate for an elective office; another may be organized to produce a product. The activities of both groups would include series of operations designed to utilize the energies of group members to accomplish the end purpose. The difference in the outcome of the group effort would be that one effort would not result in a material product and the other would (although if the candidate won, the outcome would be tangible). If a group were organized for the purpose of maintaining high standards in the professional training of teachers, it would be much more difficult to relate the activities of the members to any end purpose of the group. Since the purpose is long-range, and in a sense continuous, the activities of members would of necessity center around subgoals, which might or might not pertain to the end-purpose of the group. It would be difficult for a group to determine the activities that would maintain high standards in the professional training of teachers, and even more difficult to determine later whether the activities actually did lead to the maintenance of high standards.

A classroom group is unique in its purpose in that it is organized to produce changes in the group members themselves. The end product, or the reason for the existence of a class group, is to develop citizens who can function effectively in a free society. As in the case of a group organized for the purpose of maintaining high professional standards of teacher training, it is difficult to determine the activities and tasks that will achieve the end purpose, and it is also difficult to determine the quality of the product produced, since there is no end point in the process.

The fact that the goals of the class group are prescribed by persons external to the group itself is not a characteristic unique to the class group; most formally organized groups have prescribed goals. The difference is that the members themselves not only create the product, they are the product. Many kinds of work groups have prescribed tasks and purposes determined by people outside the actual work groups; however, because the class group is unlike many other groups in that it is organized to produce changes in the members themselves, the tasks and activities that members must perform are unlike the tasks of many other work groups.

The class group also differs somewhat from other work groups in member composition. For one thing, the members of class groups are more homogeneous in many respects than workers in most other groups. The members of class groups are usually similar in age and interests, and they usually have similar needs and desires. The composition of other work groups is often haphazard. The members of many work groups may be alike only in that they possess somewhat similar knowledge and skill, and in other ways they may be very different.

Classroom groups differ from most work groups in that membership in the classroom group is mandatory. In few other groups are members compelled to participate. Members in industrial work groups may not have complete freedom to leave a group at will, since economic or other circumstances may oblige them to remain even though they do not like the group or the leader or the task assignment. The fact remains, however, that in most work groups the members are not compelled by law to remain in the group. In most instances the workers have freedom of choice. Members of a classroom group cannot leave under any circumstance, since attendance is compulsory. This involuntary membership is a specific, distinct characteristic of a class group.

The control or leadership of a classroom group is not unlike that in other groups. Most work groups do not have control over the selection of a leader, nor do they have any more recourse from his leadership practices than do children in the classroom group. While the tasks of a leader of a class group vary widely from those of leaders of other kinds of work group, the problems of control and use of power are quite similar to those found in other work groups.

A class group is located within the structure of an institution. Many small work groups are located within large organizations. In this respect class groups and other work groups are not too dissimilar.

The features of a class group, then, which distinguish it from other work groups, lie not so much in its organization or its leadership, but in its goals, tasks, and the fact that membership is mandatory. However, each type of work group differs in some ways from every other kind of work group. Though it differs in some features, since it is essentially a work group, the class group may be said to have many characteristics in common with other work groups.

Questions for Study and Discussion

1. Some people argue that a classroom of children is not a group because the individuals in the group may not share common motives or goals. Evaluate this argument.

2. How and to what extent did membership in childhood play groups influence your interests and your social behavior at the time?

3. To what extent has membership in different groups influenced your attitudes toward teaching as a profession? Toward professional behavior?

4. What are likely to be some of the effects of isolation from play groups upon children?

5. Describe some play group activities you have observed. What were the probable effects upon individual behavior?

6. Are there ways teachers might make use of the childhood gang for educational purposes?

Suggestions for Further Reading

Benne, Kenneth and Grace Levit. "The Nature of Groups and Helping Groups Improve Their Operation," *Review of Educational Research,* 23:289–308, October 1953.

Laing, James M. and Paul F. Munger. "The Group Process Concept," *Education,* 80:231–234, December 1959.

Redl, Fritz. "Pre-Adolescents—What Makes Them Tick," Jerome Seidman (ed.), in *The Child, A Book of Readings.* New York: Rinehart, 1958, pp. 609–620.

Trow, William Clark, Alvin Zander, William Morse, and David Jenkins. "Psychology of Group Behavior: The Class as a Group," *Journal of Educational Psychology,* 41:322–337, October 1950.

Waller, Willard. *The Sociology of Teaching.* New York: Wiley, 1932, Chapter XII, "Crowd and Mob Psychology in the School."

Whyte, William F. "Corner Boys: A Study of Clique Behavior," *American Journal of Sociology,* 46:647–664, March 1941.

Wilson, Gertrude. "What Is a Group?" *Journal of the National Association of Deans of Women,* 12:103–104, March 1949.

Part II # Characteristics of Classroom Groups

Chapter 4   # Group Cohesiveness

CLASS groups vary with respect to the degree of unity and the amount of friendliness exhibited by the children who comprise the membership. Although teachers are aware of these differences in "groupness," why they occur is difficult to explain. Why, for example, do the members of one fifth grade class work better together, seem happier, and show more enthusiasm for engaging in school tasks than do the members of the fifth grade who come along the following year? Why is it that at times class group members show a lack of harmony when working on a common project, and then become strongly united when they believe another class is granted more privileges? Similar examples are observed every day in classrooms, and it is difficult to understand the reasons for the many variations of cohesiveness.

Chapter 3 indicated that research in the area of small-group behavior has isolated a number of group properties and dimensions that are significant to the understanding of group behavior. The property of cohesive-

51

ness may be identified in groups, but it is difficult to isolate for it exists in varying degrees and has many aspects. It is related to other properties in numerous ways, and the nature of the relationships determines to a large extent the degree of cohesiveness that a given group possesses.

The importance of developing a "good" group feeling has been stressed frequently by educators. Although the term cohesiveness is seldom used, there is frequent reference to the values to be gained by establishing shared feelings of "we-ness" or "belongingness." These latter terms imply friendliness between the children in the class, and they imply that the children have a good feeling about the group as a whole even though each individual member may not hold strong feelings of friendship for every other child in the class. However, although the importance of developing a friendly group feeling is frequently stressed in education, very little understanding is provided regarding the determinants of this condition. Knowing the values to be gained from developing a strong feeling of friendliness does not provide the teacher with the knowledge necessary to make the group attractive to its members. Descriptions of cooperative class groups in the literature do not help teachers understand why a class of children is cooperative or why the group members may suddenly become quarrelsome and uncooperative. The descriptions do not account for fluctuations in group spirit, nor do they explain why some class groups are attractive to members while others are not. Teachers need to understand why it is that a class of children may suddenly become indifferent to the project at hand when previously there was much enthusiasm. They wish to know why it is that children, who for some time have exhibited unfriendly feelings toward one another in the classroom, suddenly become very genial and friendly in their relationships with one another. Describing friendly class groups and stressing the value of developing cooperative class groups does not adequately provide a foundation for understanding the psychology of group behavior.

This chapter attempts to clarify the concept of cohesiveness, to recognize the forces operating in the group that affect cohesiveness, and to suggest practices that may increase group unity and friendliness.

The Nature of Cohesiveness

The first step in developing an understanding of class group cohesiveness is to develop certain concepts regarding the nature of this group characteristic. The literal definition of cohesiveness is "the tendency to stick together and be in accord." Educators have described it as a condition where children in the class are strongly motivated to become involved in group activities and in group affairs. The class atmosphere is friendly and happy, and children show their awareness of the existence of the group by speaking of *my* grade and *my* class, and by saying *we* work and *we* play. Although cohesiveness may be observed, described, and appraised, it does not lend itself to a single, specific definition. Objective or operational terms fail to cover a number of the abstract qualities that characterize cohesiveness. Definitions have been given, but any short concise statement fails to be inclusive and to make the meaning of the term clear. Usually brief descriptions are unable to encompass the multiple meanings inherent in the concept, and they sometimes employ illusive and subjective terms. But an adequate conception of cohesiveness can be formulated by describing a number of conditions that exist when a group possesses this characteristic.

Operational Definitions

A number of operational definitions have been formulated for measuring the amount of cohesiveness in a group at a given time. Cohesiveness has been defined in terms of the forces acting upon the members to cause them to remain in the group; the number of friendship ties that exist; the extent to which members of a group function as a unit and are free from dissension, conflicting interests, and disrupting forces; and the degree to which the members share the same norms in the area of social behavior.

Cohesiveness has been defined by Bonner [1] as a system of interlocking roles initiated and sustained by standards either already existing or evolved by members of a group in the course of striving for a common goal. Cohesiveness has been referred to as integration, which in turn is defined as the ability to maintain structure and function.[2] Various conceptions of cohesiveness were examined by Gross and Martin,[3] who concluded that cohesiveness should be defined in terms of the resistance of a group to disruptive forces, both internal and external. Another analysis in the area of cohesiveness found that there were three different aspects of this characteristic that could be distinguished: attraction to

[1] Hubert Bonner, *Group Dynamics: Principles and Applications*, New York: The Ronald Press Company, 1959, p. 69.

[2] Ralph M. Stogdill, *Individual Behavior and Group Achievement*, New York: Oxford University Press, 1959, p. 213.

[3] Neal Gross and W. E. Martin, "On Group Cohesiveness," *American Journal of Sociology*, 57:546–554, 1952.

the group, including resistance to leaving it; motivation of members to participate in group activities; and coordination of the efforts of members.[4]

Operational definitions are practical and useful for purposes of measurement, but of necessity such definitions do not include intangibles, which must be determined by inference. While the term cohesiveness may be appropriately applied to groups whose members are united by many friendship ties or to groups whose members are attracted to the group itself, the concept cannot be restricted to those characteristics that can be observed, recorded, and counted. Some elements of the concept are abstractions and can be inferred or deduced only from instances of behavior.

Behavior Indicating Cohesiveness

A classroom group will not always give evidence of being cohesive, nor will it do so in all situations. When thirty or more children are grouped in the same room for several hours a day, there are bound to be occasions when disagreements, arguments, and various other types of conflict occur. Does a quarrel over an incident that happened during the play period indicate the group is not cohesive? Does a vigorous disagreement over plans for a group project show a lack of group solidarity? Are there, in fact, specific behaviors that indicate group unity?

There is no systematic knowledge available concerning cohesiveness in classroom groups, but an analysis of the general nature of cohesiveness and a study of the investigations involving cohesiveness in general provide a number of clues about the kinds of behavior that indicate that a class group may be characterized as having unity or cohesiveness.

At times, situations arise that cause groups to show evidences of extreme solidarity. For example, the following situation was reported by a fifth grade teacher. In this instance, because of threat from an outside force, the group, which may or may not have been strongly cohesive previously, became so when a threatening situation became a reality.

THE SAFETIES

In our school, sixth graders are awarded the privilege and honor of taking turns at being "Safeties." A Safety wears a special cap and an arm band, and two Safeties each are stationed at crosswalks on the four corners of the school block in the morning, at noon, and after school. Lights

---

[4] Dorwin Cartwright and Alvin Zander, *Group Dynamics: Research and Theory*, Evanston, Ill.: Row, Peterson & Company, 1960, p. 72.

direct the traffic and Safeties direct the children. If children do not obey and start across the street while the light is yellow, or if they walk outside the white lines, or if they loiter or run, they are reported to their teachers. Some of the Safeties do a good job, but there are a number who glory in their authority and, figuratively speaking, wield a big stick.

This particular incident happened immediately after class started one morning. The door opened and two Safeties came in literally dragging two of our fifth grade boys. They reported these boys had stepped outside the white lines. Both fifth grade boys jerked loose and loudly and angrily denied the charge. Both talking at once, they claimed some other sixth graders had given them a shove, and that they had accidently stepped over the line. The two Safeties shook their heads and denied this was so. About this time the whole class erupted. There were angry shouts of "Big Head!" "Bully!" and other names. Such things as, "All you do is shove us around!" "You think you are so smart!" The Safeties continued to look smug and superior, and I asked them to leave and said we would settle this affair at a later time. There was no use attempting to begin a lesson, because by this time the children were reciting every case of unfair treatment they believed they had received at the hands of the Safeties. They were all convinced that the sixth graders took delight in picking on them, and that they ganged up on them to get them into trouble. The two boys who had been the most recent victims were patted on the back and consoled, and were made heroes for the day.

How children band together when their group or members of their group are attacked by outsiders was illustrated in the foregoing incident. This aspect of cohesiveness is easily discernible. The degree to which members are friendly and helpful to one another also indicates unity, but often the actual behavior is less obvious than when the group is defensive and members unite and form a solid front when faced by an enemy. The following incident was observed by a supervisor who was visiting a third grade social studies class. Although only a few of the class members were directly involved in the incident, it appeared that the reaction of the committee leader reflected the over-all friendliness and concern that the children felt for one another.

THE MAP MAKERS

In the back of the room a committee was working on a large floor map showing an area of the community. Rodriguez was the chairman and his job was to supervise the layout of the map. Everything was progressing smoothly until two boys who were working on the north section stood up to get a long range view of their work. It was then they noticed what Sol was doing. Voices grew a little loud and they could be heard saying to Rodriguez, "Look! Sol is making the railroad tracks too fat! It's going to spoil the map!" Sol kept on working and Rodriguez took no action. Others stopped working and joined the protest. "Fire him, Rod! Give him something else to do!" Rodriguez shook his head slowly and said to the disturbed committee, "No, we don't fire him. We just teach him how to make those tracks skinny." The children seemed to hesitate only an instant, and then two boys dropped to their knees beside Sol and began to show him how to hold his brush to draw a narrow line. The others, apparently satisfied that everything was under control, went back to work without another word.

Planning together and carrying out the plans indicates cohesiveness. A sixth grade class was losing some of the time allotted for art because the procedure for passing out the water, paper, and other supplies was too slow. The class planned a new routine for passing supplies efficiently and quietly. The class wanted the plan to work and it did work, because everyone cooperated. Class groups indicate they are cohesive when they are able to plan together and to solve problems of mutual concern.

Sharing the same behavioral norms is another indication of cohesiveness. At times teachers become concerned over this aspect of group unity, because the norms may not be the precise standards of behavior that teachers desire. On the other hand, when members of a cohesive class group agree to certain standards of behavior, they adhere to these standards and a result can be a much improved learning situation, even though the standards may or may not be the teacher's idealized standards.

Positive Consequences of Cohesiveness

Research findings indicate that a high degree of cohesiveness in a group contributes to a number of positive behavioral correlates. Again, these findings have implications for education even though they did not come out of research into actual classroom group situations.

Cohesive groups, because they function relatively free from dissension and conflict, have more time for work. When quarrels and conflicts occur individual productivity is lowered. Even when steps are taken to prevent wasted class time, the issues involved in the dissensions occupy the thoughts and dissipate the energies of many children. There are numerous reports from teachers that express their concern over the time lost from class lessons because children are involved in group dissension. The following incident is representative.

THE UNFINISHED FIGHT

The group I have always comes into the room after recess with an unfinished fight on everyone's mind. The children don't want to settle down to work, but instead they want to continue the argument. The quarreling is apt to break out again any time of the day. It is a problem because we always miss about five minutes of spelling every day. Then, too, some children never seem to put the fight out of their minds so it is very difficult to get them interested in school work.

As this description indicates, it is extremely difficult to motivate children and get them to concentrate on school work when fights and quarrels break out in class groups.

It is not uncommon for educators to claim that when class groups are cohesive the children will be motivated to work harder and learn more. It must be pointed out that although numerous studies have determined that cohesiveness is an important factor in learning and productivity, it can operate with both favorable and unfavorable effects. For example, it has been found that when the predominant group influences are toward increased productivity, cohesiveness tends to strengthen the influences and to heighten productivity. On the other hand, when the predominant influences in the group are to restrict production, then cohesiveness acts to lower productivity.[5] Other studies showing effects of cohesiveness have found that highly cohesive groups adhere to a work group norm for either *high* or *low* productivity. The findings indicate that cohesiveness as such does not increase individual learning, but the findings do suggest that when cohesive class groups manifest interest and enthusiasm for school tasks, individual members in the group will be stimulated to greater efforts. It has been observed that children in happy cohesive class groups, when highly motivated, work with zeal and encourage and help one another with the tasks at hand. Individuals are encouraged and inspired to do more because they are affected by the force of enthusiasm that arises from the total group. Also, when a group develops good working standards, cohesiveness provides the group with power to exert pressure upon members to conform. In this way cohesiveness helps to create a good learning situation. Studies consistently show that cohesiveness enables groups to influence members. When members like the group and the other members of the group, they conform more to the opinions of the group.[6]

It has been shown that cohesive groups are more able to operate under stress than are groups lacking in cohesiveness. Because cohesiveness involves morale and the feeling of belonging together and of identifying with others, it provides security for members. It is an agent making for

[5] Stanley Schachter, Norris Ellertson, Dorothy McBride, and Doris Gregory, "An Experimental Study of Cohesiveness and Productivity," *Human Relations*, 4:229–238, 1951.

[6] Leonard Berkowitz, "Liking for the Group and the Perceived Merit of the Group's Behavior," *The Journal of Abnormal and Social Psychology*, 54:353–357, May 1957.

persistence and group self-maintenance. Unity enables groups to resist disruptive forces, both internal and external, with much more success than do groups whose members are less unified. This implies that when class groups are cohesive the children are more able to withstand interruptions, outside distractions, and changes. It is not uncommon in the elementary school to have a work period interrupted by a messenger, a custodian, or a parent, or by an animal wandering into a door left open. Outside distractions occur, such as sounds of sirens, lawn mowers, low-flying planes, or other children having physical education. Although daily routines are established, the daily program is subject to many changes. For example, assembly programs, television specials, health examinations, paper drives, and many other things disrupt the established routines. More difficult for groups to adjust to than the things listed are changes that involve disappointment or produce anxiety. Cancellation of a field trip or loss of a regular teacher for a substitute might be examples of more severe changes.

The following report by an eighth grade teacher calls attention to another kind of change, one that is experienced to a greater or lesser degree by every class group.

NEWCOMERS TO THE CLASS GROUP

I am teaching this year in a school that has a large number of transfers. The pupils who come and go are from families of migratory farm workers or other transient workers. This has posed problems that I had not experienced before in previous jobs. Before I took this position the principal of the school told me that most of the behavior problems arose because of a failure to assimilate this short-term pupil population into the established class group.

I have found that the additions to the class and the withdrawals create an unrest. The most difficult job has been to find ways to get the permanent pupils to accept responsibility for helping newcomers. Then there is the problem of lessening the anxiety of new pupils, and helping them learn what behaviors are expected and what are not expected or tolerated by the school or the regular class group members.

Cohesive class groups can better withstand additions and withdrawals in membership, but if a cohesive class group is not guided toward acceptance of new children, it may act as a clique and shut out all outsiders. Resistance to newcomers can create unpleasant classroom incidents. Some evidence from research shows that newcomers to groups are admitted and integrated with greater facility when the members are informed that change is expected. It appears that expectation makes the adjustment to change easier.[7] Teachers who help class groups plan at the beginning of the year for integrating newcomers may find the assimilation process much less difficult. There is less threat to the regular group members and less rejection of new students when the class group is prepared for newcomers.

The Relation of Cohesiveness
to Other Group Properties

In Chapter 3 it was shown that a group differs from an aggregation or other collection of individuals because a group possesses a minimum, at least, of each of the following properties: (1) a multiple personnel with some feeling of identification and some degree of cohesiveness; (2) a system of interaction; (3) an organization or structure; (4) some common motives or shared goals; (5) some power to standardize behavior; (6) an observable pattern of behavior resembling what is called personality in an individual. The degree to which each of these properties exists in the group affects all the other properties and the degrees to which they exist. The extent to which a group is cohesive, then, is affected by the other group properties, and conversely, the natures and degrees of the other properties are dependent upon the degree to which the group is cohesive.

Interaction and Communication

It has been found that when techniques are used that limit or curtail pupil-to-pupil communication, or if verbal interaction in the classroom is channeled between the teacher and individual students, groups develop little unity. When communication and interaction are fostered and encouraged, cohesiveness increases. Bovard [8] found that the amount of verbal interaction that took place among class group members affected members' liking for one another. When communication was encouraged the interaction induced a positive feeling toward the group. This positive feeling pertained to individuals in the group and to the group as a whole. In classes where interaction was fostered by a number of specific techniques such as deflecting back to the group questions asked the teacher, cohesiveness was heightened. There was an absence of threat in

[7] Robert C. Ziller, Richard D. Behringer, and Matilda J. Jansen, "The Newcomer in Open and Closed Groups," *Journal of Applied Psychology*, 45:55–58, 1961.
[8] Everett W. Bovard, Jr., "Interaction and Attraction to the Group," *Human Relations*, 9:481–489, 1956.

the atmosphere and reduced feeling of isolation, even though the group was composed of members of mixed races and of mixed socio-economic statuses.

Numerous other studies reveal that the amount of interaction and the frequency of verbal communications have a direct relationship to the degree to which a group is cohesive. The implications for the elementary classroom group are clearly evident. When children are given opportunities to plan together, when they are encouraged to discuss their problems, and when techniques are used to foster oral communication, unity in the class group will be heightened. Also, when communication between children is very restricted, the amount of unity is decreased.

Structure of Class Organization

Cohesiveness is affected by the structure of the group. Clique formation, or the presence of subgroup rivalry, will decrease the cohesiveness of the total group, though cohesiveness may be high in each subgroup or clique. If the structure formation involves rivalry for power and prestige, and if rival leaders develop feuds that involve members of the class, group unity suffers. If group members are struggling for status, and do so at the expense of other group members, resentment is generated and affects group unity and solidarity.

A study involving a number of groups in a housing community found that a major dimension in which the groups differed was the extent to which the total groups were structured into subgroups.[9] The data showed that when three or more persons chose one another exclusively, the subgroups become cliques. The presence of cliques was found to make a less cohesive total group, but subgroups loosely formed did not affect group cohesiveness. It is important for teachers to note that a class group can have unity even though a number of small friendship groups exist within the total class organization. Because of the size of classroom groups there are always a number of friendship clusters. Sociograms reveal these groupings, but the figures that show each child's preference for work and play companions do not necessarily provide evidence of cleavage in the total group. They reveal, in most cases, the individuals who make up the small subgroups. They show which children like each other somewhat more than others in the class group and who may have more opportunity to interact inside and outside of class. However, if these friendship groupings are mutually exclusive, there is cleavage in the total group and the degree of cohesiveness is low.

[9] Leon Festinger, Stanley Schachter, and Kurt Back, *Social Pressures in Informal Groups,* New York: Harper & Brothers, 1950.

The results of a study by Kelley [10] showed that cohesiveness and group attraction were significantly affected by the kind of structure in the group. Experimental hierarchical groups were created in which some members were given high-status positions while others were assigned low-status positions. Some of the high-status members were assured that their positions in the hierarchy were secure. Other *highs* were told they might be moved to lower-status positions at any time. The individuals with low status were treated in a similar manner. Some were told they might be promoted while others were convinced that they would not be allowed to improve their positions in the structure. The study demonstrated that when high-status members faced "demotion" and low-status members faced the impossibility of improving status, the condition contributed significantly to a decrease in group attractiveness. Individuals who were secure in their positions of high status and members who felt they might rise in status were most attracted to the group and to the members in it. It was concluded that high status with security of position and low status with the possibility of upward locomotion both operated to develop interlevel friendliness. Low–nonmobile and high–mobile conditions seemed to result in hostility when members perceived persons at the other level either as threats to desirable positions or as occupants of coveted but unattainable positions.

If the structure of the classroom group is organized by the teacher into high and low groups according to ability, and if children perceive that there is no likelihood of advancement from low to high, the children in low groups will probably find the class group unattractive. Informal classroom studies find that children in the low and middle reading groups aspire to friendship choices within the high group. High-group members choose other high-group members. It may be concluded that permanent groupings in reading or in other areas will detrimentally affect the cohesiveness of the total class group. Other studies involving status hierarchies provide additional evidence to support the hypothesis that the practice of separating children into more or less permanent ability groupings may substantially affect the extent of total class cohesiveness and the degree of liking children have for the class group. Thibaut [11] found that interteam hostility developed when teams (subgroups) were forced to operate on an unequal basis. Children in low groups who perceive that it is unlikely that their positions will improve may develop hostile feelings toward the group as a whole. A study of the reactions of group

[10] Harold H. Kelley, "Communication in Experimentally Created Hierarchies," *Human Relations*, 4:39–56, 1951.

[11] John Thibaut, "An Experimental Study of the Cohesiveness of Underprivileged Groups," *Human Relations*, 3:251–278, 1950.

members toward aggressors who differed in status found that low-status aggressors received greater rejection than high-status aggressors.[12] A child's status in the class group is a matter of importance to him. Not only does his status affect how others will react toward him, but it exerts a direct influence upon his pride, self-concept, and satisfaction with the group. Although small groupings are necessary for effective teaching, they can be organized informally and can be varied so individuals of superior ability and those with inferior ability can at times coordinate their efforts and work together. A pleasant, friendly class atmosphere cannot be developed or maintained if a formal differentiation is made that brings subgroups into unfavorable comparisons with one another. Cohesiveness depends to a large extent on members liking the group; therefore, the structure must be such that members feel comfortable, and it must be one in which their contributions can be recognized.

Motives and Goals

When members share common motives, and when they work together for goals that are shared, cohesiveness is heightened. Research in child growth and development has demonstrated that child behavior is meaningful only when viewed in relationship to other factors operating in a social setting. Although there are other determinants, the social setting causes needs and offers ways in which these needs can be satisfied. On the basis of studies it can be stated that almost all children, if not all, strongly desire to identify with others of their age groups. Children enjoy belonging to peer groups and derive satisfaction from "groupness" or "belongingness" as such; thus, children in elementary classroom groups have at least one motive in common—they want groupness and they desire to be a group. Many children may value group affiliation more than they do achievement.

It has been stated before that one characteristic that seems to be common to most groups is that the individuals comprising the group have some common interest, aim, purpose, or objective. Although it is possible for a group to be a group with members sharing but few motives, a group cannot be described as cohesive unless members share common motives and goals. Because children come to their class groups with strong desires to be a group, and because they have a high degree of uniformity in many respects, they tend toward cohesiveness. However, the more that children share the same values, the more they share common goals, and

[12] John Thibaut and Henry Riecken, "Authoritarianism, Status and the Communication of Aggression," *Human Relations,* 8:95–120, 1955.

the more they view things from the same perspective, the more cohesive they will be.

Group Standards or Norms

Children who are cohesive share common or similar norms, and sharing of group norms is therefore an important index of group cohesiveness. The sharing of norms is not an important factor in creating cohesiveness; rather, the relationship is one in which cohesiveness affects the operation of group norms. The more cohesive the group, the more pressure it can exert upon members to make them conform to the norms of the group; stated another way, the potential power of a group is a function of its degree of cohesiveness. Research suggests that when cohesiveness is highly valued by the group, the members tend to exert pressures upon some individuals in an effort to integrate them into the group. In classroom groups that are highly cohesive, the children make greater efforts to agree and greater efforts to make changes toward agreement than do groups low in cohesiveness. The intensity and vigor that children exhibit when discussing what is "fair" and "not fair" in their play situations is an example. Noncohesive groups develop few behavioral standards and have little power to induce members to agree to certain standards.

Factors Affecting Cohesiveness

A complete conceptualization of cohesiveness requires some understanding of the factors that prevent group unity or that bring about friction and hostility. Many of the group behavior problems teachers face in classrooms are created by the same disruptive forces that impair group unity. For example, in contrast to the many classroom groups characterized by cohesiveness, there are some classes of children, such as the one described in the following example, that appear to lack all semblance of solidarity. The children in these classes exhibit such behaviors as frequent disagreements over small incidents, numerous interruptions caused by unpleasant remarks, and sudden eruptions of hostility. Teachers reporting such incidents sometimes seem more concerned over the time lost than they do over the lack of unity and the causes for it; some are more disturbed by the difficulties encountered when trying to teach such a noncohesive class than they are over the noncohesiveness itself or its causes.

SPECIAL PRIVILEGES

Quarrels between parts of the class are one big headache. One incident that happened recently caused accusations and fighting because a part of the class seemed to receive a special privilege and others didn't. We were studying about shipping in our fifth grade unit, and we were making a drawing of a harbor, using the opaque projector. The ones who didn't get to draw began to argue. They said some of the children drawing had been given opportunities to do other interesting things before, and they had not had a turn. Half the period was wasted getting the quarreling stopped. The children not drawing were not satisfied at all by assurances that they would get a turn next time.

Undoubtedly a number of conditions contributed to the lack of cohesiveness in this class group, but it seems evident that a knowledge of factors that create disruption and dissolution in groups is essential to teachers if such behavior is to be analyzed or understood and if remedial practices are to be employed.

Member Satisfaction and Group Attraction

Research has shown that group cohesiveness depends to a large extent upon member satisfaction with the group. In fact, much of the research relating to cohesiveness has involved investigating and measuring group attractiveness. This concept—group attractiveness—may be considered in two ways. It may be viewed from the standpoint of the individual and the forces that attract him to the group, or from the standpoint of the group and its power to attract members.

Why is a child attracted to a classroom group? Elementary education emphasizes the importance of the class group to the child. There is general agreement that classrooms should be "good" societies, and that a child needs a "feeling of belonging" if he is to develop to his greatest potential. Investigators of group behavior note group influence upon individual pupil development. For example, Bovard states, "The time may come when we will consider the kind of classroom experience the individual has had to be second in importance only to family experience in determining how he will relate to others, and to himself." [13] Although the development of adequate, adjusted personalities is extremely important and should not be minimized, we are at this time

[13] Everett W. Bovard, Jr., "Psychology of Classroom Interaction," *Journal of Educational Research*, 45:215–224, November 1951, p. 223.

exploring the needs of children in relation to the attractiveness of the class group rather than in relation to personality development.

For a class group to be attractive to a child, it must satisfy some personal needs such as his needs for affiliation, acceptance, recognition, and security. If the class group makes a child feel he is not liked or wanted, if the group makes him feel he is not able or successful, or if the group makes him feel he lacks worth or is insignificant, the group will have little or no attraction for the child. However, because a growing child has a strong need to belong, to be accepted by his peers, and to experience some success, he may not reject the class group for some time, but instead he will continue to seek acceptance and a place in the group. The fact that low-status individuals continually seek acceptance increases cohesiveness in some class groups. However, an individual who "goes along" with the group in a frustrated attempt to gain acceptance would in all probability leave the group if such a course were open to him. Viewed from the standpoint of the individual then, a class group is attractive only to the extent that it satisfies some of his personal needs; however, it appears that because individual children have such a strong desire to be a part of a group, cohesiveness may exist at a fairly high level in spite of factors that significantly reduce group attractiveness.

What power does a group have to attract members? What sources of attraction does a class group possess? We have stated that an individual child has needs that can be satisfied by membership in a class group. The power of the group and its attractiveness depend upon these individual needs. A class group is attractive to the extent that it fulfills the needs of the children who are members. A child who is a valued member is more likely to find the group attractive than one who is not valued. Dittes [14] found that a member who was made to feel well accepted was more attracted to the group than a member who was made to feel he was not accepted. The study showed that the effect of high or low acceptance was much stronger with an individual who was low in self-esteem to begin with, because such an individual had a stronger need for acceptance than others. In part, this explains why a child who is not accepted by the group does not decrease the overall unity to a great extent. His need for acceptance is great; therefore he tries to win acceptance by adhering to the group's norms and by sharing common motives and goals.

The activities of a class group may affect its attractiveness. However, regardless of how interesting or appealing certain class activities may be,

[14] James E. Dittes, "Attractiveness of Group as a Function of Self-Esteem and Acceptance by Group," *Journal of Abnormal and Social Psychology*, 59:77–82, 1959.

if a child's contributions are not valued, or if he is made to feel that his performance is of a low level or not needed, the interesting activities will not increase group attractiveness for the child. The idea is expressed frequently that if class work is made interesting and exciting, and if children are kept busy, few problems of class behavior arise. There is some truth in this statement, but there are related factors. Interesting activities must also contribute to each child's success, or provide recognition for him, or add to his sense of personal worth, or they lose their appeal. Interesting activities add to group attractiveness only to the extent that they satisfy needs.

There are some sources of attraction that are not primarily directed toward the individuals in the group, but are due to the group's characteristics or properties. In a previous section, the relationship of cohesiveness to other group properties was discussed. Whether a child likes his class group depends upon the structure, the tasks, the goals, and the other children who make up the membership. However, the teacher, the communication patterns, and the prestige of the class in relation to other classes also have some bearing upon whether a child finds his class attractive. When these characteristics support the individual, group attractiveness is enhanced; in turn, group attractiveness increases cohesiveness, but contributes to cohesiveness only if this satisfaction leads to positive, constructive behavior. Stogdill [15] points out that a group member may exhibit a high degree of satisfaction while in the process of playing around, wasting materials, dissipating group resources, and otherwise contributing to group dissolution. This kind of member satisfaction with the group does not contribute to cohesiveness. Also, even though one child likes the class very much when he behaves in a destructive manner, his behavior may detract from the group attractiveness for others, thereby again decreasing the over-all cohesiveness.

A child's expectations may affect whether he likes the class and the children in it. A child who comes to school believing that the class group will probably provide satisfying experiences will look for the sources of group attraction. A child who expects to have unsatisfying experiences will look for sources of dissatisfaction. Experiments show that the perceptions of individuals concerning group attractiveness can be influenced by the simple procedure of pointing out the various attractions that the group has and the advantages of membership.

[15] Ralph M. Stogdill, *Individual Behavior and Group Achievement*, New York: Oxford University Press, 1959, pp. 219–220.

Cooperation and Competition

Cooperative teaching practices versus competitive teaching practices is an issue frequently discussed in education circles and by others interested in education.

Child psychologists have been concerned over competitive practices because of the effects upon individual personality development. Group psychologists have been concerned with the question of cooperative versus competitive practices in relation to their effects upon learning and group processes. The investigations, in many instances, reveal the effects of each kind of practice upon the behavior of the group and upon group attraction and cohesiveness.

An investigation by Deutsch [16] clearly disclosed the effects of cooperation and competition upon the group process. He found that a situation in which the group members were in a cooperative relationship was more attractive than one in which they were competing. Cooperative classroom groups were created by telling the members that all would be given the same grade depending upon the overall quality of each group's work. The competitive groups were told that each member would be graded on his merits relative to others in the group. The cooperative groups displayed many behaviors indicating high cohesiveness. Compared to the competitive groups, the members liked one another more, made more attempts to influence one another, and were more friendly in their behavior. It was demonstrated that the cooperative groups possessed a number of characteristics which indicated high cohesiveness. There was coordination of effort, diversity in amount of contribution per member, subdivision of activity, attentiveness to fellow members, good communication, orderliness, and good group function. The results regarding most of the activities were found to favor cooperative behavior. Deutsch called attention to some practical implications of the study. He said that there was some indication that competition produced greater personal insecurity through expectations of hostility from others than did cooperation, and suggested that educators might well reexamine the assumptions underlying their common usage of a competitive grading system. He questioned whether a competitive grading system produced the kinds of interrelationships among students and the personal security that were in keeping with the important objectives of education.

A research designed to extend and further investigate the findings

[16] Morton Deutsch "The Effects of Cooperation and Competition upon Group Process," in D. Cartwright and A. Zander (eds.), *Group Dynamics: Research and Theory,* Evanston, Ill.: Row, Peterson and Co., 1960, pp. 414–448.

of the foregoing study sought to find if the lack of competition would reduce anxiety and lessen tension in a problem-solving situation and thereby increase productivity.[17] The problem-solving performances of groups of college students were compared under four conditions of reward: (1) rewards given to *individuals* with no competition involved, (2) rewards given to a *group* with no competition involved, (3) rewards given to *individuals* on a competitive basis, and (4) rewards given to *groups* on a competitive basis. The students were involved in discussions of problems in human relations. The measurement of the quality of the discussion made it clearly evident that the noncompetitive treatment was superior to the competitive.

From these and other studies it seems that cohesiveness and mutual acceptance promote communication and result in increased motivation and greater productivity. This appears to be particularly true when the task involves group discussion. Some research evidence, at least, strongly suggests that competitiveness arouses fear and anxiety in members and inhibits communication. Such findings have implications for teaching practice. For example, developing the skill of solving problems growing out of social situations is one of the more difficult tasks required of teachers. Although discussion periods in social studies usually involve the whole class group, and rarely, if ever, do teachers set up competitive situations between subgroups, the task of motivating and encouraging all members to participate is difficult. It seems that if the class group is cohesive, more children will participate and make contributions. On the other hand, if individual contributions are compared in a way that makes some children feel their remarks and contributions are better or worse than others, anxiety and tension will result. Anxiety and tension act to reduce the amount and quality of individual performance, which in turn impairs the adequacy of the group solution. It seems, then, that skill in group problem solving can be developed and improved by avoiding competition that includes comparisons and by treating each contribution with equal respect.

A study made with fourth grade children investigated the effects of cooperation and competition on the cohesiveness of the groups.[18] The results showed that working together under cooperative conditions increased members' liking for the group and the cohesiveness of the group.

[17] Lee Keith Hammond and Morton Goldman, "Competition and Non-Competition and Its Relationship to Individual and Group Productivity," *Sociometry*, 24:46–60, March 1961.

[18] Beeman N. Phillips and Louis A. D'Amico, "Effects of Cooperation and Competition on the Cohesiveness of Small Face-to-Face Groups," *The Journal of Educational Psychology*, 47:65–70, February 1960.

However, competitive conditions did not necessarily decrease cohesiveness. In the study they reported that under competitive conditions with a reasonably even distribution of rewards, there was no decrease or increase in cohesiveness.

That cohesiveness is increased when individuals work together rather than in competitive situations was demonstrated further by Sherif.[19] The experiment involved groups of eleven- and twelve-year-old boys in a camping situation, and tension and conflict were produced by competition. At the beginning all of the boys were housed together, and as expected, they quickly became friendly. After a few days the boys were divided into two groups and the competitive element was introduced. One group could achieve its goal only at the expense of the other group. This competition resulted in the development of hostile attitudes of one group toward the other. An attempt was made to integrate the antagonistic groups by involving them in activities that were in themselves pleasant and that required social contact between members of the opposing groups. This attempt was not effective in reducing the tensions. A second attempt at integration made it necessary for the competitive groups to work together. For example, in one instance the members of both groups had to work together and cooperate in order to secure a much desired film, for it was made impossible for either group to obtain it alone. The results showed that working together and striving for common goals increased friendliness and reduced the conflict.

Teachers who face problems such as the following one can readily see the implications of this study for teaching practice.

TEAM CONFLICT

Last year I set up permanent teams for baseball by dividing the class in half according to their seating positions. After several games I noticed much bickering, arguing, and fighting. Strife seemed to develop very soon between the two groups. As the games continued, the antagonism grew worse. Every day I talked with them about proper sportsmanship, and finally began threatening them by saying they would lose their game period unless the fighting stopped.

I realize now why some of the intergroup conflicts developed, and know I might have stopped it by having the whole class work together for some much desired goal. I might have alleviated some of the conflict also by changing teams frequently so that subgroup loyalty wouldn't have become so strong.

[19] Muzafer Sherif, "Superordinate Goals in the Reduction of Intergroup Conflict," *American Journal of Sociology*, 63:349–356, 1956.

Cohesiveness can be destroyed in a class group if the group is split into competing subgroups. Tension and conflict result, causing unpleasant working conditions for the children and teacher and reducing the time spent on curricular activities. Knowledge of how to reduce conflict and tension is important to teachers. It is most important to know that when class groups are required to work together for something they desire and that can be obtained only if they work together, conflict is reduced and cohesiveness is increased.

Restrictive Practices

The term *restrictive practices* is used here to mean practices that affect group processes negatively. They could be practices that manipulate structure so that status hierarchies develop, they could be practices that prevent group interaction, or they could be practices that threaten the group or prevent it from reaching its goals. Since the leadership and teacher control practices are studied in detail in Chapter 9, the discussion of restrictive practices in this chapter is limited. The only objective at this time is to mention some ways restrictive practices affect cohesiveness.

Cunningham [20] observed the various reactions of class groups to teachers' control practices. She noted that classes with teachers who used restrictive procedures responded in several decidedly different ways. Some groups exhibited active negativism and open hostility. In some groups there was tension and the members were fearful. Some classes were docile, but the children were dependent upon the teacher. Some classes were apathetic and indifferent and the children lacked enthusiasm and interest.

Groups that are openly hostile toward the teacher or toward the restrictive practices are also highly cohesive in most cases. Many times class groups that appear fearful also show evidence of being cohesive. Docile groups that are highly dependent upon the teacher are generally low in cohesiveness. Apathetic classes, because of infrequent interaction, may show no signs of cohesiveness.

Research provides some explanations for the various group reactions to restrictive practices and for the differences in degrees of cohesiveness.

Group unity is usually thought of as developing from agreeable experiences. In some groups, however, cohesiveness is increased when the group is threatened, when it is attacked, or when it is blocked from reaching desired goals. When a teacher is perceived as threatening, or when he employs practices that continually thwart the group, the mem-

[20] Ruth Cunningham and Associates, *Understanding Group Behavior of Boys and Girls*, New York: Bureau of Publications, Teachers College, Columbia University, 1951.

bers of the group unite. The more highly cohesive they become, the less restrained they are in expressing their hostility. Techniques were used in one study to arouse mild to strong degrees of hostility.[21] To arouse strong hostility, the groups were treated in an unjust and arbitrary manner. Sarcastic remarks were addressed to the groups and disapproval of them was expressed. The results showed that the highly cohesive groups released more than twice as much hostility as did the groups low in cohesiveness. It was concluded that the greater the cohesiveness of a group, the greater its power and the less restrained its members will be in expressing hostility.

Threat, which causes fear and tension, may also result in cohesiveness. The group becomes a source of security for members. A study of the effects of threat and frustration on group cohesiveness, involving two teams of boys in a summer camp, showed that strong frustration increased group unity.[22] It seems that when members of a group are threatened they seek emotional support and therefore they form closer relationships and cooperate with one another. Thibaut [23] found that members of groups that were unfavorably treated displayed an increase in attraction to the group. It appears that sharing the same misfortune improves interpersonal relations. Members may see themselves as similar to others, or they may turn toward one another to relieve their fears.

Groups that react to restrictive practices with docile acceptance and dependency upon the teacher are most likely threatened in such a manner that uniting offers no solution. The threats may be disguised in such a way that the children cannot cope with them. For example, when teachers control children with constant, gentle reminders such as, "Miss Bee would be very unhappy if anyone talked while we were reading," or "The *nice* boys and girls are sitting up straight, and they make Miss Bee *so* proud!" the children feel threatened but do not know why. They do not perceive the teacher as threatening since she never scolds or gets angry. They become very dependent upon such a teacher and seek security and approval from this source. The group does not unify, because for the most part the interaction is between teacher and pupil and there is little between pupil and pupil.

When the group members view the situation in the classroom as completely hopeless, and they cannot see a way of avoiding the threat or a means for reducing it, the group as a whole becomes apathetic and in-

[21] Albert D. Pepitone and George Reichling, "Group Cohesiveness and the Expression of Hostility," *Human Relations*, 8:327–338, 1955.

[22] Albert D. Pepitone and Robert Kleiner, "The Effects of Threat and Frustration on Group Cohesiveness," *Journal of Abnormal and Social Psychology*, 54:192–199, 1957.

[23] John Thibaut, "An Experimental Study of the Cohesiveness of Underprivileged Groups," *Human Relations*, 3:251–278, 1950.

different. Members interact infrequently and very little cohesiveness develops, if any.

In summary, school children cannot leave their classroom groups. They must remain even though the situation is so restrictive that it is extremely unpleasant or even intolerable. For the most part, adults can leave their places of work if the situation becomes intolerable. If they find themselves in a place that frustrates them, they may find it difficult to leave, but at least they have this choice. Usually, students at other levels of the school program can change their classes or revise their schedules so certain situations are avoided. In almost all cases, elementary school children have no choice but to remain. When the class restrictions are difficult to endure, they seek ways of relieving their frustrations. They may unite, since a single individual—because of fear of retaliation—must conceal some of his hostility. A group is less vulnerable, so individuals together can more openly express their hostile feelings. To counteract fear, they band together seeking security from fellow sufferers. When the source of the frustration is not evident and surface conditions appear serene and pleasant, the children may seek to relieve their insecure feelings by becoming passive and dependent. Cohesiveness decreases. When the situations seem hopeless, they protect themselves by reacting with indifference, and no cohesiveness is generated.

Developing Cohesiveness

In a study involving some groups of elementary school children, cohesiveness was developed by: (1) creating an awareness in children that a personal need could be fulfilled by functioning with the group; (2) emphasizing the personal gains that could be attained through belonging to the group; (3) stressing the group's potential for providing personal prestige; and (4) using cooperative techniques.[24] The experiments tended to suggest that the procedures did create highly cohesive groups.

Various external devices for increasing cohesiveness have been analyzed in research studies. These studies have implications for teachers who wish to develop unified groups in classrooms. The following are some of the means that have been found useful for developing cohesiveness.

1. Heightening the pupil's awareness of the various attractions the class group offers.

[24] Charles E. King, "The Applicability of Small Group Knowledge to the Classroom Situation," *Sociology and Social Research*, 45:18–23, October 1960.

2. Stressing satisfactions that are to be derived from working with other members of the class.

3. Telling the group as a whole what a good group it is when warranted.

4. Emphasizing the group's prestige (they are now *first* graders, *eighth* graders, *juniors*, etc.) when suitable.

5. Dramatizing the many new and interesting things they will learn, and beginning with an attractive activity on which the children can work together.

6. Having the group plan together some phases of their daily activities.

7. Getting favorable evaluations of the classroom group from an outsider (administrator, supervisor, another teacher) when appropriate.

A positive corollary of cohesiveness is member satisfaction with the class group. Group attractiveness leads to cohesiveness; it is also true that cohesiveness makes a group more satisfying to its members. As the following incident illustrates, cohesiveness can influence productivity.

YOU CAN DO IT!

I teach a group of seven-year-olds. In this group I have several children who are rather low in ability, and who do not respond in the same way as the more alert ones do. The children soon recognize this and know the ones who have difficulties.

The incident I am referring to happened one morning in my classroom. I had put up a chart with a poem which we had decided to memorize. The poem had been up several days. Each morning several children recited the poem from memory. All of the children had recited except for about four of the slower ones who had not asked for a turn. In this group is a little boy, Roger, who not only is slow, but also has difficulty with his speech. This particular morning Roger timidly put up his hand to recite the poem. He walked to the front of the room and began to speak. Together the class and I held our breath hoping he would be able to perform successfully.

He did quite well in reciting—very well, in fact, and as he neared the end and the children realized he was over the hurdle their faces began to light up and there were smiles all over the room. When Roger uttered his last word, there was a spontaneous outbreak from children throughout the room. "We knew you could, Roger!" Some clapped as they called, "Good for Rog!" and "He did it—we knew he could!"

The behavior of the children in this class indicated that the atmosphere was warm and friendly and that the children liked one another. Since the individuals in the class group as a whole were considerate and concerned over one of their members, it can be inferred that the atmosphere was one of mutual trust and understanding. It seems certain that a child not so well endowed for learning as the average in the classroom would be encouraged and inspired to do his best in such surroundings.

Questions for Study and Discussion

1. Observe a classroom or children's club for language that indicates group cohesiveness or the lack of it. Particularly listen to the children's language references to cohesiveness, such as "my class . . . ," "our work . . . ," "our class . . . ," etc.

2. Diagram the interlocking roles of a group that you know well. (Refer to Bonner's definition of cohesiveness.) It may be a group of which you are now or were recently a member, or it may be a group that you observe as a nonmember.

3. Distinguish between internal forces and external forces that may be disruptive to a group.

4. Do subgroups within the total group weaken group cohesiveness? Could they strengthen group unity? Can you think of examples of subgroups that could in some way strengthen the group's cohesiveness?

5. Give examples of group activities that motivated the members to participate in the group.

6. How useful for the classroom is the idea of cohesiveness that is based upon the motivation of pupils to participate in group activities?

7. Would the fifth grade class that was involved in the incident "The Safeties" show cohesiveness in other situations? on the playground? the cafeteria? etc.?

8. In a book devoted to elementary school curriculum or methods, locate and quote a part that gives the author's viewpoint on classroom or group atmosphere. Analyze the implications.

9. From your experience or observation, describe an incident in which a cohesive group was able to operate or continue work despite a disturbing condition or happening. If the upsetting influence had been increased in intensity, or if it had been prolonged, how might the group have behaved?

10. Prepare a checklist or a scale to guide your observation of a group when you wish to evaluate its cohesiveness. Refer to the section in this chapter, "The Relation of Cohesiveness to Other Group Properties," for ideas to include.

11. Why is a class group attractive to a child? Give as many reasons as possible.

12. Discuss the degrees of cohesiveness in groups that are: (a) docile and dependent on the teacher; (b) openly hostile toward the teacher.

Suggestions for Further Reading

Bass, Bernard M. "Feelings of Pleasantness and Work Group Efficiency," *Personnel Psychology*, 7:81–91, Spring 1954.

Berkowitz, Leonard. "Liking for the Group and the Perceived Merit of the Group's Behavior," *Journal of Abnormal and Social Psychology,* 54:353–357, May 1957.

Cohen, David, John W. Whitmyre, and Wilmer H. Funk. "Effect of Group Cohesiveness and Training upon Creative Thinking," *Journal of Applied Psychology,* 44:319–322, October 1960.

Dineen, Mary A. and Ralph Garry. "Effect of Sociometric Seating on a Classroom Cleavage," *Elementary School Journal,* 56:358–362, April 1956.

Grossack, Martin M. "Some Effects of Cooperation and Competition upon Small Group Behavior," *Journal of Abnormal and Social Psychology,* 49:341–348, July 1954.

Heber, Rick F. and Mary E. Heber. "The Effect of Group Failure and Success on Social Status," *Journal of Educational Psychology,* 48:129–134, March 1957.

Keedy, T. C., Jr. "Factors in the Cohesiveness in Small Groups," *Sociology and Social Research,* 40:329–332, May–June 1956.

Libo, Lester. *Measuring Group Cohesiveness.* Ann Arbor: U. of Michigan, 1953.

Pepitone, Albert and Robert Kleiner. "The Effects of Threat and Frustration on Group Cohesiveness," *Journal of Abnormal and Social Psychology,* 54: 192–199, March 1957.

Pepitone, Albert D. and G. Reichling. "Group Cohesiveness and the Expression of Hostility," *Human Relations,* 8:327–338, 1955.

Phillips, Beeman N. "Effect of Cohesion and Intelligence on the Problem-Solving Efficiency of Small Face-to-Face Groups in Cooperative and Competitive Situations," *Journal of Clinical Psychology,* 50:127–132, October 1956.

Phillips, Beeman N. "Effects of Cooperation and Competition on the Cohesiveness of Small Face-to-Face Groups," *Journal of Educational Psychology,* 47: 67–70, 1956.

Phillips, Beeman N. and Louis A. D'Amico. "Effects of Cooperation and Competition on the Cohesiveness of Small Face-to-Face Groups," *Journal of Educational Psychology,* 47:65–70, February 1956.

Sherif, Muzafer. "Experiments in Group Conflict," *Scientific American,* 195:54–58, November 1956.

Stendler, Celia, Dora Damrin, and Aleyne C. Haines. "Studies in Cooperation and Competition: I, The Effect of Working for Group and Individual Rewards on the Social Climate of Children's Groups," *Journal of Genetic Psychology,* 79:173, 197, December 1951.

Taguiri, Renato and Nathan Kogan. "Personal Preference and the Attribution of Influence in Small Groups," *Journal of Personality,* 28:257–265, September 1960.

Zander, Alvin, Ezra Stotland, and Donald Wolfe. "Unity of Group, Indentification with Group, Self-Esteem of Members," *Journal of Personality,* 28:463–478, December 1960.

Chapter 5   Interaction and

                                                    Structure

THE behavior of a group is determined to a large extent by the patterns of communication that develop and by the nature of the structure (or structures) that form as a result of the interaction. The communication patterns within which groups work affect total group behavior, and the positions that individuals occupy in the group structure affect their individual responses and actions.

Throughout this book we are concerned with the many types of group behavior that arise in the classroom, and all these various kinds of behavior are actually the products of interaction. In other words, the outcomes of group members' reactions to one another are the group behaviors upon which attention is focused. This section is not concerned with *specific* types of behavior growing out of interaction, but rather the focus is upon the *positioning of members* as a result of interaction (structure) and the *form* of interaction (communication).

When individuals interact over a period of time, an informal structure arises. However, the class group has a formal structure as well. Members are placed in various groupings and are expected to do certain things according to these groupings. Research indicates that members of class groups may relate to one another in certain ways according to this formal structure, but that their interrelationships will also be affected by pressures stemming from the informal structure. The influence of group structure on member behavior and member satisfaction with the group is documented by numerous studies. Studies show also that the functioning of the group as a whole is affected by the extent to which the group is organized into special subgroups or cliques, which is part of the informal structure. Also, the patterns of behavior that develop in class groups are affected by the communication practices. Studies reveal that the nature of the informal structures that characterize a class group is determined to a large degree by the group's communication processes. These findings and many others make it apparent that some knowledge of structure and communication is essential to the understanding of group behavior.

The goals of this chapter, then, are: (1) to analyze and develop concepts relating to interaction and structure; (2) to report the significant findings from research; and (3) to make applications of the concepts and findings to classroom groups.

Analysis of Interaction

Any identifiable incident of class group behavior involves interaction. Such behavioral incidents are, in fact, examples of the interactive behavior of individuals in a class group. However, as previously stated, we are not concerned at this time with the total process of interaction, but rather the object is to examine the way interaction takes place and to note certain factors that influence patterns of interactions in class groups.

Meaning of Interaction

Interaction refers to the relationship between two or more persons in which the actions of each person affect those of the other person in the situation. If one person's behavior is described in order to illustrate interaction, this description would include how the individual acts toward others and how the others react toward him.

Bonner [1] defines social interaction as "a type of relationship between two or more persons in which the actions of one are affected by the actions of another."

Another way of describing what is meant by interaction is to say that when individuals form a relationship, "they emit behavior in each other's presence, they create products for each other, or they communicate with each other." [2]

According to Stogdill,[3] interaction means that in a group composed of two members, A reacts to B and B to A in such a manner that the response of each is a reaction to the behavior of the other. In groups of larger size, the interaction pattern becomes very complex.

The following example describes reactions of two individuals to each other and effects of their reactions on the rest of their group.

ACTION AND REACTION

During the noon hour on the playground, Charlie spit on Joe. There were two factions in the class. Charlie was the leader of the minority group, while Joe was an important member of the popular group in the class.

Later, as the class came in from the playground, Joe waylaid Charlie in the lavatory. He had prepared wet paper towels which he used to slap Charlie. The result was a fight of considerable proportions. Of course, there was an audience. Each boy had his own group backing him. Finally a teacher appeared and the fight was stopped. The discord continued in the class for some time, however, and it was extremely difficult to suppress further outbursts between the two factions.

In this incident, Charlie reacted to Joe by spitting on him, while Joe responded by slapping Charlie with wet paper towels. The reactions of the two individuals were similar—that is, both were aggressive. However, series reactions in interaction are not necessarily the same. Had Charlie spit on a timid youngster, he might have responded to this act by running away to avoid a fight, or he might have reacted by reporting the incident to the teacher. Had this occurred, the reactions of other group members to the two individuals would have been different.

Homans [4] has proposed that interaction is the group's behavior that

[1] Hubert Bonner, *Group Dynamics: Principles and Applications.* New York: The Ronald Press Company, 1959, p. 35.
[2] John W. Thibaut and Harold H. Kelley, *The Social Psychology of Groups,* New York: John Wiley & Sons, 1959, p. 10.
[3] Ralph M. Stogdill, *Individual Behavior and Group Achievement,* New York: Oxford University Press, 1959, p. 18.
[4] George C. Homans, *The Human Group,* New York: Harcourt, Brace & Company, 1950, pp. 109–121.

arises from its internal system, as differentiated from the behavior that arises from its external system—that is, the group's behavior as it reacts to a particular environment. In explaining the process of the growth and development of group interaction, he suggests that if frequent interactions between members of a group take place, then the interaction increases the liking of members for one another, which leads in turn to further interactions. He suggests, also, that interaction and friendliness are associated only if authority does not enter into the situation (that is, if some members do not have authority status). Also, interaction is accompanied by friendliness among members of a group only if the group as a whole is successful in its environment. A further point emphasized is that the more frequently persons interact with one another, the more alike in some respects both their activities and their sentiments tend to become.

When children meet together in the class group for the first time, some degree of uncertainty pervades the situation. There is a certain amount of jockeying for position. During this time the members explore the limits of behavior. Some test the authority and methods of the teacher, and while this is going on, members are assessing one another as well as the teacher. Because of the size of the class group, subgroups—or small friendship groups—form. Individuals interact and there is interaction between these subgroups. As is the case with most groups, class groups go through stages of group formation and growth. This broad pattern of interaction has been described as "the changing networks of relationships." Thus, within the class group there may be many cliques or subgroups, and one child may have two or more sets of relationships in these separate, though interrelated, networks. In the early formation stage of the class group, the relationships change rapidly. Later these networks change more slowly.[5]

In the beginning stages of class group formation the interaction is generally two-way—that is, between pupil-pupil or teacher-pupil. In a very short time, however, children begin to know what to expect of each other person in the group and of the teacher. They become more sure of themselves and more comfortable in the group setting. Any major changes in this network of developing relationships may cause the group to disintegrate for a time because the group cohesiveness and morale have not developed sufficiently to enable the group to withstand change and disruption.

[5] Henry S. Maas, "Understanding Group Processes," in *Fostering Mental Health In Our Schools,* Association for Supervision and Curriculum, Washington, D.C.: National Education Association, 1950, Chapter 17, pp. 286–299.

CHANGE OF CLASSES

Due to crowded conditions, we had a shift in classes. This took place during the third week of school. We made a shift from a complete third grade class to a third–fourth grade combination.

The principal came to announce to the class the names of those students who were to be involved in the change. Everything went smoothly until Bill's name was called. Bill promptly burst out in tears. Then the group reacted. Up to this time all the children were in control of themselves, but as soon as Bill began to cry the group that was involved in the change immediately began to beg not to be changed and to act in a very upset manner. Those who were not changing also showed they were upset. They kept asking if the class could not remain together. It seems that if these shifts in classes do not take place during the first few days of school, the children become very disturbed over the change.

Observation reveals that children behave differently in one group from the way they do in another group, and they behave differently in a group from the way they do when they are alone. The presence of other people elicits different responses than those that characterize the behavior of an isolated person. This is because the actions of each person affect all the other individuals in the situation.

Many factors affect these relationships. Children in class groups act in certain ways because of the ways they perceive the situation. What they have learned, or their past experiences, determine to a great extent their behavior in the class group. How they feel toward others is also an outcome of past experience and affects their group relations. The nature of the group organization partially determines the interactive behaviors in the classroom. Thus, the interaction in a class group is determined by many things, including the perceptions of the individuals who make up its membership and the environment in which the interaction takes place.

Elements of Interaction Patterns

Interaction involves several aspects and elements, and these must be related in some way if patterns of interaction are to be described in an understandable manner. We have noted that whenever individuals interact, certain broad patterns of behavior emerge. Mutual liking of members, for example, provides a general pattern of interactive behavior, but only a broad framework is indicated by this pattern. The determining elements and the means by which interaction takes place are not specified.

Interaction cannot be treated as a product of the group more or less independent of the individuals composing the group. Neither can it be described without taking into account the situation in which it occurs.

Thus, to describe group interaction patterns, both the characteristics of the members and the nature of the group environment must be considered, for interaction patterns are determined in part by such factors as age, sex, and social acceptability of the members, and by such environmental influences as the group organization, the communication practices, and the size of the group.[6]

Although reciprocal behavior (how individuals act toward others and how others act toward them) is an important aspect of interaction, there is another developmental aspect that is equally important. As a result of the interaction of group members, a structure emerges. This is to say that there is a patterning of positions in the group. In the case of the class group, there is a formal structure (or structures) to which members are assigned positions, and within this formal organization develops an informal structure (or structures). Both the formal and the informal structures determine to a large degree the patterns of interaction that develop.

The ways individuals relate to one another in the group, and the structures that emerge, are affected by the communication network. This communication network affects, and is affected by, member relationships, the nature of the group, and other factors in the environment.

Any discussion of the interaction children have in a classroom situation must give consideration to both the physiological and psychological characteristics of the individuals involved and the factors affecting the situation in which the interaction occurs, and structures, too, must be examined with these factors in mind. Children will like one another more, and be more satisfied with the group, if the structuring is somewhat flexible. On the other hand, if interaction is severely curtailed in the classroom—that is, if communication between group members is severely limited or if it is mostly between pupil and teacher, this factor will determine to a large extent the patterns that will develop in the group. To summarize, the group situation and the interests, attitudes, and motives of the group members are interdependent—all determine to some degree the kind of interaction patterns that will occur.

The Development of Structure

The term *structure* describes the phenomenon of members of a group being located in particular respects relative to other members. In general, the term refers to ways members interrelate and to the patterns that are formed; it may, however, refer to prescribed patterns of relationships—

[6] A. Paul Hare, *Handbook of Small Group Research*, New York: The Free Press of Glencoe, 1962, pp. 167–168.

that is, a structure organized in advance. Sometimes the term structure is used to distinguish parts of groups—that is, the subgroups and cliques found within larger group formations. What is meant by structure? How does structure originate? Once these questions are answered, examination can be made of the formal structuring of class groups and the effects of these structures upon individual and group behavior.

Meaning of Structure

Structure in a group is sometimes conceived as a network of varied roles, statuses, and reciprocal expectations. The *roles* that individuals assume are defined by the *functions* he performs or the general nature of his contribution to the group. *Status* implies a hierarchy of positions. Both achieved and ascribed statuses in groups are contingent upon group expectations—that is, the mutual acknowledgment among members regarding the value of each position. Figure 2 shows the structure of a classroom committee.

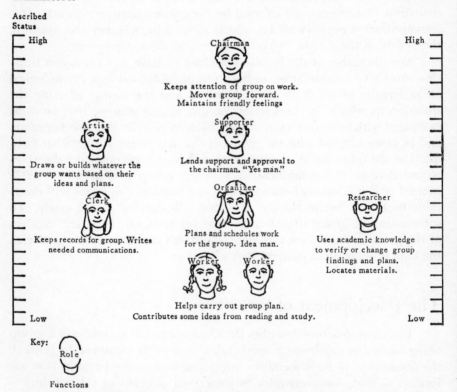

Ascribed Status

High — Chairman — High

Keeps attention of group on work.
Moves group forward.
Maintains friendly feelings

Artist

Supporter

Draws or builds whatever the
group wants based on their
ideas and plans.

Lends support and approval to
the chairman. "Yes man."

Clerk

Organizer

Researcher

Keeps records for group. Writes
needed communications.

Plans and schedules work
for the group. Idea man.

Uses academic knowledge
to verify or change group
findings and plans.
Locates materials.

Worker   Worker

Low   Low

Helps carry out group plan.
Contributes some ideas from reading and study.

Key:
Role
Functions

Fig. 2. Structure of a classroom committee engaged in preparing a report—showing roles, functions, and ascribed status (hierarchy).

Sometimes structure is described in terms of a network of *positions*. Each position is conceived as part of an inclusive system of positions, and each carries with it definite prescriptions for behaving. The expected behaviors of persons occupying certain positions constitute the roles associated with the positions.[7]

Stogdill[8] defines both status and function in terms of a particular position rather than for any given occupant of the position. He defines role according to the pattern of behavior that an individual exhibits. He suggests that at least three factors seem to operate in structuring a group's expectations about a member's role. The first relates to the status and function of the position the member occupies; the second comes from the group's demands upon the member as the result of changes in the group's requirements; and the third comes from the other members' perceptions of the kind of person the member in question is.

According to Sherif,[9] one of the evidences of structure is "the appearance of relative, interdependent roles for individual members in a hierarchical order at relative distances from a leader."

When speaking of structure, use a number of terms to indicate that each group member can be located in relation to all other members according to some criterion of placement. The most common terms relating to an individual's position in a group are: status, rank, position, and role. Sometimes an individual's location in a group is identified by stating that he belongs to a certain subgroup or clique, or that he is a central figure or a marginal member in the group. Because of their familiarity with sociometric techniques, teachers use such terms as "leaders," "stars," "isolates," and "rejectees" to indicate children's positions in structures; or they may say a child is popular or not popular.

Youngsters also develop their own names to indicate an individual's position in the structure. These names also indicate expectancies concerning roles and categories into which individuals are grouped. McGuire and Clark[10] found that such names as the following were assigned to individuals to designate acceptance and position in the structure: "wheels" (the top crowd, or the ones who run everything); "brains" (students, or those who take little interest in anything except studies); "mice" (the quiet ones who are inoffensive and ineffectual); "drips" (would-be wheels who make others uncomfortable); and "dopes" (would-be brains who arouse antagonism).

[7] Theodore M. Newcomb, *Social Psychology*, New York: Dryden Press, 1950, pp. 276–270.

[8] Stogdill, *op. cit.*, p. 128.

[9] Muzafer Sherif, *An Outline of Social Psychology*, New York: Harper & Brothers, 1948, p. 101.

[10] Carson McGuire and Rodney A. Clark, "Age Mate Acceptance and Indices of Peer Status," *Child Development*, 23:141–154, 1952.

Generally speaking, group structure is usually thought of as a hierarchy of statuses in which the group awards certain members more and other members less status. The same criteria that determine "liking" and "disliking" are factors in determining status. Status may also be affected by such things as sex, age, material possessions, looks, social class, and abilities that contribute to aspects of the group's purpose. In some groups of children and adolescents, status may be determined by physical size, or by the possession of the only football to which the group has access, or because some individuals talk more and in louder voices than others.[11]

Structure is also thought of as the group's distinguishable parts, as indicated by the existence of subgroups or cliques. The following incident is an example of a subgroup structuring. In this case, membership in an outside group distinguished some members of the classroom group and set them apart from others; on one day of the week, at least, this particular structure was evident.

THE BROWNIE GROUP

Thursday is Brownie meeting day and all the girls that belong to this group wear their Brownie uniforms and hats to school on this day. These girls are always rather excited and have some trouble keeping their minds on school work. They are more interested in what the Brownies are going to do after school.

Many of the girls belong, and new girls join all during the year. I have noticed recently that on Thursdays, Brownie girls are together more on the playground, and this past week they were excluding the non-Brownies in their play and activities.

The Brownie girls kept talking about a "hike" they were taking, and about the special treats they were having to celebrate a birthday. Then the hurting remark came. "You can't play with us because you don't belong to our Brownie Group!" The non-Brownies were very disturbed and of course they came to me because these girls on other days play well together.

Friday they were all happy again and playing together, but somehow, I don't feel they will ever be the same on Thursdays, and I hope it does not eventually cause a permanent split in the group.

Children and other young people attach particular importance to uniforms and insignia that indicate "belonging," and sometimes these marks become the objects of great striving. Possession of uniforms or insignia in children's groups is important because these things bring recognition to the persons who have them. In adult groups, the possession of a Phi Beta Kappa key, for example, indicates that the owner possesses

---

[11] Dorwin Cartwright and Alvin Zander, *Group Dynamics: Research and Theory*, Evanston, Ill.: Row, Peterson & Company, 1960, p. 648.

certain abilities and skills that are acknowledged bases of high status in some segments of society. However, uniforms, insignia, and the like are often prized by children and other young people not because they indicate special accomplishments but simply because they identify an individual as being a member of a particular group. They give him a feeling of "belonging."

Formal and Informal Structures

All formal groups have organized structures established for the group. A characteristic of all formal work groups is differentiation of roles and responsibilities regarding the aim, task, or goal of the group. The purpose of organizing and structuring any work group is to see that the group can reach its goals effectively. In many work groups the leadership function is an important element in the organization structure. Developing this structure involves grouping individuals in a manner that will best achieve the goals. Development of a structure also involves the problem of grouping in a way that will best promote cooperation and allow the leader to function effectively. Thus the responsibilities or duties of members are set down in the formal structuring of work groups. In short, the established structure sets down in advance a patterning of positions and the responsibilities of the leaders, and it determines the relationships of participating members to one another.

The formal structuring does not alone determine the role expectations of members, however. Members themselves establish expectations for one another as well as for the organization as a whole. This is true regardless of the kind of work group involved or the characteristics of members of the group. The formal structure may have a great influence upon the kind of interpersonal relations that develop, but it does not determine in advance all the additional types of expectancies that arise. Within the formal structure, an informal group develops. When this informal group is cohesive, and when member relationships are congenial, this informal structure provides many satisfactions to the group members. It frequently influences group productivity, or it may operate to protect the members against leadership practices that they interpret as menacing to their welfare.

Organization of the Class Group

It must be recognized that class groups frequently represent highly formalized structures. Often the class group organization is firmly predetermined and is completely independent of, or separated from, individual desires or preferences.

One factor that creates or necessitates a differentiation of positions in formal organizations is that different members have different abilities. Also, formal structures are developed to permit leaders to function effectively—that is, to help group members perform their tasks and to see that the purpose of the group is achieved. At times it seems that class groups are structured for the primary purpose of enabling teachers and administrators to carry out their tasks with the greatest facility, rather than to enable pupils to best perform their tasks. Of course it could be argued that if the prescribed structure of the class group facilitates the work of the teacher, then the pupils will be given more attention and thus learn more. However, this argument is debatable. Again, it often seems that new types of structures are devised in districts because a new change in structuring or grouping usually draws some attention to a district and to its administration. Whatever the basis of the structuring, however, the reason generally advanced is that it is done to best care for individual differences and to best help individuals achieve their maximum developments.

Havighurst and Neugarten [12] suggest that this structuring or sorting by the schools is based upon two factors: the child's ability and his social class background. They claim that the educational system (though not intentionally) tends to treat children of higher social status differently from those of lower status. There seems to be ample evidence to substantiate their point of view. An examination of a few of the grouping practices commonly employed in various sections of the country suggests that these formal structures in the schools foster a kind of caste system. High in the caste system are those children with mental abilities best suited to the academic work of the school. Low in the caste system are those children whose mental abilities are not best suited to academic work, or those children who are not motivated to achieve what they are capable of achieving. Many of the children in the "low groups" come from backgrounds that are "impoverished" in the sense that they do not provide experiences that prepare children for the tasks required by the school curriculum.

GROUPING OF PUPILS. Class groups have been structured (or grouped) in a variety of ways over the years and no attempt will be made at this time to summarize all these grouping practices. For purposes here, it is sufficient to examine but a few of the common methods employed in various sections of the country.

Methods employed in structuring or grouping students in the secondary schools place varying emphasis on: (1) grouping by type of

[10] Robert J. Havighurst and Bernice L. Neugarten, *Society and Education*, Boston: Allyn and Bacon, 1957, p. 230.

curriculum; (2) segregating in classes on the basis of ability as revealed by various test scores; (3) grouping by sex; and (4) grouping in ways most convenient for teaching logically organized subject matter.[13] In secondary classrooms, interaction is often curtailed, and further structuring occurs as a result of such practices as (1) arbitrarily assigning pupils to seats by alphabetical order; (2) segregating students who are "too friendly" by placing them in separate classes or seating them apart; (3) forbidding talking without first obtaining permission; and (4) organizing class discussion so that communication is from student to teacher or teacher to student.

At the elementary school level, if the school is large, having 80 or more pupils per grade, it is not uncommon for children to be grouped according to intelligence quotients into three grade sections of somewhat equal size. One grade group may range in IQ from 70–92. The average ability grade may range from 93–110. The high grade group might range from 110–140 or higher. For these three sections of each grade, made more homogeneous with respect to IQ, curricula and methods of teaching are usually differentiated. For the middle group, the curriculum is an approximation of the expected for the average grade-level. For the highest group, the curriculum is usually enriched, and the goals of achievement extended. For the lowest group, the curriculum may consist of the minimum essentials, and academic goals are more limited.

Whether "homogeneous grouping" is practiced by grouping children into different classes, it is common practice to divide each classroom group into ability groups and to arrange the curriculum on difficulty levels according to the ability level of each group of pupils. Usually three ability groups are formed within the classroom—a high, middle and low, and although many factors in numerous combinations are used as a basis for these groups, intelligence tests or achievement tests are usually the determining factor. This method of structuring the class greatly complicates class organization, since often a teacher has three or four different ability groups in one room. In some cases the class may be divided into groups for each of several curriculum areas—for example, for reading, spelling, and arithmetic.

Even though ability grouping is not employed in all areas of the curriculum, it is a common practice to group (or structure) pupils in the elementary school according to reading achievement. The plan of dividing the class into three reading groups according to achievement is widespread, although other plans for organization are advanced from time to time. The three-group reading plan structures the children into

[13] Lindley J. Stiles and Mattie F. Dorsey, *Democratic Teaching in Secondary Schools,* Philadelphia: J. B. Lippincott Company, 1950, pp. 414–415.

low, average, and high groups. Supposedly, the grouping is flexible—that is, a child in a slow group who improves is moved to the next higher group. However, flexibility in this case is more theoretical than practical. Basic reading texts are designed and arranged to introduce skills and vocabulary gradually. A new skill is not introduced until a child has mastered a previous skill, which thus serves as a foundation. For example, a child is not asked to deal with syllabicating words until he has developed some understanding of vowel rules. When a child is moved from a low group to a middle group, it becomes necessary for him to move from one text to another. All groups do not finish their texts at the same time. If a child is moved to the middle group, he would of necessity jump or skip the material that the middle group has previously covered. In many instances he would lack the foundation for learning new skills that the middle group has already acquired. Therefore, although educators and teachers advocate flexible grouping in reading and in other areas, the procedure is not practiced as frequently as it is advocated. In fact, in some sections of the country, it is not uncommon to find a class of children seated permanently at tables according to high, medium, or low placement! Even though the "lows" may be average or high in arithmetic or in some other subject, or the "highs" may be low in some areas, a hierarchical structure is determined by reading achievement and emphatically emphasized by placement at tables.

EFFECTS OF GROUPING PRACTICES. Research shows that status structures that provide little opportunity for upward locomotion cause hostile feelings in individuals and dislike for the group. For example, as said earlier, hierarchy was created experimentally in groups by Kelley,[14] who assigned some members to central or nonmobile positions and others to peripheral or mobile positions. Each of the positions was associated with high or low status. In the study it was demonstrated that low-status–nonmobile conditions and high-status–mobile conditions produced a significantly lower degree of attractiveness than the opposite experimental conditions—high-status–nonmobile and low-status–mobile. In other words, the individuals in the low group who perceived that there was no way for them to be moved to a higher position, and those in the high group who were always faced with demotion, found the group relatively unattractive. The liking of members for the group was affected by this kind of structuring.

Kelley concluded that high status with security of position and low status with possibility of upward locomotion both operated to develop interlevel friendliness. It was found that the low–nonmobile and high–

---

[14] Harold H. Kelley, "Communication in Experimentally Created Hierarchies," *Human Relations,* 4:39–56, 1951.

mobile conditions were definitely more detrimental to the group's total cohesiveness than were the other status–mobility combinations investigated. Again repeating, this was explained in terms of hostility that resulted from perceiving individuals at the other level either as threats to desirable positions or as occupants of coveted but unattainable positions.

Although it is difficult to determine the precise effects of high, medium, and low reading groupings upon either individual or group behavior, it would seem that such structuring does have a negative affect upon total group cohesiveness. It would seem also, that such structuring would emphasize children's feelings of defeat, anger, and bewilderment. While no one would deny that children with reading difficulties need specialized instruction, it would seem that assigning them to a clearly perceived low-status position in the group structure will only increase their frustration. For example, it has been found that the children with reading disability show a significantly greater proportion of dependence, aggression, and withdrawal reactions while reading than do children without such difficulty.[15] Also, evidence suggests a relationship between peer prestige status and reading achievement status. It seems that this holds true irrespective of the socio-economic level of the school community.[16]

No child wants to be continually reminded that he cannot read, and with this self concept he is likely to feel inadequate and perhaps rejected, and he is likely to become a disturbing factor in the classroom. No children wish to be placed in a low-status position. It is reported, for example, that children in both low and middle first grade reading groups aspire to friendship choices within a high reading group. Members in the high group make friendship choices among other high group members.[17] Teachers of other grade levels, in conducting sociometric studies in their class groups, have substantiated this finding. Of course, it must be recognized that other factors are functioning in this situation, and that such studies do not indicate to what degree the high, middle, and low group organization is a determining factor.

Group studies show that differential attractiveness of positions in the group exerts forces on members to change their positions. When there appears to be no means to move toward attractive positions, the morale of the group suffers. It is possible for the formal structure in classrooms to have quite explicit paths set up for advancement from one work

---

[15] Gladys Natchez, "Oral Reading Used as an Indicator of Reactions to Frustration," *Journal of Educational Research,* 54:308–311, April 1961.

[16] O. V. Porterfield and Harry F. Schlichting, "Peer Status and Reading Achievement," *Journal of Educational Research,* 54:291–297, April 1961.

[17] Lois V. Johnson, "Direction of Friendship Choices in First Grade Reading Groups," unpublished manuscript, University of Illinois, 1947.

group to another, whether these groupings are in reading, arithmetic, or other subjects. This practice is far more desirable than practices that create work groups in which there is no apparent likelihood of change. When it appears to group members that there is no clearly defined means of changing position in the structure, studies show that low-status members become hostile and aggressive.

Incidents of class group behavior problems written by teachers reveal that certain class structurings contribute to certain group behaviors that teachers consider to be problems.

THE LOW GROUP

My third grade class was working some arithmetic problems. The class was grouped according to achievement—that is, the children were placed in groups of high, medium, and low achievement. At the time this incident occurred, the low and high groups were working some problems at their seats while I instructed the middle group.

Before very long a child in the low group called out, "I'm on problem two!" Soon another child in the low group said, "I'm on problem three!" This started a whole rash of announcements by the members of the low group. The high group was very annoyed, and they were soon remarking to the low group, "Keep quiet," and, "Don't call out!" Also a few remarks were made by high-group members that indicated they were scornful of these low-group members' abilities. For example, a high-group member said, "With those easy adding problems you should be finished!" Another high-group member said, "Well, who cares how much *you've* done! Keep still so we can *really* work!"

As any teacher knows, remarks can be made during an incident of this kind more quickly than a teacher can stop them. In this case, the low group was admonished and told they were not to call out because it disturbed others. The talking stopped, but some low-group members continued to signal or give indications about the progress they were making, and this caused some disruption.

Thibaut and Riecken [18] studied the reactions of group members toward aggressors who differed in attributed status. It was found that low-status members were less intense in their rejection when overt communication was directed toward members of high status. On the other hand, high-status members were more intense in their rejection of low-status members. Thus the children in the low arithmetic group spoke out in class and annoyed the higher groups, but these low-status members did not directly communicate their aggressive feelings to members of

[18] John Thibaut and Henry Riecken, "Authoritarianism, Status, and the Communication of Aggression," *Human Relations*, 8:95–120, 1955.

the higher groups. On the other hand, high-status members were quite outspoken in their anger toward the low-status aggressors.

Members regarded as "low" in status receive other indications of rejection. Judgments of performance tend to be related to the status of members. Sherif [19] found, for example, that boys consistently overestimated the performances of high-status member of their group and underestimated the scores of those of low standing. (The boys were in a summer camp. They were eleven and twelve years old, well-adjusted normal boys of homogeneous background.)

It has been observed that those members of a group who anticipate low ratings for themselves tend to overestimate the sociometric status of others; those with high self-expectations underestimate the status of others. Those who underestimate their own status tend also to have relatively low self-expectations. [20]

Harvey [21] found, also, that the lower a member's status in the group, the more his performance was underestimated by others in the group. The higher the status, the more his performances were overestimated, and the greater were the expectational demands upon him. The subjects in this study were adolescents who were members of well-defined cliques. The data showed that the higher an individual's group status was, the more he tended to overestimate his future performance with reference to a given task, and the lower an individual's status was, the less likely he was to overestimate his performance and the less the group tended to overrate his performance.

The problem of grouping has been debated from a philosophical standpoint for many years and many experiments have been tried and are continuing to be tried. So far, all of the various ways of grouping according to some aspect of ability have only enlarged the range of differences in other areas. In view of some of the findings from sociopsychological research, it seems that any one of the formal organized plans that places children in clearly indicated low, middle, and high groupings will seriously retard learning in one area or another. In some instances, for example, children with high intelligence quotients have been placed in rooms for the "gifted." In many cases, these classes are also divided into high, medium, and low groupings for purposes of instruction. There are cases where children in the "low-gifted" group have asked to be put back into regular classrooms where they will not have the stigma of

[19] Muzafer Sherif, "Experiments in Group Conflict," *Scientific American*, 195:54–58, November 1956.

[20] Herbert Schiff, "Judgmental Response Sets in the Perception of Sociometric Status," *Sociometry*, 17:207–227, 1954.

[21] O. J. Harvey, "An Experimental Approach to the Study of Status Relations in Informal Groups," *American Sociological Review*, 18:357–367, 1953.

being low-group members within their class groups. Parents have been known to request that their children be transferred back to regular classrooms since the experience of being low-group members seemed to make them anxious and unhappy, and since the children preferred being "high" in a regular classroom. Objective evidence is lacking, however, concerning whether a large number of children react in this manner.

For data on the question of the possible threat of homogeneous grouping to pupil self-esteem, Luchins and Luchins [22] asked 190 homogeneously grouped fourth to sixth grade children which sections they would prefer if they were permitted to choose. When the children were interviewed it was evident that every child was aware that his class was labeled bright, average, or dull. In each section, at least 75 per cent of the pupils expressed preference for the highest section. Only four per cent of the bright and 25 per cent of the dull children chose the lowest section.

It seems safe to assume from the present evidence that a rigid practice of structuring classes according to ability seriously affects children's attitudes toward themselves, toward others, toward learning, and toward school. Since some of the most urgent problems of our society involve human relations, delinquency, and mental health, the time may come when we must decide whether we are paying too high a price for academic learning. The classroom experience determines to a large degree how children relate to others and how they regard themselves. It would seem that thoughtful citizens of a democracy given a choice would want first of all for the schools to develop healthy, independent, self-respecting, law-abiding citizens, with the goal of academic learning placed second in the list. Learned delinquents, learned neurotics, or even learned dependent individuals cannot for long perpetuate a free society.

What is the answer to grouping? It is very true that when children are advanced from grade to grade with age mates irrespective of their achievement, many curricular and instructional difficulties are presented to the teacher. In groups such as this, children vary widely in levels of achievement, and the rates at which they master concepts and skills vary. The higher the grade level the greater the range in mental ages and achievement of the children.

One proposal suggests that if children of the same chronological age get along reasonably well even though there is a spread in mental ages, they continue on the next year in the same age group.[23] This proposal

[22] Abraham S. Luchins and Edith H. Luchins, "Children's Attitudes Toward Homogeneous Groupings," *Journal of Genetic Psychology*, 72:3–9, 1948.

[23] Carleton W. Washburn, "Adjusting the Program to the Child," *Educational Leadership*, 11:138–147, December 1953.

emphasizes *no single standard of achievement*. Each child would master a common core of subject matter—reading, arithmetic, language, spelling, and other universally needed and used skills, but he would do so at his own rate. He would work individually on these areas at certain times during the day. Most of the time, however, he would work in the group, discussing, listening, doing research, and helping to plan and execute projects.

Although the emphasis throughout this book is upon groups and the behavior of groups, it is not proposed that group learning is superior to individual learning, or that many types of problem-solving are not best achieved by individuals alone. Certain academic skills (as opposed to social skills) must be learned individually and taught individually. In these skill areas children work at their own rates. In reading, for example, some of the work can be individualized. Some of the time children can work in teams of two or three, the teams not always formed on the basis of reading achievement but perhaps made up of friends who like to work together. Small groups may work with the teacher or pupil–teachers.[24]

It must be stressed at this time that because of varying needs and abilities, and because teachers must work with individuals, it is usually necessary to divide pupils into small work groups. The problem of organizing such groups is difficult. Of course, the nature of the task or activity must be considered, but if classes are of reasonable size, it seems possible for individuals needing particular help in certain areas to be grouped in various ways from day to day. In many cases the members of the class may be involved in the formation of these groupings—that is, they may choose to work with the teacher in a group formed to remedy a skill deficiency, or they may choose on some days to practice by themselves.

Students may at times help one another by working in groups of two or three. Pupils can learn to give help and to receive help, the two-way process helping to make it possible to receive help without developing dependency or feeling threatened. In fact, sometimes the most important help a child can receive is from some of his classmates who accept him and provide him with emotional support when the learning task is painful and when he has not made as much progress as others. There is no doubt that methods of grouping need further investigation. However, a teacher can control the amount of stress and frustration created by low, middle, and high groupings by varying the bases of grouping and by varying the kinds of grouping.

[24] Donald D. Durrell, *Improving Reading Instruction*, New York: World Book Company, 1956, pp. 125–134.

Interaction and Communication

The pattern of communication or the communication network is a key factor in interaction because it is through some kind of communication that interaction takes place. Newcomb [25] suggests that interaction is a form of communication and proposes that many of the phenomena of social behavior that have been assembled under the label of interaction might be more accurately studied as communicative acts.

There is considerable evidence to substantiate the idea that communication plays a central role in determining the kind of behavior that a class group will exhibit. For instance, some of the behavior problems teachers frequently describe appear to be the results of tension or frustration. Failure in communication may cause this tension or frustration, while good communication may relieve them. Likewise, communication barriers may explain the inability of some groups to achieve harmony, or these barriers may be responsible for the difficulties some groups have in establishing desirable behavior standards. In addition, poor communication may explain why some teachers cannot reach their students and why they cannot help them to work to their greatest potentials.

The communication pattern not only determines the frequency, duration, and direction of member communications, but in many instances may restrict the content. This is to say that what is said, how it is said, and to whom it is said are determined by the communication pattern.

Most of the studies exploring the effects of various communication patterns upon group performance, morale, individual satisfaction, and other aspects of group and individual behavior have been conducted in small laboratory groups. Some experimentation has been concerned with channels of communication and with solving communication problems that arise in large organizations. Since these group organizations and their problems are quite unlike the small classroom group organizations and their problems, the findings appear to have little significance for classroom groups. However, such studies as those relating to member position in the communication structure and to one-way and restricted communication do seem to have implications for teaching practice. Findings from studies concerned with seating and spatial factors provide some clues about ways that patterns and outcomes of class group interactions can be guided or controlled to achieve certain desired goals.

[25] Theodore Newcomb, "An Approach to the Study of Communicative Acts," *Psychological Review*, 60:393–404, September 1953.

Feedback in Communication

Research seems to indicate that in a classroom situation where the communication is mostly one-way (that is, the teacher communicates to the class but there is little opportunity for the class to communicate back), the accuracy of the communications is reduced. If members of the class group are restricted in their responses; if they do not communicate to the teacher because of apathy, lack of opportunity, fear, or some other reason; if they do not acknowledge in some way that the message is received; if they do not question; if they do not communicate their negative reactions, then confidence is reduced for both the teacher and the class group. There is a tendency on the part of the class group to feel some hostility toward the teacher. Studies show that an initial period with feedback improves accuracy; the members of the group learn to understand how the teacher communicates and to interpret the teacher's communicative acts. After an initial period there may be less need for feedback. Experience in communicating with a particular group improves the teacher's skill in sending (if feedback is encouraged), and experience improves the abilities of members to receive communications.

A number of studies confirm these statements. For example, Leavitt and Mueller [26] were concerned with finding how the transmission of information from one person to another was influenced by the return of the information from the receiver to the sender. The investigators had noted that it was taken for granted in the lecture hall (or classroom) that transmitting information from the sender to receivers was an efficient process. The researchers hypothesized that sending information was an inefficient process unless there was feedback to the sender so that he could determine what progress he was making in sending the information.

The findings of the study showed that when the receiver could feed back the information freely to the sender, the accuracy of the information transmitted and the total communication process improved appreciably. This process seemed to permit the participants to learn a mutual language, and once the mutual language was learned, it obviated the necessity for a large amount of feedback.

Evidence seems to show that if a teacher initiates some act that is interpreted by the group as unfriendly or hostile to the group, and if the children are not allowed to communicate their feelings, the group members develop strong hostile feelings. In that case opportunity is not pro-

[26] Harold J. Leavitt and Ronald A. Mueller, "Some Effects of Feedback on Communication," *Human Relations*, 4:401–410, 1951.

vided for teacher and class members to develop mutual understandings. Because of this one-way process, other problems may develop that affect teacher–group relationships. If, however, the teacher makes a statement or announces a decision that is not accepted by the group and the members are allowed to communicate back to the teacher their feelings, the act of communicating back acts as a catharsis. After such an experience the children usually show greater friendliness toward the teacher. A study by Thibaut and Coules [27] found that communicating back to an instigator of hostility had this effect. This investigation attempted to determine the role of communication in the reduction of interpersonal hostility. It was found that overt acts of aggression tended to be reduced when group members were permitted to communicate with the instigator of the hostility. It may be inferred that when a group leader (such as a teacher) has aroused some hostility in group members and when the members are allowed to communicate their feelings, the hostility is reduced, for after such a feedback of hostility the members show increased friendliness toward the person who initially aroused the hostility. Of course, group hostilities toward individuals in the group also may be reduced if the group is allowed to communicate its feelings to the individual directly.

The following example has many implications regarding feedback in communication, particularly where problems of group behavior are concerned.

DANIEL

At recess and noon the play equipment is passed by a monitor to any child who wants to take it to the play area. Other children are to be allowed to play if they are present when they are organizing for a game.

There is one boy in the class who is very domineering, so usually whatever game he wants to play he gets the ball and manages to control the ball and say who will play, and play is by his rules, which deviate from the regular rules of the game.

The children have complained several times about how Daniel cheats and controls the game. With Daniel in the room, but without mentioning him directly, we discussed and wrote on the board some standards to observe to be a good citizen and how we should play fair, wait our turn, etc. This helped, but not for long.

In a short time it was reported again that Daniel was not playing fairly. I asked the assistant principal to talk to Daniel about his actions,

[27] John W. Thibaut, and John Coules, "The Role of Communication in the Reduction of Interpersonal Hostility," *Journal of Abnormal and Social Psychology*, 47: 770–777, October 1952.

his bossiness, and his unfair play. I talked to the class while he was out of the room and they agreed that a good thing to try would be for all to walk away from the game and go play with someone else when he started cheating.

This led to the following incident. This week about ten girls stayed after school to tell me how they had been walking away from the game when Daniel didn't play fair but that some boys usually stayed on and played or he got friends from other rooms to play with him.

I asked them what they thought we should do. They said he should be told directly how they felt. They decided to write a letter to Daniel telling him that his citizenship was not what it should be and to make a list of rules for him to abide by and then to have the class members sign the letter if they agreed he needed improvement in the items listed. The girls composed the letter and did an effective job.

After the last recess, I sent Daniel to the office with some material and I quickly explained to the class what these girls had done. Then I read the letter to the class and told them if they agreed with the girls that Daniel needed to improve in the standards listed, to sign quickly and pass it on to their neighbors. I pretended to be busy but kept a close watch. Each child signed his name. However, I did see several of Daniel's friends hesitate a few seconds before signing. All the class signed, however.

When Daniel came back to the room I gave him the letter and told him to read it and see how his friends expected him to behave in the future. I told him how they had all signed their names as proof that they expected him to be a better citizen.

Poor Daniel looked crushed (but he really is spoiled by always getting his way so I hope this will help him to improve his actions).

As for the class, they were so excited and jubilant over what they had done they bubbled over. They all felt they had accomplished a great deal. Before going home they told me, "Good night. Have a nice week-end," and made other pleasant comments two or three times each.

It will be noticed immediately that the class not only had strong feelings about Daniel but also had some resentment against the teacher because she was not able to control his behavior. It would seem from the research evidence that if the class members had been given the opportunity to communicate their feelings directly to Daniel during the first discussion period, the hostile feelings toward him might have lessened. Also, this procedure might have prevented the development of resentment against the teacher. From the group reaction that followed the presentation of the letter—that is, the friendly comments made to the teacher, one might wonder whether resentment toward the teacher was not stronger than resentment toward Daniel. Because teachers are very concerned about each individual and his development (and rightly so), it is seldom that the expression of criticism—even honest criticism— is permitted in the classroom. It would seem that signing a letter behind

Daniel's back was more damaging to him than a direct approach would have been. Faced with direct accusation, he would at least have had opportunity to defend himself. As it was, the letter gave him little chance to express his point of view. He was issued orders without having the opportunity of hearing what individuals had to say about the matter. Some of Daniel's friends might have pointed out his good attributes, which would enable him to accept the dictates of the group without complete loss of pride and status. As it was, Daniel must have felt he did not have a friend in the group.

It seems that if the group is permitted to communicate feelings in an organized discussion in cases such as the one involving Daniel, the social relationships of the class will be much improved. Teachers usually restrict such communication by saying, "We do not criticize others," or by implying in some way that within the classroom walls criticism of individuals is never directly expressed. Mutual understanding is difficult to achieve when communication is severely restricted. Problems keep recurring. Reminders to groups such as "Do not make unkind remarks about others," often result in a build-up of hostility which is expressed outside the classroom. Of course, children need to learn the difference between just and unjust criticism. By reminding children not to make unkind critical remarks, teachers are generally thinking of remarks that are uncalled for and unjust. There is a difference, and this children must learn, but honest criticism should be given honestly—not behind a person's back, or in "poison pen letters" or the like.

The behavior of the class group in the preceding incident corresponds with the findings of another study that was concerned with communication in group situations.

The sources of pressure to communicate in the group were identified by Festinger,[28] who found that members of groups communicated more when there was discrepancy in group opinion. When uniformity existed, there was no pressure to communicate. The magnitude of the pressure increased in relation to the degree of relevance the item had to the functioning of the group and it increased monotonically with the increase in the cohesiveness of the group. (In the case of Daniel, we saw that the group gave evidence of a strong desire to communicate their feelings to him.) The findings of Festinger's study showed, too, that not only did the pressure to communicate increase as the perceived nonuniformity within the group increased, but also the force to communicate was strongest toward those whose opinions or behaviors were most different. Communications tended to be addressed mainly to those mem-

[28] Leon Festinger, "Informal Social Communication," *Psychological Review*, 57: 271–282, September 1950.

bers within the group whose opinions were extreme. When a person was not wanted in the group, or when he was perceived as a nonmember, the force to communicate decreased. From these findings we might assume that Daniel was not completely rejected by the group. He was considered a member, although the group desired that he conform more to the group's standards of behavior. However, another pressure to communicate was noted by Festinger and may apply in the situation involving Daniel. He observed that the existence of an emotional state also created a force to communicate but that little experimental work had been done upon the problem. Perhaps the emotional state of this class group was the force that prompted this group's strong desire to communicate. Whatever the reasons, such incidents occur quite frequently in classroom groups. It would seem from the studies that teachers might reduce the problem and prevent a series of other problems from developing by conducting discussions in which members are permitted to communicate their feelings in a two-way process. Restricting the expression of criticism toward a person who is creating problems in social relationships seems to intensify group hostility toward the individual and create some hostility toward the teacher. The restriction of direct criticism in the classroom does not spare an individual from becoming the object of group hostility. In fact, it appears that in time he might face total group rejection if communication is reduced. It is by means of communication that mutual understandings are developed. Daniel needed to understand the group's strong feelings and the group needed to understand some of Daniel's problems.

Feedback is also important in task performance. A study by Pryer and Bass [29] compared the effectiveness of groups that were given correct knowledge of results of the group's success in attaining task goals with groups that operated without feedback. They found that group interest in the task was greater with feedback. During the group discussion periods, groups not receiving feedback exhibited more boredom and discouragement than did those groups that received feedback. These "no-feedback" groups were distracted from the subject more often than groups receiving feedback. Groups receiving feedback "learned to learn."

Teachers are better able to help groups in learning situations if they encourage feedback from the groups. Teachers sometimes are puzzled about why their performances are ineffective and why they are unable to achieve certain results with class groups. Unless a teacher is guided by continuous feedback, it is difficult for him to know whether a modifi-

[29] Margaret W. Pryer and Bernard M. Bass, "Some Effects of Feedback on Behavior in Groups," *Sociometry*, 22:56–63, March 1959.

cation of pace is necessary, or whether his delivery is ineffective, or whether the level of abstraction is too difficult, or if the cause is some other factor. Group responses help teachers determine whether individuals in the groups are able to proceed toward desired goals. Without feedback, teachers cannot adequately determine if pupils are encountering difficulties in the instructions or where the difficulties lie.

Cunningham [30] described a specific incident in which the teacher attempted to have the children make some relationships between what they had been reading and their own actions or behaviors. The children were unable to make appropriate responses. Cunningham noted that another approach might have helped the children recognize these relationships, for in the situation described, the semantics of the teacher in presenting the problem and the concepts seemed unclear to the children. Although it was not interpreted as such, the example given seemed to be one in which the sender (teacher) did not communicate enough with the children (receive enough feedback) to determine why they were unable to make the relationships. Although it appeared that the lack of ability to respond was mainly caused by difficult concepts, the lack of response could have stemmed from the way the topic was presented to the group. Various approaches and constant feedback might have enabled the teacher to determine why the children could not recognize the relationships, or if the lack of appropriate responses was caused by the way the problem was presented to the class.

Feedback that indicates only if pupils understand what is expected of them is not enough to improve a teacher's performance. Feedback must also indicate the particular misconceptions that pupils have and whether the teacher needs to change his approach to the teaching task.

After examining the problem of feedback and the performance of student teachers, McNeil [31] concluded that student teaching will improve if feedback includes: (1) indication of the extent to which children understand the lesson; (2) knowledge of obstacles encountered by children; and (3) explanation of how teaching performance can be modified.

When the group engages in problem-solving operations, feedback is necessary to increase the efficiency of group discussions. The problem-solving activities of a group involve proceeding toward a goal. This involves both direction and movement. Group members need to know if they are moving toward or away from the goal, and they need to know

---

[30] Ruth Cunningham and associates, *Understanding Group Behavior of Boys and Girls*, New York: Teachers College, Columbia University, 1951, pp. 281–282.

[31] John McNeil, "An Experimental Effort to Improve Instruction Through Visual Feedback," *The Journal of Education Research*, **55**:283–285, March 1962.

where they are in relation to the goal. A group can utilize feedback to determine the progress it is making.

Jenkins [32] noted that feedback was important to the operations of groups because groups had to be made aware of their rates of progress if they were to improve. Without knowledge of progress, members of groups became aggressive toward one another or escaped the situations through apathy and boredom.

Effects of Various Factors upon Communication

The leader of a group is an important factor in communication because the practices of the leader tend to control the frequency and duration of any single member's contribution and the patterns and directions of the communication in the group as a whole. Besides leadership, there are other factors that affect the communication network. These factors are related to group cohesiveness, group structure, group size, and spatial locations.

LEADER INFLUENCE. Some teachers tend to believe that assigning a pupil to lead the class group in discussions is more "permissive" than guiding the discussions themselves. Research indicates that in groups as large as classroom groups, the practice of assigning or sharing leadership with group members tends to result in a decrease in group satisfaction and cohesiveness. More interest and enjoyment in discussion is achieved when the group leader (teacher) tries to insure equal participation for all members, and when the leader injects questions and statements that keep the discussion "on the track." Lack of effective leadership in large group discussions often creates a frustrating group situation.

Preston and Heintz [33] compared two types of leadership, which they called "supervisory" and "participatory." The supervisory leaders did not participate in any of the discussions and limited their responsibility to seeing that the group completed the work with reasonable expedition. In other words, they did not enter into any part of the discussion unless the group wandered afield. The participatory leaders, on the other hand, injected comments that regulated and managed the thinking along certain lines. They also injected statements to insure that both majority and minority opinions were examined and to prevent the

[32] David H. Jenkins, "Feedback and Group Evaluation," *Journal of Social Issues*, 34:50–60, 1948.
[33] Malcolm G. Preston and Roy K. Heintz, "Effects of Participatory vs. Supervisory Leadership on Group Judgment," *Journal of Abnormal and Social Psychology*, 44:345–355, 1949.

group from being influenced by extreme prejudice. These participatory leaders, then, performed certain functions designed to permit the groups to have free and full communication. The groups under participatory leadership found the group discussions interesting and meaningful, and the members were friendly toward one another and found the experience enjoyable. Both the leaders and group members showed interest and enjoyment in the task and believed the groups to be efficient and productive. The members under the supervisory style, however, tended to regard the discussions as not interesting and not worth while. They did not enjoy the tasks or consider the groups to be efficient or productive.

A teacher skilled in guiding discussion can affect the amount and quality of communication appreciably. A pupil leader, on the other hand, because of lack of skill, generally restricts communication and is unable to regulate and guide discussion. Often this lack of skill produces a mechanical question–response type of discussion, which is ineffective in developing group productivity of high quality. Often he is unable to summarize at appropriate times and therefore cannot keep things going at a proper pace. A teacher is aware of some of the difficulties pupils have in putting ideas and feelings into words. At appropriate times they can aid the pupils by saying such things as, "Do you mean—?" By restating the thought the pupil was trying to communicate, the teacher may be able to see that the content of the pupil's contribution is more clearly understood by others in the group. A teacher, too, in guiding discussion, watches various reactions of members. By noting *how* things are said, meaning is clarified and this aids a teacher in guiding group discussion. A pupil, however, is concerned primarily with his own performance. His level of communication may not be as high as some of the members in the group that he is directing. For this reason the situation may become a very frustrating one for the group. A pupil leader may be very effective in maintaining "discipline," but this usual authoritarian approach is the main reason why pupil leader discussions are often so restrictive and frustrating. (Because pupil leaders are often able to squelch spontaneous comments and "keep order" they may be assigned this task.) Although guiding discussion as well as participating in discussion are skills that must be developed, it is suggested that pupil leaders be used in small discussion groups such as committees. Guiding large group discussions, however, is a task best performed by the teacher.

COHESIVENESS AND COMMUNICATION. The communication level varies positively with the degree of group cohesiveness.[34] Therefore, if it is

[34] Albert J. Lott and Bernice Eisman Lott, "Group Cohesiveness, Communication Level, and Conformity," *Journal of Abnormal and Social Psychology*, 62:408–413, March 1961.

known that a group is highly cohesive, it can be predicted that the level of communication also will be high—that members will communicate frequently with one another.

Numerous studies have found that cohesiveness is related to the amount and kind of verbal interaction within a group. Highly cohesive groups show fewer individual differences in the amount of member participation than do groups low in cohesiveness. When groups engage in frequent verbal interaction, this process generally induces a more positive feeling toward the group. This is to say that attraction to the group as a whole increases in proportion to the amount of verbal interaction among members. This seems to come about because individuals seek security, and verbal interaction aids perception and understanding, which in turn often improve interpersonal relations.

Studies that have examined the effects of various types of teaching procedures upon group behavior have found that frequent interaction increases an individual's liking for the group. Also, communication patterns that involve all group members in discussions improve group atmosphere. Bovard,[35] for example, contrasted the effects of two teaching procedures. One, termed "group-centered," fostered verbal interaction by a number of specific techniques, such as seating students in a circle and deflecting teacher-directed questions back to the group. The other procedure, called "leader-centered," employed techniques that limited or curtailed student-to-student conversation and all verbal interaction was channeled between the teacher and the individual student. It was found that in the group-centered classes there was more spontaneity of behavior and barriers were broken down. There was no significant atmosphere of threat or isolation, and students formed a group that was strong, friendly, and cohesive, even though it was composed of mixed races and mixed socioeconomic groups.

COMMUNICATION AND STRUCTURE. As mentioned earlier, Kelley studied some of the driving and restraining forces that acted upon various communication contents in a group as a result of the group's being structured as a status hierarchy. It was found that the more unpleasant a person's position was in the group structure, the stronger were the forces on the person to communicate irrelevant content. This communication of irrelevant content seemed to serve the function of permitting the occupant of an undesirable position to escape from it. The experiment showed also that there were restraining forces acting upon high-status persons against expressing any content that tended to lower their statuses. The hierarchy of levels tended to produce certain restraints against communicating criticisms of persons at other levels, yet the

[35] Everett W. Bovard, "Interaction and Attraction to the Group," *Human Relations,* 9:481–489, 1956.

high-status persons seemed to have greater freedom to express whatever criticisms they had directly to other levels than they did to criticize members of their own levels.

Other studies of high-status and low-status subgroups find that when discrimination in favor of high-status subgroups continues, the low-status members increase the total amount of communication addressed to high-status members. One explanation advanced for this trend is that when low-status members perceive that the possibility of becoming a high-status member is slight, they increasingly resort to communication to high-level persons as a substitute means of satisfying their desire to become high-status members.

Another finding related to status structuring and communication is that communications attributed to high-status persons are more readily accepted than those attributed to low-status persons.

Whether a group member desires to participate and communicate with other group members is directly related to his position in the group structure. If he does not perceive that he is accepted by other group members, his emotional reactions may lead to a restriction of his participation in the affairs of the group.[36]

GROUP SIZE. The size of the class group is no doubt a limiting factor in communication. Although elementary school class groups are large, the group members work and play together for many hours a day. This no doubt negates, to some extent, the limiting effects of class size. The members of secondary class groups, however, may meet together for as little as 50 minutes a day and may have no further contacts with one another. The size of the group in the secondary school, and the size of the school, does limit the amount of communication that can take place between members.

As group size increases, the average member of the group has fewer chances to speak and intermember communication becomes more limited. It is also more difficult for members to make their contributions at appropriate times. For example, a seventh grade class was discussing a current topic in which the interest of members was high. Concurrent with this, the group was examining its discussion procedures. Finally, after waiting his turn for some time a boy spoke out saying, "How can I wait my turn to speak when by the time it comes around we are way past the point I wanted to talk about?"

This is the problem in all large group discussions. Satisfaction with the discussion and the group decreases as the size of the group increases. As size increases it becomes more difficult for each member to keep track

[36] Helen Hall Jennings, *Sociometry in Group Relations,* Washington, D.C.: American Council on Education, 1948, pp. 67–73.

of the discussion and still keep his own contributions in mind. With some individuals, as size increases, there is more inhibition of impulses to partcipate; thus there is not only an actual restriction of time per member, but also the possibilities of feelings of threat and of inhibition.

The size of a group relates to several group factors that in turn affect communication. Large groups have more members; hence, there are more individual differences among the persons comprising a large group. A large group that persists over a span of time develops an informal status hierarchy even though there is an organizational structure laid down for the group. As we have seen, the communication in the group is affected by the structure, and it is also affected by the ways members feel about one another. Therefore, as the size of the group increases, these interrelationships gain in complexity. There is a tendency for large groups to be less cohesive than small groups. In small groups, each member is better able to interact with every other member. Also, large groups have a greater tendency to split into subgroups or competing factions than do small groups.

Interaction within different sized groups was studied by Hare,[37] who found that in larger groups there was less opportunity for members to participate and less satisfaction with group discussions. Because the larger group size limited interaction and communication, individual members often felt that their opinions were not important and not worth presenting.

In groups that exceeded twelve members it took much longer to reach consensus than it did in smaller groups and there was a greater likelihood that members would break into conflicting subgroups. It was found, too, that with an increase in the size of the group there were changes in the nature of the interaction; also, leadership skill was found to be much more important than in smaller groups. Although leaders in small groups tended to have more influence on group decision than did leaders of larger groups, their individual skills as leaders were not an important factor in their influence.

Hemphill [38] found that the reported behaviors of leaders who were rated as superior "differed significantly in terms of the size of the group in which they functioned." In larger groups there was greater tolerance for more "leader-centered," or dominant, behavior. Members of large groups exhibited a significantly greater tendency than those in small groups to approve a more directive type of leadership. Although educa-

[37] A. Paul Hare, "A Study of Interaction and Consensus in Different Sized Groups," *American Sociological Review*, 17:261–267, June 1952.

[38] John K. Hemphill, "Relations Between the Size of the Group and the Behavior of 'Superior' Leaders," *Journal of Social Psychology*, 32:11–32, 1950.

tors stress "permissive" or democratic leadership practices, the evidence indicates to some extent at least that the larger the class size, the more directive and dominant a teacher must be. The evidence indicates also that the larger the group the more the leader needs skill. This suggests that perhaps the success or lack of success of beginning teachers is in some degree related to the sizes of the class groups that are assigned to these beginners.

SPATIAL FACTORS. The teacher usually sets the standards for the form of the group communication pattern in the classroom. This imposed pattern (or patterns) may limit group performance or it may result in significantly better performance, depending upon the nature or the pattern and the natures of the tasks or operations.

Stienzor [39] studied the spatial factor in small discussion groups and found that persons in groups were more likely to interact with others if they could see them as well as hear them. The findings indicated that interaction between persons in groups was not only affected by the content of what was said but by such nonverbal factors as gestures, postures, and the total physical impressions that individuals made on one another. Certain implications of significance to group leaders emerge from the study. When a high level of interaction and a greater extent of participation by members in a group is desired, the leader may place expressive individuals opposite quiet ones. When there are a few persons in the group who tend to monopolize the discussion, seating them next to each other may tend to decrease the interstimulation.

Leavitt [40] explored the relationship between the behaviors of small groups and the patterns of communication in which the groups operated. It was found that the positions that individuals occupied in a communication pattern affected their behaviors in those positions. They also affected an individual's chances of becoming a leader, his satisfaction with his contribution to the group, and the quantity of his activities.

Centrality (the most central position in a pattern or the position closest to all other positions) was found to be the major characteristic of communication patterns which was most clearly correlated with behavioral differences. Persons who were central tended to be more satisfied and the satisfaction increased with time, and the opposite was true of persons in peripheral positions. Where centrality was evenly distributed and there was no leader, there was high activity and high satisfaction with the group. When frustration did occur, it was the result of the

[39] Bernard Stienzor, "The Spatial Factor in Face to Face Discussion Groups," *Journal of Abnormal and Social Psychology*, 45:552–555, July 1950.

[40] Harold J. Leavitt, "Some Effects of Certain Communication Patterns on Group Performance," *Journal of Abnormal and Social Psychology*, 46:38–50, January 1951.

group's inadequacy and not the inadequacy of the environment. When a person's position was found to be low in centrality relative to other members of the group, that position was found to be a follower position and there was little opportunity for the member to experience prestige, activity, or self-expression.

As a pattern, the circle was most satisfying to the members and the wheel pattern was the least satisfying. This latter pattern operated by sending all information to the leader who was in the middle who then sent the information back to the group.

Before any conclusions can be drawn from this experiment, the limitations in terms of task and group size must be considered. For example, Leavitt found that the circle was most satisfying to most group members, but this experiment was conducted with small laboratory groups and each group member was given a specific task to perform. A circle in a large class group does not necessarily provide the greatest satisfaction to members, and it may not be the pattern most conducive to effective communication. Observation of class group discussions at times when members are arranged in a large circle reveals that frequently this seating pattern acts as a restraint upon communication. There is great distance between members, which does not foster member-to-member interaction. It is difficult to prevent all comments from being directed to the leader. Shy children, or those who have difficulty formulating thoughts or who have trouble expressing their thoughts, do poorly in this arrangement. This appears to be because these children can see that they are in full view of all the other members and they are more self-conscious than they would be in other arrangements. It is not possible for them to achieve the kind of anonymity they need for full freedom of expression.

Observation of classroom groups during discussion periods also reveals that when children are given a free choice of position—that is, when nothing is said about seating, they will move toward the leader and form a tight, compact group. It has also been noted that when shy children are toward the front of the group, they contribute more freely to the discussion. Since improvement in oral expression is an important school objective, all the factors involved in the process deserve consideration by teachers. This is an area in which research is sorely needed. Although many experiments have been conducted with seating in classroom groups for the purpose of improving interpersonal relations and reducing cleavages, few if any have been conducted to determine the best arrangement for conducting class group discussions. Informal experiments by teachers at various grade levels could add to knowledge in this area.

When member characteristics are discussed in Chapter 8, some of the research studies dealing with seating and its effects upon interpersonal relations will be reported. However, since the class seating arrangement is an important factor in determining the large patterns of interaction that develop in the group, the topic of spatial factors cannot be left without examining the general topic of seating in the class group.

Various studies show that the seating arrangement within a classroom definitely has a bearing on the behavior of the children within the room. Frequently, educational literature deplores a seating arrangement that has children placed in rows or columns. Stressed previously was the fact that general patterns of interaction cannot be considered without taking into account the type of task or activity that engages the class at the time. When members of the group are involved with individual tasks, perhaps the best seating arrangement is one that limits communication and social access. Since many times during the day the members of the group are working individually, seating by rows may be the arrangement that provides the best working atmosphere. (Elementary school teachers frequently report that they believe each child in the classroom needs a private work space of his own—one that he does not have to share with others.) However, at other periods during the day, when the teacher and group must work together, the arrangement by rows makes it necessary to change the seating so member–member communication and teacher–group communication are not unnecessarily limited. Organizing a series of moves whereby 30 or more children change their locations is a problem that plagues many teachers. Unless such maneuvers are well planned and quickly executed, much time is wasted.

Planning such moves is one problem, but seating may be further complicated by the size of the space available and the character of the equipment. Rows of permanent seats, unless the space is large and other means of seating is available, presents an almost insoluble problem. Tables also cause difficulties (in addition to their basic shortcoming of providing little privacy for individuals who need, at times, to work alone). They cannot be moved quickly and without some confusion, and they cannot be placed in a pattern that is conducive to an all-class discussion. Many classrooms are built and equipped in such a way that flexible seating arrangements are provided. Teachers who do not have to cope with lack of space or inflexible furniture have only to decide when and how to use different seating arrangements. Findings from various studies should provide teachers with some clues that will influence their decisions, although research does not provide answers to all the specific problems teachers encounter in seating. It is well to keep in mind that permanent seating by ability causes anxiety and frustration and hinders learning. Planning, discussion, and some activity periods are best conducted in a pattern that allows for two-way communication.

When children need to work alone, the arrangement should provide for islands of privacy. Since both group instruction and individual instruction are required for the maximum development of individuals, it is desirable that seating arrangements be variable to permit adjustment to the nature of the tasks and activities.

Communication in the Classroom

Communication is dual in nature. Teachers who succeed in achieving a general pattern of cooperative group behavior always develop two-way communication systems. Children are given opportunities to express themselves, so mutual understanding is built between members in the group and between members and teachers. In these classes, not only are children given opportunities to express themselves but the teachers are especially attentive to what the children are trying to communicate. They are usually able to figure out what the children are trying to say even though the meanings might be obscure. Although teachers who are successful in establishing generally cooperative behavior patterns do not always know the reasons for their success, it is, in a large part, due to their recognizing the importance of two-way communication and to their ability to receive as well as send messages. They are not only concerned with seeing that their messages are clear and received by the members of their classes; *they are also attentive to the messages they receive.* Successful teachers consciously or unconsciously recognize that to help children learn—whether the learning is in the area of skills or content or whether it pertains to attitudes and values—it is as important for the teacher to know what the children are saying as it is for the children to understand what the teacher is trying to say to them.

One reason why beginning teachers have difficulty in establishing desirable behavior patterns is that they are more concerned with communicating *to children* than they are with receiving communication *from children.* There are a number of factors that contribute to this condition. For one thing, many demands are placed on these teachers by administrators and others, and they tend to become anxious and self-concerned about these demands. Also, children have many ways of expressing themselves other than verbal language, and because they vary widely in their use of oral language, it is not always easy to figure out what they are trying to communicate. If the meaning is obscure, and if the teachers are pressed by other matters, or feel insecure, they do not spend sufficient time in trying to interpret what the children are trying to communicate. Even though a procedure is established that appears to provide an opportunity for children to question, discuss, or plan, if what is said is not interpreted and understood by the teacher, the process is a mechanical one and serves no purpose. Many times the procedure employed in discussing a problem or evaluating a lesson, for example, is a one-way process. The way the problem is presented, the tone of voice, and other subtle factors indicate to the children that certain responses are required. Therefore, they dutifully answer. The procedure of asking for statements from children in a manner that indicates a certain response is desired is a one-way pattern of communication. Many misunderstandings arise unless a true two-way pattern is established.

Communication between pupil and pupil is important in establishing a friendly cooperative class group. However, the schools have inherited a philosophy from the early days of our country which states, "Children should be seen but not heard." In some places teachers who prevent pupil-pupil communication and who have silent classrooms are considered "good" teachers. Thus, teachers in such situations are under pressure to prevent talking between pupils. Of course, lessons cannot be taught if children are engaged in friendly conversation at the time, if the room is noisy, or there is a lack of attention, but children are usually reasonable. Given a chance to make decisions they will usually agree that there are appropriate times for pupil-pupil communication and lesson time is not one of them. To forbid any talking during the long school day, however, is unreasonable.

The class in the next example appears to be a cooperative, hard-working group. The teacher's statements, however, indicate that she felt that the class behavior left something to be desired. It is reasonable to assume that this teacher was under pressure to have a completely quiet, nontalking class. Either her own attitudes toward talking caused her to view her group as too talkative, or a prevalent school attitude was responsible.

THE CHATTERING CLASS

The chief problem of the members of this sixth grade group is that they talk as they enter the room, and as they change from one activity to another.

This is a good work group. During study and work time the boys and girls work quietly and efficiently. They conduct good discussions and do good committee work.

At the end of each play period they usually wait quietly in the corridor until the door is opened for them to enter the room. The minute they walk through the door into the room they begin to chatter. They chatter until the class president asks them to stand for the pledge of allegiance to the flag. As soon as this is finished, they begin to chatter again.

When the class treasurer is ready to take the lunch and milk order, the president again must call the group to order.

When the work for the first class begins and they get settled down, they work very well.

When a class period ends, they chatter and are noisy as they put away materials and get other materials ready for the next class. As soon as they get work started, with the exception of two or three individuals, they work quietly and efficiently.

Some remedies have been tried, but they work only for a time.

During talking periods, the only time they get quiet without being reminded is when the telephone rings. Immediately all chatter stops. If anyone does continue he or she is quietly but firmly "shushed" by the group.

Maybe there's a reason for this, but if so I haven't found the answer.

From the description given of the behavior of this group, it appears to be a happy, friendly, responsible group. If talking between individuals stops when a class is working, if it stops when the class is called to order, and if it stops when such things as the ringing of a telephone occur, it seems that the class group is behaving in a controlled, responsible manner. One conclusion that might be drawn from the incident is that perhaps the children are given too few opportunities during the regular class period to discuss and exchange ideas. Because there is little opportunity for them to communicate during organized periods, they satisfy their needs to interact and communicate when there is no work in progress.

Another important reason for establishing an effective two-way communication system stems from the need that group members often have to express themselves about problems that trouble them. Class groups frequently develop a need to settle problems that affect group unity, and situations often arise that need clarification.

The teacher in the next example evidently recognized that at times a class period must be devoted to settling serious issues that are of concern to the group. She also seemed to know that an attempt to force the class to settle down to work at the time of the described incident would prove futile and that little or nothing would be accomplished unless the problem were settled or at least considered.

THE BADGES

One day the children came in from recess in a state of excitement. It concerned the boys mostly, but then there are more than twice as many boys in my classroom as there are girls. Everyone tried to talk at the same time and it took several minutes to calm them down enough so that I could get even an inkling as to what had happened. It seemed that Tom had brought several tin badges to school. He had passed them out to different individuals to wear, and this gave them the privilege to play in a certain group. Then it occurred to Tom to ask the boys to pay him for the badges if they wanted the privilege of continuing to use them and to belong to the group. The boys argued about the price he asked of ten cents each for the larger ones and five cents each for the smaller ones. Finally, though, it was settled and the boys brought the money from home and gave it to Tom. All were happy for a few days and Tom was in control of the playing. Eventually resentment of his leadership developed but he wouldn't relinquish his post. Then the boys began to complain about the quality of the badges and demanded their money back, and Tom refused to refund it. At this point it became a whole class situation, with many siding against Tom. On the day the trouble came to a head, one boy had thrown his badge down and stamped on it saying "it was no good anyway." Others said the same badges could be bought for less at a store. Tom maintained that the badges were not in as good condition as when the boys bought them and that he shouldn't have to refund the money. Most of the children, even though they were not involved in the deal, had quite definite opinions about the whole situation. Feelings against Tom were strong among the boys, but most of the girls were in agreement with Tom. They felt he should not have to refund the money.

The teacher does not report whether a settlement was reached, or if unity was restored. There were several issues involved in this incident. Had the teacher been able to help the class recognize the basic issue— that is, Tom's method of gaining leadership control with the group's cooperation, the lesser issue regarding the return of the money might have been seen in a different light. Also, some valuable social understandings might have developed from such a discussion. The boys might have learned that they were largely responsible for what had occurred. Tom might have learned why his leadership was rejected. The girls might have learned to look for underlying causes. In fact, the class as a whole might have gained better understanding of how to reach a solution to a problem of this nature.

Children often reveal their attitudes about situations, other individuals, or themselves in nonverbal ways. We know that a child who continually seeks approval from the teacher is anxious and fearful. This behavior reveals something about the child to the teacher. The behavior of a group of children can communicate many things to a teacher also, even though nothing takes place on a verbal level. If a sigh runs through the group when a particular announcement is made, it reveals something about the group and its reaction to the announcement. If many glances are exchanged between pupils, or if a ripple of derisive laughter spreads through the group, these behaviors tell the teacher something about the group at that moment. For example, what does the behavior of the group of first grade children in the following example suggest? Although all the factors are not revealed, the group reaction permits some fairly accurate predictions.

NONVERBAL COMMUNICATION

It was shortly after 11:00 on a warm Friday morning. Eleven children from an afternoon first grade class had been added to this class the day before, making a total of 35 children.

As the children came quietly into the room and went to their seats, the teacher announced that it was time to write the story to go with the study film they had seen earlier that morning. A child had his hand up and was called upon by the teacher. This child suggested that perhaps they should review the discussion that had followed their seeing the film. Many points were rediscussed by the class group.

It was then that the paper was passed out and the children were asked to take their pencils from their desks. At this moment one boy dropped his pencil, and since it was rather large and the class was quiet, the pencil made a fair amount of noise. Immediately, without exception, the entire group dropped their pencils. The pencils were not all dropped at once, but this desire to drop pencils seemed to move in a wave throughout the classroom.

Communication between a teacher and the group involves an interpretation by the teacher of the behavior of the group. If a class group as a whole behaves in a way that seems contrary to what the members have been told, a teacher should analyze the situation before assuming that the children share the teacher's understanding and are misbehaving because of conscious intent.

If problems in group behavior are to be prevented or solved satisfactorily, and if change in group behavior is to be achieved, the lines of communication in the classroom must be open. Certainly little communication will take place in a quiet classroom. If communication is constantly suppressed, the group is very apt to become chronically frustrated. When a group is thwarted in this way, adequate communication is further blocked by feelings of hostility and resentment. Such conditions are unfavorable to the curricular learning and very favorable to the development of many types of group and individual behavior problems. When it is possible for children to communicate freely when they feel there is a need, many problems are avoided or solved. A teacher's job is not to restrict or prevent communication, but to see that communication patterns are developed that facilitate learning and promote good relations. This is not to say that there should be no restrictions or controls, for this would lead to disorganization and confusion. It means that teachers must recognize when there is need for communication and learn to use a two-way system.

Questions for Study and Discussion

1. Discuss the relationship of "interaction" and "structure" in theory and in practice.

2. Describe the beginning stages of the formation of structure for a group that you know well or in which you have participated. Tell of the kinds of behavior that different members showed in their attempts to locate places for themselves in the group structure.

3. Why do groups in formative stages take different lengths of time to establish structures? Why does it take some groups longer, etc.?

4. Discuss the importance for individuals and for the group of the ascribing of role and status to members in early formative stages of the group.

5. Analyze a group that you know well, or have known well in the past, for (a) the ascribed roles and/or statuses and (b) the real roles and/or statuses as you saw them. Make two lists and connect the name (which may be fictitious) in the first list with a line to its place in the second list.

Ascribed Roles	Real Roles
1.	1.
2.	2.
3.	3.
4.	4.
5.	5.

6. Investigate the current terminology used by elementary or secondary students to indicate the positions of individuals in the group structure. Note whether the terms are newly developed or whether they are of longer standing.

Suggestions for Further Reading

Back, Kurt W. "Influence Through Social Communication," *Journal of Abnormal and Social Psychology,* 46:9–23, July 1951.

Borosage, Lawrence. "A Basis for Viewing Communication," *The National Elementary Principal,* 46:6–12, May 1962.

Bovard, Everett W., Jr. "Group Structure and Perception," *Journal of Abnormal and Social Psychology,* 46:398–405, July 1951.

Cohen, Arthur R. "Upward Communication in Experimentally Created Hierarchies," *Human Relations,* 11:41–53, 1958.

Crook, Robert B. "Communication and Group Structure," *The Journal of Communication,* 11:136–140, September 1961.

Deutsch, Morton, "Task Structure and Group Process," *American Psychologist,* 6:324–325, July 1951.

Deutsch, Morton. "Social Relations in the Classroom and Grading Procedures," *Journal of Educational Research,* 45:145–152, October 1951.

Exline, Ralph V. "Interrelations Among Two Dimensions of Sociometric Status, Group Congeniality, and Accuracy of Social Perception," *Sociometry,* 23:85–101, March 1960.

Festinger, Leon. "Informal Social Communication," *Psychological Review,* 57:271–282, September 1950.

Festinger, Leon, and John Thibaut. "Interpersonal Communication in Small Groups," *Journal of Abnormal and Social Psychology,* 46:92–99, January 1951.

Havighurst, Robert J. and Bernice L. Neugarten. *Society and Education.* Boston: Allyn, 1957.

Hearn, Gordon. "Leadership and the Spatial Factor in Small Groups," *Journal of Abnormal and Social Psychology,* 54:269–272, March 1957.

Howells, Lloyd T. and Selwyn W. Becker. "Seating Arrangement and Leadership Emergence," *Journal of Abnormal and Social Psychology,* 64:148–151, February 1962.

Jenkins, David H. "Feedback and Group Evaluation," *Journal of Social Issues,* 34:50–60, 1948.

Jensen, Gale E. "The Social Structure of the Classroom Group: An Observational Framework," *Journal of Educational Psychology,* 46:362–374, October 1955.

Klein, Josephine. *The Study of Groups.* London: Routledge & Paul, 1956.

Larsen, Otto N. and Richard J. Hill. "Social Structure and Interpersonal Communication," *American Journal of Sociology,* 63:497–505, March 1958.

Lloyd, R. Grann and others, "The Relationship Between Academic Achievement of Pupils and the Social Structure of the Classroom," *Rural Sociology,* 21:179–180, June 1956.

Raven, Bertram H., "Social Influence on Opinions and the Communication of Related Content," *Journal of Abnormal and Social Psychology,* 58:119–128, 1959.

Ross, Donald H. and Bernard McKenna. *Class Size: The Multi-Million Dollar Question.* Study No. 11, Institute of Administrative Research. New York: Teachers College, Columbia University, 1955.

Sherif, Muzafer, Jack B. White, and O. J. Harvey. "Status in Experimentally Produced Groups," *American Journal of Sociology,* 60:370–379, January 1955.

Silberman, Harry F. "Effects of Praise and Reproof on Reading Growth in a Nonlaboratory Classroom Setting," *Journal of Educational Psychology,* 48:199–206, April 1957.

Stephan, Frederick F. and Elliot G. Mishler. "The Distribution of Participation in Small Groups: An Exponential Approximation," *American Sociological Review,* 17:598–608, October 1952.

Stotland, Ezra, Nickolas B. Cottrell, and Gordon Laing. "Group Interaction and Perceived Similarity of Members," *Journal of Abnormal and Social Psychology,* 61:139–147, November 1960.

Thelen, Herbert A. *Dynamics of Groups at Work.* Chicago: U. of Chicago, 1954.

Ziller, Robert C. "Communication Restraints, Group Flexibility, and Group Confidence," *Journal of Applied Psychology,* 47:346–352, 1958.

Chapter 6   # Group Norms

As a group of children work together and engage in repeated interaction over a span of time, a structure forms and norms for behavior
develop. In fact, the concept of the term "group" indicates that there is
some distinctive pattern of behaviors that distinguishes members of a
particular group and differentiates them from members of other groups.
Although there may be no explicit norms during the early formation of
a class group, a set of standards soon develops and certain ideas are
formed regarding how members are expected to think, act, and even
feel in particular situations. Without some norms a group could not
function long.

Just as the larger society could not exist without some basic norms
such as are established in manners, conventions, mores, and the law, so
a small society (or a class group) could not continue without some standardized modes of behavior. Some normative standards are established by
the school and the teachers. Many are developed by the class group itself.

As interaction continues from day to day, the children come to share expectations about what is right or desirable. Shared expectations or norms may arise around almost any facet of group life, and once formed, the group puts strong pressure upon the members to conform. Membership in the group demands a certain amount of behavioral conformity to the norms.

Since the concept of the group norm is central to the understanding of group behavior in the classroom, these questions must be answered: What are group norms? How are they formed and how do they operate? Can the uniform behavior that characterizes members of a particular class be changed? Can a teacher so influence the class that group pressure is utilized to improve the learning situation?

In this chapter we shall discuss what is meant by norms, how they are formed or established, and how they operate as inducing agents to produce certain common kinds of behavior that can be observed in schoolroom situations. In a later chapter some specific techniques for changing undesirable norms to more desirable ones will be examined.

The Nature of Group Norms

What do we mean when we speak of the norms of a group? An examination of children's group behavior reveals and illustrates a number of kinds of peer-group influence. Norms relating to fashions or fads are easily recognized. If blue jeans are in favor, few boys will wear corduroys. If short hair is the current style, few girls wear their hair at shoulder length. Sometimes an unusual fad will appear in a class group and the children will exhibit temporary normative behavior.

THE LEMON FAD

Suddenly one day the children in my fifth grade class came to school with cuts of fresh lemon in their lunch boxes. At nutrition time and at lunch the children would chew on these pieces of lemon. Since some rules existed concerning what could be eaten at nutrition time, the class was told that lemons were not acceptable. The children answered, "The rule has always been that we could eat fruit. Lemons are fruit." Several lessons were planned that stressed proper diet, but this approach did nothing to change the behavior. Appeals were made to the children to return to more sensible eating habits, but, if anything, this action only encouraged more children to bring lemons. Children who did not eat at school came back after lunch at home chewing on quarters of sour lemon. Then one day as quickly as this fad began, it stopped, but another took its place. For a while, quite a number of children brought sandwiches made of bread, butter, and slices of raw green pepper.

Group influence of the kind described is readily discerned. However, classroom groups often exhibit behaviors that cannot be so easily traced to the fact that a norm is operating in the situation. Often a norm that is exerting pressure upon children to conform is difficult to distinguish. For example, incidents such as the ones in the following examples are characteristic of class groups having established their own particular norms for specific situations. The behaviors that result from such norms are usually viewed by teachers as group failure to conform to the standards established by the group itself. Actually, standards or norms established by the groups themselves *are* operating and the publicly stated standards are those desired or imposed by the teacher.

THE DIRTY PLAYGROUND

A problem that I find very difficult to control arises because of a dirty playground situation. The playground is constantly dirty and in need of cleaning. The method of cleaning the yard is for the principal to select a class each day to go outside and pick up the papers and straighten the benches. The choice of the class is announced each morning over the intercom system.

Every time my class is selected, the same thing happens. The children show intense resentment. They all begin to talk at once and claim they are not responsible for the mess on the playground and should not have to clean it up. Although they are given an extra ten minutes before their physical education period, they still become very hostile and almost defiant. It is almost impossible to get the children to quiet down and start on the class work.

In an effort to improve the situation we discussed the situation on a day when we did not have to clean the yard. The children decided that when their turn was announced they would accept the situation calmly and cooperate with the request. They set up a list of standards they would follow, including how they would act on the playground when picking up the papers. However, in spite of the standards that they agreed to follow, the next time the announcement came stating that it was their turn to clean up the yard, the same disorder prevailed. The resentment was just as strongly expressed and the cooperation on the playground was practically nil. The children are asked frequently to review their standards but up until now this has proved a useless procedure.

A number of factors contributed to this class group's behavior, but the concern at this time is directed toward the reaction of the children to the request to clean up the yard. The response of the class group appears to have become standardized, but when the class was asked to set standards for behaving, the children undoubtedly gave answers they knew the teacher wanted and would accept. The standards were perceived by the group members to be those of the teacher and not of the group, and the children continued to behave according to previously established ways of behaving. Similar behavior is reported in the next example of classroom behavior. The class responded in a standardized way to a specific situation. Again, behavioral guides were established by the teacher with the class group, but these guides were not followed and did not serve as a means for changing or improving the behavior of the class group.

TALKING WITHOUT PERMISSION

The most common type of classroom behavior whose guidance and control take time and patience on my part is talking without permission. We have developed a good guide to follow, which states in positive terms when we should speak and not speak and the practices to follow to gain permission to speak, but this class will not follow the standards.

The children in this class begin to talk at any time and it does not matter what subject we are studying. It varies somewhat as to how the children react. Usually one child will suddenly ask a question, which starts the whole thing. Often the question isn't very pertinent but the others will join in and will ask any number of questions without raising their hands or waiting for others to finish speaking. Then some people turn and answer questions even though the questions have been directed to the teacher. Finally the majority of the class members are talking, which increases the hub-bub and confusion. I suspect they do this because they are doing some work that they don't particularly enjoy, but whenever someone asks some insignificant question the whole class seems to react in this manner.

Once in a while the pattern changes. Someone will speak out and ask a question and the class members create just as much confusion by telling everyone to keep quiet and not ask questions. Of course this disturbs the quiet atmosphere of the class just as much as the asking of questions.

Definitions of the Term "Norm"

The meaning of the term *norm* can be inferred from the various illustrations cited. Norms evolve from group interaction and may include customs, traditions, codes, values, standards, rules, fads, and fashions. They are concerned with expected behavior in matters of consequence to the group.

Thibaut and Kelley [1] define a norm as a behavioral rule that is

[1] John W. Thibaut and Harold H. Kelley, *The Social Psychology of Groups*, New York: John Wiley & Sons, 1959, p. 129.

accepted, at least to some degree, by members of the group. According to this conception, acceptance of the norm by all the members of a fairly large group is not essential, although it is necessary that a sizable number accept it. Also, a norm does not exist unless there are agreements among members about what behaviors the individuals in the group should, or should not, enact, and unless social processes are used to produce adherence to the norm.

According to Sherif and Sherif,[2] norms of any description represent standard generalizations concerning expected behavior of group members in situations of consequence to the group. Involved is the implication that evaluations are made of modes of behavior relating to persons, objects, or situations. They are not formed in relation to every kind of behavior nor for all possible situations, but norms are of importance to the group at specific times.

Norms are not the behavior itself; rather, they represent what people in groups think behavior ought to be or what they expect it to be.

Norms are described by Bonner[3] in terms of what norms do. They represent the controls of the behavior of group members. He points out that just as society could not exist without some kind of established rules for behavior, so a group cannot exist without having some frame of reference to guide the interaction of the individuals belonging to the group. Norms are a regulator of behavior for members of a group.

Characteristics of Norms

One of the distinguishing features of norms is their evaluative nature. They refer to desired behavior, or ideal conduct, or preferred ways of thinking and believing. They more or less stipulate what is most valued and what is best to believe. Once norms become established they provide a reference point by which members may guide their actions, reactions, ambitions, and aspirations. They help individuals perceive and judge what is "right" and what is "wrong"—what is "appropriate" or "inappropriate" or what may be approved or disapproved.

Characteristic of this evaluative aspect of norms is that they specify the amounts or degrees of expected behavior and the times and places where it is expected. For example, a class group may expect certain behavior from members relating to talking during class periods. This expectancy, or norm, governs the amount of talking considered appro-

[2] Muzafer Sherif and Caroline Sherif, *An Outline of Social Psychology*, New York: Harper & Brothers, 1956, pp. 240–242.

[3] Hubert Bonner, *Group Dynamics: Principles and Applications*, New York: The Ronald Press Company, 1959, pp. 50–51.

priate in certain specific instances. In social studies discussion, a child's behavior may be disapproved because he talks too much and monopolizes the conversation. Another child might be censored because he talks too little during sharing periods. Sometimes groups expect members to conform to a rule of no talking during study periods but believe that talking is appropriate during the time immediately preceding dismissal.

This specification of the amounts or degrees of the behavior expected and of the times and places at which the behavior is appropriate is the quantitative dimension of norm behavior. Norm behavior is also characterized by a qualitative dimension.

Some behaviors are considered better than others. For example, a class group norm may govern the topics considered appropriate for discussion in the classroom, or it may operate to disqualify the use of certain words, even though the same words may be part of the ordinary conversation outside the schoolroom. A child's behavior may be disapproved because he brings up a subject that the members feel should not be discussed in class. A child may use a word considered inappropriate but not too "bad," and this may evoke but slight disapproval. However, the use of highly descriptive but questionable words may provoke a strong expression of disapproval or even cause the group to punish the individual. This qualitative dimension of norm behavior may differentiate between boys and girls in specifying what is acceptable and what is unacceptable behavior. In this sense the norm specifies the "best" or ideal behavior for certain situations and for certain individuals; it also differentiates between behaviors considered poor, better-than-poor, and best.

A certain behavior area may involve a number of attitudes, values, and beliefs. A teacher's attitudes, values, and beliefs may or may not correspond with those held by the children in the class group. Even if they do correspond, the teacher may rank their order of importance differently from the way the children do. Thus the teacher's judgment of the "best" behavior in a certain situation may differ from that of the children.

In the following incident the teacher and the children differ in how they judge the behavior of two individuals.

BRASS KNUCKLES

A fight had taken place one night long after the children had reported home after school. Two boys in the class had become involved in an argument which ended in a fist fight. Ned received the worst of it. He had a black eye and a long cut on one cheek. Walt escaped without any visible signs of the struggle. The next morning at school Ned described the fight to his classmates and said that Walt had used some brass knuckles during the scrap. Walt, on the other hand, had his side of the story. He said Ned offered him a jacknife if he would lend him his bicycle, and then refused to keep his side of the bargain. He would not give up his knife, but instead tossed Walt a dime for the use of the bike and told him to "take it and like it."

The teacher heard the bare outline of the story before the children came into the room. It was evident to her that the class was full of unrest and uneasiness when they came in after the opening bell. In order that the class could settle down and begin the class work, she took some time to review the incident. She began by saying that a bargain is a bargain and when we make commitments we live up to them. The class members listened and appeared to agree but did not seem inclined to discuss the matter. The children quieted down and the teacher thought the discussion had settled the issue. As lessons began, however, she noted that Walt was the recipient of a number of "dirty" looks, and that muttered threats were issued in his direction. The group was orderly enough, but it was plain that the children were far more concerned over the fight incident than they were with the lesson at hand. The teacher was at a loss to explain the tense atmosphere. She thought the discussion had more or less settled the right and wrong of the issue to the satisfaction of the group. However, it was rather obvious that it had not done so.

Finally, when it seemed that no learning was going to be accomplished for the day, the teacher stopped the work and asked the children why they continued to be disturbed over an incident that did not concern them directly. Eventually the problem came out into the open. The class disclosed that they felt the use of brass knuckles was unfair and that Walt was to be condemned and punished for using them. To this group the unfair fight was the issue and the fact that Ned did not live up to his bargain was of lesser concern. To them the payment of a jacknife (and it was established that it was a very good knife) was too high a price to pay for the use of a bicycle and a dime was sufficient payment.

The conduct of the participants in the fight was of much more importance to this class than whether the bargain was kept. The teacher failed to recognize the values that her class group stressed until the children were given the opportunity to thoroughly discuss the incident. Undoubtedly there were some children who did not at first hold any strong opinions regarding the use of brass knuckles, but as the feeling of other members became evident to them they tended to shift their judgments and values in the direction of the majority opinion. Not only do members of a classroom group tend to shift their opinions and beliefs in the direction of conforming to the norms of the group, but the members tend also to exert pressures designed to induce such conformity. The "dirty" looks and the threats directed toward Walt were attempts to structure his behaviors and beliefs to coincide with those of the group.

Norms have another characteristic in that the amount of approval or disapproval varies between certain limits. Sherif has termed this the range of tolerable behavior. The range may be narrow—that is, the group will tolerate very little deviation—or the range may be broad. Since norms do not apply to all members in equal degrees, this characteristic of norm behavior indicates the limits of behavior that the group will tolerate for various individual members. A well-liked member may be allowed to vary from the expected behavior pattern as long as the behavior is of little consequence to the group, whereas a fringe member may be held to strict conformity to norms; however, a member who is not accepted at all may be ignored to the extent that the group does not establish a limit for his behavior. The group may have no expectancies established for these nonaccepted members, and their behaviors will go unnoticed unless they interfere with the group in some way. There may be some norms to which leaders in the group are expected to conform at all times. Other norms may be less strictly applicable to the leaders than to others of the group. And even though a group may tolerate in a well-liked individual behavior that ranges close to the disapproval level, it may act quickly to bring the member into stricter conformity with the norm should it be inconvenienced by such far-ranging behavior. The class group in the next example allowed one member a certain degree of latitude in his behavior during discussion periods. When the group was made to suffer because his actions ranged too far from the norm, the group refused to tolerate his behavior and restricted his range considerably.

THE TRANSGRESSOR

Ed is a brilliant child, well liked and admired by all of the pupils in the class. However, one of his failings is to distract the class group during discussion periods by making occasional funny remarks. Sometimes his interruptions are barely noticed by the group; at other times they laugh but go right on working. Recently during a class planning period, Ed continually interrupted with remarks that completely threw the discussion off the track. Ed then went into an act that made the children laugh and forget all about the work at hand. The group was punished for condoning this behavior, and this seemed to change the sentiment of the group entirely. The next day Ed again tried to attract the attention of the group but failed miserably. The children completely ignored him. A few gave him a look as if to say, "Why don't you be quiet!" He has made a few feeble attempts to get a rise out of the class since the time he was completely squelched, but the children pay absolutely no attention to him. In fact, they won't even consider his serious attempts to join in the discussion. Outside of class the children seem just as friendly toward him as they ever were.

Evidently they became tired of putting up with his foolishness during discussion periods.

Intensity is characteristic of norm behavior. Norms about behavior that is of vital concern to the group will evoke high degrees of feeling in the members whether the specific reaction is one of approval or disapproval. The more the group values a particular standard or belief the more strongly will members attempt to enforce conformity. The intensity, or strength of the forces that the members place on one another to obtain uniformity in behavior and belief, varies according to whether the members view the behavior area as important in accomplishing the group's purposes. The degree of intensity exhibited by group members varies also according to the amount of satisfaction the group provides its members; also the greater the group's attraction the more intensity the group will exhibit toward conformity and nonconformity. In areas where the behavior is of little importance to the group, or when the group is not satisfying or its attraction is relatively lacking, the amount of approval or disapproval elicited by appropriate or inappropriate behavior will be low in intensity.

A child may receive a great amount of approval for defending a smaller child who is bullied by a larger child if this behavior is expected by the group; conversely, a child who breaks the code may be punished severely or even ostracized for a time. Jackson [4] suggests that the classroom atmosphere may be very threatening unless the children in the classroom exhibit the same strong feelings of approval as they do of disapproval. Unless children accord approval and reward for behavior considered appropriate or ideal in the same and with the same intensity as they distribute disapproval and punishment for behavior regarded as inappropriate, life in the classroom will be essentially threatening for individuals.

GROUP CODES. Norms that are well established and that require member conformity at all times are *codes*. It is common knowledge that preadolescents, adolescents, and even adult members of certain gangs and organizations follow a commandment or a code that prohibits "squealing" on other members of the group. Even when a member is personally resentful of another member, he must not tell an outsider anything concerning this member. Codes regulate member behavior in certain definite, specific situations. Where a code exists, the group exerts rigorous pressure upon members to conform to the code.

[4] Jay M. Jackson, "Structural Characteristics of Norms," in Nelson B. Henry (ed.), *The Dynamics of Instructional Groups,* Fifty-ninth Yearbook of the National Society for the Study of Education, Chicago: University of Chicago Press, 1960.

Studies Revealing the Existence of Norms

A number of studies have substantiated the finding that in the process of interaction, group members develop and hold in common norms, attitudes, opinions, and modes of behavior. The observed uniformity of behavior has been found to develop from some power that the group is able to exert over its members, and once norms and standards have been established the uniform behavior is difficult to change. These studies not only reveal the existence of norms, but they provide further insight into how the individuals' perceptions and even their opinions can come to reflect those of the group.

A series of experiments by Asch [5] showed that when some persons were led to believe that everyone in the group saw B as larger than A (even though this was erroneous), the individuals then had a strong tendency to agree with the judgment, and in many instances did so with a confirmed belief in the false judgment. The groups studied were comprised of seven or eight individuals each. The subjects were asked to compare and to match lines of various lengths. All the members except one were instructed by the experimenter to respond erroneously. A single uninstructed member was then confronted by a situation in which he perceived all other members of the group to be in error; to put the situation another way, the one "naive" subject was faced with a conflict between his senses and a desire to join the majority.

Approximately one-fourth of the 50 uninstructed subjects gave correct responses even though they were a minority. Approximately one-third of the subjects agreed with the majority and against the evidence of their senses for more than half the time. The other individuals fell between these two extremes. Those who yielded did not all do so in the same way or for the same reasons. A few subjects yielded completely but were unaware that their estimates had been displaced or distorted by the majority. These persons came to perceive the majority estimate as correct. Most of the subjects in the investigation seemed to yield because of a distortion of judgment. They suffered from doubt and lack of confidence, and came to feel that their perceptions were inaccurate and that those of the majority were correct. Some subjects yielded even though they did not believe they were wrong but had overmastering needs not to appear different from or inferior to the others. These subjects suppressed their observations and voiced the majority position with awareness of what they were doing.

[5] S. E. Asch, "Effects of Group Pressure upon the Modification and Distortion of Judgments," in E. Maccoby, T. Newcomb, and E. L. Hartley (eds.), *Readings in Social Psychology*, New York: Henry Holt and Company, 1958, pp. 174–183.

The experiments by Asch were later refined by Crutchfield.[6] In his investigation he found that about one-third of the responses made by a group of individuals were strongly influenced by the majority opinion, even when that majority opinion was clearly false. Some persons were swayed on almost every item by what they thought to be solid group opinions. The personality characteristics of these individuals were analyzed. They tended to be individuals who were defensive, rigid, and moralistic. They had little understanding of themselves and always wanted to maintain good "fronts." They had very great respect for authority and were unable to tolerate ambiguity. They lacked self-confidence and tended to become confused under stress. The independent group had characteristics of a different sort. They were nondefensive, unaffected, and spontaneous. The persons who were able to resist the group influence were those who were confident, open, secure, and expressive. They were active, persuasive leaders in whom others had confidence and who had confidence in themselves.

Further insight into how the group affects the opinions and perceptions of individuals is provided by Sherif,[7] who experimented with individual and group reactions to the "autokinetic effect." This is the name for a condition that exists when, in a darkened room where there are no visible perceptual standards by which an individual can orient himself, he will invariably perceive a fixed point of light as moving. (The light will appear to move back and forth, though it actually does not do so.) The subjects in Sherif's experiment were exposed to the autokinetic effect, which provided an ambiguous stimulus situation. After a series of observations that were made through an experimental peephole, each subject reported how much the light seemed to move. Each individual's responses eventually centered around a norm for him. Some said two inches, some said three, and so on. After a norm for each individual was clearly established, the subjects were put into groups and again asked to give their estimates of movement. The group members did not consult one another to agree on a norm but rather continued to give their own estimates and hear the estimates of others. In this situation a new norm emerged. This new group norm differed from the previous norms of the separate individuals. The norm was established through a series of mutual modifications, which—according to the subjects' later reports—were not consciously intended.

[6] Richard S. Crutchfield, "Conformity and Character," *American Psychologist*, 10:191–198, 1955.

[7] Muzafer Sherif, "Group Influences upon the Formation of Norms and Attitudes," in E. Maccoby, T. Newcomb, and E. L. Hartley (eds.), *Readings in Social Psychology*, New York: Henry Holt & Company, 1958, pp. 219–232.

After the group norm had been established, the individual subjects were again asked to record in private their judgments concerning the autokinetic effect. It was found that the subject now perceived the situation in terms of the range and norm of the group, even though he faced the situation alone. The finding showed that the effect of the interaction situation was not just an immediate one. The norm formed during interaction with others became the individual's own norm.

Group influence upon the judgments of children was investigated by Berenda,[8] who found that children were more influenced in their judgments by the alleged opinions of other children than they were by the opinions of teachers. It was found that in groups made up of similar ages there was considerable acquiescing to majority opinion, even when the majority was known to be wrong. When an individual child was opposed by eight of his classmates who gave incorrect judgments on simple perceptual material, the individual tended to change his judgment in the direction of the majority. There was no relationship found between IQ or personality traits. Children who tended to be leaders and children who tended to be followers both followed the group. When the teacher tried to change the judgment of an individual, she had some influence with younger ones. Older children became more cautious and more accurate. It was also found that the more ambiguous the stimulus situation, the more the individual tended to follow the group.

Sources of Class Group Norms

The norms and expectancies that class groups develop come from a number of sources. Children acquire certain attitudes and expectations toward school from their family groups—their first attitudes toward teachers, principals, subject areas, and schoolroom practices are generally acquired at home. Parents may warn children that if they do not do certain things or if they do certain things the teachers will punish them. Sometimes parents boast of their childhood exploits and include their rewards or punishments in their descriptions contributing toward the formation or expectations. Children entering a new grade may have older brothers and sisters say to them, "Wait until you get fractions!" or something similar, so they come to believe that some subject areas will be difficult and unpleasant. Neighborhoods, too, are influential in shaping the norms that eventually arise in the classroom. The neighborhood may place a high value on education and hold the school in high esteem. When the community displays positive attitudes toward the school,

[8] Ruth W. Berenda, *The Influence of the Group on the Judgments of Children*, New York: Teachers College, Columbia University, 1950.

these attitudes are reflected in the behavior of the children in the school. The major source of norm behavior, however, originates in the school itself.

Formation and Functioning of Norms

As members of class groups continue to interact over periods of time, they come more and more to share expectations about how members should act, feel, and think. These shared expectations may arise around any aspect of school life. Each child, as he becomes a part of the class group, becomes increasingly aware of how he is expected to react to the teacher, to various subject areas in the curriculum, to other members in the class group, and to situations in the classroom. He becomes aware of behavior that will be approved or applauded by the group and behavior that will be rewarded by the teacher. He will note that some kinds of behavior may gain approval from the group but disapproval from the teacher and vice versa.

The work of Sherif, mentioned previously, clearly indicates that norms are set up in the course of interaction. His demonstrations with the autokinetic phenomenon showed that when individuals lacked a standard of judgment for estimating the amount of movement of the light, each subject established a range or norm for movement which remained consistent during subsequent trials. When several individuals were brought together they established a new frame of reference or a new norm. This norm then remained consistent for the group and for individuals of the group when tested separately.

Although individual children come to school with many expectations regarding what should or should not be done, what should or should not be liked, and numerous other beliefs, there are no established class group norms in operation when they meet for the first time in the class. As the children work together in the classroom and play together on the playground, a new system of expectations, definitions, and sanctions evolves. In the process of interaction, the children come to share expectations and beliefs and to sanction certain behaviors. In their work and play they come more and more to conform and to behave alike.

How can the similarities in the behavior of children in class groups be explained? Three suggestions have been presented by Cartwright and Zander.[9] (1) Members come to know, perceive, and to do things in a similar fashion because they are in the same environment and are af-

---

[9] Dorwin Cartwright and Alvin Zander, *Group Dynamics: Research and Theory,* Evanston, Ill.: Row, Peterson & Company, 1960, p. 167.

fected by the same stimuli. (2) Persons in groups act alike because each individual wishes to be sure he is understanding and interpreting events around him correctly, so in periods of uncertainty he accepts the opinions of members he likes and trusts. (3) Individuals in groups come to behave in a similar fashion because there are forces that press on them to make them conform.

Belonging to a certain classroom group does determine for a child many of the things he will see, think about, learn, and do. To a large extent he will see the same events, observe the same facts, and hear the same interpretations as the other children in the room. When he is uncertain of his own reactions to events that occur, he will get his cues from others in the group whom he believes are more sure and correct in their interpretations. Then too, both overt and subtle pressures are applied that bring him around to thinking and believing much the same as others in the group.

It seems plausible that children in class groups behave in similar fashions because as individuals they are similar in many respects, and that because they are alike in many ways, children often perceive objects and events in similar manners. Although children are nonvoluntary members of their class groups, the individuals assigned to the various grade levels are alike in many ways. Though the children in a classroom may come from mixed neighborhoods and hold different values and beliefs regarding some areas of behavior, in other areas they hold no firm convictions and are still in the process of forming attitudes, ideas, and opinions. Children in the elementary school are continually facing new situations about which they do not know what to believe or "what they are supposed to believe." Sometimes what is a new situation to one child is a familiar one to the next child, and so the youngsters learn from one another. Since children in a particular class group are of a similar age, they have many similar interests and needs. They are more or less uniform in their desire to be accepted by their age-mates. Even those children who reject the school as an institution rarely wish to be excluded from all friendship groupings or to be outcasts from the class. When a new situation or a new event occurs, children turn to those who appear to know to help them with an interpretation.

Although the processes underlying norm formation in elementary classrooms have not been adequately explored, some reasons other than those cited might be offered to explain why certain norms emerge in classroom groups. It seems that some norms are imported from other relationships. They are tried out, and if they are found to be adequate for the new situations and if they make the behaviors of the group members more predictable, the norms are accepted and used. In some instances they seem to form in a process of trial and error. An event arises which requires some response from members of the group; if they find their reaction is not appropriate or workable, they try another; or if the first reaction is suitable, they continue to follow this way of behaving because it works or because it is rewarding in some way. Thus the members of class groups establish consistent behavior patterns for particular situations or events when they occur. In the next example, the children do just this.

THE BIRD WATCHERS

During the spring my first grade class became very interested in studying the birds of the surrounding area. We were very fortunate in having two linnets build a nest outside our window. The children were thrilled to have the birds so near. Every time the father bird would go "food-shopping" for his youngsters he would come very near our window. The first time this happened a child said softly, "Look! There's the papa bird!" Someone else whispered, "Sh-h-h—don't scare him!" From then on everytime the father bird came near the classroom window the children would become exceedingly quiet and would stay that way until the bird flew on to search for food elsewhere.

The norm that developed in this case defined what the group expected in the way of behavior from its members when the bird flew near the windows of the classroom.

Another reason might be offered to explain how norms form in class groups and cause members to behave in similar fashions: norms may emerge accidently. When a group is confronted with a new situation and the members have no standard or frame of reference to help them select an appropriate response, the first reaction exhibited may be interpreted as the approved response. To explain further, it might be that each individual child feels that he is the only one who is unsure of the correct response. When a situation occurs, each member of the group hesitates and waits while he seeks a clue. Some slight movement or action may be interpreted as a sign of group approval or disapproval. Someone may clear his throat and just as quickly someone else may make a disapproving sound and it may seem to the individuals that every other member disapproves. They respond to the situation according to their perceptions of group acceptance or nonacceptance. The description of "The Election" in the following example describes a class group that was faced with a new event. It seems that most members of the group had no clear frame of reference by which to guide their responses. Evidently the appropriate behavior had not been defined or clarified by either the teacher or a previous group response, so class members reacted in the way they perceived that others in the group reacted to the situation.

THE ELECTION

The fourth grade was conducting an election of class officers for the first time. Prior to the election, the children had been given some instruction in procedures and were advised to prepare nomination speeches.

The nominations were in progress. Several children had stood, addressed the chair, and had nominated one of their friends for the office of president. Usually the speeches were short and followed the same pattern. "I nominate my friend Charles because he is a good citizen. I think he will make a good president because he always minds the rules and doesn't get into trouble."

Several names had been nominated by the time Joe was recognized. He read his short nomination speech from a piece of paper that he held in his hand. Obviously someone at home had helped him prepare his speech, which went as follows:

"The person I wish to nominate for president of the fourth grade class has several qualities to recommend him. If you elect him president, he will not boss people around and act smart. He will give everyone a chance and not just give all the good jobs to his friends. He will see that the business of the room is run fair and square. This is what I would do if I am elected president, so I nominate myself, Joe Smith."

The proverbial pin would have made a crash immediately following Joe's nomination. For a moment no one seemed to breathe. Then someone gasped and a faint titter followed. Then everyone exploded. Children hooted and laughed and made remarks about "someone dumb enough to nominate himself."

Quiet was quickly restored with an order to stop the commotion and to listen. The children were told that elected officials often announced their intentions to run for office and that Joe's speech was not unlike many campaign promises. The children, however, were not convinced. Although the hooting and laughing stopped, the children continued to look at Joe with expressions that showed they believed he had committed a ridiculous act. Poor Joe sat through the ordeal, his discomfort revealed by his flaming red face.

Attempts were made later to establish procedures that would allow children to announce their intentions to run for office, but this action was never accepted by the class and no one again ever nominated himself or even indicated openly that he wished to run for office.

Frequently class group norms are formed in these slightly or greatly unstructured situations. If the situation is new or the conditions are vague and unclear, the action the group takes must be selected among the alternatives available. When the group makes a selection, a frame of reference or a standard for behavior is established, which is perceived by members as being the desired way of acting in that specific situation. Thus in the case of "The Election," the group was faced with a situation for which they had no standards to guide their actions. The members had at least three alternatives. They could continue with the nominations and find out at a future time if nominating oneself was appropriate, they could approve the behavior by noting it was a good speech or by other means, or they could show disapproval by ridicule. In the silence immediately preceding the laughter the group was in a state of suspension while members sought clues to guide their responses. In that instant each individual may have felt unsure what his reaction should be. Someone laughed, others followed, and in that moment a norm was formed that provided a reference point for individuals in succeeding elections.

As children work and play together they come more and more to behave alike and norms for the class group become standardized. In many instances, group norms that were originally shared become assimilated by members and become individual norms. These individual norms are constantly reinforced because of being shared by other members of the class group. In this way children's original expectations and beliefs undergo changes. This explains why some children who have been "good citizens" in one class suddenly become "poor citizens" in another class the following year. The expectations and beliefs of these individuals about what is good and what is poor behavior have been modified in the new group situation.

At times, the process of norm formation and the difficulties involved in establishing what is right or wrong, expected or not expected, or approved or disapproved, leads to group behavior problems that are difficult for teachers to guide or direct. Often these kinds of behavior problems arise on the playground and are brought into the classroom. Children bring to school a number of expectations relating to games and play situations from their neighborhood play groups. Since there is a relatively small amount of time allowed for free play at school, children often have difficulty in establishing shared feelings about how members should act when they play particular games. As a consequence, children frequently come into their classrooms after the noon hour or recess in unsettled states because there has not been sufficient time for them to establish what is right or wrong in a specific instance. Many teachers state that for them the most difficult type of behavior to guide or control occurs immediately following noon or recess. They cite numerous incidents that describe excited discussions or quarrelsome sessions that evolved from incidents that happened during free play periods. Most teachers conclude that these situations are difficult because the children are not ready or willing to begin work and that it takes considerable time and effort to get a class to settle down and devote their attention to school tasks. Teachers report that when the children are quieted, they begin their work with reluctance because their real interest and attention is upon the unfinished discussion or argument. Teachers frequently ask how to handle such situations without resorting to threat and punishment.

At these times children are attempting to develop a system of expectations and definitions. They are trying to establish what is right and wrong or fair and unfair. Probably much less time would be taken from the subject areas of the curriculum if teachers would help the children in their class groups develop fair and workable standards to which they could all agree. When situations of this type occur, the children are distracted and are unable to give their full attention to lessons. Very little may be accomplished for the remainder of the day if the teacher does not provide time for the children to interact and establish agreed upon standards for the troublesome situation. Also, unless the behavior is discussed and the expected response agreed upon by the members of the class group, the same group reaction may occur over and over, day after day. In the long run, the teacher will find that much less time is lost from the subject area of the curriculum if the children are helped during class time to develop norms for their free play periods. For teachers who believe that improving social behavior is not the responsibility of the school, but who do believe that skill in discussion techniques is one important learning to be developed, the situations that arise on playgrounds provide excellent discussion topics. Discussion skills can be taught at the same time that playground problems are being solved and that desirable standards of conduct are being agreed upon.

Processes Producing Conformity

There are several types of influence that in varying degrees may operate to induce conformity to the class group norms. One type of influence involves positive sanctions. The group bestows rewards and gives approval to individuals who conform. Commendation is employed rather than censure. The group chooses children for various committees, elects them as class officers or turns to them for advice and counsel. In numerous ways the group makes the individuals feel they are approved and accepted. When this type of pressure is used by class groups to bring the members into conformity, it is often so subtle that individuals, the teacher included, are unaware of the pressure and the changes that are being effected in behavior. Such subtle pressures often produce highly conforming individuals who develop an unquestioning loyalty to the group and its standards, beliefs, and expectations. Personal value systems may be modified to a large degree. What the group sanctions, the individuals approve. What the group condemns, the individuals discard.

Research has provided evidence that groups in which members can freely interact without fear of ridicule or scorn produce a high conformity to group norms. In an experiment conducted by Bovard,[10] two groups were organized, one having a group-centered and the other a leader-centered pattern of control. The group-centered control produced an atmosphere which was permissive and which had an absence of situations that were threatening to individuals. The group having the greatest amount of latitude in behavior was also the one that had the most conformity in member behavior. It was suggested that because there was a great amount of verbal interaction among members who were group-centered, they always knew what was expected of them. The conformity zone was clearly indicated, and therefore the group had more power to alter perceptions in the direction of a common norm than did a leader-centered structure. It appears that groups composed of members who like one another, and who employ positive rather than negative sanctions, also have members who exhibit more uniformity with respect to specified opinions and modes of behavior than do groups composed of members who are less friendly and who employ negative sanctions.

The process of identification also acts as a means of inducing conformity. This is another subtle type of pressure that causes individuals to conform to class group norms, and it stems from the desire of children to be a part of or identified with the class group. Identification may be defined as the psychological merging of self with another person or with a group. It causes an individual to think, feel, and act as he perceives or believes the group or person with whom he identifies thinks, feels, and acts. A child who is eager to be accepted by classmates will behave in the ways he perceives the group expects him to behave, even though some of the behavior patterns incur the displeasure of parents or teachers.

The literature relating to child growth and development has either explicitly stated or implicitly assumed that it is normal for preadolescents and adolescents to join groups and to accept unquestioningly the peer group standards and codes, even though the standards conflict with parental norms and values. Children's need to form groups, cliques, and

[10] Everett W. Bovard, Jr., "Social Norms and the Individual," *Journal of Abnormal and Social Psychology*, 43:62–69, January 1948.

gangs is frequently stressed. In the course of establishing a strong identification with a peer group, a loyalty develops to the peer group behavior standards. Thus, this need for identification and the strong desire felt by children to be accepted and approved by classmates act as forces that guide children to follow the behavior paterns that are recognized by the group as binding upon all alike.

The need for identification may cause children to support judgments or behave in ways that they do not privately accept. They support what they believe to be the opinions held by the majority of the members or by the most powerful members or by the members whom they most desire to be like. Usually when the class group is characterized by positive satisfactions, there will be less discrepancy between privately held opinions and public statements. In other words, a group that is satisfying to an individual produces actual change in individual beliefs, and outward behavior. Often, the group produces behavioral conformity by means of the threat of punishment. The individual who so strongly desires to identify with the class group is faced with possible ostracism if he does not conform. Because he fears and dreads the thought of nonacceptance, behavioral conformity results even though the group does not in reality threaten the individual.

Fear of disapproval provides a very strong motive for following the dictates of the group regarding certain ways of behaving. A child who might otherwise violate his group's standard for behaving in one instance stops short when he considers the possible consequences if he follows the dictates of his own conscience and behaves contrary to the norm.

A substitute teacher reported an incident that illustrates this point.

FEAR OF DISAPPROVAL

The substitute was called to a school to take a fifth grade class whose teacher had been involved in an accident on the way to school. The class had been only partially supervised up to the time the substitute teacher arrived. The group was reading when she walked into the room. At the precise moment when she began to introduce herself to the class, 36 books were dropped to the floor. Unfortunately for the class, the principal walked into the room at this moment. His response to this behavior was, "This class will remain in this room for sixty minutes after school and I will stay with you." The substitute learned later that this class had established a reputation for making the situation difficult for substitutes.

Later in the day, one of the girls came to the desk of the teacher and said, "Miss B., I dropped just a tiny pad when the others dropped their books. I really did not think it was a very nice thing to do when we didn't even know what you were like. I want you to know that I am sorry for what the class did and I don't think we should act like that."

The teacher responded by saying, "Since you didn't drop a book and since you really disapproved of the behavior, I will speak to the principal. I don't think you should have to stay in after school."

To this the girl quickly replied, "Oh no! I must stay in with the others! What would they think of me if I didn't? I only wanted you to know that I didn't approve of what was done and didn't think it was a nice way to act toward you."

Conformity to norms may be exacted by the use of openly negative or restricting forces. This may involve meting out punishment to individuals who fail to conform. Rewards may be withdrawn or the individuals may be subjected to mild "kidding," ridicule, or scornful remarks. The group may threaten expulsion or it may temporarily ostracize a member for not conforming to a certain approved norm. Compliance may be forced by "ordering" recalcitrant members to comply, or conversely, "forbidding" them not to. The range of negative pressures extends from mild disapproval to extreme condemnation and removal from membership in the group. The extent of the punishment depends upon the importance of the norm to the group, and the status of the individuals who are the recipients of the influence attempts.

At times children use cruel and harsh measures to bring about conformity. In the next example a group of children in an upper grade classroom threatened a member because he did not take action against his little brother, who had annoyed the older group.

LITTLE MONSTER

Randy is a third grader and is a problem on the playground. He runs through the games, grabs balls, and is generally a big nuisance. His older brother, James, is in my class. After several days of being annoyed with Randy, the children decided to do something about it. They came in one day after recess and proceeded to take James to task. They told him in angry tones to "keep that little monster from interrupting our games or else—." James wasn't very successful and the very next day Randy grabbed a ball and went running off with it. The children took out their anger on James. After another outburst in which they blamed James for Randy's behavior, they stopped talking to James altogether. Later it came out that some of them jeered him all the way home.

The social influence processes, or the types of social power that are exerted by some group members upon others, have been distinguished by French and Raven.[11] They identify and define five major types of power to explain how pressure is exerted upon individuals to make them conform. These five types of power are: (1) reward power, which may be the promise of rewards or the use of actual rewards; (2) coercive power, which is use of punishment or the withholding of rewards; (3) legitimate power, which stems from internalized values in members that others have the right to prescribe behavior for them; (4) referent power, which comes from the desires of individuals to identify with other individuals or with the group; (5) expert power, which is based on the perception by some that someone else has superior knowledge or ability in specific areas.

Occasionally there are individual children who may not conform to a certain norm for behaving even though the strength of group pressure is very great and the threat of expulsion for nonconformity is apparent. One reason may be personality differences. Crutchfield's experiments explored the differences in personality between the ready and slow yielders to the group norm.[12] Another reason may be that one individual may vary from another in his definition of the situation because of differences in backgrounds or in positions within the group structure.[13] Some children may receive more pressure than others, and some may be better able to perceive that they are receiving pressure.

It has been found that when the group norm conflicts with a firmly established set of values, individuals in the group are not apt to conform to the group norm or to change their behavior to any great degree. A finding, reported by Festinger and Thibaut,[14] showed that a greater conformity to the group's standards for behaving was obtained when members did not consider the behavior very important. When the issue was relevant to a member's value system, there was less conformity to the norm. In other words, those group members who attach a great degree of importance to the area of behavior, and who hold contrary values concerning the behavior in question, are not so apt to conform or to change their behavior to any great degree even though the group places great pressure on them to conform. Those individuals who do not attach a very great importance to the issue or behavior area are much more likely to change and conform to the group norm.

[11] John R. P. French, Jr., and Bertram Raven, "The Bases of Social Power," in Dorwin Cartwright (ed.), *Studies in Social Power,* Ann Arbor: Research Center for Group Dynamics, University of Michigan, 1959, pp. 150–165.

[12] Richard Crutchfield, "Assessment of Persons Through a Quasi Group-interaction Technique," *The Journal of Abnormal and Social Psychology,* 46:577–588, 1951.

[13] Raymond L. Gorden, "Interaction Between Attitude and the Definition of the Situation in the Expressed Opinion," *American Sociological Review,* 17:50–58, 1952.

[14] Leon Festinger and John W. Thibaut, "Interpersonal Communication in Small Groups," *Journal of Abnormal and Social Psychology,* 46:92–99, January 1951.

Factors Affecting the Conformity Process

A strongly cohesive classroom group produces more conformity to norms than one that is low in cohesiveness. Findings from a number of studies show that the extent of group power over members is directly proportional to the amount of cohesiveness that the group possesses. In an experiment involving groups that differed in cohesiveness, Back [15] observed that members of highly cohesive groups attempted to influence each other more and were more receptive to influence than members of low-cohesive groups. He found also that members of the highly cohesive groups were affected more by group pressure and changed considerably, whereas members of low-cohesive groups were less affected by pressure, compromised more, and changed but slightly. Other research findings indicate that members of cohesive groups take on the views of their fellow members more often. They adhere more closely to group standards and are more apt to protect the group norms by exerting pressure upon or rejecting individuals who do not conform.

Children who are strongly attracted to their classroom groups are also more apt to adhere closely to the group standards. According to Bovard [16] and others, the greater the extent to which a member values group affiliation, the greater likelihood he will permit the group to structure his expectations. Gerard [17] found a greater convergence of opinion in groups with high attraction than in those with low attraction. It is suggested that groups whose members are not allowed to leave (such as classroom groups) develop more overt or noninternalized conformity than groups whose members remain because they are attracted to it.[18] If a group is engaged in important or attractive activities, individuals tend to yield to group pressure.

The personal traits or characteristics of the children in a class group affect the extent of pressure that the class group can exert upon them. Children who strongly desire status within a group will conform to the norms when conformity is a condition for attaining status. Sherif [19]

[15] Kurt W. Back, "Influence through Social Communication," *Journal of Abnormal and Social Psychology*, 46:9–23, July 1951.

[16] Everett W. Bovard, Jr., "Conformity to Social Norms and Attraction to the Group," *Science*, 118:598–599, 1953.

[17] Harold B. Gerard, "The Anchorage of Opinions in Face-to-Face Groups," *Human Relations*, 7:313–325, 1954.

[18] Dorwin Cartwright and Alvin Zander, *Group Dynamics: Research and Theory*, Evanston, Ill.: Row, Peterson & Company, 1960, p. 180.

[19] Muzafer Sherif, "A Preliminary Study of Inter-group Relations," in J. H. Rohrer and M. Sherif (eds.), *Social Psychology at the Crossroads*, New York: Harper & Brothers, 1951, pp. 388–424.

describes how the boys in his camp groups who strongly desired popularity exhibited overconformity to norms in an apparent effort to increase their acceptance and improve their status in the groups. Newcomb [20] and others present evidence that the extent to which an individual conforms to a group is related to the extent of his identification with other reference groups whose normative values are similar to the norms of the group. Experimental evidence indicates also that prior experience that confirms an individual's value system strengthens his ability to withstand pressures exerted by the group. Persons with weak opinions are more apt to conform to group norms than those with strong ones. Individual conformity to group opinion regarding a matter of fact is related to the degree of certainty of the individual's initial judgment and to the accuracy of the group opinion. When an individual is aware that rewards will follow approved behavior, or if he knows that unpleasant reactions are apt to follow resistance to norms, he is more apt to conform. Thus, an individual's knowledge or his ability to perceive possible group reaction to conformity or nonconformity affects his behavior. Some individuals are more prone to perceive that the group is putting pressure upon them than are others.

Deviation from Norms

Deviation from norms implies digression from some *expected, prescribed, or established way of behaving.* Therefore, the behavior of a class group, subgroup, or individual cannot be characterized as "conforming" or "deviating" unless there is a rule or a standard in existence that prescribes the expected behavior which serves as a criteria by which the actual behavior may be evaluated. To analyze conformity or deviation meaningfully, it is necessary to refer to specific norms, whether they be those of a particular school, teacher, or classroom group.

GROUP DEVIATION FROM NORMS. Class groups may conform to many of the norms that regulate the overall school population but deviate from others in certain instances. Classroom groups within the school may develop norms that are diverse or contradictory to school norms in some respects. For example, there are often regulations governing conduct in the school auditorium. Most classes may abide by these regulations and it may be said that a norm for behavior in the auditorium exists. However, one class in the school can, and sometimes does, develop a norm for behavior in the auditorium that differs from that of the whole school population. What appears to be deviation by this class group is in fact

[20] Theodore M. Newcomb, *Social Psychology*, New York: Dryden Press, 1950.

conformity to its own group norm. When class groups conform to the regulations set by the school they have either accepted these norms as their own standards for behavior or they have not developed norms to govern their behavior for the particular situations.

Sometimes a certain school practice results in the standardization of children's behavior and in the establishment of certain expectancies regarding what is correct or not correct. Often when the school attempts to make changes in the regular practice, the teachers and administrators are surprised to find that the children will not accept or conform to the requested changes. The next example describes a class group caught in such circumstances. The school had established certain practices governing the play activities of the boys and girls. A time came when it was necessary to change the customary procedures. The attempt to change was met with strong resistance by the group. On the surface, the refusal to change appeared to be nonconformity, because it was expected that children would accept and follow a request made by the principal of the school.

BOYS VERSUS GIRLS

The boys and girls from the three upper grades in my school are separated for the physical education program. Also at noon and recess the boys and girls play separately. This happens because each group is assigned its own play space. Because of these arrangements for play periods and physical education, it is not customary for boys and girls to play together in their free time, nor is it customary for activities such as games and sports to be taught to combined groups of boys and girls. As a result of this practice of separating boys and girls, the following incident occurred in my class.

It was just before dismissal time for physical education. The principal came into the room and announced that the physical education supervisor had come that day to instruct a combined class of boys and girls in folk dancing. I was asked to take the class to the auditorium for instruction. No sooner had the principal left the room than a boy spoke out and asked to be dismissed from dancing and instead be allowed to go and play with the boys from the other classes. This request was immediately followed by similar ones from a number of girls. When the requests were denied, it seemed that everyone spoke out demanding to be excused from the lesson. Soon it was open rebellion. At the same time, the children began asking permission to leave the room for any number of reasons. Then the boys began saying they would not dance with the girls because no other class in school did so and the girls responded by stating the same thing. When the class was told that on succeeding days there would be other grades asked to participate in similar activities, the group responded that they would not be the first ones to be singled out. Finally when they saw they would not be excused, there was insistence on the part of both boys and girls that they at least be taught folk dancing separately and not together. The class was still in a state of general confusion when the supervisor and principal arrived to see what was delaying the group.

This example of group behavior illustrates how a way of behaving may become standardized and how sudden attempts to change the behavior may be met with extreme resistance on the part of the group. The school practices regarding physical education and play periods had built up a belief in the minds of the children that boys and girls were to play separately. The sudden request to change to a new way of behaving caused open rebellion. The class members refused to deviate from standard practices, though it might appear to the casual observer that the group members were nonconforming and defiant, since they would not comply with the request.

Many times class groups deviate from norms set by the teacher. Following is another example of a class group that is apparently nonconforming in that the class members do not follow a behavior pattern desired by the teacher, but that is actually conforming to its own norms for behaving.

UNCONTROLLED CONFUSION

We have carefully set standards regarding what we do when we change from one activity to another. We go over these every day in class using up a good deal of time doing so. In spite of the time spent in attempting to establish good working standards, there is always a great deal of noise when we change activities. If anyone happened to walk into this room when the children are changing from one lesson to another, he would think that no attempts had been made to help the children decide on good working habits. Pencils drop, books slam, and children talk and move around. Left to themselves the children would never get ready for the next activity. The only thing that works is to tell them that they have so many minutes to get ready and that the rest of the wasted time will be made up after school. The question is, how do you get the class members themselves to want to follow the standards they suggest but then ignore?

The teacher in this case had certain beliefs or expectations about how children should behave when they change from one lesson to another. In an attempt to obtain class group conformity to the normative order she desired, she set standards for the group to follow. The children, on the other hand, had developed another way of behaving; they had established their own norm. The teacher appeared to believe that the standards suggested by the children during classroom discussions were really their own standards, based upon their own beliefs and attitudes, when what had actually happened was that when the teacher called upon the children to establish behavior standards, they recognized the answers the teacher would accept and they said what they believed she wanted them to say.

Charts of group standards (see Figures 3 and 4) are commonly displayed in classrooms. At times it may be observed that the group behavior is not consistent with the statements on the chart. When this condition prevails it implies that the stated standards stem from the teacher and that they do not reflect the beliefs and opinions of the children in the group.

HOW WE WORK

We work quietly.
We do our own work.
We stay in our seats.
When we finish
  we read
  we write stories
  we listen at the listening post.

Fig. 3. A standards chart from a primary grade.

OUR BEHAVIOR CODE

We share with others.
We cooperate with the group.
We respect the opinions of others.
We recognize property rights.
We respect majority decisions.
We consider minority opinions.
We act on the basis of responsible
  thinking.
We exercise self-control.

Fig. 4. An upper-grade standards chart.

Subgroup Deviation

A subgroup within the classroom group may deviate from the norms of the larger group. Some members may conform to the subgroup norm even though the way of behaving might deviate considerably from the norm for behavior set by the larger class group. Members who attempt to deviate from the subgroup norm in the direction of the norm of the larger group become the recipients of active disapproval of the subgroup. At the same time, the subgroup as a whole is made a target for expressions of disapproval from the larger group if its members do not conform to norms of the larger group.

THE THREE BAD EGGS

There are three boys in our class who always stick together, and who are not very well liked by the other children. They aren't well liked because they often do things that the class does not approve of or that result in our class getting into trouble. On the playground the children call them "the three bad eggs." Sometimes the epithet slips out in the classroom and the children must be reminded that we don't call one another names.

Last week soon after our class came in from physical education period, the principal came in and asked who in our room had written on the newly painted corridor walls. No one answered but the eyes of a number of children turned toward one or another of the trio. John is the weak one of the group and just follows along with the other two boys. When the principal said to him, "John, did you write on the walls?" he blurted out, "I don't have any lipstick. I didn't do it." His two friends glared at him and then began to squirm when he turned to them and said, "Well, you guys know I don't have the lipstick!"

The principal said, "John, who said anything about lipstick?"

John was completely flustered. One of his friends said in disgust, "Oh, you dumb-bell!" With that the principal took the three boys outside, but it was some time before the class quieted down because they were once again very indignant over the behavior of these three boys.

Conflicts within class groups tend to be generated when there are subgroups whose members do not conform to the standards of behavior set by the larger class group. Conflicts between the members of the larger group and the subgroups are often disturbing and disrupting. The classroom group, in the situation just described, appeared to suffer from frequent disruptions because of the existence of a subgroup that had established norms of its own.

Conditions Producing Deviant Individuals

Several conditions may exist to cause individuals to deviate from the norms of their class groups.

1. *Lack of communication prevents the child from perceiving the regions of behavior that are approved or disapproved.* The system of communication in

the class group may be weak with respect to this individual, so that he has little opportunity to know what the group expects in the way of behavior from him, or he is unable to communicate effectively with others and thereby receives an inaccurate perception of the norms.

2. *The class group is unattractive to the child.* Needs for friendship and group affiliation may be satisfied by membership in outside play groups or gangs. He has few positive feelings toward the group and very little desire to be like its model members.

3. *Deviating from group norms is rewarding in itself.* The child receives praise and approval from the teacher, parents, or others for *not* following the group norms, and this may be more rewarding than group acceptance and approval.

4. *The group norm runs counter to a highly prized conviction concerning right and wrong.* Certain attitudes and beliefs acquired from the family or other sources are valued more highly by the child than those that the group expects him to accept.

Although these types of conditions provide some reasons why individuals deviate from the norms of their class groups, it appears that children more often deviate because of lack of communication than from any of the other three named causes. Even though the group is unattractive, or deviation is rewarding, or the norms run counter to highly prized convictions, most children cannot withstand the pressures of "kidding," ridicule, or ostracism, and sooner or later they conform, at least overtly, to the norms of the group. Usually the children who continue to deviate are those who do not accurately perceive the norms. They may be strongly motivated to conform but limited in their communication abilities and therefore unable to anticipate what the group expects or desires.

Patterns of Deviant Behavior

Individual deviations from a group norm must be examined in relation to the range of permissible behaviors that is characteristic of the particular norm and that is implied in its operation. Deviation refers to behavior that is outside the limits of behavior that the group will tolerate. It is not merely a variation of usual group behavior; it is behavior that the members consider to be *quite* different, or undesirable, threatening, or disloyal. An individual deviant is one who behaves in a way that is completely outside the range of behavior that has been established for a particular norm.

It seems that many of the problems in group behavior that teachers say are difficult to control or guide occur when class members are placing pressure upon individuals to make them conform to group norms. When deviation occurs, the group communicates its disapproval either by trying to change the individual's beliefs through arguments, or by using ridicule, scorn, or threats. Group studies have shown that members of groups communicate more when there is a discrepancy in group opinion or in member behavior.[21] When uniformity exists—that is, when everyone conforms—there is little pressure to communicate. The magnitude of the pressure increases in relation to the degree of relevance the item has to the functioning of the group. Not only does the pressure to communicate increase as the perceived nonuniformity within the group increases, but also the force to communicate is strongest toward those whose opinions are most different. Communications tend to be addressed mainly to those members within the group whose opinions are extreme. When a person is not wanted in a group, or when he is perceived as a nonmember, the force to communicate decreases.

Certain group norms may apply to all members equally, while some norms may vary for members according to their status levels. It has been observed by Thibaut [22] and others that high-status members, or those well liked and well accepted by others in the group, exhibit a greater freedom of action than do members low in status. Individuals who are highly rated by others tend to deviate on certain occasions. They are more spontaneous in their reactions. However, it has been found also that members with prestige conform to the norms which are conceived by the group as highly relevant to group purpose. Though they may deviate in some specific instances, they usually do not deviate from norms that are of particularly great importance to the group.

In the next example a well-liked group member deviated from the group norm. It is not possible to tell whether the individual acted as he did because he held principles that ran counter to the norm or whether his behavior was only the spontaneous reaction of a secure, self-confident member of the group. It is interesting to note that the deviant asked the group to excuse his actions by stating that he did not like to violate the group's expectancies. His partial apology revealed that he was aware of the norm and the nature of his assertion indicated that he seemed not to fear that the group would take strong action against him because of his deviation.

THE TRAITOR

About 16 to 20 children in my third grade class eat their lunch in the cafeteria every day. Since I am on regular cafeteria duty, we are the first

[21] Leon Festinger, "Informal Social Communication," *Psychological Review*, 57: 271–282, September 1950.

[22] John W. Thibaut, "An Experimental Study of the Cohesiveness of Underprivileged Groups," *Human Relations*, 3:251–278, 1950.

class to go through the cafeteria line, and we are usually the first class to finish eating. When a child has completed his lunch, he leaves the cafeteria in order to make room for other classes, which come in at 10-minute intervals.

Jimmy, a third grader from another classroom, always comes in a little later and tries to sit with my third grade. He is not very popular with the children in his own room. Evidently he is not liked by my third graders either, but it was quite a long time before I became aware of this fact.

One day I noticed that the children in my class were acting in a quiet, sly manner. There was some whispering accompanied by an air of suppressed excitement. All the seats at their two tables were not filled and the children were trying to fill the seats. They were motioning to children from another class to fill the chairs. When all the spaces were filled the excitement seemed to subside. I noticed, also, that when a child had finished eating, he looked around for someone to fill his vacant place. A child who had finished eating did not leave his seat until there was someone available to take his place at the table. I did not know the reason for this behavior, which was repeated for several days, until one day I noticed that the children were watching the door. When Jimmy came in the excitement became intense. Up and down the line the word was whispered, "Here he comes!" The places at the third grade tables were all taken, and as soon as Jimmy was settled in another part of the cafeteria the tense excitement subsided.

Then one day, John—who was a very popular member of his class—proved to be a traitor to his group. Jimmy came in much later than usual. He headed straight for a third grade table. John had just completed his lunch. As he stood up he saw Jimmy standing nearby looking for a seat. John offered him his place at the lunch table. There was a loud gasp from the group and all eyes fastened on John with glares of surprise and anger. John stood with his tray in his hands for a minute, evidently noting the wrath his action had aroused. He started to leave and then turned back and said to the group in an apologetic tone, "You know what? I hate myself!"

When a well-accepted, valued member of a classroom group deviates from a norm the children rarely reject the individual or even subject him to severe forms of discipline. Observation reveals that the group reaction is usually the transmitting of feelings of astonishment, disappointment, or uneasiness to the deviant. Rarely is he threatened unless the norm is very important to the group. Research findings suggest that when a well-accepted group member deviates from a norm the group may choose one of several alternatives.[23] The group may reinterpret his behavior so it is no longer threatening. The deviant's behavior may be excused on the grounds that he did not realize what he was doing or he did not mean to do it. The group may change the norm so the act of

[23] Dorothy Stock, R. Whitman, and M. Lieberman, "The Deviant Member in Therapy Groups," *Human Relations*, 2:341–371, 1958.

deviation becomes one of conformity rather than one of nonconformity.

There seem to be times when influential members of classroom groups deviate from established ways of behaving and these deviations initiate changes in the group norms. John's behavior in the previous incident may or may not have caused the group to change its behavior. Most likely it did not, since he indicated to the group he wished forgiveness. Had he remarked that he felt sorry for Jimmy or that he thought the group was behaving unkindly toward him, the group members might have discarded or reinterpreted the norm in question.

There are children in class groups who deviate widely from some group expectancies or norms but who conform in areas considered highly important and are therefore accepted. Cunningham [24] described a child who was a "sissy." However, since he could write and produce assembly programs and since this ability had high status value, he was accepted even though he deviated in mannerisms and dress.

Children who deviate because they are unable to perceive what the group expects or the kind of behavior it will approve often have intense desires for group approval and applause. These children often upset the group and create problems of group control because their behavior arouses group anger and hostility, which is evidenced in ways that disturb ordinary classroom routine. The following incident describes a child who wished approval but who lacked perception of what the group would approve, and it reveals how this behavior upset the class and created a situation that was difficult for the teacher to handle.

THE FLAG SALUTE

The day before Flag Day we had a lesson on the flag. We discussed what the flag represented and reviewed the history of our flag. In particular we discussed what the flag stood for and why we honored it. The class was interested and the discussion was lively. Toward the end of the lesson the class considered the meaning underlying the words of the flag salute.

Ronnie was a boy who was always trying to attract attention and get the approval of his classmates. Just as the class was about to begin the flag salute, Ronnie stepped forward, clicked his heels together, and with arm extended shouted, "Zieg Heil!"

For a second there was absolute silence in the room. It seemed that every individual was too shocked to move or speak, but following this period of silence came a violent reaction. There were cries of "That's not funny!" and "Get out of here. We don't want you around." Two youngsters standing close by began shoving him, saying "Get out, you traitor!" and

[24] Ruth Cunningham and associates, *Understanding Group Behavior of Boys and Girls,* New York: Teachers College, Columbia University, 1951, p. 137.

"We don't want any communists in here!" (The children classified all un-American acts as communistic.) A number of children moved toward Ronnie as if they were actually going to hit him or push him around further.

This all occurred very quickly. I hesitated a moment, wondering how to handle the situation, but there was not time to think as the children were becoming increasingly violent. I went over to Ronnie and asked him to step outside for a few minutes to think over his action. The children were then asked to take their seats, but it was difficult to quiet them.

The class completely rejected Ronnie and his behavior. Even when he came back into the room and, without coercion, told the class he was sorry for what he had done, the group would not accept him. They stopped addressing any remarks to him and they completely ignored him for the rest of the time school was in session.

The behavior of the child in this situation appears contrary to some research findings relating to individual conformity to norms. In a laboratory experiment, Dittes and Kelley [25] found that in making both simple perceptual judgments and more complex social judgments, subjects who were not quite fully accepted by their groups adhered to group norms more closely than did fully accepted members. This heightened conformity of fringe members was observed not only for judgments made in public but extended even to judgments held privately. This strict conformity to group norms, particularly in public, by persons least accepted by their groups resulted presumably because these individuals perceived overt conformity as a means of preventing total rejection by their groups. Further confirmation comes from the research conducted by Jackson and Saltzstein,[26] who also demonstrated that judgments of members who were not accepted by the group were more highly influenced by majority opinion than were those of fully accepted members. It appeared that such conformity might be derived from a "need for social reassurance" or be related to lack of confidence, because nonaccepted individuals experienced loss of confidence in their abilities to make required judgments and hence depended disproportionately upon the group for their judgments. These members identified with accepted group members and conformed to their judgments.

It seems probable that some individuals are unable to predict the group response to certain actions or to perceive what is expected of them in certain situations. When they react to an event in a manner

[25] James E. Dittes and Harold H. Kelley, "Effects of Different Conditions of Acceptance upon Conformity to Group Norms," *Journal of Abnormal and Social Psychology*, 53:100–107, 1956.

[26] Jay M. Jackson and Herbert D. Saltzstein, "The Effect of Person-group Relationships on Conformity Processes," *Journal of Abnormal and Social Psychology*, 57:17–24, July 1958.

similar to Ronnie's response in the flag incident, they believe their actions will receive group approval. Although these individuals may conform highly in situations where the norm or standard is clearly defined,
they are limited in their ability to perceive what the group expects in
new situations where expected behavior must be inferred. This may be a
major factor in their nonacceptance by the group. Then, too, the position held by an individual in the group's structure affects his perception.
It was found by Festinger and associates [27] that persons with peripheral
positions in the communication structure often possessed different information, which led to misunderstanding and conflict. The findings indicate that when an individual is not accepted by the group he is placed
in a position where he is less able to observe the range of behavior that
the group will tolerate. Thus he is a victim of a circular effect. The more
he is rejected for lack of perception, the less he is able to perceive. Conversely, the individual in a central position receives more accurate information and is better able to perceive what the group expects.

Recommended practices for handling children who are isolates like
Ronnie or fringe group members have led teachers to work with these
children individually in efforts to change their behavior. Teachers recognize the need of these children for acceptance and approval and they
usually understand why they clown and attempt to attract attention. In
an effort to make them feel important and increase their statures in the
eyes of other class members, teachers often place these individuals in
desirable positions. They are made monitors, or chairman of committees,
or their achievements are given special recognition. The fact is that
these practices generally make these children more unacceptable to the
group because further group resentment is aroused. Also, such practices
do not get at the basic causes of the difficulties. Children like Ronnie do
not understand what is expected of them by the group. When they
exceed the limits of acceptable behavior, procedures need to be followed
that involve the whole group. If instead of isolating Ronnie, the teacher
had redirected the group members to a discussion of why they felt so
strongly about Ronnie's behavior, it is conceivable that two important
things might have resulted.

First, the hostility of the group would have lessened by encouraging
the members to communicate their feelings and beliefs. It has been
found [28] that overt acts of aggression tended to be reduced when group

[27] Leon Festinger, Stanley Schachter, and Kurt Back, *Social Pressures in Informal
Groups,* New York: Harper & Brothers, 1950.

[28] John W. Thibaut and John Coules, "The Role of Communication in the
Reduction of Interpersonal Hostility," *Journal of Abnormal and Social Psychology,*
47:770–777, October 1952.

members were permitted to communicate with the instigator of hostility, and following the communication there was increased friendliness toward the person who initially aroused the hostility. When not permitted to communicate, group members in the cited study exhibited few friendly responses toward the aggressor.

Second, by hearing the group members state their beliefs, Ronnie would have obtained evidence from which he could modify his perceptions and be better able to assess group reaction toward his behavior in the future. Direct communication by the group to the individual can act as an influence to produce changes in the child's perceptions and values, and this type of influence is far more effective than that arising from displays of group disapproval or actual aggressive action. Unless the group is guided toward helping the child increase his understanding of why his behavior is unacceptable, he may heighten his acts of bravado in an increased effort to gain attention. Ronnie was undoubtedly left in a state of worse confusion than he had been previously, and he was also faced with total group rejection. Total utilization of the group was needed to help Ronnie understand the reaction to his behavior and to increase the probability that group hostility would be lessened.

Teachers are often faced with disturbances caused by a child's deviating from group expectancies or norms when the group expects or the norm demands some ability that the individual does not possess. The following example of group reaction is typical of many that teachers report.

THE UNACCEPTED

Some time ago we began square dancing in our fifth grade as part of our physical education program. We have followed the practice of having the boys choose the girls one day and the next time having it be "Ladies' Choice." Whenever it is the boys' turn to choose, it always happens that one girl, Peggy, is left out. No one wishes to dance with her, and she seems not to be liked or accepted by any of the children in the class.

One day after this had occurred several times she began to cry after we came back into the room. She put her head on her desk and sobbed and said everyone hated her. The rejection was too much and she was completely miserable. I sent her out to the nurse's room to rest and compose herself. While she was gone we had a class discussion. We talked about all her good qualities and also brought out the reasons why she was not liked. The main objection from the boys seemed to be that when it was her turn to choose a team for games she was not able to pick the right people and therefore the sides were unbalanced. The girls said she didn't pay much attention to how she looked and was pretty awkward in both games and dancing. There were probably deeper objections, since Peggy's IQ is only 82, but these were the ones the children said caused them not to like Peggy. After more discussion they reached the conclusion that these objections were not really serious and that they could help her overcome some of her faults.

Peggy is now getting along very well and seems much happier. A group of girls got together and made a special effort to help her. She has been willing to let the boys help her choose teams when it is her turn. So far, she has never again been left out of the dancing. The children have really cooperated in their efforts to help her.

In this case the solution to the problem was not too difficult. The teacher was able to get the cooperation of the group to help Peggy, but often the situation is more complex. Sometimes the child is handicapped physically, is of a different race or nationality, or comes from a very poor family and does not possess the material things that children admire or expect. It is not always realistic for the teacher to attempt to change group expectancies in instances of deviation. Neither is it possible, in most cases, to change the deviant individuals themselves. The task of the teacher is to help the group to respect and make use of the resources that such individuals possess. This is not accomplished by lecture or appeal, but by creating a setting where individuals who are handicapped, whether by physical deformity, personality adjustment, or prejudice, can make contributions to the class group. Most children have strong urges to achieve status in their class groups and to be well accepted. There are some children, however, who appear to be unconcerned over the fact that they do not belong and that they are rejected by their groups. The reasons for this apparent lack of desire for affiliation and companionship are not always clear. Sociometric studies have shown that individuals tend to prefer persons in the group whom they perceive to be similar to themselves, particularly in social values. It is possible that rejected members do not perceive that others in the group are similar and that therefore they have no desire to be accepted. It has been found that when members are made to feel they are not highly valued they place a lower value on group membership and conform less to the norms.[29] Since membership in a group serves purposes other than satisfaction of the desire for belonging, it may be that individuals who are rejected and who appear unconcerned over this rejection find that the group goals and their own goals are not in harmony. Realization of their own personal goals is more important than securing acceptance from

[29] Harold H. Kelley and M. M. Sharpiro, "An Experiment on Conformity to Group Norms Where Conformity Is Detrimental to Group Achievement," *American Sociological Review,* 19:667–677, 1954.

the group members. If the normative behavior demanded by the group has no intrinsic value to the individual, he will have little motivation to perform it. An individual will conform to the degree that the group can give him what he wants. If he wishes something other than acceptance and status, and if following his own goals is more rewarding, he will be unlikely to conform to group norms.

The following incident is an example of group reaction to a member who is completely rejected by the children in the class.

THE BOOKWORM

We have a girl in the class who is not liked by the children because she is "bookish" and always knows the answers. She never appears to show off or act superior, but the children seem to resent the fact that she invariably gets the highest scores and rarely makes mistakes. Most of the time the class as a whole ignores this girl (Ellen) entirely. If we are planning something and she makes a suggestion, the class members behave as if her comments were not heard at all. If an attempt is made to force the class to consider her proposals, the children invariably reject them completely without discussion or consideration of any kind. Generally her ideas are better than other suggestions, but the fact that she made them causes the group to disregard them entirely. Ellen herself always appears self-possessed and never gives any indication that it matters to her that the others in the room pay no attention to her or to her suggestions. When the children act as if they do not hear what she says or when they flatly reject her ideas, she makes no move to force herself upon the group. In fact she seems to prefer to remain in the background and follow her own interests and pursuits. However, it is not possible for her to remain in the background at all times, and when she is drawn to the attention of the children in some way, the situation is very difficult to control.

For example, the other day it was her turn to give an oral report utilizing the wall map. She had just started her report when she pointed to the map to illustrate a point. The map rolled up, hit the bracket, and fell to the floor with a loud crash.

The class reacted as a unit. The children began to laugh loudly and derisively. Unkind remarks were exchanged concerning the report and slurring statements were made concerning Ellen herself. These comments were not addressed to Ellen but were exchanged between class members. The children were admonished to be courteous and to pay attention to the speaker. The map was replaced in its bracket and Ellen began again. It was necessary to interrupt her report several times and command the class to pay attention. It did no good however, and the behavior did not change until another child got up and began his report. During the whole incident Ellen remained completely calm and poised.

Whenever Ellen comes into the picture, the class reacts with behavior that is impossible to control.

The degree to which a child will wish to be identified with a class group is dependent upon whether the other members manifest characteristics, behaviors, customs, and skills that he values. Ellen, in the preceding case, may or may not have been as unconcerned over her rejection as she appeared to be. However, it could be that Ellen found that praise for good scholarship was more rewarding than group acceptance, and she therefore made no effort to gain approval from the group.

Consequences of Deviation

Whatever the cause of deviation from a class norm, when an individual deviates the children frequently become very talkative and the atmosphere in the room often appears disorderly. Schachter [30] found that the communication addressed to a deviant increased the more the group perceived the differences that existed between the group and the deviant. Also, the more relevant the issue, the more extensive was the communication directed to the individual. One reason for the increased talking and apparent disorder is that members tend to communicate to the deviant in an effort to influence him and make him change his behavior or opinion. Most teachers have experienced this phenomenon, though they may have been unaware of the causes for the disruptions.

As we stated earlier, it has been found that the more unpleasant a person's position is in the group structure, the stronger are the forces on him to communicate irrelevant content.[31] The child who deviates frequently and as a consequence has low status in the group tends to make remarks that are of little consequence to the group's purpose but which serve to create a talkative or noisy atmosphere in the classroom. This situation may be observed frequently in class groups. The "problem" children talk out for no apparent reasons, though the actual cause has been inferred as serving the function of permitting the person holding an undesirable position in the group to escape from it.

The consequences of deviation may be very great to an individual child. The child who will not yield to group pressure in certain instances because he holds firmly established attitudes and values must have great courage if he is to continue to stand by his own beliefs and

[30] Stanley Schachter, "Deviation, Rejection and Communication," *Journal of Abnormal and Social Psychology*, 46:190–207, 1951.

[31] Harold H. Kelley, "Communication in Experimentally Created Hierarchies," *Human Relations*, 4:39–56, 1951.

principles. The teacher needs to support him and his stand, for few children can undergo group disapproval for long periods without this state of affairs having adverse effects upon their attitudes toward school and school work. The marginal or rejected member who cannot live up to group standards usually lacks the sense of security that is necessary for successful achievement in school work. When he cannot achieve as well as is expected of him, he often develops a feeling of failure, which further increases his inefficiency. Tensions are aroused, which cause the child to expend his efforts to reduce the tensions instead of employing his energies to complete school tasks. In his struggle to gain acceptance, he creates situations in the group that affect other members, and frequently a classroom condition develops that is not conducive to learning. The group becomes less attractive to other members, because the deviate inflicts his needs and tensions upon the group. Since it is usually impossible to change the deviant, the teacher can improve the situation only by attempting to get the group to reduce its demands.

Questions for Study and Discussion

1. Some elementary school groups develop fads, or series of fads, relating to handwriting, clothing, jokes, games, etc., while other groups develop few fads or customs of their own and adopt few from other groups. Discuss the possible reasons for this and describe the probable differences in group characteristics in the different cases.

2. Referring to the Sherifs' definition of norms, explain and illustrate kinds of behavior that are "of consequence" to the group.

3. Describe an instance of either similarity or dissimilarity of school norms and class group norms. If the norms of the school and the norms of the class group are dissimilar, what types of behavior problems can be predicted?

4. Recall or observe a lesson in an elementary classroom and identify some instances of norm behavior. Were the group norms and the teacher's norms in agreement or disagreement? Were the norms or standards ever referred to openly by the group members or the teacher? Was there evidence that the teacher had been able to develop with the class group desirable norms for behavior?

5. A chart of standards for behavior is commonly displayed in classrooms. They have varied titles such as "How We Work," "Our Room Standards," or "The Central School Rules." From your knowledge of group norms, discuss the values and limitations of preparing and displaying such charts.

6. From your experience or from observation, describe an effective group norm that was accepted by part, but not all, of the group. Why was it effective? What reasons may be advanced to explain why a few members of the class did not conform?

7. From your experience, describe an instance where a well-accepted group member deviated from a group norm. Include in your description: the kind of group, the approximate chronological ages of members, and the group norm involved. Analyze the group reaction and cite the possible causes of the deviation.

Suggestions for Further Reading

Berkowitz, Leonard. "Effects of Perceived Dependency Relationships upon Conformity to Group Expectations," *Journal of Abnormal and Social Psychology,* 55:350–354, November 1957.

Deutsch, Morton and Harold B. Gerard. "A Study of Normative and Informational Social Influences upon Individual Judgment," *Journal of Abnormal and Social Psychology,* 51:629–636, November 1955.

Dittes, James E. and Harold H. Kelley. "Effects of Different Conditions of Acceptance upon Conformity to Group Norms," *Journal of Abnormal and Social Psychology,* 53:100–107, July 1956.

Festinger, Leon, Harold B. Gerard, Bernard Myovitch, Harold Kelley, and Bert Raven. "The Influence Process in the Presence of Extreme Deviates," *Human Relations,* 5:327–346, 1952.

Festinger, Leon, Stanley Schachter, and Kurt Back. "The Operation of Group Standards," in Cartwright, D. and A. Zander (eds.), *Group Dynamics: Research and Theory.* Evanston, Ill.: Row, 1960, pp. 241–259.

Gerard, Harold B. "The Anchorage of Opinion in Face-to-Face Groups," *Human Relations,* 7:313–325, August 1954.

Goldberg, Solomon C. "Three Situational Determinants of Conformity to Social Norms," *Journal of Abnormal and Social Psychology,* 49:325–329, July 1954.

Hardy, Kenneth R. "Determinants of Conformity and Attitude Change," *Journal of Abnormal and Social Psychology,* 54:289–294, May 1957.

Harvey, O. J. and Conrad Consalvi. "Status and Conformity to Pressures in Informal Groups," *Journal of Abnormal and Social Psychology,* 60:182–188, March 1960.

Jackson, Jay M. and Herbert D. Saltzstein. "The Effect of Person–Group Relationships on Conformity Processes," *Journal of Abnormal and Social Psychology,* 57:17–25, July 1958.

Kelley, Harold H. and Edmund H. Volkhart. "The Resistance to Change of Group-Anchored Attitudes," *American Sociological Review,* 17:453–465, August 1952.

Lippitt, Ronald, Norman Polansky, and Sidney Rosen. "The Dynamics of Power," *Human Relations,* 5:37–65, February 1952.

McKeachie, Wilbert J. "Individual Conformity to Attitudes of Classroom Groups," *Journal of Abnormal and Social Psychology,* 49:282–289, April 1954.

Menzel, Herbert. "Public and Private Conformity Under Different Conditions of Acceptance in the Group," *Journal of Abnormal and Social Psychology,* 55:298–402, November 1957.

Rommetveit, R. *Social Norms and Roles.* Minneapolis: U. of Minnesota, 1953.

Schachter, Stanley. "Deviation, Rejection and Communication," *Journal of Abnormal and Social Psychology,* 46:190–207, April 1951.

Snyder, Aaron F., Walter Mischel, and Bernice Eisman Lott. "Value, Information and Conformity Behavior," *Journal of Personality,* 28:333–341, September 1960.

Wiener, Morton, Janeth T. Carpenter, and Bruce Carpenter. "Some Determinants of Conformity Behavior," *Journal of Social Psychology,* 45:289–297, May 1957.

Chapter 7   # Group Goals

CLASSROOM groups seek to achieve goals, as do all working groups. Some goals are predetermined and prescribed, such as curricular content, that is, indicated in curriculum guides, courses of study, and textbooks. Other goals are those that the group develops or creates in the process of the class interaction and they may encompass or they may differ from the prescribed goals. Goals that relate to the psychological well-being of the group, as a group, may exist concurrently with the prescribed curricular goals.

Goals prescribed for school classes are not single, monolithic points toward which the total group membership is expected to expend effort over a period of time; rather, there is a mélange of larger and longer range goals to which shorter term and lesser efforts contribute. There are also smaller goals that are independent of the dominant goals.

Both group goals and individual goals coexist in the classroom. Individuals pursue their aims in what they may perceive to be isolation from the group. The attainment of skills in a subject field—spelling or arithmetic, for example—is seen by the learner as his individual goal requiring his individual effort, the results or products of which are his personally. Group goals are those that the learners in the classroom accept as affecting the group, to which they give their efforts, and whose results or achievements are group products or outcomes. Just as individual goals and group goals occur daily in classrooms and can be recognized as such, so does an interplay of individual and group goals occur. When a class decides upon a goal that requires independent individual actions, there is a fusion of the learner's effort and goal for himself with his effort for the group goal. A further variation is seen when the more able students assist the less able student on an individual basis to promote both the individual's achievement and the group goals. To summarize, goals as found in the classroom are individual goals, group goals, and combinations of the two.

Group goals, then, are not the only goals operative in the classroom. They are a group property that affects the behavior of the group and of the individuals in the group. They direct, channel, and guide behavior to the degree that the goals are accepted, understood, and desired by the group; when this occurs the goals serve to motivate, energize, mobilize, and change behavior.

This chapter will attempt to define and develop the concept of group goals. The discussion will examine sources of goals, how goals are formed and established, factors influencing group goal achievement, and how goals operate to produce certain behaviors that can be observed in classrooms.

The Nature of Group Goals

Behavior is often viewed as goal-oriented, and this concept is frequently applied to educational practice. Although theories differ, the term *goal* is used most frequently in the literature to refer to a condition or a state that leads to the termination of motivated behavior. Groups, and individuals as well, operate in terms of goals. The drive to action is furnished by goal-seeking. Despite the importance given in education to understanding and directing individual goals, and despite the fact that it is advocated more and more that some goals be established with the total group, the relation of group goals to class group behavior is seldom explored in the educational literature. One reason for the little attention given to this may well be that it is exceedingly difficult to examine, or it may be that educators assume that a group goal is a sum of individual goals, which may or may not be true.

Group Goal Concepts

The essential feature of a goal is that it specifies a preferred condition or a desired state and it guides behavior toward the attainment of this condition or state. A goal refers to objects or consequences that either a person or a group of persons seeks to achieve. Expectations are involved—that is, it is expected that when the end point, or the target (goal), is reached, the results will be satisfying. Although there is general agreement that a group goal, as well as an individual goal, steers activities in a particular direction, conceptualizations of the *group goal* differ. Various group goal concepts have been advanced, which define and describe group goals in different ways. This section of the chapter explores three conceptualizations and attempts to relate them to class group behavior.

COMPOSITE INDIVIDUAL GOALS. Some discussions of group goals refer to them as composites of similar individual goals. In some instances, children in classrooms do appear to seek the same goal even though they do not communicate verbally or reach a consensus regarding the goal that they seem to seek. For example, when children are required to remain seated at their desks for long periods of study, the majority may desire activity at the same time. This desire to release excess energy may cause a large number of children to behave in a similar manner. The following behavioral incident, described by a fifth grade teacher, is used to examine further the composite group goal concept.

UNPREMEDITATED BEHAVIOR

At certain times during the school day, usually during a study or work period, I become involved with the problems of individual pupils. After a while I become aware of the fact that the previously quiet and stationary group of pupils is noisy and many individuals are wandering about the room. It appears to happen quickly, unobtrusively and almost unaccountably. I have forced myself to try to observe and to track down just how this behavior arises.

It usually starts, it seems, with an apparently casual, unpremeditated move of *one* pupil. Then, almost automatically as if by some prearranged signal, other children casually arise and move to other parts of the room. They do such things as walk to the globe, the encyclopedias (as if they were looking something up), the pencil sharpener, the water fountain, or other pupils. It is astonishing to suddenly look up and find children out of their seats and in all parts of the room as if this has occurred by magic! Once this class migration is well under way, it is time-taking and somewhat difficult to restore the classroom to its original quiet, studious atmosphere.

When it is one of the less studious pupils who initiates this behavior, it seems as if it is almost planned and deliberate. However, close observation proves that most often it is started by one of the pupils considered most studious and well behaved. The minute one person begins this meandering to some other part of the room, one at a time others start rising and moving to other parts of the room. Often they stop on the way to visit with friends.

I've tried to determine if the pupils sense a sort of termination of the lesson, or if they sense a time to relax. While the behavior appears to be unpremeditated, still it seems as if a signal is flashed to each person in the group which tells each one it is time to stop work and to move around the room. It is a problem—mainly because it shortens the study and teaching time. Getting them back into place and getting them to start to work again involves many minutes.

On the surface it seems justified to explain this behavior in terms of a composite group goal. The majority of individuals in the group do appear to seek the same goal—a release of excess energy. Children in a class group, because they are of the same approximate age, have similar interests, and are influenced by the same room environment, often seem to have highly similar goals (or even identical goals). However, because most of the children in the room desire to release energy does not mean that the children desire to change conditions for the group as a whole. Similarity of individual goals does not provide an adequate definition for a group goal. The basic difficulty involved in viewing the group goal in this manner is that *individual goals* specify consequences the individual wishes to attain for himself; *group goals* specify consequences that are desired for the group as a whole. That each child in the group desires a condition for himself that is similar to the desires of the other individuals does not justify the assumption that collectively the children in the class are seeking to achieve this condition for the group as a whole, nor can it be said that the goal is shared and therefore a group goal. Discussions of teaching practice frequently include suggestions regarding the setting of goals, and sometimes the proposal is made that group goals can be established if individual goals are *shared*. The children in the above example seem to have the same goal, but it is difficult to conceive that sharing such a goal creates a group goal. In fact, it is difficult to think of a group goal as resulting from a pooling of a number of individual goals even though they are similar, because such a pooling or sharing would not necessarily specify a preferred condition for the group as a whole.

AN OPERATING CONSENSUS. Another conception of group goals stresses consensus. Thibaut and Kelley [1] agree that individual and group goals

[1] John W. Thibaut and Harold H. Kelley, *The Social Psychology of Groups,* New York: John Wiley & Sons, 1959, pp. 256–257.

resemble one another in that goals, whether group or individual, designate that some action will be taken toward putting a given task in a particular state. According to their view, however, the resemblance ceases at this point because group goals require some degree of consensus before they can be prosecuted by enough of the group members to warrant their being called group goals. These authors conceive group goals as being related to tasks. Members of a group meet and decide to take some action. They define an end-state (goal) toward which they will work and reach a consensus about the quality of the outcome. The members reach a consensus also, about how the goal is to be reached. This conception then, considers group goals as representing "an operating consensus about a desirable state of a given task." These goals are developed by explicit processes or deliberate acts of decision. Although the differences are pointed out, the similarities between goals and norms are noted. Both are dependent upon consensus and both affect group behavior in somewhat similar ways. Consequently, when goals are conceptualized in this manner, it is often difficult to distinguish between norm and goal behavior.

In the following example, the question could be raised whether the group set a goal or whether a norm was established.

SPELLING

When this fourth grade started out in September, we created two groups in spelling. Not more than a month passed before the children in the low group got together and decided that they could take all the words and still make good grades. They have been able to maintain the standard they set for themselves. During the past months many new children have joined the class, some of them are of low ability. Every time a new pupil enters the class, the group manages to make it known that, "We just don't miss our spelling words." The result of this class pressure is that very few words are missed in spelling. Even a few boys who are reading at a second grade level usually manage to spell all the words correctly by the end of the week.

It is not uncommon for teachers to interpret such behavior as goal behavior. Actually, the members of the "low" group set a standard or norm. Joint action was not required to put a given task in a desired state. In other words, the task (spelling correctly) did not call for group action but only individual performance. The behavior exhibited is very similar to that observed in factories where the workers set a standard for how much or how little is to be produced. In this case, the established norm for individual performance was high. It is conceivable that some children would find it very difficult to maintain such a standard. All the individuals in the above example probably did not have individual goals of learning to spell correctly. With some, the individual goal was possibly to achieve or maintain group approval and acceptance. Although it is important for teachers to understand how group goals form, if the group goal concept is limited to the formulation process, it is conceivable that teachers might continually believe they are establishing group goals while they are actually attempting to set norms.

GOALS AS PURPOSES OR CONSEQUENCES. A third approach to the group goal concept is favored by Cartwright and Zander.[2] They do not consider the means by which a group sets a goal as the important factor, but propose that a group goal be defined at the group level of description in a manner similar to the way an individual goal is defined at the individual level. The group is viewed as an undifferentiated entity, and this permits consideration of the similarity between a group goal and an individual goal. Certain major features of this conception are described in terms of group locomotion. The group, as an entity, has a location in an environment. When a group goal exists, some location in the group's environment is preferred more by the group than another location. The group directs its activities toward reaching the preferred location. When a group attempts to move toward a preferred location, it is usually necessary to engage in a series or a sequence of activities that will lead the group to the desired location. This is thought of as the path taken by the group to reach the goal. Several alternative paths to the same goal may exist. The decision as to what path the group will take to reach the goal may be accomplished without the participation of all of the members. In fact, some members may not be aware that there is some consensus among the members of the group as to the way the goal is to be reached. In other instances, the group decides on the path and how the tasks will be performed.

This approach to group goals provides a clear definition of group goal operation. The construction of the concept makes it possible to visualize the processes involved. This is particularly true when the goal is explicit and openly agreed upon and the path to the goal is reasonably clear. A fairly common classroom activity can be used to illustrate the major features of this conception. For example, a classroom group decides that it is time to change a bulletin board. The theme agreed upon is "Good Books." (The classroom group now has a goal. The path to the goal is not yet clear; if the group is to move toward the goal it must plan and perform a series of activities.) A number of suggestions are made in the planning period about ways the theme might be devel-

[2] Dorwin Cartwright and Alvin Zander, *Group Dynamics, Research and Theory*, Evanston, Ill.: Row, Peterson & Company, 1960, pp. 349–352.

oped. They include, among others: the use of book jackets, a display of book reports, a pictorial literary map. (Each suggestion represents an alternative path to the goal.) The group decides to illustrate five selected books, and committees are organized to perform these tasks. (By group decision, the path to the goal and means of reaching the goal are specified.) Each time a committee completes its task, the group moves nearer the goal. When all five books are illustrated and mounted on the bulletin board, the group goal has been reached.

The illustration given is perhaps too simplified, for the goal is clear and the alternative paths are not diverse in nature. The situation is much more complex when the goal is ambiguous or when the path to the goal is hazy. For example, a class group wishes to be recognized as the grade with the best citizenship record because the P.T.A. has announced it is giving a plaque to the class with the best citizenship record. This plaque will hang in the front hall with each child's name engraved upon it. But "good citizenship" has not been defined clearly by the P.T.A. What must the group do to achieve such a record? The group goal is to win the plaque, but the path to the goal, or the steps to be taken to reach the goal, are difficult to determine. Is group effort required; that is, to win the plaque must the class work together on such tasks as cleaning the yard or other similar responsibilities? Does it mean that each individual must change his way of behaving? If the latter suggestion seems a more likely path to the goal, does this mean that in order for the group as a group to reach the goal, standards for individual behavior must be established?

This conception of a group goal becomes complex when the paths to the goal are not clearly defined; nevertheless, such a conception makes it possible to examine a specific class group goal in terms of needed group operations. Moreover, the progress a group makes toward the goal can be examined at any given time or at any given point in the process. This is of particular benefit to a teacher who must help the class group reach desired goals.

The differences in these three conceptions are obvious. In the first instance, group goals are not differentiated from individual goals. If a number of individuals in the group have the same goal, then it is presumed that a group goal exists. Since group goals are a source of influence on member behavior, this conception does not account for the fact that a group goal can induce a member to act in support of it even though it differs from the goal an individual has for himself. This conception makes it difficult, also, to explain group action in terms of goal-seeking behavior. For example, how can an individual goal, though multiplied, induce *all* members to seek to achieve the goal? If group goals are composites of individual goals, how can a teacher help each individual to formulate an identical, acceptable, workable goal?

The second conceptualization stresses the fact that before a goal can be considered a *group* goal, a number of members must reach agreement that they wish to undertake certain tasks in order that some desired objective be reached. Therefore, goals become group goals when enough members agree that they wish to combine their efforts and work on tasks that will produce certain desired outcomes. In one way this view is simple to conceptualize. A goal is thought of as some end point or some desired state that requires united action by group members. If they agree to work to achieve this state, then a group goal exists. Individual motives, attitudes, and interests are not involved, since once consensus is reached, the group goal becomes the force that induces individuals to perform certain tasks and activities. However, groups often agree upon a goal that does not clearly specify the tasks and activities required. How the goal operates in this situation is not easily described if the group goal is conceived as an operating consensus involving putting a given task in some desired state.

The third conceptualization views the goal as a preferred state or an end point that a group desires to reach, just as an individual has an aim or objective that he desires to attain. When a group goal is conceptualized as being similar to an individual goal, and when the group is viewed as an entity that engages in goal-seeking behavior much as does an individual, then it is possible to describe group-goal behavior quite specifically. Conceived in this way, it is also possible to differentiate between norm setting and group-goal development. When the group goal is conceived as some end point that the group desires to reach and that requires the performance of a series of operations before it can be reached, the teacher's role in guiding group-goal-seeking behavior is more easily determined. For these reasons, when class group behavior is examined in relation to group goals, the class group will be viewed as an undifferentiated entity, which engages in goal-seeking behavior at the group level much in the way an individual engages in goal-seeking behavior.

Goal Characteristics

Since a group goal can be considered as similar to an individual goal, the same general definition may apply to both individual and group goals.

A goal is sometimes defined as that which when attained will satisfy a need or an expectation, or it is defined as some point or some condition in the environment that an individual strongly desires to reach or attain. A goal is defined by Newcomb [3] as, "a state of affairs toward which behavior is directed." The term *goal* is a way of describing the directional aspect of behavior, for a goal, as such, does not actually exist in the environment. It is an end point of a specific sequence of behavior. These definitions clarify one aspect that is extremely important to the understanding of group goals; that is, a goal is defined as a state of affairs *toward* which behavior is directed, although some behavior is directed *away* from a certain state of affairs in the environment. The explanation given is that goal behavior is toward some end point because there is no way of avoiding something without going toward something else, and that to avoid an undersirable goal, behavior will be directed toward another that is more desirable.

A teacher is concerned with directing and guiding behavior *toward* certain goals, while the class group may be concerned with directing behavior *away* from these goals. Although there are some important differences in behavior that is goal-directed and that which is directed away from a goal, the group goal concept is more easily understood if it is recognized that the group directs its energies toward a substitute goal when it wishes to avoid a nonaccepted goal.

Whether a goal is an individual goal or a group goal, its general characteristics are the same. To clarify thinking later when the complexities involved in group goal formation and operation are examined, a goal's general nature is reviewed at this point.

LONG-RANGE AND/OR REMOTE GOALS. Goals refer to objectives or consequences that a person or a group seeks to achieve. These consequences are expected, in many cases, at some future time. Some individual goals are quite remote—so far off in the future that the paths to attainment are very hazy. For example, a boy in high school may desire to become a foreign newspaper correspondent. His end goal is quite far distant, but it exerts an influence upon his choice of extracurricular activities and upon his selection of courses. He writes for the school newspaper, takes French as an extra subject, and makes a special effort to do well in his English classes. Another boy with the same goal does not plan the steps necessary for him to reach his goal. He desires to become a foreign newspaper correspondent but he becomes wrapped up in more immediate goals such as becoming a member of the football team. His elective courses

[3] Theodore M. Newcomb, *Social Psychology*, New York: Dryden Press, 1950, pp. 77–83.

are selected because other members of the team are taking them. Class group goals are never as far off in the future as this. For one thing, the class as a group exists within a certain time span. This limits planning, so group goals are not remote, though some may have fairly long ranges. Long- and short-range goals may be differentiated not only by time, but by the length of the path necessary to reach the goal. The goal may be long-range because a number of operations are required before it can be achieved, or the goal may be short-range because relatively few steps are needed before it is reached. A goal may appear to be far off because the ways to attain the goal are ambiguous. When compared with some individual goals, the goals of the class group are usually short-range, but some major class goals are more distant than others in the sense that they cannot be achieved in one process or in one day. The following example distinguishes the differences between long- and short-range goals.

THE EXHIBIT

At the first of the year it seemed that this fourth grade was taking a long time to settle down and really get to work. The turning point came though, about a month before we had Parents' Night. (We have an open house for parents in the fall and again in the spring.) Several weeks before Parents' Night we began talking about some of the things we might put up in the room to show our parents what we were doing. The children did not exhibit much enthusiasm until one day when one of the boys, Jim, brought in some shells he had gathered at the beach. The shells sparked a general class discussion. We were studying our state in social studies, so we switched from a study of the history to a study of the physical geography, which included the coastal area. The suggestion that we make a shell exhibit came from the class. The children brought their shells, made maps, and wrote stories. The exhibit was a big success and from that time on the class seemed to really get to work. There was much less playing around and more interest shown in accomplishing the school work.

Completing a shell exhibit can be considered a major or long-range goal in this instance, although the time period extended over only a few weeks. The goal was not long-range in the sense of the tasks required to achieve the goal being difficult to distinguish. The maturity of the individuals in a class group will also be a factor in determining how distant a goal is for the particular group.

Subgoals or intermediate goals. The goal of the fourth grade class group was to make an exhibit for their parents. Although the procedures they followed are not explicit in the description of the incident, to achieve the goal the group—and individuals in the group—had to complete a number of tasks and activities. Each task and activity involved a subgoal—sometimes called *task* goals, *intermediate* goals, or *process* goals. In fact, the sessions of group planning for the incidents required an objective or goal, the purpose of such sessions being to decide on the appropriate steps that would lead to the completion of the exhibit. For example, the subgoal of one planning session might have been to decide on what maps were to be made, who was to make them, and how they were to be made. Again, this new subgoal or process goal required that the group members perform a series of operations such as drawing, coloring, and mounting the maps. These were only some of the steps in a series of steps required to reach the major goal—the completion of an exhibit.

THE MULTIPLE NATURE OF GOALS. If it were possible to view each action taken by a group as if the action were directed toward a single goal, goal behavior would be much easier to explain. However, this is not the case. Goals usually have a multiple nature, and it is therefore seldom possible to regard each action as directed to one specific goal. To use the shell exhibit as an example, the major goal is the completion of the exhibit and the group expects that the results will be satisfying because the exhibit will demonstrate to the parents what the group can accomplish. However, the group members may have a number of end purposes in mind. The group as a whole may be seeking teacher approval for working so well, or the members may collectively desire to work on the exhibit because by doing so, work on more unpleasant tasks may be avoided. A knowledge that other grades in the school will view the exhibit may arouse the desire to achieve the respect of children in upper grades. Individuals strive for self-enhancement; groups, too, seek prestige. All in all, the exhibit undoubtedly involved many goals.

DIMENSIONS OF GOALS. Goals may vary in their dimensions—that is, they may vary in force, degree of strength, or dominance. To illustrate, the goal of making an exhibit appeared to exert considerable force in directing group action. The same goal, in another class situation, might not have had much strength. The teacher reported that the first discussions concerning what might be done for Parents' Night did not arouse much enthusiasm. Certain projects were suggested but they had so little force that no group action was taken. In such a situation, several ideas or goal objectives might be discussed, but one or two might be more dominant than others. Sometimes some goals assume such importance that they transcend all others, even though the negated goals may have been dominant under different circumstances. The behavior described in the following incident can be interpreted as an example of a task goal that had so little force that the individuals in the group did not complete their individual tasks.

Invariably during the sixth grade art period the following behavior occurs. I usually begin the period by stimulating a discussion, by having group evaluation of a previous lesson, or by giving a demonstration of some aspect of the new lesson. At this time, the class is usually very attentive and the children usually show considerable interest as well as a readiness to tackle the project. They start out in a business-like way and seem to know exactly what they want to do. Sometimes a few discussions start at the point when they get their materials, but these discussions are generally constructive and to the point. The group begins work, but after some time has passed it seems that a large number of individuals begin to show interest in what a neighbor is doing and lose interest in their own project. Word spreads that something exciting is being done in another part of the room. Everyone wants to see it and visiting and confusion begins. Some decide to change what they are doing. Talking becomes louder. There is moving about and general restlessness and few seem interested in finishing the projects that are underway. Before I know it there is a general disruption of what could be very good work.

Although the task goal was individual rather than group (the members of the class were not working together to achieve something desired by the group as a whole), something seemed to occur in the class group that caused the goal to lose strength. It could be that the expectations that the pupils had when they began the work were in some way thwarted and they therefore began changing their original productions. It could be that each individual started out with a clear expectation of the picture or project that he wished to complete but had no clear idea of how to proceed in order to achieve his expectations. Perhaps if the individuals in the group had perceived that others accepted the task goal and expected that all would complete the task, the behavior might have been different. Had the teacher provided a group incentive (the finished pictures or objects to be used to decorate the classroom, or used in a group art exhibit), the task goal might have gained more strength. Or, if the teacher had checked with individuals or the group at various stages of the process to see if the tasks were going forward according to expectation, the behavior might have been different. It seems very possible that although the individuals in the group had clear ideas of what they wished to achieve, the force of the goal diminished because either the majority of individuals did not know how to perform the needed operations or else their expectations were set at too high a level.

Operational and Nonoperational Goals

It has been proposed that goals should be distinguished according to whether they are operational or nonoperational.[4] A goal is operational if there exists some basis for relating the goal to various kinds of group activities that will achieve the goal. It is nonoperational when there is no basis for relating the goal to possible courses of action. One of the problems of curriculum development is to set specific objectives and to select appropriate activities that will contribute to the attainment of these objectives. For example, "to teach the basic facts in addition" is operational because a number of appropriate activities can be expected to move a class of children toward this goal. On the other hand, "developing good citizenship," is nonoperational and requires the development of subgoals or objectives that more clearly define the tasks required to develop good citizenship. At this point a problem arises, for often teachers are presented with subgoals or objectives that are also nonoperational. Although "honesty" and "dependability" are characteristics of good citizens, "to develop traits of honesty and dependability" are not objectives that define the tasks or activities that lead to their achievement. The large number of nonoperational goals that are used as the basis for much educational literature is the major source of teacher dissatisfaction when they state that, "education classes are not practical," or that they are "too theoretical."

A class group that decides upon a nonoperational goal must employ some criteria other than the goal to determine the activities. The class that desires to win a plaque by becoming better citizens, for example, cannot hope to win unless operational subgoals are selected. Various group members, in this case, are apt to become frustrated by the apparent limitations to group action. What tasks or activities can the group engage in that will make each member of the group a better citizen? Unless, as was suggested before, some service to the school or the community can be performed that is interpreted as good citizenship, there are few activities that the group as a working unit can perform which will lead the class toward winning the plaque. When a group in this position is unable to make progress toward its objective because the goal is nonoperational, the activities of the group may become directed toward controlling the behavior of certain individuals in the group who appear to be hindering group progress. The group may develop standards to control behavior, but since the behavior itself is not clearly defined, it is likely that group

[4] James G. March and Herbert A. Simon, *Organizations,* New York: John Wiley & Sons, 1958.

integration will be highly disrupted as time for the plaque presentation approaches.

Task and Nontask Goals

Once the group has agreed upon a goal or subgoal, a number of steps or operations are usually required before the goal can be reached. We have defined the goal as an end point toward which activities are steered and have noted that sometimes the goal quite clearly stipulates the activities or tasks that must be performed, while in other instances the necessary operations are not specified by the goal. Sometimes the group activities take a different course even though the path to the goal is quite clearly delineated. The relation of tasks and activities to goals is viewed in a number of ways. Different proposals are advanced to explain why goals differ in the nature of their relationship to group activities.

GROUP MAINTENANCE. The group is regarded in some instances as a system that tends to maintain itself in balance. Group operations are described in terms of goal direction, integration, and morale. Group integration is defined as the extent to which structure and operations are maintained under stress, and morale describes the degree of freedom from restraint exhibited by a group in operating upon a goal objective. These factors are related; a group devotes some of its energies to maintaining the group as well as to performing tasks. The more time and effort a group has to devote to achieving integration or to resisting disruptive forces, the less time it has and the less able it is to work toward task goals. Vigorous action toward a goal—morale—might be expected to be closely related to productivity. However, a group may exhibit high morale and integration and still be low in productivity because of the difficulty of overcoming obstacles in the way of group progress.[5]

GOALS OF THE INFORMAL GROUP. At times the varying nature of group activities is explained by distinguishing between differences in group structure. Jennings [6] uses the concepts of "psyche-group" and "socio-group" to distinguish the structure of informal, spontaneously formed groups from that of formal working groups. The psyche-group is described as an interpersonal structure that often is found developed within the socio-group (a group formed for the express purpose of performing cer-

[5] Ralph M. Stogdill, *Individual Behavior and Group Achievement*, New York: Oxford University Press, 1959, pp. 196–201.

[6] Helen Hall Jennings, "Leadership and Sociometric Choice," in E. Maccoby, T. Newcomb, and E. Hartley (eds.), *Readings in Social Psychology*, New York: Henry Holt & Company, 1958, pp. 483–489.

tain tasks). The socio-group, then, is organized around goals of task performance, while a psyche-group is organized around goals of achieving satisfaction from associating with congenial people. It seems that at times the motivation to establish satisfying group relations is stronger than the motivation to perform tasks. In particular this appears to be true when socio-groups (classroom groups) are not organized or led in ways so that the members experience satisfying interpersonal relations. It is not un-common for a teacher to find that he has difficulty in mobilizing a group to work for a task goal even when there appears to be consensus regard-ing the desirability of the goal. Many times this is because the informal group organization is directing its energy toward developing satisfying group relationships.

THE "HIDDEN AGENDA." Thelen [7] suggests that a distinction be made between group activities that are directed toward the accomplishment of task goals and other kinds of group activities. Activities of goal-seeking nature are called *work*. Other kinds of activities are called *problem solv-ing*. A group *works* when there are publicly stated and generally shared goals; it is characteristic of *work* activities that they are easily observed. Members make decisions openly and know where the activities are lead-ing. However, when a group is in the process of *working* or moving toward a task goal, it sometimes faces problems that are not explicitly for-mulated and that arise because of shared anxieties relating to membership and other adaptations to the group. They are hidden and are consid-ered the "hidden agenda" of the group. The activities of the group that are directed toward solving problems of human relations are not con-sidered *work*. This term is reserved for purposive goal-directed behavior. Activities directed toward the hidden problems of the group are called *problem-solving* activities. If the work engaged in by a group to achieve its publicly stated and shared goals is interrupted, the activities may change direction—not because the group seeks other goals, but because of hidden problems of group relations that create disruption in cohesive-ness and morale. At these times the group acts as if guided by a particular purpose, but this conception views these activities as problem-solving behavior and not as goal-seeking behavior.

There are similarities among all these various conceptions of rela-tionships between group goals and group activities. Goals steer group activities in certain directions, but there are times when the members of a group desire to develop more satisfying conditions or relationships. Problems or conflicts occur which disrupt task-oriented behavior. Group activities then organize around the "goals" or the problems of achieving

[7] Herbert A. Thelen, *Dynamics of Groups at Work,* Chicago: The University of Chicago Press, 1954, pp. 276–278.

harmony or satisfaction. There is considerable agreement that a group directed toward accomplishing a certain clearly stated task, if unable to maintain satisfying member relations, will attempt to reestablish "groupness." Group activities may take a different direction because of these hidden difficulties or unstated problems. There is disagreement whether these group-saving activities can be called goal-seeking behaviors. However, in describing the behavior of class groups in relation to goals, it appears to be useful to conceive goals as being of two kinds: task goals and nontask goals. The task goals are the clearly formulated and agreed-upon goals that designate that certain activities will be undertaken so certain tasks will be put in particular states. Nontask goals are not clearly formulated or overtly expressed, but they may designate that groups will engage in certain activities to maintain group integration. Since these goals are not tangible, the groups may appear to make little or no progress in any direction. Activities directed toward achieving nontask goals may be considered as activities organized to establish "groupness" or to achieve group stability. It seems that if groups, particularly classroom groups, are not led in ways that allow the members to experience satisfying group relations, task goals are superseded by nontask goals. This conception accounts for a number of kinds of group behaviors that can be observed in classroom groups. The class in the following example is diverted from the task goal and the group activities seem to be directed toward solving some problems in human relations.

COMMITTEE WORK

An incident of classroom group behavior that was difficult to control or guide occurred during a social studies period. This was a combined A-B6 class engaged in completing a culmination project on Central America and South America for presentation to parents and faculty before graduation. This culminating activity included both social studies and science projects. There were eight groups with an average of five in a group working on the following projects: a physical map made of salt and flour, a picture map of products, a political map, a population map, a mural, a weather map and instruments, and a diorama of the solar system. In previous social studies periods, before the students had begun to work on these projects, groups had made outlines of the materials needed, named the chairman, and had specified the duties to be performed by each member. Students had been given opportunities to choose the projects upon which they wanted to work.

The incident occurred when some members in several groups refused to cooperate and work in their committees. Several pupils played around, which caused a disturbance that affected the whole working area. Other pupils were influenced to become lax or else they attempted to stop the disturbance, so only more confusion resulted. It finally became necessary to

halt all committee work because nothing was being accomplished and evaluate the behavior of some of the individuals in the class.

Goal Acceptance by the Group

A class group goal is some consequence that members of the class
group are willing to work together to achieve. This goal, or consequence,
may be defined in terms of a condition to be obtained, a response desired
from another person or another group, or a general feeling, such as
enjoyment, excitement, or the shared pleasure of success.

Any goal accepted by members of a group consciously or unconsciously induces motivational forces upon members and the magnitude
of the influence varies among goals and among members. When most of
the group members are not committed to the same goal, there is continuous friction in working. Subgroup structures committed to different
goals induce disintegrating forces into the total group structure. Furthermore, when group goals are not fully accepted, the goals of the group have
little power to influence the behavior of members and there is very little
task-oriented group behavior.[8]

It was pointed out in the previous section that in the final analysis,
prescribed classroom goals refer to individuals. It was mentioned, however, that there are times when educational goals are more easily
achieved if the class members, as a group, accept a subgoal that steers
individual behavior toward performing tasks that are necessary if certain
desired educational goals are to be attained.

What does group goal acceptance imply? What factors influence the
acceptance by a group of a goal? To answer these questions, another
common classroom practice is presented as an example.

The children in a class group, with teacher guidance, decide they
wish to ask a resource person to come to the class to give them first hand
information about some area currently under study. If a relatively large
number of children accept this goal it becomes a *group* goal. Acceptance
of the goal means that each individual believes that a good outcome will
result from having a resource speaker. The class group may anticipate
enjoyment only—that is, the consequences expected by the children may
not be related to the improvement of certain skills or even to obtaining
more knowledge of the topic that is being studied. However, acceptance
of the goal does imply that the children are willing to perform tasks
that will lead to goal achievement—in this case, bringing the speaker to
the class. Since the tasks and activities required to bring the speaker to

[8] Ralph M. Stogdill, *Individual Behavior and Group Achievement*, New York:
Oxford University Press, 1959, p. 78.

the class involve skills that the teacher desires the members to use, the group goal steers members toward performing in these desired skill areas. The group, with the teacher's help, can plan the tasks that are needed to bring the resource person to the class. These tasks may include: getting permission to have the resource person come to the class; inviting the person; planning the introduction; constructing questions; thanking the speaker, and perhaps a number of other related activities. As stated before, the goal of the group may be only that the members have an enjoyable, interesting time. The teacher, however, has no such single goal. The teacher desires to develop oral language abilities, to improve writing skills, to extend knowledge of courteous behavior, to improve discussion skills, besides extending the children's knowledge in the content area. If the group actually accepts the goal of bringing the speaker to the class, members will be motivated to perform the needed tasks. Without a group goal each individual child might not feel the need to practice making announcements, writing invitations, etc. The group goal exerts an influence over the behavior of members since "good" group members are expected to work toward goal attainment even if their preferred goals are not selected by the group.

A study by Horwitz [9] showed that a member's desire to attain a group goal did not depend upon whether the individual was in favor of accepting the goal in the first place. Even though the goal was not accepted initially, after group acceptance the member usually agreed to the group decision and became motivated to see that the goal was achieved. In this study, the members identified highly with the group, which accounts in part for this finding. Most children desire acceptance by their class groups; therefore, a class group decision to perform tasks that will lead to group goal attainment usually produces the same effect as the one observed in Horwitz's study.

It is important for teachers to note that goal acceptance alone may not produce the results they desire. For example, class members may decide with much enthusiasm that they would like a speaker to come to the class, but they may expect the teacher to make all the arrangements. The goal acceptance must include acceptance of the idea that the arrangements are made by the class, or teacher goals will not be achieved. In fact, the acceptance of a goal by a class group means that certain activities must be performed by the group if the goal is to be attained, but the acceptance of the goal includes the willingness to enact certain behaviors that will lead to goal achievement.

[9] Murray Horwitz, "The Recall of Interrupted Group Tasks: An Experimental Study of Individual Motivation in Relation to Group Goals," *Human Relations*, 7:3–38, 1954.

If all the members of the class are willingly to perform tasks that otherwise they might resist doing, the goal must have widespread acceptance. The group members must be given opportunity to exercise group power in order to attempt to gain complete acceptance of the goal. Acceptance may be achieved by group discussion with a maximum of participation throughout the group, so that hesitant members perceive that the group as a whole is motivated to perform the tasks and achieve the goal.

Cohesive groups, because they are more able to influence members, are more apt to get goal acceptance and insure a high degree of behavior in accordance with the necessary task performance. Studies testify to this fact. Experiments by Back,[10] Schutz,[11] and others show that when groups are attractive to members—that is, when groups mediate personal need satisfaction, when members like one another, and when groups have prestige, these cohesive groups exert great influence upon members to accept group goals and to perform necessary tasks. Schachter [12] and associates propose that highly cohesive groups, as compared with less cohesive groups, will attain more conformity to work goals whether the conformity is directed toward increasing output or restricting it.

In his study of the effects of cooperation and competition upon the group process, Deutsch,[13] found that task-directedness, or the group force in the direction of a goal, was stronger in a cooperative group than in a competitive group. There was greater communication of ideas, coordination of efforts, and friendliness when members were working together on a task and toward common goals than when members were working toward individual goals and individual task completion.

When groups are cohesive it seems that eventually there is actually genuine acceptance of group goals by members who initially resist goal acceptance. When the desire of the majority of members is communicated to the unaccepting minority, the latter members come around to accepting the majority-approved goal. Cohesiveness, then, has the effect of causing undecided or unaccepting members to acquiesce when they perceive that the goal is accepted by the majority.

A class group may resist putting a goal in a desired state for a num-

[10] Kurt W. Back, "Influence through Social Communication," *Journal of Abnormal and Social Psychology,* 46:9–23, July 1951.

[11] William C. Schutz, "What Makes Groups Productive?" *Human Relations,* 8:429–465, 1955.

[12] Stanley Schachter, Norris Ellertson, Dorothy McBride, and Doris Gregory, "An Experimental Study of Cohesiveness and Productivity," *Human Relations,* 4:229–238, 1951.

[13] Morton Deutsch, "An Experimental Study of the Effects of Cooperation and Competition upon Group Processes," *Human Relations,* 2:199–232, 1949.

ber of reasons. Some of the reasons may be because members do not have clear understandings of the goal or of the path to the goal. Sometimes the group resists a goal because the tasks required do not seem to be within the group's range of skills, or the activities are more undesirable than the goal is desirable. The leadership pattern employed can either facilitate or hinder the acceptance of a group goal.

Investigators who varied the clarity of the group goal and of the path to the goal found that an individual will resist goal acceptance if the goal and the path are not clear. Raven and Rietsema [14] manipulated experimental conditions with tape recordings to produce one condition in which the group goal and path were clearly perceived, and another in which the goal and the path to the goal were unclear. The group member who clearly perceived the goal and the path to the goal was found to experience a greater feeling of group belongingness, particularly as manifested in an involvement with the group goal. Also, the member with a clear understanding of the group goal was more interested in his goal-related task than a member who had an unclear understanding of the goal and of the way of reaching it. It would appear that if a number of members of a class group do not have a clear picture of a goal or do not see a means by which the goal can be reached, the group as a whole will resist accepting the goal.

It is important that teachers recognize the necessity for group discussion concerning both the nature of the goal and the means of reaching it. Discussion procedures are essential for several reasons. They enable teachers to clarify points that are not clear to some members. Also, it is by means of discussion that goals that are more acceptable to a larger proportion of children in the group are selected. There is a need for an actual exchange of opinions about the desirability and attainability of a goal. Studies by Bovard [15], Rehage,[16] and others indicate that when a leader of a group acts in a manner that is understanding and that facilitates participation, the group is able to set up cooperative task goals and is more productive in making and carrying through plans than it would be without this kind of leadership.

When class groups have task goals imposed upon them, there is often no group initiative to work or to continue with work unless the

[14] Bertram H. Raven and Jan Rietsema, "The Effects of Varied Clarity of Group Goal and Group Path upon the Individual and His Relationship to His Group," *Human Relations,* 10:29–47, February 1957.

[15] Everett W. Bovard, Jr., "Group Structure and Perception," *Journal of Abnormal and Social Psychology,* 46:398–405, July 1951.

[16] Kenneth Rehage, "A Comparison of Pupil–Teacher Planning and Teacher-Directed Procedures in Eighth Grade Social Studies Classes," *Journal of Educational Research,* 45:111–115, October 1951.

teacher uses threat or force. If the pattern employed by the teacher does not provide opportunity for the group to achieve satisfactory relations, the motivation to achieve satisfying group relations is sometimes more powerful than the motivation to perform the group tasks.

Lippitt and White [17] found that in children's groups where task goals were a matter of group planning and decision, the children began work and continued to work on planned group projects whether the leader was absent or present. In situations where task goals were imposed on the members, there was no group initiative to start new work or to continue with work already under way unless the leader was present. The class in the next example indicated that it had initiative whether the teacher was present or not.

ACCEPTING RESPONSIBILITY

The class "Speak Your Mind Club" (usually referred to by the students simply as "Our Club") meets on Fridays. A different child serves as chairman each week and the class plans its own program. Everyone is encouraged to participate.

One week, the teacher was absent for three days. When he returned on Friday, he assumed that the club would not meet since the students had not been given an opportunity to set up an agenda during his absence. "But we planned on our own during lunch period as a surprise for you," the chairman told him. Several students announced that they had invited their parents. (It has been the custom to invite a few guests to each meeting.) Although the teacher felt somewhat nervous about having guests at this surprise meeting, it was obviously too late to call it off. However, the students had accepted responsibility for their own meeting and had done an excellent job of planning. Students who had not been assigned special roles in the meeting were responsible for seating and introducing guests. The students later expressed much pleasure in the success of their meeting and reported that their parents were impressed.

In another instance, a teacher told the children in her class they were to paint Easter pictures for the bulletin board. As the children painted, the teacher arranged a caption and otherwise prepared the display to her liking. Since the teacher wished to be "democratic," she told the children they could vote on the best picture, which would then be placed on the bulletin board. When the voting took place, the group enthusiastically selected a picture of a prehistoric monster, which also

[17] Ronald Lippitt and Ralph K. White, "An Experimental Study of Leadership and Group Life," in Eleanor Maccoby, Theodore Newcomb, and Eugene L. Hartley (eds.), *Readings in Social Psychology*, New York: Henry Holt and Company, 1958, pp. 496–511.

featured a large egg. The teacher who reported the incident concluded by saying she did not understand why the group behaved as it did after the children had agreed upon an Easter theme before they started work.

It seems evident that although the theme was accepted, the tasks required to carry out the theme were imposed upon this group. As stated before, acceptance of a goal also requires acceptance of the required tasks. The goal in this case was to prepare a bulletin board featuring an Easter theme. The bulletin board could have been arranged in a number of ways. (There were several paths to the goal.) However, goal acceptance in this case evidently did not include discussion and acceptance by the group of the means for reaching the goal. The result was that one member, at least, did not draw a picture that is commonly considered as representing Easter (except perhaps for the egg). Although other children presumably did draw Easter pictures, the group voted to place the prehistoric monster on the bulletin board. Why the class group acted in this fashion cannot be determined; however, it is clear that although they agreed to work on an Easter theme, the task or the means by which the goal could be reached was not accepted by the majority of the children.

An experiment conducted by Horwitz and Lee [18] attempted to show why individuals in groups changed behavior after engaging in the activity of discussion and decision making. They concluded that as a result of decision making, motivational energy tended to be channeled into action, and that in the absence of decision making, motivational energy tended to be channeled into wish fulfillment. It appeared that when groups acted on the basis of consensus, and when members were allowed to decide among alternative paths before they engaged in activities toward a goal, the process involved a mechanism for controlling the disposition of motivational energy and this mechanism directed the energy toward action. In groups where the decision-making step was short-circuited by an authoritarian leader who made the decisions and told the members they were obliged to follow the decisions, the motivational energies of the group were channeled into wish fulfillment. The psychological environment or the morale of the group was affected, and there was no strong striving toward the goals set by someone else.

Effects of Goals

The process of interacting in order to achieve a common goal produces differential effects upon individuals and upon the group as a whole.

[18] Murray Horwitz and Frances Lee, "Effects of Decision Making by Group Members on Recall of Finished and Unfinished Tasks," *Journal of Abnormal and Social Psychology*, 49:201–210, April 1954.

This means that working for goal attainment causes individuals to change in perception, thinking, emotion, and action. In fact, the major influence on children in the classroom is interaction with others, whether the interaction process is directed toward goal achievement, establishing norms, or developing satisfying member relations. Interaction with others can either stimulate or retard pupil growth, and knowledge of the effects of the group working to achieve a common goal can help teachers improve the quality of individual behavior and individual learning.

A teacher's choice of whether to use direct or indirect influence in group planning for goal achievement affects the behavior of individuals and the general pattern of group behavior. It has already been noted that goals exert pressures upon children to perform certain tasks and activities that they might not perform willingly if they were not working for a group goal. Since a group goal requires task-goals in most cases, group planning involves the setting of these task goals. The kind of influence a teacher exerts is highly important, for the practices teachers employ in the planning sessions affect both the total group response and the nature of individual participation.

Some of the effects of goals upon individual behavior are examined in this section, as well as the part the teacher plays in producing these effects.

Group Goals and Individual Performance

A class group with a definite common goal, the attainment of which necessitates discussion, planning, and execution, usually becomes more cohesive because of this interaction process. Group norms, which regulate the behavior of members within the group in matters of consequence to the group, tend to become stabilized. Thus, when the group is inclined favorably toward school task objectives, a group's positive stand in this direction usually creates an attitude change in individuals who previously reacted negatively toward some of the goals and tasks of the school. The satisfaction derived from group membership contributes to this change. A child who does not find the group attractive undoubtedly will not be as influenced by a group goal as one who does. However, participation in group goal setting usually increases a member's satisfaction with the group. The act of goal setting itself, then, often increases an individual's liking for the group. A child who wishes to be accepted and to belong to the group usually accepts a goal he perceives that the majority of members wish to attain, because working with others gives promise of personal satisfaction. Or, the desire for group acceptance causes a member to respond to the group's influence attempts because failure to conform could bring about group rejection. Thus, a pupil who perceives that others in the class expect all persons to work for the goal and to facilitate group operations will often show high interest in group tasks and will exhibit a desire to work on the tasks and to complete them successfully, whether or not the tasks themselves are appealing.

FACTORS AFFECTING MEMBER PARTICIPATION. A number of factors seem to influence how readily a member accepts a group goal or is influenced by the group's acceptance of a goal. It seems that members who do not participate in goal-setting and planning are less motivated to participate in task performance than those who actively participate. The effects of active and passive group participation was explored by Willerman,[19] who found that the differences in motivation in active and passive group members had a definite bearing upon the total group behavior. Members who participated actively were more satisfied with the group and, of course, were more dominant in motivating group behavior. On the other hand, passive participants were less satisfied with the group and less ready to accept group decisions.

Since active group members often are more skilled in communicating their ideas and feelings, teachers must guide group discussions so that these verbal members do not monopolize the discussion and thereby create a number of passive participants. Such guidance is not easily achieved, since many of the active members may be high in a number of abilities. It is exceedingly important that teachers facilitate communication and make sure that all persons have opportunities to contribute if they wish to do so. Even though some suggestions are not so pertinent to a problem as others, each contribution should be given equal consideration before it is discarded. When teachers direct the group toward considering various aspects of individual contributions, the group can be helped to consider the usefulness of the contribution and not be swayed solely by the personality and verbal ability of the person making the contribution. Some studies show that more talkative group members are more successful than less talkative ones in getting their groups to select their solutions to problems. Teachers with much experience in working with classroom groups know that children who are both high in social acceptability and in ability to express ideas clearly and with enthusiasm are apt to be very successful in influencing the group even though their ideas are not as good as those of less vocal and less popular members.

Most teachers face problems pertaining to the use of direct influence in cases where the class ignores good proposals made by unpopular members in favor of poor proposals contributed by popular members. Should

[19] Ben Willerman, "The Relation of Motivation and Skill to Active and Passive Participation in the Group," *Journal of Applied Psychology*, 37:387–390, May 1953.

the group be allowed to make "poor" decisions when the members have the opportunity to consider better ones? How can a teacher by indirect means cause the group to give fair consideration to all proposals? These questions are extremely important, since both group and individual reactions are involved.

According to the findings of research, in general, the social status among children of elementary school age will tend to rise following involvement in a common small group experience. However, if the group experiences failure in an activity, the social status of individuals will tend to decrease, although the effect appears to be temporary except when the group experiences success. One study concerned with the effects of success and failure on social relationships found that the experience of working together increased the liking of members for one another, but the effects were more permanent when the group experienced success.[20] It seems probable that a child will become more acceptable to a group if the teacher makes it possible for him to actively participate in a successful group project. Direct influence by the teacher in the form of assigning a particular child to a responsible position or telling the class that the member's contribution should be accepted or valued will probably be rejected by the group. Indirect influence undoubtedly will be much more effective in most cases.

In the Heber study,[20] the groups under success conditions had a significant and permanent increase in status rating. One point of significance to teachers was that praise and acknowledgement of group success was important in determining the feelings group members had toward one another. The praise was given to the group as a whole and not to individual members for their contributions.

It seems that in a constructive group interaction situation in which mutual agreements on experiences and preferred activities are emphasized, the group members come to perceive others as more similar to themselves.[21] When a teacher is aware of status structures in the group— that is, aware of the ratings members assign to one another regarding such qualities as leadership, quality of suggestions, etc., the knowledge can be used to implement group effectiveness, group morale, and pupil participation.[22] Individuals not accepted to any degree by their peers can be helped to gain a higher social acceptability rating if, by indirect

[20] Rick F. Heber and Mary E. Heber, "The Effect of Group Failure and Success on Social Status," *The Journal of Educational Psychology*, 48:129–134, March 1957.

[21] James Bieri, "Changes in Interpersonal Perceptions Following Social Interaction," *The Journal of Abnormal and Social Psychology*, 48:61–66, January 1953.

[22] Isidore Bogen, "Pupil-Teacher Rapport and the Teacher's Awareness of Status Structures within the Group," *Journal of Educational Sociology*, 28:104–114, November 1954.

methods, a teacher guides the group toward an examination of the contributions made by these individuals in goal-planning sessions. This
examination of all contributions should improve the group's ability
to select the best ideas and utilize the resources of the best informed
members.

Awareness by teachers of the effects of leadership status on individuals is also important. Some studies of adult groups indicate that individuals who influence their groups in discussions of task-performance,
or in problem-solving activities, are also persons who are popular in
social situations. Findings indicate also that when a group accepts an
individual as a leader, the individual recognizes this and attempts to
hold his position by constantly initiating ideas that will gain group response. Teachers have undoubtedly noted this effect in their class groups.
Whenever ideas are called for, those children who perceive themselves
as leaders always come up with suggestions even though they have little
to offer in some instances. They seem to have a need to play a leadership role regardless of whether they have something to contribute to the
point being discussed. Since class sizes are usually large, this tends to
deprive many other individuals who might wish to contribute. They not
only have less opportunity because a few always contribute, but they
perceive that the group looks to these few for this role. Teachers must take
care that such behaviors do not become characteristic responses in their
class groups. For one thing, individuals who customarily initiate most
of the ideas become upset if the routine is broken. They are apt to
become aggressive if they are not the ones who have the most opportunity
to be heard. They see their position as being threatened. Then too, the
group product is apt to be superior if all ideas and contributions are considered.

There seem to be a number of factors, including group size, that
cause groups to fail to utilize the resources of the most knowledgeable
members. At times it has been maintained that the group power structure,
or status system, is the cause for this failure. Other times it is said that
group pressure toward uniformity frequently interferes with the group's
utilization of the best information presented by members. It is the
opinion of some that a teacher will often contribute to this failure by
directing the group's attention to the contributions made by a few
selected children in the group. Whatever the causes for this failure to
utilize the best contributions, it seems that a teacher can minimize the
effects by using practices that indirectly cause a group to consider all proposals and all the resources of individuals in the group.

GROUP INFLUENCE UPON LEVEL OF ASPIRATION. Experimental evidence
suggests that a child's level of aspiration is influenced by the standard of

performance within his group. Therefore, if the group sets high but reasonable standards for task performance, a child will most likely raise his standard of performance to that expected by the class. However, the evidence indicates that the individual must also be given knowledge of where he stands with respect to the group. Anderson and Brandt [23] set up an experimental group and a control group and attempted to motivate children in different ways. Both groups were given a simple cancellation task to perform. On successive days the children in the experimental group were given their relative standings in class, whereas the children in the control group were not provided with such information. Each child in the experimental group knew where he stood with respect to the group, and was asked to set a standard for himself on the task. The experimental group was significantly superior to the control group in achievement of the task. It appeared that the motivation produced by knowledge of where one stood in the group was related to this difference in achievement. This conclusion is consistent with data from other studies that indicate that if an individual has knowledge of how he is doing, the knowledge tends to enhance performance and motivation for improvement. Another finding was that children who were in the lowest ranks of actual achievement set goals considerably above past achievements and those in upper ranks set goals considerably below their preceding achievements. This evidence seems to indicate that some groups, at least, set a standard for achievement toward which group members tend to move. This last finding presents a strong argument against using groups, in all instances, to set goals for task performance. Many task goals must be of an individual nature, since the group norm may lower the high achiever's level of aspiration.

When a group sets a level of aspiration for its members, it is more often accepted by a member as a personal goal if the activity is relevant to the group than when it is nonrelevant. Stotland and others [24] examined the effect of a specific level of achievement upon an individual's evaluation of his performance when the achievement was relative to a level of aspiration established by the group. The experimenters studied the aspirations and self-esteem of individuals working alone or in groups under conditions of induced failure and success. The subjects were told that the group had either low or high expectations for them in completing a performance task. It was found that failure on a relevant

[23] Harold H. Anderson and H. F. Brandt, "Study of Motivation Involving Self-Announced Goals of Fifth Grade Children and the Concept of the Level of Aspiration," *Journal of Social Psychology*, 10:209–232, 1939.

[24] Ezra Stotland, S. Thorley, E. Thomas, A. R. Cohen, and A. Zander, "The Effects of Group Expectation and Self-Esteem upon Self-Evaluation," *Journal of Abnormal and Social Psychology*, 54:55–63, January 1957.

task generated a poorer self-evaluation than when the task was non-relevant. In other words, when group expectations were high, it induced the member to evaluate his performance poorly. Group expectations did not affect self-evaluation when the performance was successful. It appears that group expectation, as a reference point, is more potent than self-esteem in evaluating self performance.

Chapman and Volkmann [25] conducted an experiment to determine if groups tended to establish a standard of performance in reference to the standards of other groups, or if groups were influenced principally by their own previous experiences. A college class was divided into four groups, and members were told that they were to take a test of literary ability. The first group was given instructions about the nature of the test; the second group was given, in addition to the instructions, the mean score obtained on this test by a group of literary experts; the third group was given the mean score of a group of college students on the test; and the fourth group was given the mean score of a group of WPA workers on the test. The students in each group were then asked to estimate their expected performances. When the mean estimates of how the students expected to do were computed, the investigators found that the second group of students, who knew the average score of literary experts, set their level of aspiration much lower than any of the other groups. The group that was told the performance of the WPA workers set their level of aspiration higher than any of the groups. Since none of the students in these groups knew how he would actually perform on the test, he was presumably estimating his performance by comparing himself with what he knew about how other groups had performed. Another group of students, in a second part of the experiment, were given similar instructions, but not until after they had taken a first form of the test. Under these conditions the students estimated their expected performances more in terms of their own previous performances than in terms of the known performances of the other groups.

Effects of Goals on Group Behavior

A previous section examined the tendency of a group to work on nontask goals rather than task goals when the group faced obstacles involving morale and group integration. Of course, if a group uses its energies upon group maintenance, it is not so productive nor does it display so many desired behavior patterns as one that does not have obstacles in its way. Groups seek to maintain stability, coordination, and

[25] Dwight W. Chapman and John Volkmann, "A Social Determinant of the Level of Aspiration," *Journal of Abormal and Social Psychology*, 34:225–238, 1939.

integration. Class groups show concern when members deviate from the group norms or do not share group motives. The group as a whole and individual members both operate to exert pressures toward maintaining the cohesiveness of the group. However, teacher practices, the organizational structures, and other factors may create internal conflicts. Sometimes power struggles develop between competing individuals or subgroups. Such struggles are disturbing to the group and decrease productivity. Teachers are most concerned with this aspect of group behavior, primarily because of the time consumed by the group in attempting to restore integration. Note the following example.

GIRL–BOY FACTIONS IN THE CLASS

In several instances the boys in this third grade class took the girls' ball on the playground. They refused offers to play together and instead they simply took the ball and ran off to play by themselves.

For some reason the playground supervisor was unaware of this, and the children came in after lunch expecting me to handle the entire situation. There were recriminations back and forth. Even when we all decided on action that would be acceptable to all, dissatisfaction was voiced. The children continued to argue and talk about the "rights" and "wrongs" of the situation. So much time is taken up by this kind of behavior that it becomes necessary for me to use a forceful "police action" to get the children back to work. Even then the problem remains on some people's minds and keeps popping up during work periods.

Internal problems sometimes arise because one member in the group fails to conform. The group then turns its efforts toward exerting pressures on the member in an attempt to restore cohesiveness. This type of integrative action is illustrated in the next example.

THE AFFAIR OF TOMMY

During our intramural game, kickball, Tommy was ruled "out." After much discussion on the playground by all concerned, I was called to make a decision. According to the rules of the game, Tommy was definitely "out."

Tommy was very angry. He accused everyone of being "cheaters." He was on the verge of tears. Some children said they thought he was very silly to feel the way he did. Tommy then said he would go home.

He stomped out of the playground. The children became very excited, and many ran to inform me about his action.

When our recess period was over the class found that Tommy had not gone home. The children went into the classroom, but they were still excited and concerned over Tommy's action. Everyone talked at once, and much advice was given Tommy. There was no use trying to begin work until this affair was settled to the group's satisfaction.

Sometimes goals are imposed on groups with the promise of a reward if the group reaches the goal. Paper drives, membership drives, and other similar situations are examples. Sometimes these situations involve group cooperation. Other times only individual cooperation is needed, yet the class as a whole is seeking to reach the goal and win the prize. As the following incident shows, sometimes these imposed goals are the cause of group disharmony and bad relations among members of the group.

REACHING FOR THE MOON

It was the annual P.T.A. membership drive. The question asked every class was, "Who will be first to reach the moon?" This was the message on the notice taken home by every child. Each child was to receive one point for each membership obtained. Each class was represented by a rocket on a chart. It moved along strings towards the moon on the basis of points earned. First to arrive at the moon would be rewarded by a class party.

Nearly every child in this particular third grade room responded with two memberships, one for each parent, thereby gaining two points for the class. One of the few nonparticipants was a child coming from a Mexican family (the only one in the room). The class landed on the moon several days before any of the others. Of course the children were looking forward to the party. At the end of the drive came the announcement that another class was to have the party. Their total number of points was higher.

The reaction of the class was one of complete disillusionment and no work was done the remainder of that day. This class, which had previously appeared to be a very cohesive group, began to blame each other for not having enough points to win. Such statements as "Mexicans never join anything!" or "Your father didn't help us!" and "It's unfair! They didn't keep their promise!" were repeated constantly.

It seems we are being very unfair to children to create situations such as this one. It's also unfair to some individuals and places a teacher in a very difficult situation. The Mexican child, through no fault of his, was the object of the group's scorn and a once friendly group lost its good feeling and pleasant relations.

Occasionally the regular work program in the room is disrupted because the group becomes involved with a short-term goal. Unless the group is able to achieve this goal, or to agree upon a satisfactory substitute, the teacher may find that it is difficult to get the class to work on school tasks.

THE TURTLE

A baby water turtle, new to the classroom, was missing one morning in my kindergarten classroom. The children were anxious to know what had happened to it. I told them I thought we had put too many rocks in the turtle's container, making it quite simple for the turtle to crawl out. As I talked, I could almost feel a wave of excitement come over the children as they realized the turtle might be hiding somewhere in the room.

After this I managed, in the face of interruptions and queries about the turtle, to call the roll and take care of our necessary daily routines. As their activity time began, I soon realized that few children had taken up their chosen jobs. Almost all of the children were looking for the turtle. Two or three with magnifying glass in hand had even slipped outside to look for it.

When the children were finally coaxed back to their jobs, little was accomplished aside from "turtle talk."

In general, it may be concluded that the less time the class group has to spend on nontask goals, the more time it will have to work on regular tasks and assignments. The less a class is involved with internal difficulties and problems, the more productive it will be, and the more it will display desirable, work-oriented behavior patterns.

Group Productivity and Group Goals

We have already noted a number of factors that influence group productivity. For example, groups in which members perceive among themselves a facilitating interdependence will show greater interest in the group task, will have a stronger desire to complete the task, and will have a higher morale than groups in which perception of interdependence is absent. Clarity of the goal, clarity of the path to the goal, and clarity of instructions all affect the extent of group productivity.

For the most part, studies show that the power the group exerts upon members to perform tasks relating to goal attainment is directly related to the degree to which the group is cohesive. However, it is not necessarily true that a happy, cohesive group is more productive. A cohesive class group can, and sometimes does, establish a low work norm. Studies of groups in industry show that a cohesive group may adhere to either a high or low work standard. However, cohesive groups tend to exhibit a high degree of concern about task performances of members and goal achievements of the group. It seems that some degree of cohesiveness is necessary for productive effort.

That cohesiveness has an effect upon productivity suggests that structure is also instrumental to goal achievement. Productivity is facilitated when the organized group structure is flexible. If the type of influence exerted by the teacher enlarges the responsibilities of the group, and allows for two-way communication and planning, productivity is increased. In short, whether members readily accept a group goal and the degree to which they become task-involved and the extent to which members are productive depend upon the nature of the group properties. The leadership pattern employed facilitates or hinders the setting up of group task goals. In fact, there is considerable research that presents empirical evidence that group goal acceptance and task performance are closely related to group properties and to the conditions existing within the group.

If a group sets up goals that are realistic in terms of the group's ability to reach the goals and then succeeds in reaching them, these experiences of success affect the probabilities that the group will accept similar goals in the future. If, on the other hand, the group sets goals that are too high and the group efforts are not rewarded by success, the chances are the group will be less inclined to accept similar goals. Class groups with histories of failure are less apt to be productive than successful groups. Successful outcomes of group projects reinforce the expectations of further success. When groups are praised for their successful achievements, the success plus the recognition bring a feeling of prestige and high status to the group. This heightens the degree of initiative and the desire to maintain this status.

Teachers use many incentives to increase productivity. It has been observed in a previous discussion that incentives are related to goal striving, and that praise of the group as a whole is a more effective incentive than praise given to individual members in the group. Interests are another type of positive incentive. Children differ in interests, but if the group is cohesive and if affiliation with the group satisfies members' desires for security, self-esteem, and the esteem of others, the group will play a large part in determining what the interests of members will be. For example, in some groups the general reaction to folk dancing may be that it is "sissy-stuff" and general dislike and lack of interest in this activity is generated. On the other hand, some groups may show a great interest in dancing, and a physical education period devoted to this activity is received with enthusiasm by the group even though some individual members may prefer, in fact, to have the period devoted to sports and games. However, only short-term benefits can be expected from the use of external incentives if they are used to overcome the effect of some group factors that decrease productivity.

Even though a group may become involved in disagreements when attempting to determine the necessary task goals, member satisfaction with the group and member support of the group's goal usually enables the individuals in the group to coordinate efforts and eventually come to a workable agreement. This point is clearly illustrated in the following report of a group at work on a task activity.

GROUP INTEGRATION

The newspaper staff was holding its weekly meeting before getting into the swing of starting the next week's paper. The subject up for discussion was the theme to be used in the annual joke paper.

The editor and her friends had decided that a western theme would be used, but they had decided to try to appear democratic about the matter. The sports editor and his reporters wanted to use a jail theme. The teacher frowned on this suggestion. The press bureau thought a Greek myths theme would lend itself to some creative writing.

The situation was getting a bit out of hand with factions using all their argumentative powers to squelch one another's ideas. Just as the group had about come to the decision that the whole project had better be given up, one meek reporter who belonged to none of the factions said, "Why don't we use an 'End of the World' theme?"

Suddenly everyone was in accord. There was no further belittling of one another's ideas. All was peaceful on the journalism front.

Although children in the primary grades do not have as much "groupness" as those in succeeding grades, even at this level the acceptance of task goals by the group tends to increase individual productivity.

It appears that when class groups at any grade level are given the opportunity to discuss the problems involved in goal objectives, they tend to accept the goals and produce more than when lessons are assigned or when there are other restraints imposed on the group. The fact that the members of the group are given an opportunity to communicate and to openly express their feelings seems to reduce the amount of time that is needed to achieve integration. Productivity seems to increase when the group is given the opportunity to identify task obstacles and to suggest ways they may be overcome. One may conclude that if productivity is to be increased in class groups, teachers must use techniques that enable class members to identify obstacles hindering task performance and to determine, to some extent, the ways they will work, even though such procedures are time consuming.

Questions for Study and Discussion

1. Find in your reading a conception of group goals and compare or contrast it with the three conceptions presented in the chapter.

2. Give an illustration of a classroom situation in which the teacher is trying to direct behavior *toward* a certain goal, while the class is attempting to achieve behavior directed *away* from that goal. Indicate specifically the teacher-goal and the group-goal.

3. Discuss the effects on group goals of one of the following: motives, attitudes, interests, incentives. Do not reiterate the material in the chapter, but select additional points.

4. What proportion of goals for a class should be operational, as distinguished from nonoperational? What would be some effects on a group of a large proportion of nonoperational goals?

5. From your experience as a member of a class, describe "work" and "problem-solving" activities according to Thelen's concepts.

6. Under what conditions are nontask goals more dominant than task goals? When are task goals dominant?

7. Observe a group discussion and note how effective in influencing the group and the group's decisions is the amount of talking by different individuals. Particularly notice the effects of the most verbal members.

8. Explain how the level of aspiration for a group goal affects members of the group.

9. Outline the steps that a teacher could use in getting a class to accept a task goal that was apparently difficult and disliked by the group.

10. Interview a child about the goals of his group. Investigate his perception of task goals and nontask goals, using terms that he understands. In reporting your interview, give the age and grade of the child, your questions and comments, and his responses as nearly exact as you can recall them.

11. Observe a class, if possible, and identify the group goals and such individual goals as are apparent while you are there. Are the two kinds of goals—group and individual—in agreement or conflict, insofar as you can determine?

12. What are some reasons for a group failing to pursue an agreed-upon goal?

Suggestions for Further Reading

Atkinson, John W., Jarvis R. Bastian, Robert W. Earl, and George H. Litwin. "The Achievement Motive, Goal Setting, and Probability Preferences," *Journal of Abnormal and Social Psychology*, 60:27–36, January 1960.

Berkowitz, Leonard, Bernard I. Levy, and Arthur R. Harvey. "Effects of Performance Evaluations on Group Integration and Motivation," *Human Relations,* 10:195–208, August 1957.

Berkowitz, Leonard. "Effects of Perceived Dependency Relationships upon Conformity to Group Expectations," *Journal of Abnormal and Social Psychology,* 55:350–354, November 1957.

Borosage, Lawrence. "A Basis for Viewing Communication," *The National Elementary Principal,* 41:6–12, May 1962.

Bovard, Everett W., Jr. "Group Structure and Perception," *Journal of Abnormal and Social Psychology,* 46:398–405, July 1951.

Deustch, Morton. "Some Factors Affecting Membership Motivation and Achievement Motivation in a Group," *Human Relations,* 12:81–94, February 1959.

Gerard, Harold B. "Some Effects of Status, Role Clarity, and Group Goal Clarity upon the Individual's Relations to Group Processes," *Journal of Personality,* 25:477–488, June 1957.

Heber, Rick F. and Mary E. Heber. "The Effect of Group Failure and Success on Social Status," *The Journal of Educational Psychology,* 48:129–134, March 1957.

Horwitz, Murray. "The Recall of Interrupted Group Tasks: An Experimental Study of Individual Motivation in Relation to Group Goals," *Human Relations,* 7:3–38, February 1954.

Horwitz, Murray and Frances Lee. "Effects of Decision-Making by Group Members on Recall of Finished and Unfinished Tasks," *Journal of Abnormal and Social Psychology,* 49:201–210, April 1954.

Loomis, James L. "Communication, the Development of Trust, and Cooperative Behavior," *Human Relations,* 12:305–315, 1959.

Raven, Bertram H. and Jan Rietsema. "The Effects of Varied Clarity of Group Goal and Group Path upon the Individual and His Relationship to His Group," *Human Relations,* 10:29–47, February 1957.

Raven, Bertram H. "Social Influence on Opinions and the Communication of Related Content," *Journal of Abnormal and Social Psychology,* 58:119–128, January 1959.

Stotland, Ezra, S. Thorley, E. Thomas, A. R. Cohen, and A. Zander. "The Effects of Group Expectation and Self-Esteem upon Self-Evaluation," *Journal of Abormal and Social Psychology,* 54:55–63, January 1957.

Zander, Alvin, Thomas Natsoulas, and Edwin J. Thomas. "Personal Goals and the Group's Goals for the Member," *Human Relations,* 13:333–344, November 1960.

Part III

Factors Influencing Group Behavior in the Classroom

Chapter 8   # Group Composition

FORCES at work in a group influence the behavior of every individual in the group. Hence, the behavior of a child when he is alone in a situation is not the same as when he is imbedded in a group, because the group modifies the individual's tendencies to a certain degree. Conversely, each individual in the group affects, to some extent, a group's interaction processes and its total behavior pattern. One set of determinants, then, that influences a group's pattern of interaction is derived from the characteristics of its members. These dimensions of personal behavior that play a part in the activity of the class group are associated with such individual characteristics as age, sex, and personality. The ages and sexes of the members contribute to noticeable variations in patterns of class group behavior. The personality of each member also determines, to a great degree, his status in the group, the extent to which he accepts others, and the extent to which others accept him. A group member's social status, and the group's pattern of interpersonal relations, are both affected by such environmental factors as ethnicity and social class. This chapter discusses variations in class group behavior that are determined, in part, by characteristics of members and certain environmental conditions.

Effects of Member Characteristics on Interaction

The previous chapters have been concerned with the ways group properties influence the behavior of members. Attention is turned at this time to certain characteristics of individual members that affect the total group pattern of behavior.

Age Differences

The number and intensity of social relationships vary among children in different age groups. Young children who make up kindergarten groups have had relatively little experience in social interaction in large group situations. They do not have many ideas concerning the kinds of relationships people can have with one another. The ability to symbolize and communicate varies greatly from child to child, though all kindergarteners are limited in this area compared to older youngsters. However, by the time children have reached the age of six years, they have progressed from a relatively unsocial stage to a much more social one. Most have learned to cooperate in play activities involving a number of children.

The age of the members of a class group affects the actions of each individual and the total pattern of group interaction. Primary teachers, for example, expect that the children in their classrooms will vary greatly in their abilities to get along well with others. They recognize that this ability is acquired only after children have had many opportunities to work and play with many individuals. Most of these teachers recognize, too, that the class group exerts a strong influence on the personality of the child, and that their class groups need careful guidance so children can learn to make adjustments to others and to accept others.

The process of socialization is developmental; therefore, as children progress from grade to grade, there is a gradual change in the type of behavior displayed at each age level. Children in the first grade lack a strong sense of group feeling (although there is more "groupness" than some claim). Adjustment to others occurs rather rapidly after the first grade, and by the time children reach the third grade, group relations are fairly well established, and group influence is becoming strong. That the desire to be accepted and to "belong" becomes increasingly important to children as they grow older has already been noted.

Age affects many other aspects of behavior. Traits that make a child acceptable vary from age to age, as do feelings regarding the opposite sex. Stability in friendships increases as children grow older. Such forms of social behavior as cooperation, generosity, sympathy, and good sportsmanship develop through the elementary school years. For example, behavior related to sharing equipment on the playground and supplies and materials in the classroom is sometimes mentioned as a problem by primary teachers, but it is rarely identified as a source of conflict by middle and upper grade teachers. Sharing behavior, of course, is learned, and children gradually come to share with others.

Sex Differences

Throughout the elementary school years a sex cleavage develops. At the third and fourth grade levels the children of opposite sex draw apart; they occasionally express verbal contempt of one another—particularly the boys for the girls. For a few years they have little in common. By the sixth grade they are beginning to make approaches to one another. In certain areas, some of the children in the sixth grade are "going steady." For the most part, however, at this age the approaches of the sexes to one another are more subtle.

Differences in behavior between the sexes are related to the traits children admire in others. By the time he reaches the third grade an aggressive boy is admired and may often be selected as a leader, but an aggressive girl is often considered too "bossy" by both boys and girls. Similarly, a boy who is quiet, kind, and thoughtful may be considered "sissy," but these traits in a girl are admired by both boys and girls. Boys are expected to be vigorous, somewhat aggressive, and willing to fight. Girls are expected to be quiet, not aggressive, and more or less "lady-like." By middle grades, popular boys and girls generally conform to the socially approved patterns for sex-appropriateness.

Girls and boys 12 to 14 years old are very interested in the personality characteristics of their peers of the opposite sex. Girls say they admire boys who know when to "kid" and when to be serious, who act their age, who are not show-offs. They should be kind, considerate, and truthful. They should have a good sense of humor and not be too shy. Boys of this age say they like girls who act like girls, who smile, and are friendly. A good sense of humor is important to boys, as is the desire to have fun, but they do not like girls who giggle. Both boys and girls of this age say neat appearance is very important.[1]

The sex composition of a class group may be important to the pre-

[1] Lester D. Crow, "Personality Traits Admired by Adolescents," *The Clearing House*, 29:25, 1954.

diction of group behavior, particularly in the middle and upper grade levels, where boys are more inclined toward aggressiveness than girls. Girls are partly responsible for the tendency of boys to "show-off" or to act aggressively. A group of girls may seem to a teacher to be angelic and very easy to manage, while the boys appear to be the source of continuous disturbance. If the teacher observes closely, she may note that the girls are approving the boys' behavior and their approval "eggs them on," even though they profess to scorn the girls.

Cultural influences bring about many of the behavior differences between the sexes. There are cultural pressures on both boys and girls to develop interests appropriate to their sexes and to behave according to certain cultural norms. Bonney [2] states that neither constitutional differences nor stages of sex development create the interpersonal attitudes that exist between and within sex groups in the classroom. He suggests that differences are most likely due to socio-economic background, the extent to which boys and girls have been separated on the playground and other places, and the extent to which sex differences have been encouraged or minimized by direct or indirect teaching.

Variations in Personality

All teachers are very much aware that interaction patterns in class groups are affected to a certain degree by the personalities of some of the members. In fact, some teachers are inclined to believe that the patterns of behavior that emerge in the group are determined entirely by a few aggressive, adventuresome, or excitable individuals. However, it seems likely that many of these individuals who appear to be "behavior problems" because of their own dominant central tendencies to behave in certain ways are actually behaving, in many instances, in response to pressures from the group. Some children, however, are relatively insensitive to the forces operating in the group, so they do behave more or less according to their own personal tendencies.

An individual's personality pattern is made up of certain specific qualities of behavior sometimes called "traits." These traits include ways of meeting problems and reactions to frustrations, aggressive and defensive behavior, and outgoing or withdrawing attitudes toward other people. These traits are integrated and organized into a pattern. Some of these traits are more predominant than others; thus, we have children we label as well adjusted, outgoing, and friendly, and others we label as

[2] Merl E. Bonney, "Choosing Between the Sexes on a Sociometric Measurement," *The Journal of Social Psychology*, 39:99–114, 1954.

maladjusted, hostile, aggressive, and withdrawing. Usually the children in class groups who are labeled "problems" are aggressive and somewhat obstreperous by adult standards. Commonly, the children who respond to the normal pressures in the classroom in socially disapproved or inadequate ways are labeled "emotionally disturbed" by teachers.

Generally speaking, one might predict that the general pattern of class group interaction would be highly favorable if the group were composed of members whose personality patterns were those that characterize the "well-adjusted," accepted child, since these children make good adjustments to both adults and other children and to groups as wholes. Numerous studies have found that children who turn their energies outward, who adjust without making disturbances, who comply with requests, and who accept gracefully what happens are well accepted by adults and by their classmates. These children are kind to others. They share what they have, are willing to take turns in games, and they show impartiality in their dealings with members of their groups. Such individuals assume responsibilities. They participate in and enjoy group activities. They feel secure in their statuses and compare themselves favorably with their peers. The personality pattern of the "well-adjusted" child is that of the expansive, energetic, objective individual who is relatively free from fears and anxieties.

Poorly adjusted children, on the other hand, show quite different personality traits. Some may be unresponsive, timid, and shy. Others may be impulsive, irresponsible, and emotionally dependent. The accustomed mode of behavior of some children at school reveals them to be suspicious, hostile individuals. Others say very little and show inhibited, withdrawn, or apathetic tendencies. Of course, a child's personality is more than a combination of certain traits such as those mentioned, but one set of characteristics may appear to dominate his behavior in such a way that other traits seem to be insignificant. For example, the teacher who wrote the following report described the characteristics that dominated Harry's behavior.

IGNORED

Harry was quite large and exceptionally heavy for his eight years, being much larger than the others in the class. If he wanted something, he grabbed it. If he wanted to talk, he talked. His idea of play was to push, shove, and pile on top of someone. At first, he was tolerated. Then after he had been shown, told, fought with, and screamed at by the children, they decided that they had had enough! Both boys and girls agreed to leave him alone. This was done both in and out of the classroom. This continued for about a week.

Harry became very upset and even began to stutter. Finally, one of the girls relented enough to talk and play with him on a trial basis, but all the rest continued to ignore him.

Personality traits that are admired by members of the class group vary from grade to grade. Tyler [3] found that first graders accepted quiet, inconspicuous children more frequently than those who were active, talkative, or aggressive. By the third grade, quiet children are often overlooked and more talkative, aggressive children are preferred and considered most acceptable by group members.[4]

A study made to determine how the social behavior of highly accepted and poorly accepted first graders differed found that highly accepted individuals were flexible in their social relationships,[5] that they conformed to classroom requirements, that they smiled often and participated willingly in cooperative group activity, that they made many voluntary contributions to the group, and that they associated with many children during free play and activity periods. The findings seem to indicate that first graders who get along well with others are confident, sociable, and adaptable individuals.

In a similar study at the second grade level, highly acceptable children in free play situations were observed to talk more frequently, to laugh and giggle more, to participate more frequently in cooperative group activity, and to play with other children more frequently.[6] Thus, as with first grade children, highly accepted children tended to be more happy, secure, confident, and adaptable than less acceptable ones.

An investigation conducted by Smith [7] to find out why certain children in a fourth grade classroom were well liked and secure in their relations with others in the class and why other children were disliked and hesitant about participating in the group found certain personality differences in these children.

The procedure followed was to have each child write the name of the child in the class he liked best and the one he liked least.

The reasons given for liking the best-liked children indicated that

[3] Leona E. Tyler, "The Relationships of Interests to Abilities and Reputation Among First Grade Children," *Education and Psychological Measurement*, 11:255–264, 1951.

[4] Donald Brieland, "A Variation of the 'Guess Who' Technique for the Study of the Adjustment of Children," *Journal of Educational Research*, 43:385–390, 1952.

[5] Merl E. Bonney and Johnny Powell, "Differences in Social Behavior Between Sociometrically High and Sociometrically Low Children," *Journal of Educational Research*, 46:481–495, 1953.

[6] Merl E. Bonney, "Social Behavior Differences Between Second Grade Children of High and Low Sociometric Status," *Journal of Educational Research*, 48:481–495, 1955.

[7] Gladys H. Smith, "Sociometric Study of Best-Liked and Least-Liked Children," *Elementary School Journal*, 51:77–85, October 1950.

children liked by others were well-adjusted, generous, and considerate, and that least-liked children were aggressive, domineering, and selfish.

The relationship between personality characteristics and social acceptability in adolescence was studied in an effort to discover the personality characteristics popular and unpopular youngsters were judged to have.[8] Those traits that showed the greatest differentiation for both sexes and at all grades were the abilities to be enthusiastic, to be cheerful and happy, to be friendly, to enjoy jokes, and to initiate games and activities. It was found, too, that those who were highly accepted by their own sexes were judged also to like the opposite sex.

The general trend of the findings concerning adolescents who are not well-adjusted is that they often, in the privacy of their own lives, are rather moody, troubled, and distressed. It has been observed, for example, that they often show symptoms of insecurity; many of them seem to be troubled by problems in their home environments and to be absorbed by difficulties in their own lives to such extents that they lack the freedom to enter into lively give-and-take with others. In a study by Kuhlen and Collister,[9] it was noted that ninth graders who were generally not socially well adjusted tended to be withdrawing, shy, and unhappy, and they tended also to be unattractive, poorly groomed, and lacking in social "know-how."

Differences in Social Acceptability

Social acceptability refers to those characteristics that contribute to whether a youngster is acceptable in his peer group. If the members of a class group are all reasonably well accepted—that is, if there are none who are extremely low in acceptability—both the quantity and the quality of interaction are increased. Individuals in the group have more influence on one another, and they are better able to withstand frustration. When members are accepting of one another, there is more cooperation between members and less conflict. Thus, the pattern of group behavior is affected to a large degree by whether the children in the class display the characteristics that make them acceptable to the members of their age groups.

A child's social acceptability depends to a large degree upon his personality, which results from his physical characteristics and his experi-

[8] Raymond G. Kuhlen and Beatrice J. Lee, "Personality Characteristics and Social Acceptability in Adolescence," *Journal of Educational Psychology*, 34:321–340, 1943.

[9] Raymond G. Kuhlen and E. Gorden Collister, "Sociometric Status of Sixth and Ninth Graders Who Fail to Finish High School," *Educational and Psychological Measurement*, 12:632–637, 1952.

ence. His attitudes, values, habits, basic motives, and frustrations determine significantly the degree to which he is socially acceptable.

Another subtle factor affects a child's social acceptability. This is the process of his perceiving and interpreting the situation in which he finds himself. Any situation is perceived or "defined" by the individual before he makes overt response. This is to say that "meaning" is formulated, and this meaning is a crucial determinant of behavior.

It was noted when personality characteristics were examined that socially acceptable children made good suggestions about activities, they were friendly and considerate, and they were usually the type considered by adults to be well-adjusted personalities. Numerous studies have been conducted to determine the factors that influence social acceptability, the constancy of social acceptability, and differences in age trends.

One characteristic frequently attributed to a person who is liked is that he likes others. Other frequently mentioned characteristics are a certain kind of freedom, spontaneity, and willingness to enter into things, which are described in terms such as, "active in games," or "you can have fun with him or her," or, "initiates games and activities." Another quality frequently noted is a kind of liveliness, cheerfulness, and gaiety, described in terms such as "enjoys a joke," or "is cheerful and happy." Fairness and good sportsmanship also are named often as qualities of persons who are liked. Frequently, also, qualities are mentioned that suggest that the well-liked person is relatively "natural" and free of pretense: he or she is "not conceited," and "enjoys a joke on himself." Tidiness, neatness, and cleanliness are also sometimes mentioned, as are qualities such as, "seems to come from a good home." It seems true, too, that popularity with peers and self-acceptance are related.

Environmental Factors Influencing Member Relations

Social relations in classroom groups may be affected by certain biases or prejudices that members have regarding those who differ in ethnic or social-class origin. Some investigators contend that persons of all ages are predisposed to like people who most resemble themselves. Children who differ in appearance, in cultural backgrounds, or who differ in other ways may not be accepted by the class group because the members have learned to give these different individuals a low evaluation. If children have not been taught to interpret these individuals as different, generally they accept them on their own merits. There are a few children, however, who lack self-acceptance, and they find it difficult to like most people.

Particularly, they may transfer their self-contempt to persons of different races, religions, or social classes.

Teachers' attitudes, preconceptions, and reactions to children may have strong influences on whether a class group accepts or rejects individuals who are "different." Invidious comparisons, high praise, or much blame given by a teacher can affect group relations. Ways in which these environmental factors influence member relations in a classroom are examined in this section.

Ethnic Origins

An influence that often affects interaction in the class group comes from differences in members' ethnic origins. Differences in race, religion, nationality, language, and culture may create cliques and subgroups that affect group harmony and the attainment of many classroom goals. Generally speaking, if some class group members are of a minority ethnic origin and the majority of members belong to a dominant racial, national, or religious group, some effects of these differences can be noted in member interactive behavior. A distinctly stratified structure may occur. Conflicts can arise between subgroups. Cleavages are often reflected in the friendship choices of pupils.

Several factors are involved in these differences in ethnic origin. On the one hand, belonging to an ethnic group may influence personality, and, in turn, social behavior. An oriental background, for example, may produce individuals who have somewhat docile, passive, and submissive external manners. These persons often place a high value on school, education, and teachers. Children of some religious faiths also may hold values and have behavior patterns somewhat different from others in the classroom group. They may disapprove of some forms of social activity such as dancing, or they may dress differently and thereby be set apart. Belonging to a minority group against which discrimination is directed because of color, can also affect personality and behavior patterns to a large extent.

In addition to differences in behavior patterns sometimes arising from differences in ethnic origins, individuals are very likely to acquire feelings of belonging to the groups in which they have been reared, particularly if they belong to the dominant group. They will feel a kinship with those who have the same background. This feeling of kinship and belonging also places a distance between persons from a dominant or accepted group and persons of different ethnic origins. For those in the minority, a hardship is created when they perceive they are regarded as outsiders. However, this attitude of preferring individuals from one's own group does not necessarily create cleavages, or lessen the total group cohesiveness. Patterns of behavior are affected only if members of the dominant group regard the other ethnic groups with dislike, distaste, hostility, or fear. Although subgroup formation may result from ethnic group affiliation, it becomes an important determinant of a poor interaction pattern only when members of ethnic groups are forced into cliques because they are excluded from other groups.

The extent of friendliness existing between children of different ethnic groups will be influenced by the attitudes that exist in the homes and in the communities in which the children live. It seems that much race awareness and many of the prejudices, including dislike of certain specific characteristics attributed to racial and ethnic groups, are developed from parental teaching and from attitudes assimilated in neighborhood play groups.

When prejudice exists in the classroom, teachers report occurrences of sudden conflict that are difficult to resolve, since the home and community structure play a part in determining how some children will relate to others.

Race antipathy is frequently manifested in children by name-calling. They use terms that are, to say the least, disparaging and degrading. Evidently their use is prompted by a desire to impress those of other ethnic and racial groups with a sense of uselessness and inferiority. The name callers, then, establish their own sense of superiority. Calling names is evidently a frequent source of classroom conflict.

NAME CALLING

At noon hour, a group of boys had been "stalking" Angel, who reportedly had hit a fellow class member, Dick, on the way to school that morning because Dick had called him a "dirty Mexican." Angel had remained within sight of the teacher on duty and had not been touched, but about four friends of Dick were after him. Angel was in my room and three of the revengeful boys were also.

The class all seemed aware of the incident and came into the room talking very loudly, except the four involved. They slammed their books down but said nothing. The class kept whispering to each other, and pointing to them, and seemed to be "egging" them on. Few seemed to side with Angel.

Social-Class Differences

The definition of what is acceptable and desired behavior varies somewhat according to the social class to which an individual belongs.

Behavior defined as appropriate in one social class is interpreted differently in another. For example, children from two contrasting socioeconomic levels were investigated by Pope [10] to determine characteristic patterns of social behavior. One group was from the lower class, the other from lower-upper and upper-middle class.

Among lower-group boys three major patterns could be discerned. The members in the first pattern, in which there were only a few boys, were the leaders who had the homage of the other boys and the companionship of the girls. They were aggressive, belligerent, and domineering. The second pattern for lower-group boys was the one involving most of the boys who were happy, sociable, able to enjoy good jokes, and considerably less aggressive than their leaders. The third pattern, the "sissy," was the one the rest could not tolerate. This pattern included the studious and classroom-conforming boys as well as what other groups would call "sissies."

Among boys of high socioeconomic status, the group leader, although active and skilled in competitive games, was not expected to be aggressive. In fact, being bossy and given to fighting tended to make him unpopular. The friendly, personable, good-looking boy who was accepted by both boys and girls was another pattern. The classroom intellectual was not actively rejected. In fact, he enjoyed a certain respect. The "sissy," in the narrower sense, belonged to still another pattern. However, he was no more acceptable than he was among low socioeconomic boys. Along with the bossy, the unkempt, and the fighter, he was not accepted.

Among the girls of the lower socioeconomic group, the type widely accepted was "the little lady," who was likeable, friendly, neat, and a good student. She was, however, not likely to be a leader. Another pattern that enjoyed prestige, but was less frequently encountered, was the somewhat rowdy, talkative, attention-getting, aggressive girl. She was apt to associate with boys in the lower group.

High socioeconomic girls, instead of having two contrasting patterns of prestige as did the lower-group girls, had but one, that of the "little lady" pattern, but with certain differences. Although good-looking, friendly, and tidy, she was more vivacious than her low-socioeconomic counterpart and she associated with boys of the group. The tomboy had no place in the group, since any form of aggressiveness or bossiness was rejected.

The results of the study made it apparent that there were distinct differences in the value systems in the two peer cultures. These differences

[10] Benjamin Pope, "Socio-Economic Contrasts in Children's Peer Culture Prestige Values," *Genetic Psychology Monography*, **48**:157–220, November 1953.

in values sometime lead to class cleavage and conflict. At times, the cleavage appears to be the result of prejudice, or a tendency of one social class group to look down upon "the common herd."

THE OTHER SIDE OF THE TRACKS

During organized play period, two girls became involved in an argument as to relative skills in playing a game of fistball. Both were outstanding athletes with excellent coordination, and each had a goodly following of peers.

The argument led to name-calling and a slight altercation that was stopped by the yard duty teacher before it became too serious. Later, when they met in the cloakroom, the two girls began fighting again.

It must be understood that both girls were acknowledged leaders of two different groups. One group was from financially and socially secure families and their leader also came from a similar background. The other girl and group came from families from "the other side of the tracks."

There was an immediate discernible line of demarcation between the two groups. Each group vigorously backed up its leader. Both sides claimed the other was at fault. There were threats of "just wait until after school," and counter-threats of a similar nature.

This split in the class is a constant source of conflict, and the fighting and arguments continually interfere with class work. It is not surprising that the one group resorts to fighting, but the girls from better homes are just as bad.

Children of the lower socioeconomic classes have more freedom of choice in selecting friends than children of the middle class because parents do not put pressure on them to choose the "right" type of friend. However, they often are not accepted in the middle-class group, so they are forced to select friends from their own group. With young children, especially, propinquity to the neighborhood is an important determinant for selection of friends. Children from lower-class neighborhoods associate with children from the same neighborhoods. The same is true for middle-class children. A study by Stendler [11] noted that there was a difference between in-school and out-of-school choices of friends made by children from differing home backgrounds. Choices within the school tended to be more democratic. However, at the highest levels in the study (sixth and eighth grades), there was little social interaction outside school between children belonging to upper-middle-class homes and children in the "working class."

[11] Celia B. Stendler, *Children of Brasstown*, Urbana: University of Illinois Press, 1949.

Teacher Attitudes

Among the factors that interfere with the acceptance of an individual by the group is the teacher's accepting or rejecting behavior. Although few teachers will knowingly reject an individual, a teacher's attitude toward certain characteristics or behaviors that a child exhibits may be noted by the group and cause the group members to perceive the child in a more unfavorable light than they had previously. Since to a large degree a child's behavior is the result of his concept of himself and how he perceives that others view him, it is logical to assume that if he feels the teacher and the group do not accept him, his behavior will reflect this attitude. The characteristics he displays that contribute to the lack of acceptance may then become intensified.

Of course, a class group frequently accepts and approves an individual toward whom the teacher shows disapproval because of his conduct in the classroom. If, however, the child is one who lacks group acceptance because he is "different" in some way, and the group perceives the teacher also seems not to accept him (for whatever reason), the group toleration of the individual becomes even less. It must be mentioned too, that if a child receives what the group believes to be excessive approval from the teacher, the group may exhibit rejecting tendencies toward this individual.

A teacher, of course, cannot be accepting of behavior that continually annoys and disrupts the class. The teacher's method of handling this behavior, however, can be other than one of attacking, degrading, or destroying the individual's integrity, either in the child's own eyes or in the eyes of the group.

Because teachers feel sorry for a child and recognize some of the reasons why the child is not acceptable to the group, they sometimes believe that they themselves are accepting, even though the group is not. Their remarks about the child, however, often disclose that they share the group's opinion of the child.

For example, a teacher was describing a class reaction to a girl who asked and was granted permission to sing a song to the class with her own guitar accompaniment. During and after the performance, the group jeered and ridiculed the girl in a sly, furtive way. In reporting this incident and expressing his concern over the group reaction, the teacher then offered an excuse for the group's behavior by saying that the girl was "skinny," "funny looking," and a kind of "goof-ball." It is quite possible that the group unconsciously recognized that the teacher shared the group attitude. It is possible, too, that the girl perceived that the teacher, as well as the group, failed to accept her.

An investigation by Back [12] showed that instructions that oriented the individuals in the experimental group to like or dislike each other altered the judged attractiveness of the individual. Generalizing this finding to teacher's practices, it can be assumed that a teacher's comments to individuals in the group, the responses given to a pupil's question, and the overall teacher reaction to individual pupil behavior will influence how the members of the group judge the attractiveness of individuals.

Groups are able to "size up" or to become aware of a teacher's attitudes and biases toward individual pupils and their behavior. Even though a teacher tries to deal fairly and objectively, if he finds it difficult to accept a pupil, the group usually becomes aware of this although the class members may not be conscious of this awareness. One reason that explains a group's ability to assess teachers' attitudes toward individuals is that teachers as a group have certain corresponding likes and dislikes of pupil behavior and personality characteristics. Children are more or less aware of these likes and dislikes.

A study by Seidman and Knapp, [13] for example, investigated students' perceptions of teachers' likes and dislikes of student behavior and found no significant differences between teachers' dislikes and students' perceptions of them. The study explored the relationship between student and teacher likes and dislikes rather than the perception of a particular teacher's like or dislike of the behavior of a particular student. For example, the questionnaire for teachers asked: (1) What are the things that students do that you like? (2) What are the things that students do that you dislike? The questionnaire given to the students was similar: (1) What are the things that persons like yourself do that teachers like? (2) What are the things that persons like yourself do that teachers dislike?

Judges categorized the responses into four categories: interpersonal behavior, individual behavior, preparation of assignments, and personality.

The students mentioned assignments more frequently than did teachers, and teachers mentioned personality more frequently than did students. The personality characteristics teachers said they disliked in students were related to temperament, untidiness, laziness, and lack of

[12] Kurt W. Back, "Influence Through Social Communication," *Journal of Abnormal and Social Psychology*, 46:9–23, July 1951.

[13] Jerome M. Seidman and Leda B. Knapp, "Teacher Likes and Dislikes of Student Behavior and Student Perception of These Attitudes," *Journal of Educational Research*, 47:143–148, October 1953.

dependability. Though it seemed that personality was intangible for some students' perceptions, the students did perceive teachers' dislikes of certain individual behaviors.

Although the study cited involved college students, a similar study at lower levels would probably reveal somewhat similar findings, since both secondary and elementary students have demonstrated that they can make consistent and stable evaluations of teacher tendencies and their likes and dislikes of pupil behavior.

The problems or behaviors that disturb and annoy teachers were the subject of an investigation by Kaplan.[14] Teachers were asked to respond to the question, "What problems or situations disturb or annoy you in your work and life as a teacher?" More than 500 items were grouped and classified and those appearing more than once were placed on a check list and submitted to a second group of teachers to determine which items were considered significant by a large number of teachers. Most of the items that were considered very disturbing or annoying related to children's social characteristics. Examples of some of the items concerned children who daydreamed and paid little attention, could not get along with others, were careless in appearance, were nonconformists, etc. Over 50 per cent of the teachers indicated that children who did not mix with others, who were timid and retiring, or who "just sat"—though they caused no disturbance—were either annoying or disturbing.

A differentiation was not made as to whether teachers were merely annoyed or whether they were disturbed because the problems were difficult for them to handle.

It seems that if teachers are annoyed by children who cannot get along with others, or who do not mix with others, or who are timid and retiring, then teachers' reactions may be easily transmitted to the group. Perceiving that these children are not well accepted by the teacher may be cause for group intolerance or rejection of these individuals.

There is reason to believe that since teachers have an unfavorable attitude toward aggressive behavior, and since boys are, for the most part, more outwardly aggressive than girls, boys receive more disapproving comments from teachers than girls. The findings of a study by Meyer and Thompson[15] confirmed this conclusion. By means of observation, and a variation of the "Guess Who" technique,[16] which measured the children's perceptions of teacher attitude, it was found that boys did re-

[14] Louis Kaplan, "The Annoyances of Elementary School Teachers," *Journal of Educational Research*, 45:649–665, May 1952.

[15] William J. Meyer and George G. Thompson, "Sex Differences in the Distribution of Teacher Approval and Disapproval Among Sixth Grade Children," *Journal of Educational Psychology*, 47:385–396, 1956.

[16] See Chapter 13 for explanation of the "Guess Who?" technique.

ceive more disapproval than girls. The study showed also that although boys received more disapproval, girls did not receive more approval.

Since aggressiveness is more or less admired and expected in boys, it is possible that a teacher's attitude and behavior toward boys who are aggressive does not affect the group negatively and cause the group to reject these individuals because of a perceived teacher attitude. It is even possible that this teacher attitude and reaction might enhance the social acceptability of such boys. This tendency of teachers to express disapproving remarks to aggressive boys could be a factor in group rejection, however, if some boys had certain personal characteristics that set them apart from others, plus a degree of aggressiveness; the group members might then increase their rejection upon noting the teacher's tendency to disapprove of the child.

Another study of teacher approval and disapproval at the fourth and sixth grade levels determined that the class groups nominated only four or five pupils as ones who received teacher approval. Four or five different pupils in the same classroom received considerable teacher disapproval according to class nominations. The children who were considered by their classmates as experiencing a high degree of teacher approval appeared to be those who were most intelligent and best adjusted. They were the children who were the most outgoing and the ones displaying the most self-confidence.[17]

If the children receiving the most disapproval were those who were least confident and least well-adjusted, the question arises as to what effects teacher disapproval had upon group acceptance of these individuals.

Studies indicate that when approval is given to the group as a whole rather than to certain individuals in the group, the group members become more cohesive and like one another better. There is some evidence that suggests that if disapproval is given to the group as a whole, the expression of disapproval also increases cohesiveness. This latter effect is accounted for by the fact that a group has a tendency to unite when attacked. Although approval and praise are generally considered by educators as the best means for encouraging individuals, it appears that unless such encouragement can be distributed evenly (which, if given honestly, might be very difficult to do), it might produce effects more harmful than good.

Teachers who are aware of the status systems in their classrooms—that is, how the children rate members on such items as *skill, power,*

[17] Albert F. DeGroat and George Thompson, "A Study of the Distribution of Teacher Approval and Disapproval Among Sixth Grade Pupils," *Journal of Experimental Education,* 18:57–75, September 1949.

respect, etc.—establish much better climates and higher group morales than do teachers who are not aware of how their pupils evaluate one another. Bogen [18] examined the relationships between pupil-teacher rapport and teacher awareness of certain status structures. Eighteen seventh and eighth grade teachers were evaluated by Wrightstone's Pupil-Teacher Rapport Scale, which measured the social climate of their classrooms. Five teachers with the highest scores and five with the lowest scores were selected for the experiment. A sociometric device was given to the children to determine the status structures in the classes. The teachers were tested for their perceptions of how their class groups would rate each child. A correlation of the scores showed that the high-rapport teachers had a greater awareness of class structure than did the low-rapport teachers. It seems that a teacher who is successful in establishing high group morale recognizes how the group as a whole evaluates its members. Or, perhaps when the morale of a class group is high, it is because the teacher is able to predict accurately group feeling toward individual members and consequently is able to guide the group toward more positive evaluations of less acceptable members.

In describing the following example of group action, the teacher reveals her failure to assess the group's choice of a leader, and furthermore she indicates that she did not correctly estimate the child's ability to fulfil the group's expectations. When the group elected for a high office a boy sne thought friendless, she not only was surprised at the group's choice but did not believe he was capable of handling the assignment.

DENNIS FOR PRESIDENT

In our third grade we have established the practice of electing a class president every month in order to give a lot of people a chance at the office during the year.

Before nominations were accepted this last time, I asked my usual question, "What qualifications do we expect a president to possess?"

The answers came back something like this. The one elected should be a child who conducts himself properly on the playground, and in the room, and one who is a good example to the other classmates. No answer indicated that the president needed to have a lot of friends to elect him, nor did the subject of popularity arise. But the previous president had been exceedingly popular, almost the "hero" type, and to an outsider he seemed to be the "overbearing and show-off" type.

[18] Isidore Bogen, "Pupil-Teacher Rapport and the Teacher's Awareness of Status Structures within the Group," *The Journal of Educational Sociology*, 28:105–114, November 1954.

The president and the vice-president, who were still in office, accepted 10 nominations and wrote them on the board. The vice-president passed out blank slips of paper for the voting. Each child wrote the name of his choice and the vice-president collected them. Votes were counted and a mark placed by the name of each candidate when he received a vote. By unanimous decision the vote went to Dennis, an extremely quiet, meek, nontalkative boy who has an air of bashfulness about him. In fact, at the beginning of school and even up to the time of the voting, I was sure that he had very few close friends.

When the last vote was counted, I had my doubts as to what would happen now that Dennis was president. To my amazement he has helped with the conduct of the class out on the playground and in the corridor. He acts with few words and mostly with motions. The respect the class manifests is wonderful. To say the least, this responsibility has changed him! I can see his bashfulness ebbing away.

Previously, I had assumed that the children would choose as their president a person who was a strong, influential leader or perhaps one of the better ball players, and Dennis is not one of these. However, he is carrying on beautifully and the class seems more than satisfied.

The teacher comments in her report that the responsibility changed Dennis, and that she could "see his bashfulness ebbing away." Only careful observation by an outsider could determine whether Dennis or the teacher changed. Perhaps Dennis was shy and inarticulate in the presence of the teacher because he recognized that she did not evaluate him highly. Or, it is possible that he had never had an opportunity to show the teacher what he could do. Evidently the group recognized his capabilities.

Another investigation involving teachers' accuracy in judging the sociometric status of pupils and their intelligence showed a relatively large spread of accuracy scores among the teachers tested. Some teachers were highly accurate in their judgments, while others were extremely inaccurate.[19] The conclusion that the least accurate teachers were unlikely to be able to meet the needs of the pupils seemed warranted. Since studies have shown that teachers' judgments of the social acceptance of children in their classes are often inaccurate, Marshall [20] investigated whether or not teachers' accuracy in judging pupil social acceptance could be improved. She organized three groups: a control group, a group trained in factual knowledge only, and a group that was given a standard for judging as well as being trained in factual knowledge. The two trained groups

[19] Norman E. Gronlund and Algard P. Whitney, "The Relation Between Teachers' Judgments of Pupils' Sociometric Status and Intelligence," *The Elementary School Journal,* 58:264–268, February 1958.

[20] Helen R. Marshall, "Training Adults to Judge Children's Social Acceptance," *Journal of Educational Psychology,* 53:27–31, February 1962.

were given the same introduction and the same description of nursery school behavior relating to preschool social acceptance. The group given a standard had additional training by demonstration of the sociometric choices of children under observation. All subjects judged the social acceptance of children twice. These judgments were then compared with the sociometric tests of the children.

After specific training, the teachers judgments were found to be improved. Accuracy was decreased, however, when the trained students had few children to observe. The investigator concluded that while teachers' judgments can be improved in this area, further study is needed to determine the best type of training.

Withall [21] discovered from a study of the distribution of a teacher's time among pupils, in which a teacher deliberately attempted to work with eight overlooked children, that it was not possible to redistribute teacher contacts evenly in the group.

When a teacher must work with 30 or more pupils, a fairly equal distribution of praise or verbal contacts is not likely for many reasons. Praise and statements to the group as a whole, however, do not single out certain individuals and leave out others, yet the effect is one of drawing the members closer together and causing them to feel they were individually praised. Praise of the group makes members more attracted to the group and more satisfied with working conditions in the group.

A comparison of high school students' behavior with that of third and fourth grade pupils showed that the secondary school students' behavior was not so closely related to teacher behavior as was that of the pupils in the elementary school. Teacher and pupil behavior in the elementary school appeared to be noticeably interdependent, whereas there was a low positive relationship between student and teacher behavior in the secondary school.[22] One might assume from this study that certain personality characteristics are more important in considering teacher qualifications for the elementary school than they are at the secondary level.

Effects upon Class Interaction

The group composition, or the combination of members' social characteristics, influences the pattern and outcome of class group interaction. If it were possible in all cases to control the membership of each class

[21] John Withall, "An Objective Measurement of a Teacher's Classroom Interactions," *Journal of Educational Psychology*, 47:203–212, 1956.

[22] David G. Ryans, "Some Relationships Between Pupil Behavior and Certain Teacher Characteristics," *Journal of Educational Psychology*, 52:82–90, April 1961.

group by selecting members (and the teacher) according to the members' social characteristics, certain conflicts could be avoided and a few important but limited educational goals could be achieved. Although certain specific objectives might be reached, it is very possible that such structuring of a class group would result in a failure to achieve many important educational goals of the longer-range and more subtle variety. For example, if class groups are organized according to the members' abilities to achieve in skill and content areas, it is difficult to develop certain attitudes that direct decision making in a free society—namely, respect for human personalities regardless of origin or circumstances of birth.

The pattern and outcome of interaction in experimental groups is often controlled by selecting the members on the basis of certain combinations of social characteristics. Thus, the interaction patterns of classroom groups can be controlled to a certain degree by selecting the children who make up the group composition on the basis of such factors as intelligence, social adjustment, task behavior (achievement), or any other desired combination. Of course, those children whose social characteristics combine in ways that leads to poor social adjustment, low achievement, or less desirable behavior patterns would of necessity have to be thrown together into classes of "poor achievers," "low abilities," or "problem sections."

Assembled in many classrooms are youngsters who differ in abilities, in personality, and in racial and social class origins. Having different values and customs, they do not share the same attitudes toward school and school objectives. The wider the range of differences, the more likely it is that conflicts will arise in the group, affecting the total pattern of group behavior. Differences in ability, in personality, in ethnicity, and social class make the job of teaching quite difficult for the teacher *unless* the teacher has considerable skill in working with groups. A skilled teacher can use the knowledge of group influence to resolve many of the problems resulting from these differences. The dissimilarities in individuals who make up the class group can then be used as resources to develop respect, acceptance, understanding, and empathy. Particularly, self-respect and self-confidence may be increased provided that class group forces are guided in this direction.

The extent of learning that takes place in a class group depends greatly on how well the group members get along among themselves and with the teacher. The more energy the group expends on nontask goals, or upon interpersonal problems affecting group integration, the less energy and the less time the group members have to devote to task goals. Numerous studies have shown that conflicts arising from interpersonal hostility are a major cause of nonproductivity. That many teachers are perturbed over problems of member relationships and group conflicts is revealed in their written reports of incidents of group behavior. They frequently comment on the amount of time that is "wasted" in quarrels and disagreements, and they express even more concern over the fact that although a conflict is halted, the children cannot (or do not) accomplish much work for some time following the conflict.

When children enter a new class for the first time, each child immediately becomes a part of a complex network of relationships that involves him and all the other members of the group. Each group member observes and interprets and judges the actions of others around him. He responds to others with feelings of liking or disliking. How he acts in the situation and how others react to him are determined by a number of factors related to his characteristics and those of the other group members. Whatever the net effect of all these factors, it is apparent to an observer of children's groups that children vary in their degrees of success in accepting and being accepted by others in their classrooms.

Questions for Study and Discussion

1. Discuss what causes age differences to produce the effects on individuals (and hence on the group) that are described in the chapter.

2. Since overage and underage children in a class are disadvantaged, make a plan to use in identifying these children.

3. Contrast the effect of sex cleavage on the classroom program at about the fourth grade level and the seventh grade.

4. Outline or diagram the personalities in a group with which you are or were well acquainted. This will require a personality description of each member. Using your outline or diagram as a basis, describe the interaction patterns that were frequent or particularly noticeable in the group.

5. Arrange a panel to discuss the dominance of certain personality characteristics over other less dominant characteristics, and the effects on group interaction. Members of the panel may present the case for age levels with which they are acquainted or in which they are interested.

6. How do children develop awareness of ethnic or other differences?

7. What responsibility, if any, does a teacher have for the out-of-school name-calling and insulting actions that occur between groups of children?

8. Summarize the desired behaviors of different social classes for an age level that you select.

9. Investigate children's choices of friends in an informal way through chats and friendly talks. Prepare the points you are interested in before the contact with the child or children. Summarize your results after the interviews.

10. Since boys receive more teacher correction and attention than girls, are girls slighted? How do girls feel about it?

11. Cite an example of a student's perception of the teacher's likes or dislikes. Was the student's perception correct?

12. In the study reported by Withall, what are possible explanations for the teacher's lack of success in giving attention to the eight overlooked students?

Suggestions for Further Reading

Allport, Gordon W. *The Nature of Prejudice.* Cambridge, Mass.: Addison-Wesley, 1954.

Alpern, Morton. "Role-Playing: Misfires and Successes," *Clearing House,* **26:** 554–556, May 1952.

Backman, Carl W. and Paul F. Secord. "The Effect of Perceived Liking on Interpersonal Attraction," *Human Relations,* 12(4): 379–384, November 1959.

Benne, Kenneth D. "More Learning Takes Place When Teacher and Students Understand the Various Roles in the Classroom Group," *NEA Journal,* **43:** 205–208, April 1954.

Bowman, Claude C. "Role-Playing and the Development of Insight," *Social Forces,* 28:2, December 1949.

Boyd, Gertrude A. "Role-Playing," *Social Education,* **21:**267–269, October 1957.

Brown, Ida Stewart. "How We Act in Groups," *Childhood Education,* **27:**156–160, December 1950.

Buswell, Margaret M. "The Relationship Between the Social Structure of the Classroom and the Academic Success of the Pupils," *Journal of Experimental Education,* 22:36–52, September 1952.

Dalke, H. Otto. "Determinants of Sociometric Selections Among Children in the Elementary School," *Sociometry,* 16:327–338, November 1953.

Davis, Allison. *Social-Class Influences Upon Learning.* Cambridge, Mass.: Harvard U.P. 1948.

Dentler, Robert A. and Kai T. Erikson. "The Functions of Deviance in Groups," *Social Problems,* 7:98–107, 1959.

Exline, Ralph V. "Group Climate as a Factor in the Relevance and Accuracy of Social Perceptions," *Journal of Abnormal and Social Psychology,* 55:382–388, November 1957.

Gillham, Helen L. *Helping Children Accept Themselves and Others.* New York: Teachers College, Columbia University, 1959.

Gold, Martin. "Power in the Classroom," *Sociometry,* 21:50–57, March 1958.

Goodman, Mary Ellen. *Race Awareness in Young Children,* Cambridge, Mass.: Addison-Wesley, 1952.

Grambs, Jean D. "Are We Training Prejudiced Teachers?" *School and Society,* 71:196–198, April 1, 1950.

Grambs, Jean D. *Group Processes in Intergroup Relations.* New York: National Conference of Christians and Jews, 1952.

Greenleaf, Walter J. "Sociodrama as a Guidance Technique," *California Journal of Education,* 26:51–55, February 1951.

Gough, Harrison G. and others. "Children's Ethnic Attitudes: I. Relationship to Certain Personality Factors," *Child Development,* 21:83–91, June 1950.

Gronlund, Norman E. *Sociometry in the Classroom.* New York: Harper, 1959.

Haas, Robert Bartlett. "Sociodrama in Education," *Sociatry* 2:420–429, December–March 1948.

Hanszen, Myra W. and W. G. Hollister. "Teaching Human Relations Through Spontaneous Pupil Play Writing and Play Acting," *Understanding the Child,* 25:103–110, 1956.

Hendry, Charles E., Ronald Lippitt, and Alvin Zander. *Reality Practice as an Educational Method.* New York: Beacon House, 1947.

Hoffman, Lois Wladis, Sidney Rosen, and Ronald Lippitt. "Parental Coerciveness, Child Autonomy, and the Child's Role at School," *Sociometry,* 23:15–22, March 1960.

Lindgren, Henry Clay. "The Effect of the Group on the Behavior of the Individual," *Education,* 73:383–387, February 1953.

Maier, Norman R. F. and A. R. Solem. "The Contribution of a Discussion Leader to the Quality of Group Thinking," *Human Relations,* 5:277–288, 1952.

Mann, John. "Didactic Use of Sociometry and Psychodrama: An Introductory Workshop on Group Dynamics," *Group Psychotherapy,* 7:242–243, 1954.

Zander, Alvin. "Group Membership and Individual Security," *Human Relations,* 11:99–111, 1958.

Chapter 9

Instructional Leadership

WHAT constitutes effective classroom leadership? Can the behavior patterns of effective teachers be distinguished? What are the effects of certain leadership practices upon interaction in classroom groups? These are recurring questions in education since the answers affect teacher training and teacher selection procedures. Unfortunately, conceptions regarding what constitutes effective teaching vary. This can be expected, since the topic of leadership in general is subject to disagreement and controversy. Educators, for the most part, do not view the act of teaching as leadership. They do not refer to teachers as leaders or examine the teaching job in terms of its leadership functions. Teaching, as performance, is more apt to be considered in terms of a set of teacher competencies or in terms of understandings and skills to be taught. Some social scientists, however, such as Hemphill, Cantor, Rogers, and Thelen, have viewed teaching as an act of leadership. Their view is that teachers are leaders and that the teaching job can be studied as a series of leadership acts or roles.

In a previous chapter, the unique combination of the characteristics of members of a group was shown to be one factor affecting class-group interaction. Perhaps leadership style has an even greater influence upon the group pattern of interaction. Considerable variations in classroom behaviors are produced by different leadership styles. The classroom leadership affects the emotional tone pervading the interaction. The ultimate aim of this chapter is to develop some understanding of the effects of various leadership styles upon the behavior of class groups. A subgoal of this chapter is to develop a kind of conceptual framework as a guide to the building of the idea that the acts of teaching are leadership acts. At the outset, therefore, let us explore some of the major viewpoints concerning leadership, and examine some of the conceptions relating to teacher performance and teacher effectiveness.

Leadership Concepts

Before examining various leadership concepts it is necessary to distinguish between leadership types. There are three different types of leadership: (1) the leader who achieves prominence because of some unique ability in a special field, (2) the leader who arises in an informal group situation, and (3) the leader who is assigned to a position of authority. Teachers are leaders of the last type; therefore, the theory and research relating to the first two types are not directly pertinent to the topic of instructional leadership, although there is considerable overlapping of viewpoints and all must be considered to some extent.

Identifying Leadership

The term "leadership" denotes a type of behavior with reference to a group. Sometimes leadership is discussed in terms of dominance, being then defined as an act or response that affects the attitudes or acts of others.[1] More specifically it has been defined as a process "whereby an individual directs, guides, influences, or controls the thoughts, feelings, or behavior of other human beings." [2] To some, leadership is a charac-

[1] Kimball Young, *Social Psychology*, New York: Appleton-Century-Crofts, 1956, p. 251.

[2] Franklin S. Haiman, *Group Leadership and Democratic Action*, Boston: Houghton Mifflin Company, 1951, p. 4.

teristic of an individual. To others it is a property of the group, the act of working through the group process to produce personality and social changes.

Some insist that the term leadership should apply only when the leader's influence is voluntarily accepted, or when it is in "a shared direction." [3] Then again, it is conceived as "the product of the interaction between the total personality of the leader and the dynamic social situation in which he has his being." [4] There are many other definitions, but the few given imply that leadership means something more than mere control or direction of a situation. These various definitions suggest, too, that there are a number of approaches to the problem of identifying or defining leadership.

Approaches to Leadership

One approach is to examine leadership according to its relationship to certain physical, intellectual, or personality traits. Those taking this position attempt to isolate certain specific personality tendencies and certain positive attributes of persons who are, or who eventually become, leaders. Although this aspect of leadership cannot be dismissed, the trait approach alone seems to be inadequate. When the studies are summarized, the findings of the investigators do not agree in most instances. Where they do agree, the differences between leaders and followers are small. A survey by Stogdill [5] covered over a hundred studies of "personal factors associated with leadership." He found there was agreement that leaders were above average in intelligence, scholarship, dependability, social participation, and socioeconomic status. However, other summaries have produced different lists which show that initiative, sense of humor, cooperativeness, and other traits are most characteristic of leadership. Part of this disparity comes from use of different terms. Many come from the use of different groups exemplifying different kinds of leadership.

Another way of viewing leadership is to examine leadership functions, or leader performance. Studies following this approach attempt to determine the general functions of leadership regardless of the type of group or situation. These functions are concerned both with task and nontask goals. The leader helps the group to establish goals and to progress toward these goals. The leader also helps the group to solve its

[3] Cecil A. Gibb, "Leadership," in G. Lindzey (ed.), *Handbook of Social Psychology*, Cambridge, Mass.: Addison-Wesley Publishing Company, 1954, p. 879.

[4] Hubert Bonner, *Social Psychology: An Interdisciplinary Approach*, New York: American Book Company, 1953, p. 399.

[5] Ralph M. Stogdill, "Personal Factors Associated with Leadership: A Survey of the Literature," *Journal of Psychology*, 25:35–71, 1948.

interpersonal difficulties and to maintain respect for individual members.

Hemphill [6] identified five functions of leadership common to any type of group. These were: (1) advancing the purpose of the group, (2) administration, (3) inspiring activity or setting the pace for the group, (4) establishing feelings of security and, (5) acting without regard for his own self-interest. The leader's function by this view is seen as a form of social interaction between an individual in the leadership position and the members of the group. Other studies have defined leader functions in a somewhat similar manner. The following requirements of the leadership act are based on a number of sources. They specify certain generalized functions of leaders and are applicable to the teacher's leadership role in the class group.

1. A leader formulates plans and policies consonant with the objectives and purposes of the group.

2. A leader analyzes, organizes, and helps the group carry out decisions and plans.

3. A leader creates and maintains group morale and solidarity.

4. A leader provides information and facilitates communication in the group.

5. A leader keeps individual purposes and activities in harmony with the group's purposes and goals.

6. A leader adheres to a consistent set of principles regarding expressions of approval and disapproval.

The behavioral or functional approach takes the view that the position the leader holds and the type of situation will determine the degree to which he carries out certain functions. Thus, while the above list can apply to the teacher in general, it does not indicate the extent to which a specific teacher takes a participatory role in specific functions or the extent to which he shares them with group members.

Another way of studying leadership is to examine the effects of certain styles or practices upon the performance and behavior of groups. Early studies were concerned with the effects of authoritarian, democratic, and *laissez faire* leadership upon group atmosphere or climate. Later studies are concerned with participatory or supervisory leadership and with their effects on accomplishment and group performance. These terms are used to describe roles fulfilled by leaders. Leadership in this sense means that the leader works with the group but responsibilities are shared. Leadership is then defined by the effect that an individual has upon group behavior; thus, leadership can be measured by the performance of the group considered as a totality.

[6] John K. Hemphill, "Situational Factors in Leadership," *Ohio State University Educational Research Monograph*, No. 32, 1949.

The idea of problem-solving leadership or participatory leadership has been explored by Cattell.[7] This approach is in line with some of the most recent research into the nature of leadership. Cattell views personality as consisting of behaviorally centered characteristics that can be measured. Thus the group leader can be described in terms of these measurable characteristics. Research has shown that participatory leadership has surpassed other methods in terms of the total effect upon the group. Groups studied have been shown to be more productive, more friendly, more highly cohesive, and more satisfied with work conditions when the leadership was participatory than when it was not.

Basic Factors in Leadership

In describing and analyzing leadership there are certain basic factors that must be considered. On the one hand, there are the factors within the act of leadership itself. That is, there are the attitudes, values, and other aspects of personality that affect the leadership act. On the other hand, situational and group factors must be taken into account. With respect to the first, it is necessary to know how the personality of the person placed in the position of leadership is organized, especially with regard to his concept of status and role. This seems to involve noting certain specific leadership traits needed in specific situations, such as the classroom. Attention certainly should be given to the nature or type of influence and control he believes he should exercise over others in particular kinds of situations. Then, too, he should be able to enact the major roles involved in communication—those of sending and receiving information and feeding back information to the group. In fact, the whole topic of personality traits or types needs to be examined in relation to the group and situational factors. Although research has not clearly defined this area, there does seem to be a relationship between basic personality types and the roles individuals enact as leaders of groups. The personality, the group, and the situational factors can be fully understood only by examining them together. Perhaps some background elements must be understood. With regard to this point, the background of a teacher, for example, may be quite important to an understanding of his present functioning. The background of a particular school situation, its organizational structure, and its functioning is important in understanding the interactional relations between the administrators and the teachers. For example, secure, independent, spontaneous personality types

[7] Raymond B. Cattell, "New Concepts for Measuring Leadership in Terms of Group Syntality," *Human Relations,* 4:161–184, 1951.

—persons who resist being managed—probably would not be effective leaders in rigid, authoritarian school situations. Another example would be a teacher with a dependent, rigid, and insecure personality who would not be effective in a school where the administration depends upon a participatory, self-directing staff.

The group and situational factors cover a wide range. They include such things as the size of the group, the nature of the organizational structure, and the stereotyped expectations held by the group members concerning leadership control. Although some persons tend to disregard the personality factor and consider leadership purely in terms of functions to be performed, it seems that personality, group, and situational factors must be taken into account. It seems that there are certain psychological elements that are particularly important in guiding group planning and group decision making, and in coordinating the activities of the group. Let us examine some of these group and situational factors.

The size of the group is an important factor affecting leadership functions. First of all, the social-distance factor operates differently in a large group from the way it does in a small group. In general, as the size of the group increases, the strength of affectional ties decreases. Each member may not feel as close to all the others in a large group. Then too, a group of large membership implies considerable individual differences among members. This means that the larger the group, the more adept the leader must be in developing and maintaining group morale. However, the larger the group and the more routine its operations, the greater the difficulty of assessing its morale and integration. It seems that group size cannot avoid affecting the extent to which the members of the group function as a unit and are free from dissension, conflicting interests, and disrupting forces.

The size seems to be an important variable too in influencing the relationship between leader behavior and the ratings members give regarding effective leader performance. One study found that the reported behavior of leaders who were rated as superior varied significantly with the sizes of the groups in which they functioned. The same study also showed that the members of large groups exhibited a significantly greater tendency than those of small groups to approve a highly structured type of leadership.[8]

Communication patterns are affected by the size of the group. The larger the group, the more skilled the leader must be in communicating and in guiding communication. Not only does the average amount of

[8] John K. Hemphill, "Relations Between the Size of the Group and the Behavior of 'Superior' Leaders," *Journal of Social Psychology*, 32:11–32, 1950.

participation per member decrease as group size increases, but the distribution of participation varies. Of course, the time available to each member for overt communication during a discussion period decreases as the group size increases, and there is apt to be less opportunity for members in the group to feed back questions or negative reactions. Accuracy and confidence are reduced for both the leader and the group members. If feedback is restricted, as it is in a large group, there is less opportunity for members to build understandings and norms by which the members manage their social relations, so social problems are more likely to develop than in a smaller group. Of course, restricted communication has an effect upon group and individual task performance as there is less understanding and acceptance of tasks.

Organizational structure is a situational factor that must be taken into account when leadership is studied. Organizations have cultural patterns that set down ways in advance for individuals to act. The organizational structures of schools, for example, define certain responsibilities and duties for teachers. But additional types of expectancies develop in the interrelationships of the administrators and the teachers. The teachers may be expected to keep a certain kind of "order." The program or equipment may be wanting according to teacher expectations. Class organization may be a source of problems. Classes may be too large, or the composition may be too heterogeneous or unbalanced. Another situational factor that affects the teacher as a leader may come from community demands, community tensions, or community disorganization. Any major community event ramifies into the school, through the administrators and to the teachers. In such situations, the teacher may be relatively powerless and impotent.

Just as the organizational structure and other situational factors set a framework within which the leaders are called upon to carry out their duties, so do individual limitations affect leadership. Some leaders may be limited in intellectual capacity; others may be skilled in certain techniques but unable to handle interactional situations. A particular individual's personality structure may not be suited to the demands of some particular situation, though it may be highly suited to different situational factors.

A teacher wrote the following report which illustrates differences in two school group situations. Although perhaps few teachers would react favorably to the first situation, there is evidence that some individuals work better and are happier in a work situation where the administrator sets the rules and clearly defines what is to be done. Others much prefer a less structured situation.

OPPOSITE SCHOOL SITUATIONS

If these comments sound like a comparison between principals, I do not mean it as such. It describes two exactly opposite situations in regards to attitudes and reactions of two school groups.

In one school where I was teaching the fourth grade, the principal had hard and fast rules with regards to pupils and staff. These rules were not flexible in any way to suit individual children or adults. The playground was supervised to death, so to speak—no freedom at all was felt by pupils or staff. Accident rate was high because everyone felt a constant stress and strain. The school group as a whole was frustrated by this constant pressure and was openly hostile and careless.

In another school, where I teach fourth grade now, the same rules prevail because it is the same district but . . . .

Here the principal administers these rules governing staff and children in a certain flexible way which constitutes no strain or stress on any individual under his jurisdiction. No one's individuality—either child or adult—is overlooked. The playground is supervised with minimum effort, the principal takes some of the playground duty to relieve the teachers. He is not weak in any way. The people involved carry out school policies because of the mutual liking established between everyone.

In the present situation, accidents are at a minimum. A very happy relationship exists in the whole school. Things are accomplished because everyone wants to do so. Pupils and staff cooperate on school policies.

The third situational factor that affects leadership is the group itself. The nature of the group affects leadership. To use a school group as an example, the culture pattern of the group must be understood. All unified school groups develop their own customs, rules, and play patterns. In some groups, acceptable, praiseworthy conduct is that of "talking back" or "sassing" the teacher. All school groups have strong feelings of what is "fair" or "unfair." It might be predicted that a teacher of a particular personality type and background might react in a way that would intensify a particular cultural pattern of a group, while another teacher would be more understanding and more able to use the group power to change the "unacceptable" customs.

Groups often hold stereotypes concerning how a leader should perform. Studies show that when leadership behavior violates the expectations of group members, dissatisfaction is created in the group.[9] Groups with highly urgent problems, for example, want direction from the

[9] Abraham Zaleznik, *Worker Satisfaction and Development,* Cambridge, Mass.: Harvard University, Division of Research, 1956.

leader.[10] Thelen and Dickerman [11] suggest that stereotypes about policies of operation often characterize groups. They identify the perceptions of members of groups at different stages of development, and they show what we have already stated: that group members hold stereotypes concerning how the leader should perform. One indication of these studies is that leadership style should be consistent with the expectations of group members.

Effects of Leadership Practice

A survey of the literature in elementary education shows that while "democratic" practices are generally advocated, these practices are seldom defined operationally. There is general agreement that before healthful social growth can take place, groups must live in a democratic atmosphere. Nevertheless, the practices that can produce a democratic classroom situation are described only vaguely. There is a tendency to equate directive leadership practices with autocracy and nondirective practices with democracy.

Some confusion arises from labeling teacher practices as "democratic" or "authoritarian." Since teachers are in positions of authority and have more knowledge than the groups they lead, it is sometimes maintained that they cannot assume a democratic role.[12] The issue is clarified somewhat by Miel,[13] who suggests that appointed leaders have responsibilities and functions to perform, and these might include directing the group when action is needed or taking steps to improve human relations. Democratic leaders, then, have power and use it when it is needed by the group, but these actions do not make the style autocratic.

Although teachers are given power and authority, it is skill rather than power that effective teachers rely upon most heavily, and skilled teachers do not attempt to force needless conformity to preconceived patterns. Power is not used in a coercive manner, although when a group difficulty requires immediate action, a teacher may have to be highly directive.

[10] Leonard Berkowitz, "Sharing Leadership in Small, Decision-Making Groups," *Journal of Abnormal and Social Psychology*, 48:231–238, 1953.

[11] Herbert A. Thelen and Watson Dickerman, "Stereotypes and the Growth of Groups," *Educational Leadership*, 6:309–316, February 1949.

[12] Franklin S. Haiman, *Group Leadership and Democratic Action*, Boston: Houghton Mifflin Company, 1951.

[13] Alice Miel, *Changing the Curriculum*, New York: Appleton-Century-Crofts, 1946.

Studies of Group Climate

In recent years the importance of the psychological atmosphere, or "climate," in which a group works has been strongly emphasized in educational literature, although experimental evidence that group climate affects productivity came first from industrial studies.

One of the most careful and systematic studies showing that group atmosphere was one of the most important single factors in increasing industrial production was conducted at the Hawthorne Plant of the Western Electric Company.[14] In a number of experiments investigating factors in production it was found that both control and experimental groups increased production. The research workers, in an effort to secure the cooperation of the workers in both the control and experimental groups, sought opinions and suggestions from members of both groups. This changed the normal authoritarian work situation and actually made radical changes in the psychological climate. The workers in both groups came to feel they were important because of the interest shown them by the research and administrative staff, and groups increased production even when very distasteful changes were made in their physical environments.

Other studies in industrial plants have considered the importance of the working climate of the group and have attempted to determine the important factors involved in climate. McGregor [15] considered the atmosphere in a work situation to be a major factor affecting the security of individuals; this, in turn, affected standards of performance.

It was felt that the atmosphere was created not by what the leader did but by the manner in which it was done, and by the leader's underlying attitude toward the individuals. Unless the atmosphere reflected genuine approval there was no security for the individuals. When the atmosphere was equivocal, or one of disapproval, group members had no assurance that their needs would be satisfied. In the absence of a genuine attitude of approval, members were fearful and insecure, and even neutral and innocuous actions of the superior were regarded with suspicion; effective discipline was impossible, high standards of performance could not be maintained, and resistance, antagonism, and ultimately open rebellion were the consequences.

[14] Fritz Roethlisberger and William J. Dickson, *Management and the Worker*, Cambridge, Mass.: Harvard University Press, 1939.
[15] Douglas McGregor, "Conditions of Effective Leadership in the Industrial Organization," *The Journal of Consulting Psychology*, 8:55–63, March–April 1944.

The experiments on autocratic and democratic atmospheres conducted by Lewin and coworkers [16] were based upon the hypothesis that the general atmosphere of the situation was, in the long run, more important for behavior and for development than even a single crucial experience. The ideology of the group determined to a high degree the goals, values, and styles of living of individuals, and the group atmosphere was determined by "leader style," or behavior of the leader.

Other studies have examined leader style and the effects of certain kinds of behavior upon the climate of the group. Flanders [17] investigated the student responses that were elicited by kinds of teacher behavior. The conclusions were that teacher behavior characterized as directive, demanding, or deprecating elicited student behavior of hostility, withdrawal, apathy, aggressiveness, and occasionally emotional disintegration. Teacher behavior characterized as acceptant, problem-oriented, evaluative or, in general, student-supportive, elicited student behaviors of problem orientation, decreased anxiety, integration, and occasionally emotional readjustment. It was concluded that the group-centered pattern of leadership created an atmosphere or climate most conducive to learning because there was a greater degree of group interaction. Where there was little interaction, the group climate might seem outwardly serene, but many individuals would give indications of feelings of insecurity.

Perkins [18] concluded that the quality of teacher-pupil relations was a major determiner of group climate. A number of implications for teacher-pupil relations were given. The initial set of feelings and relations that were established in the classroom appeared to determine the kinds and amounts of learning that followed. When the climate was group-centered, the members' reactions were more objective and problem-centered. The group climate appeared to determine the amount of learning that took place and was the key determiner of whether the emotional needs of the group were satisfied.

Studies have found that members of congenial groups were more accurate in perceiving "task-oriented behavior" in their group members than were members of noncongenial groups. Individuals in congenial groups were more accurate in social perception and were higher in task-motivation than were individuals in noncongenial groups.[19]

[16] Kurt Lewin, Ronald Lippitt, and Ralph K. White, "Patterns of Aggressive Behavior in Experimentally Created 'Social Climates,' " *Journal of Social Psychology*, 10:271–299, May 1939.

[17] Ned A. Flanders, "Personal-Social Anxiety as a Factor in Experimental Learning Situations," *Journal of Educational Research*, 45:100–110, October 1951.

[18] Hugh V. Perkins, "Climate Influences Group Learning," *Journal of Educational Research*, 45:115–119, October 1951.

[19] Ralph V. Exline, "Group Climate as a Factor in the Relevance and Accuracy of Social Perception," *Journal of Abnormal and Social Psychology*, 55:382–388, November 1957.

Another recent study examined the influence of the school and the interaction of the class group to determine the effects of each on climate.[20] It was found that it was the class as a unit or the conditions within the class that were largely responsible for the classroom climate. Classes with good climates had more social contacts. The children interacted socially more and expressed themselves more freely during the formal work of the classrooms than children did in classes with poor climates. Teacher-pupil rapport was better in the well-adjusted than in the poorly adjusted groups. The pupils and teacher interacted more, and the interaction was warm and friendly rather than aggressive or competitive. There was more interest and enjoyment shown by pupils, and when the pupils' role was clear, there was no confusion. Children were relaxed rather than tense. They were confiding and friendly rather than strained and fearful.

It was concluded that more desirable behavior is shown in the classes where the climate is good. Where the climate is poor, children are more distant from the teacher, are more disconnected as a social group, and have a poor attitude towards school as a whole. Also, there are indications that the type of classroom climate produced is not so much dependent upon the surroundings or the setting of a school but upon what goes on within the class. In general, the school surroundings and the home backgrounds of the pupils, as well as individual personal attributes of pupils and teacher have their influence; however, it is the interaction of these factors in a classroom situation that has more immediate relevance for the classroom climate and the learning process.

The study conducted by deGroat and Thompson [21] delineated the classroom atmosphere from the children's point of view. Pupils assessed teacher behaviors by nominating fellow students on such items as "Here is someone who is often praised for having his assignments done on time," "Someone whom the teacher often scolds for whispering," "Someone who is often praised," and similar statements. Twelve items involving teacher approval and twelve items involving disapproval were used with two sixth-grade groups. Four or five pupils in a typical classroom of thirty to thirty-five children received from 35 to 70 per cent of the total nominations for teacher approval, while four or five different pupils in the same classroom received 25 to 40 per cent of the nominations for teacher disapproval. The study indicated that some teachers, at least, aimed directives, questions, and comments to a few individuals more often than to members of the group as a whole.

[20] D. V. Connor, "Behavior in Class Groups of Contrasting Climate," *The British Journal of Educational Psychology*, 30:244–249, November 1960.

[21] Albert F. deGroat and George Thompson, "A Study of the Distribution of Teacher Approval and Disapproval among Sixth-Grade Pupils," *Journal of Experimental Education*, 18:57–75, September 1949.

An examination of the research into the effects of climate on group behavior indicates that group members behave differently in different kinds of social and emotional climates, and that leader behavior can alter the climate. Teachers and other group leaders whose underlying attitude is a concern for developing individual and group abilities create climates that are favorable to cohesiveness and self-direction; on the other hand, leaders whose underlying attitude or orientation to individuals and groups is to restrict behavior and to initiate all action themselves create conditions leading to (1) apathy and submission with much dependency and little self-direction or initiative, (2) hostility and rebellious behavior. Those leaders whose attitude is one of unconcern for the group and who ignore or fail to help individuals and groups achieve their goals create conditions characterized by general feelings of frustration and discontent, low cohesiveness, and low morale.

In classroom situations where conditions of good climate exist, there is opportunity for students to express themselves freely; moreover, studies show that teachers in such groups have skill in encouraging all group members to contribute freely. In a good climate, the teacher has skill in helping students to become interdependent rather than dependent entirely upon the teacher–leader. The control and influence techniques used in emergency situations, or when students have to be restricted because of limitations set by other groups, do not depend upon the use of authority, but upon the use of techniques that enable students to understand the situation and develop their own guides for action.

Teacher-Centered versus Group-Centered Leadership

Contrasting styles of leadership in classroom situations have been called "teacher-centered" and "learner-centered," or "group-centered."

To determine whether a class was teacher-centered or learner-centered, Withall [22] sought to develop an instrument whereby the social-emotional climate in a learning situation could be assessed by means of a categorization of teacher remarks and a description of the resultant pattern of statements. From the analysis of statements teachers made in classrooms, the climate of the situation was determined. A class was categorized as teacher-centered when the statements were directive, repressing, disapproving, disparaging, or defensive. A class was said to be learner-centered when the statements were clarifying or reassuring.

[22] John Withall, "The Development of a Climate Index," *Journal of Educational Research*, 45:93–100, October 1951.

A number of studies have contrasted experimentally the effects of leader-centered and student-centered teaching in small groups. Results of the studies have shown that in classes where responsible participation by the student was permitted and encouraged, academic learning proceeded about as usual when measured by conventional tests, but personal growth and adjustment improved significantly. Asch [23] experimented with leader-centered and student-centered groups and found that the student-centered group was significantly more satisfied with the group and the class than was the teacher-centered group, although the latter group made higher scores on an objective examination. In a similar experiment conducted by Faw,[24] members of the student-centered group preferred that technique to leader-centered practices and this group made higher grades on objective examinations than did their leader-centered counterpart.

A study was made by Bovard,[25] who organized two experimental groups differing in leadership technique. He found that the group-centered unit fostered verbal interaction and obtained the most conformity from members when the group demanded it. The leader-centered unit was restrained and members' perceptions were not altered to any great extent. The conclusion was drawn that a greater modification of perception could be obtained from group-centered classes than from leader-centered classes.

Further support for the superiority of group-centered teaching was found in a study by Rehage [26] in a teacher-group planning situation. This study covered a period of 30 weeks in two eighth grade social studies classes at the University of Chicago Laboratory School. In the experimental group the teacher and pupils worked out the specific objectives together and decided on the means to attain them.

When the results were analyzed, the experimental group was "markedly superior to the control group in their ability to discriminate between reasons that supported their choices of action and those that did not." The study showed that better working relationships could be effected more quickly in the pupil-teacher planning group than in the traditional teacher-oriented classroom.

The findings revealed also that well-defined subgroups persisted in

[23] Morton J. Asch, "Nondirective Teaching in Psychology: An Experimental Study," *Psychological Monograph 65*, No. 4, 1951.

[24] Volney E. Faw, "A Psychotherapeutic Method of Teaching Psychology," *American Psychologist*, 4:104–109, April 1949.

[25] Everett W. Bovard, Jr., "Group Structure and Perception," *Journal of Abnormal and Social Psychology*, 46:398–405, July 1951.

[26] Kenneth J. Rehage, "A Comparison of Pupil-Teacher Planning and Teacher-Directed Procedures in Eighth Grade Social Studies Class," *Journal of Educational Research*, 45:111–115, October 1951.

the control class, while subgroup structure in the experimental class modified perceptibly. The experimental group carried out some group projects that were suggestions of relatively low-status members, and these members also organized some of the group efforts. The experimental group developed an interest in cooperative work, and leadership roles were given and accepted with consideration of the requirements of a problem rather than on the basis of status alone.

The purpose of a study by Anderson and Kell [27] was to determine if quantitative and qualitative differences existed in attitudes about participation between student-centered and teacher-centered groups. They hypothesized that members of a student-centered group would tend to have more similar attitudes about themselves as participants than would members of a teacher-centered group. They assumed that in a student-centered group, the leader would encourage group interaction, which would tend to result in group cohesiveness, from which a common core of attitudes were developed, whereas in a teacher-centered group the instructor was more likely to interfere with the communication of ideas and expression of feelings, thereby reducing group interaction and cohesiveness.

The findings showed that the student-centered group had a tendency toward positive attitudes, and that the teacher-centered group revealed a significant split in attitudes, one constellation of attitudes implying self-confidence, a lack of defensiveness, and a desire for active participation, and the other constellation implying inactivity and anxiety about participation. From these results, the investigators concluded that more intragroup similarities in attitudes about participation could be expected in student-centered than in teacher-centered groups. The teacher-centered group also revealed more negativity. The student-centered group tended to facilitate changes in the direction of developing a core of positive attitudes. The teacher-centered climate tended to prevent changes in attitude.

In an investigation conducted in a college class, Bills [28] attempted to ascertain if students taught by the traditional lecture-discussion method differed in their understanding of the content of a course from a group of students taught in the student-centered method. From the findings of the study it was concluded that there was no significant difference in the knowledge of the course content between the two groups, but that the attitudes of students in the student-centered group toward the course

[27] Robert P. Anderson and Bill L. Kell, "Student Attitudes About Participation in Classroom Groups," *Journal of Educational Research*, 48:255–267, December 1954.

[28] Robert E. Bills, "An Investigation of Student-Centered Teaching," *Journal of Educational Research*, 46:313–320, December 1952.

were significantly more positive than those in the lecture-discussion group. Also, the opinions of the student-centered group revealed that they believed that the course was of personal value, but the students in the lecture-discussion group did not concur with this opinion.

A study by Wispe [29] challenged some widely accepted conclusions of group-centered teaching. The problem was to find:

(a) the effects of "directive" and "permissive" teaching,

(b) the reaction of students to the two kinds of teaching methods.

"Directive" teaching was defined as subject-centered, formal, and highly structured. "Permissive" teaching was student-centered, informal, and unstructured.

The findings showed that student-centered groups were characterized by student participation, student-director interaction, keen interest, humor, and mutual acceptance. The teacher-centered groups were more course-relevant, and displayed the other characteristics to a lesser degree. However, although the student-centered sections were enjoyed more, the teacher-centered sections were preferred by most of the students because they were clearly defined and because the students presumed they were aided more in preparing for examinations. The two groups showed no significant differences on the final examination when taken as a whole, but when the two teaching methods were examined for their effects on the students, it was found that the directive groups helped the poorer students more than did the permissive groups.

A survey of research of student-centered and teacher-centered leadership practices was conducted by McKeachie,[30] who concluded that experimental studies were not in agreement. He gave as examples the findings of two studies, one that showed that a student-centered class scored higher in achievement and another that showed that a teacher-centered group scored higher.

Those who analyze the controversy concerning group-centered versus teacher-centered methods generally conclude that those favoring the teacher-centered methods are more interested in course-related material and achievement scores while group-centered proponents are primarily concerned with individual development and emotional needs, hence the discrepancies in the findings.

The general research on leadership seems to indicate that one pattern of performance is not effective in all types of situations and with all

[29] Lauren G. Wispe, "Evaluating Section Teaching Methods in the Introductory Course," *Journal of Educational Research*, 45:161–186, October 1951.

[30] Wilbert J. McKeachie, "Student-Centered vs. Instructor-Centered Instruction," *Journal of Educational Psychology*, 45:143–150, 1954.

kinds of groups. The pattern used in any specific instance must suit the needs of the individuals at the time and take into account the nature of the situation.

Comparisons of Different Leader Styles

Because of the various interpretations given to the term "democratic" and because the research dealing with democratic leadership is often designed to provide empirical support for an ideological point of view, a number of researches have been conducted to determine what practices bring forth the best results without using the democratic or authoritarian base. The studies comparing different leadership practices demonstrate that it is possible to identify different styles of leadership and to determine the consequences of each style.

The findings of the study by Kahn and Katz [31] showed that effective leaders (in terms of productivity and morale) tended to delegate authority and decisions, and to develop group pride and cohesiveness. They helped the group to achieve goals as well as to maintain itself as a group. They found that good leaders possessed the skills and understandings necessary for performance of the group tasks as well as the ability to help members satisfy needs important to them.

An experiment conducted by Fox [32] attempted to determine the effects of variations in style of leadership. It was found that the "positive" group leader was able to achieve verbal unanimity by discouraging emotional conflict and involvement on the part of group members, by providing objective information, and by encouraging constructive compromise rather than "majority" rule. The "negative" leader was able to achieve verbal unanimity through persuasive imposition of ideas, by adroitly exploiting emotionalism, and by utilizing group social pressures.

The positive leadership style consistently required more time, but this style resulted in a group atmosphere that was more permissive and friendly, in greater member satisfaction with the leader, and in greater group member satisfaction and acceptance of group solutions. The results seemed to indicate that the positive leadership style had superior capacity to change the attitudes and behaviors of group members.

Another study comparing two contrasting styles of leadership found that a participatory type of leadership was more effective than a super-

---

[31] Robert L. Kahn and Daniel Katz, "Leadership Practices in Relation to Productivity and Morale," in Dorwin Cartwright and Alvin Zander (eds.), *Group Dynamics: Research and Theory*, Evanston, Ill.: Row, Peterson & Company, 1953, pp. 613–628.

[32] William M. Fox, "Group Reaction to Two Types of Conference Leadership," *Human Relations*, 10:279–289, 1957.

visory type in changing attitudes. Participatory leaders attempted to develop a good group climate, to encourage the expression of opinions from all members, and tried not to impose their opinions on the group. The supervisory leader used authority to see that certain group orders were carried out. The group members under the supervisory type of leadership not only did not change attitudes or opinions as readily, but they were less satisfied with the meetings.[33]

Two styles of leadership in discussion groups were examined to find if they would be differentially perceived by the group members.[34] The group discussion topic was concerned with a film the group members had viewed. One type of leadership was termed "directive," the other was called "nondirective." Briefly defined, the directive role required that the discussion leader serve as a professional "expert" for the group, interpreting and explaining points that were made in the film, responding directly to questions from the group, and venturing his own opinions whenever an appropriate occasion arose. In the nondirective situation, the leader refrained from interpreting the film, reflected questions and comments from individuals back to the group, and limited expression of his own viewpoint as much as possible. The effectiveness with which these contrasting roles were played was determined from examination of questionnaires completed by the group members at the conclusion of the discussions.

In the groups in which he played a directive role, the leader received significantly more favorable ratings than in those groups where he employed a nondirective approach. The directive leader was rated as significantly more interesting, frank, satisfying, purposeful, enlightening, industrious, and persuasive, and significantly less permissive, than the nondirective leader.

When the group members were classified as high or low participators, it was found that the low participators were distinctly more favorable to directive than to nondirective leadership. The high participators did not react in significantly different fashion to the two leadership conditions, although they also tended to be less favorably disposed to the nondirective leader.

There is considerable agreement that discussion groups are less satisfying to members when the leader does not play a directive role. It appears that unless the leader can skillfully guide the group, the members

[33] Malcolm G. Preston and Roy K. Heintz, "Effects of Participatory vs. Supervisory Leadership on Group Judgment," *Journal of Abnormal and Social Psychology*, 44:345–355, July 1949.
[34] Richard H. Page and Eliott McGinnies, "Comparison of Two Styles of Leadership in Small Group Discussion," *Journal of Applied Psychology*, 43:240–245, August 1959.

become involved with procedure and cannot devote their energies to discussing the topic. Again one might conclude from the above study that the type of leadership practice employed depends to some degree upon the situation and the nature of the group.

Marcus [35] investigated the question of how cohesion was related to: (a) the group-oriented leader and (b) the procedure-oriented leader. The subjects studied were members of a metropolitan welfare department. Cohesion was defined as "attraction to the group, including resistance to leaving it." An interview technique was used to provide information on the workers' attitudes toward the supervisors. It was found that workers under procedure-oriented supervisors were more cohesive, the reason being that the procedure-oriented supervisors were not liked. When the workers needed help they went to their peers. This interaction caused the groups to unify and develop their own norms. Workers under group-oriented supervisors felt freer to go to their supervisors and their expectations were more consistently met. The investigators concluded that negative feelings that were developed toward supervisors found expression in rebellion and the frustration led to greater cohesiveness. Positive feelings developed toward supervisors found expression in group harmony, but the members felt no need to form strong ties in order to defy the supervisor. Because of less interaction among members on the job, a group with a group-oriented supervisor will improve on the job and production is higher. Cohesiveness, while not disfunctional, may actually hinder efficiency if it is a reaction against the supervisor.

It must be mentioned that whatever style of leadership a group has, if for some members it is a style not consistent with their expectations, it will affect their reaction to the leader. The members may try to build a clique within the group, they may attack the leader, or they may refuse to do much of anything. For example, a case study that examined conditions that facilitated work groups was conducted by Zaleznik.[36] One of the conclusions stemming from the study was that failure of the group leader to behave according to expectations created uncertainty in the group and posed a learning problem. The formal leader's behavior became a source of constraint to the group when the group code of how a leader should behave was violated. Sufficient evidence was found to support the idea that even a minimum accommodation to the group process on the part of the formal leader went a long way in establishing a happy, comfortable work group. Here the "minimum" consisted of not

[35] Phillip M. Marcus, "Supervision and Group Productivity," *Human Organization*, 20:15–19, Spring 1961.

[36] Abraham Zaleznik, *Worker Satisfaction and Development*, Cambridge, Mass.: Division of Research, Harvard University, 1956.

preventing informal leadership from emerging, and not imposing tensions on members in their relation to the leader.

Sanford [37] concluded from a study of the leader-follower relation that followers developed both specific and general attitudes toward authority and the way it was exercised. In a concrete situation the attitudes and needs of the followers were background determiners of their reaction to the leader, but situationally determined needs were also present from time to time. It was observed that the more psychologically significant the group goal, the greater the emphasis upon the leader's competence to assist in achieving the goal. It was observed also that in groups where the goal was not highly important or visible, there was a preference for leaders who met psychological needs.

Leadership in the Classroom

Leadership has been defined in many ways, but by most definitions a teacher can be considered as a leader of the class group. One reason for the failure of educators to study the teacher as a leader and to examine the teaching act as a series of leadership functions may be because the terms "leadership" and "leadership practice" often connote dominance or force. Also, there is a prevalent belief that democratic teaching is a process of leading rather than directing. The fact is that a teacher must in a psychological sense direct and influence a class group in many areas, even though the recognition of this reality is often avoided by calling the acts initiated by teachers "teaching procedures" or "learning practices."

Even the most easy-going group discussion leader, supervisor, or teacher in some way influences and controls the behavior of others. There are various ways by which a teacher carries out the teaching assignment and helps pupils attain educational goals, but though the methods and degrees of directiveness and control vary with teachers and situations, teaching is an act of leading, and the teacher is a leader.

The Teacher As a Leader

A teacher is a person who occupies a position of responsibility in coordinating and organizing the activities of the members of the class group in their tasks of attaining certain educational goals. The functions the teacher performs are complex, but when the job is conceived as leadership, the many interrelated aspects are more susceptible to examination.

[37] Fillmore H. Sanford, *Authoritarianism and Leadership*, Philadelphia: Institute for Research in Human Relations, 1950.

For example, student and group responses to certain leadership practices can be explored. A particular leader practice can be viewed in terms of its effect on group morale and integration. This moves away from such indeterminate, hazy, nonspecifics as "atmosphere" and "climate," which are not easily translatable into terms indicating appropriate teacher behavior. When the teacher is conceived as a leader, it is easier to clarify the dimensions by which the teacher affects the members of the class group. Although research has not been able to relate *leadership*, in general, to any specific personality traits, leadership qualities and characteristics can be evaluated in the situational context of the classroom. Therefore, the teacher can be conceived as a leader, and several aspects of successful leadership can be identified. Applying knowledge of leadership characteristics to the prediction of teacher success in given classroom situations improves the quality of the predictions.

It is generally conceded that a prospective teacher must acquire understandings and skills relating to interaction of the teacher and individual pupils. Granted that this is important, this dyadic relationship must operate within the framework of the teacher's leading a group of thirty or more youngsters. Although teacher training emphasizes the teacher–pupil relationship, in actual practice teacher effectiveness is primarily judged by teacher success in leading the whole group. The ability of a teacher to lead and guide children singly toward educational goals is estimated by administrators and others as being of little value unless this skill is accompanied by the ability to relate to and to lead the entire class. The thesis presented throughout this book is that a successful teacher must demonstrate *versatility* as a competent class group leader. Unless a teacher can lead the group, it is very doubtful whether individual children in the group will be able to fully achieve the basic skills, understandings, work habits, or other educational goals for which the group was organized.

Since a teacher is placed in the position of being the formal leader of the group and is given power and authority to direct and guide the group, the theory and research relating to leader effectiveness in non-classroom organizational situations may be applicable to the classroom. Also, the theory and research should be of interest to those concerned with teacher selection and training, since leader practices have been found to produce the greatest effect on group interaction if selection and training are combined. This means that training and experience can aid persons placed in positions of leadership, although personality characteristics are related in a complex way to various leadership styles.

The general overall leadership pattern that characterizes a particular teacher usually reflects the behavioral goals of that teacher, whether the goals are in the subject area or in the area of social behavior. Some teachers, and laymen as well, believe "good" behavior is obtained by enforcement. They believe children and young people should be made to "mind." Children who are quiet, docile, and submissive, and who accept rules and regulations without question, are approved and rewarded. Those who exhibit other characteristics and who do not obey rules or who question the rules are disapproved and punished.

There are other teachers and laymen who desire well-behaved individuals and class groups, but in contrast to those who believe good behavior is achieved by enforced discipline, they wish to achieve socially desirable behaviors by developing attitudes and beliefs in the children so they tend of their own accord to behave in socially approved ways. The latter individuals, who believe that part of the teaching job is to help children develop desirable behavior patterns, usually recognize that enforcing conformity to rules and regulations does not change "poor" behavior patterns, nor does this practice develop "good" behavior. They recognize, also, that strong policing practices do not develop a respect for law and order or a respect for the rights of others.

Although it seems that many teachers are in the latter category as far as their deep-seated convictions are concerned, many of them use practices that are more consistent with the beliefs of the persons in the first category. There are several reasons for this apparent contradiction of belief and behavior. First, many teachers do not know how to develop or instill the attitudes and values that lead to socially desired and approved behavior. Second, teachers who receive classes that behave in undesirable ways do not know techniques for changing already established behavior. Finally, teachers are expected by the administrators and the community to require good behavior from the first day school is in session. They are not always given the time and opportunity to develop desirable behavior patterns. They are under constant pressure and this pressure is reflected in their control practices. Another factor enters into the picture. Not only do pressures stemming from the situation influence teacher practices, but preoccupations with personal problems and personal needs also influence the teacher's pattern of behavior. The factor of individual motivation on the part of the teacher should not be overlooked. The success of a teacher may depend upon whether he is motivated by ego-demands, a desire for dominance, prestige interests, or creative needs. For example, if the teacher desires or enjoys power to any great degree, it will be an important determinant of the practices that he employs in the classroom. When class groups develop behavior problems, some teachers take a calm, objective approach, while others become frustrated and their views of the situation are colored by personal needs and problems. The approach a teacher takes to group problems is influenced by his personal needs and basic attitudes.

The functions of leadership in the classroom are complex, for the teacher must function on a number of fronts. Within the complex pattern of the classroom the teacher must have positive social relations with the whole class group as well as an understanding of the abilities and weaknesses of each individual member. This requires *consideration and social understanding.* Certain standards of behavior must be maintained in the group so each individual child can perform to his potential. This dimension of teacher leadership might be called *integration.* Then, too, the teacher must be able to organize. *Organization* is a most important quality of teacher leadership, because the teacher's own work must be organized, as well as the work of the group and the work of each individual member. *Motivation* and *achievement* are further dimensions of instructional leadership. With the group, or with individuals separately, the teacher sets levels and standards of achievement. A final dimension might be called *social awareness,* or the ability to recognize the interaction processes in the group. These dimensions of teacher leadership—consideration, integration, organization, motivation, achievement, and social awareness—approximate Hemphill's [38] list of nine different dimensions of leadership.

Studies of Teaching Procedures

A number of investigations deal with a variety of aspects of leader practices in the classroom. The studies range from investigations of the effects of punitive practices upon children's behavior to the effects of rewards and positive evaluations. A number of these studies are examined at this point to show what research studies indicate are the effects of certain practices. It seems that the control practices discussed in educational literature often spring from a philosophical base—for example, teachers should be "firm but considerate," etc. The consequence of the philosophical orientation is that teachers can glibly state what should be done but have no clear understanding of what constitutes "firm" or "considerate" behavior, or the effects of certain teacher practices upon class behavior.

An exhaustive study by Anderson and collaborators [39] explored the effects of dominative practices upon individual children. The findings revealed that teachers using dominative practices received noncoopera-

[38] John K. Hemphill, "Situational Factors in Leadership," Columbus: Ohio State University Bureau of Educational Research, Monograph No. 32, 1949.

[39] Harold H. Anderson, "The Measurement of Domination and of Socially Integrative Behavior in Teachers' Contacts with Children," *Child Development,* 10:73–89, June 1939.

tive and conflictive responses from their pupils more often than did teachers using integrative practices. The dominating teachers tended to induce dominating roles among children in their relations with other children. Teachers whose behavior toward the children was integrative or cooperative tended to call forth cooperative conduct both in relation to the teacher and in relation to other children. This finding has been substantiated to a degree by other studies.

To determine the influence of punitive and nonpunitive teachers upon childrens' attitudes about school misconduct, Kounin and Gump [40] studied three elementary school first grade classes in a large city. Children in classes with punitive teachers were compared with those in classes of nonpunitive teachers. They found that children with punitive teachers placed greater emphasis on their misconducts. They stressed such factors as violations of school and classroom standards, while children with nonpunitive teachers were more concerned with such factors as not learning, achievement losses, and the like. The investigators concluded that compared with children who had nonpunitive teachers, the children with punitive teachers were apt to show more aggression in their conduct. They were more unsettled and were less concerned with learning and school values. They had less faith and less trust in the school, and therefore less tendency to internalize school values.

The study implies that the values and attitudes of teachers are reflected in the behavior patterns of the children in their classrooms. Punitive teachers tend to create a sense of guilt-feeling among children and this leads the children into counter-aggression. They are more conflicted in making rational distinctions about their misconducts. This tends to direct children toward placing their emphasis in negative areas, which hampers their adjustment and social growth.

Kindergarten classes were observed from the first day of school to determine how different types of control technique used by a classroom teacher affected the children who were disciplined and the children who were watching the behavior corrections.[41] The teacher's control techniques were classified in three ways:

1. Clarity   How clear were the teacher's instructions as to the behavior she wanted to stop? Was she general or specific? To what degree was she general or specific?

[40] Jacob S. Kounin and Paul V. Gump, "The Comparative Influence of Punitive and Nonpunitive Teachers upon Childrens' Concepts of School Misconduct," *Journal of Educational Psychology*, 52:44–49, February 1961.

[41] Jacob S. Kounin and Paul V. Gump, "The Ripple Effect in Discipline." *Elementary School Journal,* 49:158–162, December 1958.

2. Firmness	How firm was the teacher? Did the pupil know she meant it? Did she touch the child, walk close to him, conveying firmness, or did she gloss over the trouble lightly?
3. Roughness	Was the teacher rough? Did she express exasperation or hostility? Did she exert pressure behind her touch or give the child angry looks, etc? (There were no shakings or spankings.)

The findings showed that when a child clearly understood what was expected of him, he responded with more conforming behavior. When the situation was unclear to the child, the response was reversed. Firmness tended to be relevant, but the observers could not predict how a child would react when a firm technique was employed. Roughness was not followed by more conforming behavior. Instead, it was usually followed by more disruption. The watching child became upset as well as the child who was disciplined. It was found that children were highly sensitive to control techniques on the first day of school. The children outwardly reacted to over 50 per cent of all incidents involving discipline. The reactions lessened on following days. The investigators concluded that four factors affected the behavior of the child watching the disciplining: (1) how long he had been in kindergarten, (2) whether he was misbehaving at the time of the incident, (3) whether he was interested in the child being corrected, and (4) the disciplinary techniques used by the teacher.

An experiment in classroom management throws light on how older students respond to certain teacher practices.[42] The study explored the question of how the handling of one student's misbehavior affected the others in the group, although the group members themselves were not threatened or punished. The experiment was conducted in the following manner. Two classes were taught by a young instructor. Two other classes in the experiment were taught by an older professor of psychology. After each class's second meeting, the students in the class were given questionnaires which sought the students' opinions and attitudes regarding the instructor of the group, the cause of racial prejudice, and the seriousness of certain misbehaviors. During the third class period the instructor lectured on racial prejudice. A student, aware of the research, arrived very late to class. Each instructor used a supportive technique with one of his classes and a threatening technique with the other. In all cases the instructors first remarked that coming late to class interfered with the class and should stop. When using the supportive technique, the instructor went on to offer help to the student with material he had missed. The

[42] Paul V. Gump, Jacob S. Kounin, James J. Ryan, "Explorations in Classroom Management," *The Journal of Teacher Education*, 12:235–237, June 1961.

threatening technique stated that the student's grade could not help but be affected by his behavior. The attitude questionnaires again were given to the groups.

The threatening technique, for both instructors, resulted in significantly lowered judgments of the instructors' helpfulness, likeability, freedom from authoritarianism, and fairness. They also raised the amount of classroom tension.

For the young instructor—not the older one—differences in the two techniques produced significant changes in ratings of the instructor's competence in his subject-area and in the freedom of the students to communicate with the instructor. None of the students changed their attitudes towards the seriousness of the deviancy (coming in late), and all groups shifted toward the instructor's position on the cause of racial prejudice.

It appears from this study that the practices used toward deviants have effects upon the group as a whole, but that the prestige of the teacher is an important factor in those effects. If teachers must take action against students who misbehave, the approach should be supportive rather than threatening.

Ostlund [43] found that severe criticism by a teacher produced a negative atmosphere. The students responded by maintaining a high degree of integration, but the group did not perform well in this atmosphere. Little progress was made toward achieving the objectives of the class.

Goldberg [44] examined the effects of positive and negative evaluations upon some aspects of behavior in groups. Specifically he wished to determine: (1) if various kinds of evaluation have significant effects upon the manner in which individual group members subsequently evaluate each other, (2) the performance of groups under various conditions of evaluation, and (3) the influence of positive and negative evaluations upon group interaction processes.

The subjects were students in an introductory speech class. The groups were given certain tasks to perform after which they were evaluated on their performances. The various groups were evaluated either all positively or all negatively. Part of the experiment led the groups to believe the positive or negative evaluations came from members of their own groups. The results of the experiment showed that both positive and negative evaluations increased productivity and both groups became more process-centered. Intergroup solidarity increased in both groups;

[43] Leonard A. Ostlund, "Group Functioning Under Negative Conditions," *Journal of Educational Psychology*, 47:32–39, January 1959.

[44] Alvin Goldberg, "An Experimental Study of the Effects of Evaluation upon Group Behavior," *The Quarterly Journal of Speech*, 46:274–283, October 1960.

however, the negative evaluations created hostility and aggressiveness in the members. The evaluations of members themselves, termed "internal evaluation," stimulated group interaction. Subjects tended to be liked by those whom they liked. Whether the evaluation was positive or negative the group tended to show more interaction after having been evaluated, and they tended to re-evaluate their group in terms of the evaluation received. The change of action on the part of individuals seemed to be based upon how their group felt about them, for the groups evaluated by the experimenter were less affected. This seems to imply that group influences are greater than teacher influences. The findings seem also to support the evidence that a negative attitude in the group, whether caused by dislike of the leader or by negative evaluations, causes the group to interact more and to become more cohesive, although cohesiveness brought about by this means may not be conducive to the most productive work patterns in all cases.

Stendler et al.[45] studied the effects on the social atmosphere of a second grade group of working for group rewards as compared to individual rewards. The conclusions were that children's positive behavior was of a lower order when children were competing for an individual prize than when they were working together in a situation in which everyone received a prize or no one received one. An individually competitive environment was found to be conducive to unfriendly, negative behavior and poor work spirit, especially on the part of the children who knew that they could not win. Competition between groups was considered undesirable because it affected the social climate of the group as well as the work spirit of some group members. Deutsch's [46] results with college students also showed that cooperative groups had greater concern for fellow members and had a higher quality of product and discussion than did competitive groups.

Several studies have been concerned with the relationship of certain teacher behaviors and group productivity. Some have been concerned primarily with the techniques that produce the greatest learning and some have been concerned with opinion change. Cogan,[47] for example,

[45] Celia Stendler, Dora Damrin, and Aleyne S. Haines, "Studies in Cooperation and Competition: I. The Effect of Working for Group and Individual Rewards on the Social Climate of Children's Groups," *Journal of Genetic Psychology*, 79:173–197, December 1951.

[46] Morton Deutsch, "An Experimental Study of the Effects of Cooperation and Competition upon Group Processes," *Human Relations*, 2:199–232, 1949.

[47] Morris L. Cogan, "The Behavior of Teachers and the Productive Behavior of Their Pupils: I. Perception Analysis," *Journal of Experimental Education*, 27:89–105, December 1958.

found that the warm friendly teacher who tended to make the children central to classroom decisions and who used techniques that integrated the group was the type of teacher whose behavior produced the most and best work.

An attempt to improve the learning situation by "democratizing" pupil attitudes and behaviors was made by Cook.[48] As part of the experiment a group management approach was employed; instead of working with separate individuals within the group, the whole group was used as the target for change.

Cook assumed that group cooperation could not be taught by a teacher who merely sat and listened, nor could it be taught by one who did all the talking. The group must be given the power of decision, the teacher guiding its use of this power in the best interest of all the class members. Such a concept of the teacher role was patterned after Lippitt's "democratic group leader." In this role, the teacher guided the class group leaders and helped them to make choices. When projects were endangered, the teacher intervened so education in the group process could proceed. Although the aim of the study was to help the group learn to work together as a self-directing team, the procedures used had the safeguard of intervention and control by the teacher when it seemed necessary.

The study did not claim to have democratized the group, but it was found that the methods produced a more stable group structure and an increased volume of social interaction.

Ray[49] found that the pupil discovery method of teaching enabled students to transfer their knowledge to other situations. Dawson[50] showed that group planning and committee work and the use of group decision to set goals was a highly productive method of teaching in the area of social studies. Kipnis[51] compared participatory leadership and lecture leadership in fifth and sixth grade classes and found that participatory leadership influenced more children to change opinions than did lecture leadership.

A teacher who sets out to persuade a class to shift opinion by using a "divide and conquer" technique—that is, talking to certain students and

[48] Lloyd Allen Cook, "An Experimental Sociographic Study of a Stratified 10th Grade Class," *American Sociological Review*, 10:250–261, April 1945.

[49] Willis E. Ray, "Pupil Discovery vs. Direct Instruction," *The Journal of Experimental Education*, 29:271–280, March 1961.

[50] George G. Dawson, "An Experience in Teacher–Pupil Planning," *Social Education*, 24:325, November 1960.

[51] David Kipnis, "The Effects of Leadership Style and Leadership Power upon the Inducement of an Attitude Change," *Journal of Abnormal and Social Psychology*, 57:173–180, September 1958.

ignoring the rest—is apt to be successful, but this practice also creates much resistance. A study by Flanders and Havumaki [52] showed that when friendly authoritarian teachers used the "divide and conquer" method, the growing group cohesiveness released inner resistance, thus forcing further teacher dominance and still greater class resistance, but when teacher and class goals were the same, teacher efforts were supported by the development of group pressure and the strongest influence forces were created.

It has been noted that attempts to exert pressure on groups to change behavior after group standards have already been established have met with decided resistance. Hartley and Hartley [53] concluded that when groups were punished for maintaining their set standards, the experience tended to weld the group more closely together. If individuals were punished for behaving according to accepted group standards, it evoked group sympathy for the individual sustaining the punishment; this generally satisfied the individual enough to render the punishment useless. Moreover, punishment of the group generally provoked enough support to counteract any pressure the punishment might have been designed to exert.

Studies of Teacher Effectiveness

For many years educators have been concerned with finding the important determiners of teacher effectiveness in the classroom. The broad, general areas that have been examined relate to teacher personality, the tasks and functions of the teacher, and the effects of teacher practices upon the behavior of their class groups. In spite of the numerous studies that have been conducted, the answers to the questions, "What constitutes effective teaching?" and, "What characteristics distinguish competent teachers?" have not been answered satisfactorily.

A major research study of teacher characteristics was prepared by Ryans [54] for the American Council on Education. The primary aim of the inquiry was to identify, analyze, and describe patterns of teachers' classroom behavior, their attitudes, viewpoints, and intellectual and emotional qualities. Three clusters of observable teacher behavior were (1) understanding and friendly versus egocentric, aloof, and restricted

[52] Ned A. Flanders and Sulo Havumaki, "Group Compliance to Dominative Teacher Influence," *Human Relations*, 13:67–82, 1960.

[53] Eugene L. Hartley and Ruth E. Hartley, *Fundamentals of Social Psychology*, New York: Alfred A. Knopf, 1955.

[54] David G. Ryans, *Characteristics of Teachers*, Washington, D.C.: American Council on Education, 1960.

teacher behavior; (2) responsible, systematic, and businesslike versus unplanned, evading, and slipshod teacher behavior; and (3) imaginative, stimulating, and enthusiastic versus dull and routine teacher behavior. The first two, which had most influence on children, are closely related to two major personality factors, extraversion–introversion and anxiety–stability. The contribution of this research is in the knowledge of patterns of behavior that relate to teacher effectiveness.

A study by Flanders [55] makes use of the interaction technique for classifying teaching behaviors. He identifies two categories of teacher talking: one is termed "direct influence," which includes giving directions, justifying authority, and lecturing; and the other is termed "indirect influence" and includes clarifying student ideas, asking questions, giving praise, and using student feeling constructively. In the study, the interaction technique provided feedback to teachers, and Flanders stated that there were significant changes in the classroom behaviors of the participating teachers during the study. He believes that feedback about their performance does bring about changes in teacher behavior.

A study of teachers' behaviors in the classroom while they were teaching and of the effects of the behaviors was reported by Medley and Mitzel.[56] Their prime focus was on the behavior with its related effects, rather than on personality. Their thesis is that what the teacher needs to know to improve his teaching and to achieve competence is what effect each teaching behavior has, so he can then modify his behavior to most efficiently achieve his purposes. The investigators were aware that the same behavior does not always have the same effects. Their research framework incorporates the setting and situation in which a behavior occurs and who exhibits it as related factors in the effects of behavior.

Heil and Washburne [57] studied teacher effectiveness to determine if certain changes took place in children under the influence of teachers and if there was a relationship between these changes and the types of children and teachers. A child population of 55 classes of fourth, fifth, and sixth grades was used with representation of low, intermediate, and relatively high socioeconomic statuses. From tests and observation of the teachers, clusters of traits were noted and three profiles, A, B, and C, were made. The children were tested and four categories arranged.

One result of the study cited by the investigators was that children

[55] Ned A. Flanders, "Using Interaction Analysis in the Inservice Training of Teachers," *Journal of Experimental Education*, 30:313–316, June 1962.

[56] Donald M. Medley and Harold E. Mitzel, "A Tentative Framework for the Study of Effective Teacher Behavior," *Journal of Experimental Education*, 30:315–320, June 1962.

[57] Louis M. Heil and Carleton Washburne, "Brooklyn College Research in Teacher Effectiveness," *The Journal of Educational Research*, 55:347–351, May 1962.

in all four categories made significantly more academic progress under Type B teachers, who were work-oriented, orderly, and self-controlling. These teachers, probably because of the clarity and structure regarding work to be accomplished, were especially effective with "opposing" and "wavering" children. The results of the Ohio Social Acceptance Scale indicated that children of all types with a Type B teacher also became significantly more friendly toward one another than did children with either of the other two types of teacher. The explanation offered was that the children felt secure due to the structuring and ordering tendencies of the teachers. The data revealed that teachers of Type A, impulsive, variable, and turbulent, obtained different results with different kinds of children. Children who were classified as "opposing" and "wavering" showed little growth under teachers of this type. The pupils with a Type C teacher, anxious, fearful, and unsure of herself, made smaller academic gains than did the pupils of the other two types of teacher. The investigators believe that teacher personality is an overriding factor in determining children's academic achievements.

The evidence from several studies of good and poor teachers was summarized and compared by Peronto [58] in an attempt to discover the patterns or clusters of characteristics that appear to be associated with effective teaching and the variations in the amounts of these characteristics that appear to be associated with teaching success or failure. He concluded that in certain qualities there was evidence of measurable differences between good and poor teachers and in other qualities there was little difference. From the studies he examined, Peronto found varying degrees of measurable difference in these seven qualities: academic and professional knowledge, interest and proficiency in teacher–pupil relationships, physical and emotional energy, emotional stability, motivation, flexibility, and dominance. Problems arising from the use of inadequate criteria and of measuring devices of questionable reliability make the evidence inconclusive. The effects of situational factors on the qualities need to be studied in future research.

Questions for Study and Discussion

1. There are diverse opinions on whether a leader can help a group achieve its task goals and also help a group maintain itself in the social-emotional, or affectional, areas. Discuss the possibility of a teacher meeting one or both needs at the age-grade level in which you are interested.

[58] Archie L. Peronto, "The Abilities and Patterns of Behaviors of Good and Poor Teachers," *Journal of Experimental Education*, 30:88–98, September 1961.

2. To what extent should a teacher show consistency in leadership behavior?

3. Are there similarities in leadership for classroom teachers and for other educators? Differences?

4. What effects do the leadership expectations of the students have on the teacher's behavior?

5. Have you seen or been a member of a group in which a leader gave no help or direction (sometimes called "laissez faire")? How, if at all, did the group organize, make decisions, and achieve goals?

6. What should be the function of the teacher–leader in situations of severe stress or panic? Clearly outline the position that will guide your actions in such situations.

7. "It is incorrect to stereotype a leader as being one type or another." Discuss.

8. Define group-centered or participatory leadership, including your statement of what it is, how it functions, and its results or values.

9. What are some of the functions that are appropriate to the teacher–leader in the classroom situation? Be as specific as possible by preparing your answer in outline, list, or brief descriptive form.

10. Contrast two teachers that you would consider "autocratic." How were they alike and how were they different? What was the effect of each on individuals and on the group?

Suggestions for Further Reading

Bell, Graham B. and Harry E. Hall, Jr. "The Relationship Between Leadership and Empathy," *Journal of Abnormal and Social Psychology,* **49**:1, January 1954.

Carter, Launor F. "Leadership and Small-Group Behavior," in Muzafer Sherif and M. O. Wilson (eds.), *Group Relations at the Crossroads.* New York: Harper, 1953.

Carter, Launor F., W. Haythorn, B. Shriver, and J. Lanzetta. "The Behavior of Leaders and Other Group Members," *Journal of Abnormal and Social Psychology,* **46**:589–595, October 1951.

Dawson, George G. "An Experience in Teacher–Pupil Planning," *Social Education,* **24**:325, November 1960.

Deutsch, Morton, Albert Pepitone, and Alvin Zander. "Leadership in the Small Group," *Journal of Social Issues,* **4**:2, 1948.

Flanders, Ned A. and Sulo Havumaki. "Group Compliance to Dominative Teacher Influence," *Human Relations,* **13**:1, 67–82, February 1960.

Gibb, Cecil A. "Leadership," in Gardner Lindzey (ed.), *Handbook of Social Psychology.* Cambridge, Massachusetts: Addison-Wesley, 1954.

Guetzkow, Harold S. *Groups, Leadership, and Men.* New Brunswick, New Jersey: Rutgers U., 1951.

Haigh, Gerald V. and Warren Schmidt. "The Learning of Subject Matter in Teacher-Centered and Group-Centered Classes," *Journal of Educational Psychology*, 48:295–301, May 1957.

Haiman, Franklin S. *Group Leadership and Democratic Action*. Boston: Houghton, 1951.

Hemphill, John K. *Situational Factors in Leadership*. Columbus, Ohio: Ohio State University Bureau of Educational Research, 1949.

Hoffmann, Randall W. and Robert Plutchik. *Small-Group Discussion in Orientation and Teaching*. New York: Putnam, 1959.

Kounin, Jacob S. and Paul V. Gump. "The Comparative Influence of Punitive and Non-punitive Teachers upon Children's Concepts of School Misconduct," *Journal of Educational Psychology*, 52:44–49, 1961.

Leeds, Carroll H. "Teacher Behavior Liked and Disliked by Pupils," *Education*, 75:29–37, September 1954.

Lewin, Kurt, Ronald Lippitt, and R. K. White. "Patterns of Aggressive Behavior in Experimentally Created 'Social Climates,'" *Journal of Social Psychology*, 10:271–299, 1939.

Lewin, Kurt, and Ronald Lippitt. "An Experimental Approach to the Study of Autocracy and Democracy," in A. Paul Hare, E. F. Borgatta, and Robert F. Bales (eds.), *Small Groups: Studies in Social Interaction*. New York: Knopf, 1955.

Lifton, Walter M. *Working With Groups*. New York: Wiley, 1961.

Lippitt, Ronald and R. White. "Leader Behavior and Member Reaction in Three Social Climates," in Dorwin Cartwright and Alvin Zander (eds.), *Group Dynamics*. Evanston, Ill.: Row, 1953.

Mass, Henry S. "Personal and Group Factors in Leaders' Social Perception," *Journal of Abnormal and Social Psychology*, 45, 1950.

Mackenzie, Gordon N. and Stephen M. Corey. *Instructional Leadership*. New York: Bureau of Publications, Teachers College, Columbia University, 1954.

Petrullo, Luigi and Bernard M. Bass (eds.). *Leadership and Interpersonal Behavior*. New York: Holt, 1961.

Ross, Murray G. and Charles E. Hendry. *New Understandings of Leadership*. New York: Assn. Pr. 1957.

Stogdill, Ralph M. "Personal Factors Associated with Leadership," *Journal of Psychology*, 25, 1948.

Stogdill, Ralph M. "Leadership, Membership, and Organization," *Psychological Bulletin*, 47:1–14, January, 1950.

Stogdill, Ralph M. *Individual Behavior and Group Achievement*. New York: Oxford U. Pr. 1959.

Thelen, Herbert, and Watson Dickerman. "Stereotypes and the Growth of Groups," *Educational Leadership*, 6:309–316, 1949.

Trow, William Clark. "The Value Concept in Educational Psychology," *Journal of Educational Psychology*, 44:449–462, 1953.

Utterback, William E. *Group Thinking and Conference Leadership: Techniques of Discussion*. New York: Rinehart, 1950.

Utterback, William E. *Group Thinking: A Workbook for Use in Discussion Courses.* New York: Rinehart, 1953.

Wrightstone, J. Wayne. "Measuring the Social Climate of a Classroom," *Journal of Educational Research,* 44:341–351, January 1951.

Young, Kimball. *Social Psychology.* New York: Appleton, 1956.

Chapter 10   # Frustration

CLASSROOM groups, in the course of their daily interaction and association, face many conditions involving frustration. Groups constantly seek to maintain a state of balance in their social interactions. To maintain this internal balance, the group environment imposes restrictions and demands that require change and adaptation. If blocking or frustration intervenes, the group must adopt a problem-solving technique to attempt to reduce the frustration.

In this chapter an attempt will be made to probe into some of the classroom group reactions to frustration. The nature of frustration is examined, and situations involving reactions to frustration are explored. The principal concern of the discussion, however, is to develop some understanding of why groups behave as they do in some instances, and to thus make it possible to prevent many of these behaviors or to help class groups make more suitable adjustments.

Nature of Frustration

This section has several dimensions—the exploration of the frustration concept and its relationship to groups; the examination of related concepts and different conditions affecting frustration; the noting of the factors contributing to frustration; and the illustration of the various aspects of frustration, using classroom examples. The means by which teachers may deal with the problem of frustration in classroom groups is left for another chapter.

Frustration Defined

Frustration is commonly defined in two ways. First, it is seen as a psychological state resulting from or accompanying failure to reach a goal or blocking of efforts to achieve a goal. Second, frustration is defined as a drive related to or induced by such failure or blocking of goal-directed behavior.

In the first definition, an individual child, engaging in activities in which he is interested and in which he is trying to succeed, meets and struggles with barriers or opposition. The opposition may take the form of rules, standards of behavior, the activities, desires and interests of others, or his own inadequate or immature abilities. A condition or action that interferes with the desired success is known as *frustration*. Sometimes the desired success is avoidance; in that instance, the failure to avoid a situation, person, activity, or whatever, is frustrating.

Frustration occurs for groups as well as for individuals. A group is frustrated when it has a goal, a plan of action, and enough cohesiveness and group morale to move toward its achievement but is blocked from the desired success because of a barrier or obstacle. According to this viewpoint, frustration for the group, as for the individual, has many causes. These may include inadequate abilities in the group, lack of resources or materials, conflicting rules or standards, etc. Some of the frustrations are relatively mild and easily overcome, while others may be so difficult that the group efforts to overcome them may be of little avail. They vary in intensity. The amount, duration, and intensity determine the extent of the tension that results.

Frustration as a drive is similar to the "internal state" idea of Brown and Farber [1] which includes the hypothesis that frustration adds to total

[1] Judson S. Brown and I. E. Farber, "Emotions Conceptualized as Intervening Variables—With Suggestions Toward a Theory of Frustration," *Psychological Bulletin,* 48:465–504, 1951.

drive or motivational level. Frustration is believed to "stir the person up," thereby adding a certain amount of drive to that which he already has. In some cases, frustration, as an added motivation, may be irrelevant in that it is not related to the original motivation—that is, the motivation that initiated the sequence of behavior.

As drives, or as additional drives, frustrations may cause a group to change its behavior. For example, the goal of a class may be to achieve high average score for the class in a subject, or it may be to put on a successful assembly program. Any happening or condition that frustrates the group may cause it to expend further effort on the same line of strategy. Or, the drive toward the goal may be changed if the change seems most promising for achieving the group's objective. In other words, the drive resulting from the blocking may cause the group to persist or to alter or to completely revise its behavior.

Maier's explanation of the frustrated person's behavior is that it is without a goal.[2] According to him, the frustrated person's behavior becomes goal-less when frustration is severe and prolonged. Task-orientation then disappears. Maier raises interesting hypotheses about the effect of the difficulty of the learning problem and persistent, rigid responses, and the use of guidance at early stages to minimize fixated responses.

Frustrations are not necessarily "good" or "bad," although typically they carry a "bad" connotation. This is probably because failure, not getting whatever is sought, is implied in the term *frustration*. The barriers or blocks that are effective in thwarting or delaying achievement are part of the failure. However, analysis of "frustration," and the attendant "failure," has led to conclusions that differ from the stereotypes. Although hopeless or prolonged frustration, especially in important personal and social areas, may have serious effects, so will failures that have no alternatives for partial or complete success.

Groups that experience severe or prolonged frustration resort to adjustment processes just as individuals do when they are frustrated. Much of what teachers view as misbehavior and nonconformity to accept standards for behavior in the classroom is the result of group efforts to adjust to frustration. Many class groups misbehave because they are continually frustrated by too much pressure, inconsistent discipline practices, unreasonable demands, and so forth. The adjustment processes may involve only subgroups, or they may involve the total group. Thwarting and frustration lead to such emotional reactions as hostility, aggression, apathy, withdrawal, and other reactions. Anxiety may be expected to result from frustration, and tensions may be expected to build in the

[2] Norman Maier, "Frustration Theory: Restatement and Extension," *Psychological Review*, 63:370–388, 1956.

group. Groups make many adjustments to reduce feelings of frustration and anxiety, and they adapt a number of behaviors to counteract stress. Many of the behavioral incidents that are reported in this chapter reveal group reactions to frustration and ways groups have adjusted to frustrating situations.

Factors Involved in Frustration

The job of developing a better understanding of why children in classroom groups behave as they do is made easier by taking a look at some of the factors involved in the frustrations found in classroom groups. Groups have needs much as individuals have needs. Some behaviors exhibited by groups are the results of internal forces operating inside the group. Other behaviors are the result of external forces exerting pressures on the group, such as the requirements of the school, the expectations or demands of the teacher, threats stemming from other groups, and many others.

A group becomes frustrated when needs, such as the need to communicate, are blocked, or the need for status is withheld, or the desire to reach a goal is thwarted. Frustrations that threaten the satisfaction of a group's needs are difficult to identify. They involve behavior that is highly complex, and a number of factors or elements are involved. For example, some groups tolerate frustration better than others. Both the ages of the members and the length of time a group has been in existence affect the way the group will react to frustrating situations.

SOURCES OF CLASS GROUP FRUSTRATION. There are several general sources of group frustration. One source stems from conflicts occurring within the group. If member viewpoints seem irreconcilable when choices are required in selecting goals and proposed forms of actions, frustration usually results since the group cannot move toward goal attainment. A second source of frustration arises from inadequacy or lack of ability to achieve desired goals, or it may be that the goals selected by the group are unrealistic in terms of the group's abilities. A third source of frustration comes from the environment, which can be limiting, deficient, or lacking.

The frustration aroused by these various sources results in different responses in different groups. For example, some class groups go to pieces when the schedule for the day is changed unexpectedly, while others adapt easily and smoothly to the same change. Some groups become upset and anxious by an examination, or even by the prospects of a test, while other groups are not affected to any great degree. Class groups react with different behaviors to many kinds of conditions, such as prospects of failure in competitive situations, difficult and lengthy assignments, time limits set for completion of tasks, inconsistent or authoritarian leadership practices, deprivations of various kinds, and many other situations.

Group goals may be a source of hostility and frustration. The lack of goals; lack of means to achieve them; ambiguous, difficult, or distant goals are all possible frustration points for groups. In an experiment with groups of well-adjusted boys, eleven or twelve years old and of homogeneous backgrounds, conditions of friction were introduced. When the two groups had conflicting goals and only one group could achieve its aims at the expense of the other, the groups became hostile toward each other. Further, in the face of such goal conflict and intergroup hostility, morale and cooperativeness within each group became stronger. Solidarity within the groups increased, but these feelings did not carry over to the groups' relations with other groups.[3]

Ambiguous situations and expectations are a frequent source of frustration for classroom groups. There may be ambiguity of the problem, the means, or the desired goal or achievement. Problem behavior that appears irrational and difficult for teachers to control may come from lack of clear understanding by the group.

In the following incident the class understood the goal and wished to attain it, but the lack of contest rules left them with little or no knowledge of how to proceed.

TRIP TO THE ZOO

A contest was put on in our school system by a club of civic leaders. The prize for the best city cleanup plan offered by a class was to be a paid trip on the train for a day at the zoo. The announcement gave the closing date and the place to turn in entries, but no further instructions or rules.

The sixth grade found out that the fifth grade in our school had incorporated in their plans some of the ideas the sixth grade intended to use. They waylaid some fifth graders on their way home from school and told them they would beat them to a pulp if they used their (the sixth grade's) ideas. The fifth graders stood their ground and charged that the sixth graders had stolen *their* ideas! A fight was averted by the chance appearance of one of the teachers.

The sixth graders then got the idea that they would send out spies to find out what other classes in other schools were doing. By checking among their members they found some children who had contacts in Sunday School and elsewhere with children from other schools. They proposed in this way to find out what other schools were planning to submit for the contest.

[3] Muzafer Sherif, "Experiments in Group Conflict," *Scientific American*, 195:54-58, November 1956.

When the teacher learned what was going on, she announced that the group could not be in the contest. Interest in the project dropped, and the class was crestfallen. In a few days, fights began in subgroups. The teacher had a difficult time.

Tests as a source of frustration are cited by teachers at many grade levels. A teacher of high school social studies reported the following class reaction.

IMPOSSIBLE CHOICES

Today was the beginning of the Interest Inventory Test, a part of the vocational unit. The test questions were of the forced-choice variety. After the monitors had distributed the tests and the instructions had been reviewed, the class quietly and calmly went to work.

Then it happened. The class "show-off" remarked loudly, "These are impossible! I don't like either one! Now what do I do? I'd rather go to jail than do either!!"

A sudden rash of giggles, laughing, remarks, quips, etc., broke out all over the room just as if an explosion had occurred.

Boredom with routines, with assignments, and with lack of a normal amount of interest and excitement in school work and life leads to frustration. It is not always severe enough, however, to cause group problem behavior for the teacher.

TOLERANCE OF FRUSTRATION BY A GROUP. All classroom groups experience frustrations from the earliest kindergarten and primary years through the oldest classes in the educational system. School routines—time schedules, prescribed ways of moving from place to place, requirements of quiet, and curricular expectations—are all possible sources of frustration. Group members learn the expectations and the associated behaviors. They learn and accept some rather quickly and easily, and these present little apparent difficulty from the standpoint of the school. The behavior may be interpreted as group tolerance of frustration. The possibility of frustration from the many common delays and interruptions that are part of any school day is always present, but there is growth in the tolerance of such frustrations. Though the curricular requirements pose frustrations, groups will tolerate drills, repetitions, and tasks they may consider dull and uninteresting. Groups also tolerate frustrations in difficult conceptual learning to different degrees and in different ways.

AGE AND REACTION TO FRUSTRATION. The chronological ages of the members of the group bear some relation to the situations that frustrate them. With age and experience, previously frustrating conditions come to be accepted. They may even become perceived as necessary. The requirements for promptness, neatness, and quietness, which with the beginning primary groups may cause group problems, later are seen by children as prerequisite to other things the group wishes to do or to achieve. They are no longer paramount in causing frustration as they become learned and habitual ways of behaving.

Kindergarten children may dislike having their play activities stopped by the opening school bell with the expectation that they immediately assemble in a designated place, are quiet, and give attention to the teacher. Most groups learn to respond quickly to this situation. They may show disapproval by making remarks to children who delay in meeting this requirement. The situation that was for a brief time a frustration becomes accepted. They will, however, show frustration reactions toward delays, or toward their inability to manipulate some materials, throughout the kindergarten year and into the primary grades and even later.

In groups with older members there is a change in the type of frustration-producing situation, with a shift that corresponds to the values of the developmental level. As academic achievement, for example, becomes more important, grades and grouping become potential sources of frustration.

At times, the whole group may react to frustration brought about because of an assignment or a change in teaching practice. The teacher of the class of middle grade children in the following incident was conscious that his procedure caused the group reaction. However, class behavior is not always so recognized by teachers.

A SPELLING TEST

Usually I prepare my class for tests by telling them what will be included, suggesting that they review or by having a class review. I always tell them when I will give the test. The other day I found that I had forgotten to announce the spelling examination that was due, but decided to go ahead and give them the hundred-word test without warning. As I was pronouncing the words, I noticed that about half of the class members were not writing any of the words that I was pronouncing. They had given up and were just sitting. The examination was just a waste of time.

A child with learning difficulties may become frustrated when he tries to cope with his inability to understand. When the whole class is composed of children who have learning problems, the situation, of course, is multiplied. To be handed an assignment which is too difficult and then be told to work it out without teacher help is highly frustrating. A class group may react in differing ways to this situation. A large number may act detached as if they did not care. They may spend the period "playing around," and this attitude may affect the behavior of others in the class. On the other hand, they may react to this frustration by developing other behavior disorders, as did the class in the next example. It may be noted that the junior high school teacher in this case may also have been frustrated. His attitude toward the group was one that is very apt to create a hostile group reaction.

A RESENTED ASSIGNMENT

I made an assignment to my slow seventh grade math class. The assignment was a page of thought problems that the students had to be able to read in order to do the problems. The reading wasn't too difficult if the youngsters put their minds to it.

After about three minutes the whole class was up at my desk wanting to know how to work the first problem. When I told them to sit down and figure it out, they were very unhappy.

Five minutes later the class was a mad-house. Children began to act up and pester their neighbors; some became irritated, and some sullen. The class as a whole was upset and irritated, and showed their resentment toward the assignment by acting as if the whole situation was entirely my fault.

It appears in this incident that the teacher was, in fact, a major source of the difficulty. Although groups need to develop independence, had the teacher helped the group with the first problem, then asked them to try the second one, with assurances that after they had tried, they would receive needed help, undoubtedly the situation would not have occurred. The group, in this case, did appear to want to work on the assignment. Groups that develop a "don't care" attitude when frustrated by difficult assignments are much harder to handle than ones that desire to work.

A class of an earlier age might be more apt to react to this situation with playful disorder, or the members might reveal their hostile feelings by shifting the blame for their inabilities and the teacher's inadequacy to some class member. They might become apathetic and quiet. Older groups, in general, seem better able to tolerate some factors than do younger groups. However, the unpleasant or uncomfortable feelings that accompany frustration should not be construed to be lessened as groups show more tolerance of frustration in certain ways. The unpleasant qualities that accompany frustration may not only persist, but they may become more intense with increasing age, consistent with development in other emotional areas. Changes in the types of frustration, in control, and in evident tolerance accompany general development.

The age of the group-as-a-group, in contrast to the age of the members of the group, relates to the tolerance of frustration. A class group with a history and continuity as a group may face frustration upsets and feelings with less disturbance because they have developed cohesiveness and norms and are able to communicate supportive feelings for one another.

DEGREE OF FRUSTRATION. Frustration varies in degree as well as in type. Groups of different ages react according to different perceptions of the degree of frustration. When a teacher makes an evaluative statement such as, "We can't put these papers up on our bulletin board. They just won't do! etc.," younger groups may question, complain, and chatter. Older groups, faced with the same criticism, would probably respond much less, because they would probably see the degree of frustration as less important. When on the morning that they expected to go on their planned field trip they were informed that the trip was canceled, the same older group would probably see the degree of frustration as somewhat greater than that involved in the bulletin board situation.

A study of frustration in boys, ages seven to thirteen, in a summer camp, was made by Pepitone and Kleiner.[4] A finding of the study was that while a reduction in frustration does not produce an increase in cohesiveness, there was evidence that strong frustration produced a withdrawal symptom. In this study the withdrawal consisted of reduced inter-team competition and increased intrateam cooperation. The degree of frustration, then, produced differential results in the groups of boys.

SEQUENTIAL REACTIONS TO FRUSTRATION. Classes have a repertoire of possible or potential responses that may be called forth in frustration upsets. A behavior that has reduced frustration for the group is likely to appear when next the group is frustrated in the same or similar way. When the response does not succeed in reducing the frustration, it is weakened and another potential response appears. Sometimes, an initial reaction to frustration materially reduces the intensity of the unpleasant feeling and the drive. In that case the subsequent behaviors, even when several behaviors occur sequentially, are relatively unimportant.

The class in Figure 5, from its fund of incipient and possible responses, tried first to meet the frustration by persisting and working harder. When that was ineffective, the response weakened and dropped out. Next, polite and compliant behavior was attempted. When it failed to resolve the frustration, it, like "A," weakened and was discarded by the group. Next, "C," a type of sullen and resentful behavior appeared. The

[4] Albert Pepitone and Robert Kleiner, "The Effects of Threat and Frustration on Group Cohesiveness," *The Journal of Abnormal and Social Psychology*, 54:192–199, March 1957.

group members were resorting to maladaptive responses that teachers view as problem behavior. Actually, the problem behavior was the series of inappropriate responses to a frustrating situation as group members attempted to achieve the goal of reducing tension.

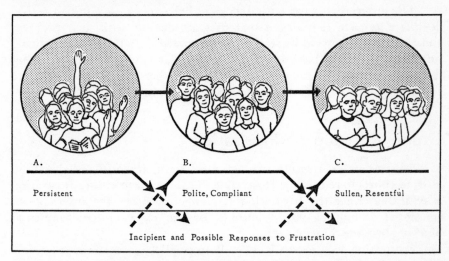

A. Persistent

B. Polite, Compliant

C. Sullen, Resentful

Incipient and Possible Responses to Frustration

Fig. 5. The appearance and disappearance of group responses to frustration. Sequence shows dominant behavior A, that is, persistent behavior by the group and the discarding of that behavior (arrow shows the decline of the behavior), and, from possible responses, the next one selected by the group is B, polite, compliant behavior. Item C is still another, or incipient, behavior.

What appears to be inexplicable behavior can become more intelligible to teachers as they see that when group members behave in certain ways they are satisfying their need to reduce the tension associated with frustration.

A sequence of group reactions to a frustrating situation was reported by a fifth grade teacher.

PERFORMANCE ON THE BLACKTOP

On one of the very hot days of the year our entire school was to be treated to a preview. Some of the actors in a show that was to be presented on the following day were to give a short performance on the playground. The children were to stand on the hot blacktop to see and hear the actors. My class was one of the first out on the playground. Because of the wait for other classes, a breakdown in the sound equipment, and a general delay, the five minutes we had expected to be out there became twenty. All the children complained loudly; many sat down to wait; some girls put handkerchiefs on the tops of their heads; others, especially boys, moved about and got into little skirmishes with one another. The whole class didn't react in the same way, but small groups clustered and groups reacted in a number of inappropriate ways.

The group that reacts with a series of behaviors is showing an active, flexible approach. It indicates that they are dealing with their problem and are working toward its resolution or toward a goal. They are seeking suitable or adaptive behavior for the particular situation. The fact that they discard one behavior and move to another means that they are evaluating the fitness of one and deciding against it.

Group Reaction to Frustration

Frustration of a group, whatever its form, intensity, or duration, leads to efforts to reduce the frustration. This action to reduce frustration is typical whether the frustration is viewed as either the internal—an emotional feeling of unpleasantness, or the external—environmental blocking by some thing or person.

Frustration in a group is difficult to predict or to assign causation. The relation of the precipitating situation (causation) to the group effects is even more complex. There is often no apparent relationship between cause and behavior. Especially are hostile acts sometimes indirectly and obliquely linked. Some expressions of hostility are not recognized as such but are simply viewed as "strange" or puzzling.

Actually there is a wide variety of ways in which hostility may be expressed by a group. Groups not only show many types or kinds of behavior in reaction to frustration, but show as well differences in strengths, immediacies, and durations of their reactions. To escape from, or adjust to, frustration, group members may react with passivity, becoming quiet, and nonresponsive. They may become apathetic and disinterested. They may withdraw either physically or psychologically, or both. They may regress and revert to more immature ways of behaving. They may persevere toward the original means and ends, working harder, putting forth more prolonged or more intensified effort. They may become dependent and ask for help. They may persist blindly or rigidly in an unproductive vein or with maladaptive behavior. They may become hostile and attack directly what they believe to be the cause of the frustration. They may reject, change, or deny the task. They may become disorganized, disoriented, or disintegrated (that is, the group may "go all to pieces"). There are other possible group responses or adjustments to frustration.

Hostile, Aggressive Reactions

Consideration will be given, in this section, to active forms of hostility. They are the reactions of groups that are most readily identified as being hostile. Active forms of hostility are usually considered to include direct verbal expressions of feelings of anger, resentment, or disapproval; or physical expressions, such as rebellion, rioting, or sabotage.

A hostile reaction in response to frustration takes many forms, as it has many, and not always apparent, causes. The response may be directed toward the person or situation arousing the reaction or it may be misplaced in the person or thing toward which it is directed. The misplaced action puzzles teachers and they wonder "Why did they do that?" Active forms of hostility often are spontaneous, but they can be caused by an accumulation of feelings gathered over a period of time. Often when hostility appears it is a quick, flashing reaction. Some classes, like individuals, may be more hostile and suspicious than others, and some may have their own typical hostile responses.

Some situations appear to the group to permit more display of hostility than others. In the following example, the class felt free to turn disapproval of an action (an expulsion of a class member) upon the teacher. The group members may or may not have recognized that the teacher did not make the decision but was merely transmitting a message. As the responsible person was not present, and perhaps knowing that the authority of "the office" could not be attacked, the class directed its hostility toward the teacher.

THE MESSAGE

There was a complete breakdown of established standards governing rights of speech and other aspects of citizenship in the 6A class. The group was engaged in the committee work organizing some past lessons and relating them to their own experiences for presentation to class when a messenger arrived from the office. The teacher was reading the rather long note that he brought, while the messenger stood waiting for the reply. He knew many of the children, and he managed to convey to them by his manner and facial expression that he was on *important business*. The teacher looked up from the note and said to Al, who was in a committee across the room, "What were you doing on the way to school, Al?" and similar questions. Al said, "Nuthin." The teacher then said, "Go to the office at once!"

Al had no more than left the room when the class—highly interested and tense throughout the little interchange—began to shout and express strong disapproval of the teacher's actions. The reaction seemed completely spontaneous.

The behavior was incited by an unjust accusation against Al and his subsequent suspension from school. The class proclaimed the boy's innocence and subsequent investigation proved that it was a case of mistaken identity on the part of the administration.

It has been observed in several studies that social support among subjects has fostered aggression against frustrating experiences. For example, Wright,[5] in a study of the influence of frustration upon the social relations of young children, found a significant increase in the cohesiveness of groups under the influence of frustration. The amount of time the group spent in cooperative behavior increased significantly, and the time spent in conflict behavior was correspondingly decreased. In other words, if a group is frustrated by a teacher or someone in authority, and members of a group see others as supporting, the group will release its aggression more openly and directly.

Another factor that may have been operative in the spread of direct aggression toward the teacher in the above example was lack of fear of consequences by group members, or a feeling of "safety in numbers." The youngsters starting the attack were supported by the rest, who may have desired approval by their peers and have thought they would gain it by joining the attackers.

In an investigation of contagious behavior, Festinger, Pepitone, and Newcomb [6] investigated the group phenomenon that they labeled "de-individuation." They observed that at times individuals seemed to obtain release in groups and were less restrained and inhibited; individuals acted as if they were hidden or submerged in the group. In an effort to determine when and why this kind of behavior occurred, the investigators found that the group phenomenon they called de-individuation was a state wherein members paid no attention to other individuals as individuals. When this condition occurred, the members felt that they were not being singled out by others. The theory was advanced that in the process there was a reduction of inner restraints; consequently, members felt cloaked in a kind of anonymity. Feeling release, hidden, and in accord with the group, an individual joined freely in behavior that as an individual he would not exhibit.

School rules and regulations are factors in causing hostile behavior.

[5] Erik M. Wright, "The Influence of Frustration on the Social Relations of Young Children," *Character and Personality,* 12:111–112, December 1943.

[6] Leon Festinger, Albert Pepitone, and Theodore Newcomb, "Some Consequences of De-individuation in a Group," *Journal of Abnormal and Social Psychology,* 47:382–389, June 1952.

Unable to attack the rule itself, to question it, change it, or attribute it to some person, classes may carry their frustrations and hostilities over to other situations.

A teacher described an incident in which the group reaction to lunch rules created a subsequent group behavior problem.

NOON RULES

Much group resentment has developed toward school in general because of our noon meal program. If the children don't sit quietly at the tables and control themselves relatively well, they are kept sitting at the tables until 12:45 or even 12:55. When this occurs the group comes into the classroom very irritated and complaining about everything that has happened on the school grounds. The group often is more quarrelsome and less willing to co-operate in group activities on these days.

Less common school rules may be disruptive and cause hostile feelings and behavior, as in the following example.

DOGS NOT ADMITTED

In the school where I teach, if any animal follows a child to school, or if any animal is on the school grounds for any reason, the Humane Society is called and the animal is put in the pound. (Three dollars to retrieve it.) The principal is not a tyrant. This seems to be a long established policy of the district. Of course the custodians must follow orders and so must the teachers. An explanation to the children about the rule does not make the situation less acute when someone's pet follows him to school. When this happens the group becomes resentful toward the principal and the teacher. The owner breaks into tears and this stops all work in the classroom. The whole thing must be explained again.

It does no good to criticize the administrative policy. A pleading note to the principal does no good. When an animal comes on the school ground, it is sent to the animal shelter. The behavior in the group is total upset and disruption. The only solution is to take the child home and explain again to the parents. The most satisfying solution is to take the child to the pound, pay the money to retrieve the animal, and the problem in the room dies down until the next time. The teacher is then the hero, the principal is the ogre, and the Humane Society is terrible!

A common finding has been that groups whose hostilities have been aroused direct more aggression toward the originators of the hostility who are lower in status than toward those who are higher. Thibaut [7]

[7] John Thibaut, "An Experimental Study of the Cohesiveness of Underprivileged Groups," *Human Relations,* 3:251–278, 1950.

reported that lower-status groups felt free to make aggressive comments to higher-status groups until it became clear they were destined to remain low in status. In collaboration with Riecken, Thibaut [8] also demonstrated that aggressive remarks were readily made toward a provoker of hostility who was low in status but less readily made when the provoker was a higher-status person.

When direct avenues of releasing hostility are lacking, and when the status of authority figures is considerable, the group may displace its hostility. In the following, the class turned its feelings against its own product—the finished writing papers.

WRECKED WRITING

This incident occurred in my fourth grade class. The class members had just completed some writing exercises that we had been practicing for several days. The writing supervisor was coming to our classroom in the next few minutes to judge the children on these particular exercises for writing awards. After the papers were completed, they were placed to the right on the desks to be picked up by the monitors. It was a windy day and cold. One of the boys went to the windows and began to open them. Papers began to fly all over the room. Children began running all over the place, scrambling and grabbing for papers—any papers, not just their own. There was screaming and laughter. By the time the papers were finally gathered together, most of them were crumpled, dirty, and ink-smeared.

Quite likely, the teacher, under pressure to get the writing papers ready for the supervisor, had put intensive pressure on the group in some way. The class did not react directly against the teacher, but instead the writing papers were the target. Direct expressions of hostility toward the teacher would probably have placed the group in serious trouble. If they had "talked back," the class members might have been punished. Also, since reaction against the teacher is considered very undesirable behavior, the members of the class could feel less guilty by reacting in the way they did. Nevertheless, the act was more or less a direct attack upon the teacher, since the supervisor would not see examples of neat writing papers. The fact that the group members laughed and took no care in gathering the papers indicated the defiance they undoubtedly felt. A class that had been praised and applauded for the writing efforts, and that felt pride in the group performance, would have been upset if the work became damaged.

[8] John Thibaut and Henry Riecken, "Authoritarianism, Status, and the Communication of Aggression," *Human Relations*, 8:95–120, 1955.

Passivity, Apathy, or Withdrawal

Passivity is one reaction that groups show to conditions and feelings of frustration. The apathetic, quiet, no-response, "stand still and see what happens" reactions are probably more frequent than appears to casual classroom observers. Teachers and others, no doubt, tend to notice and report the more vigorous and obvious reactions. The quiet response is less noted unless a noncooperative action becomes a problem to a teacher who is working toward curricular or other educational goals.

The reaction of apathy may have several meanings. It may be the group's expression of hostility, embarrassment, uncertainty, or lack of understanding of what is required or how to behave.

Some forms of hostility seem to be passive but are, in actuality, direct expressions, for the intent to damage or injure someone is fairly obvious. They may appear passive because they often involve *not* doing something, yet they are acts of deliberate, conscious defiance. Even apathetic, disinterested, or withdrawn behavior on the part of the group may sometimes be a deliberate and direct form of hostility. Complete apathy and lack of interest shown by a group when a teacher is trying in every way to arouse interest and get a response is very damaging to the teacher's morale.

Some class groups seem to habitually react to thwarting by venting their hostility directly. Other groups seem to habitually react by withdrawing or by showing passive resistance. Some groups may alternate in their reactions. It has been suggested that when groups become passive or withdrawn they are accepting the situation as futile, and therefore they waste no energy on hostile behavior. The groups wait, and when hostility does emerge it is when the groups feel that something may be gained by their efforts.

What we call passivity, then, can take several forms as a response to frustration. It can be used as a way of resisting or defying something, as shown in the following incident.

A kindergarten class was outside working in the school garden. A number of adult observers were expected to visit the class. The teacher described what occurred in this manner:

SIT-DOWN ON THE JUNGLE GYM

As the adults came along the fence toward us, I went forward to greet them. After I had them situated so they could observe the children working,

I turned just in time to see the last child reach the top of a tower gym. There all the 32 children sat in complete silence—unspeaking and unmoving—staring down at the visitors. My requests and commands to come down went unheeded. I tried just waiting and that didn't work, either. They would not move or speak until the visitors left. Needless to say, there was no observing that day.

Such passive, quiet resistance as a way of dealing with frustration was effective, although unusual in such extreme form for a group of this age. The imitative aspects of the behavior were apparent in the total group participation, and the action was accomplished so quickly and quietly that the teacher said it was done while her back was turned. The extent of the hostility and group solidarity was shown in their apathy to, and noncompliance with, the teacher's requests that they come down from the jungle gym and work in the garden.

It is a reasonable assumption that the children perceived visitors as a threat. The aspects of the threat can only be conjectured: threat to their usual activity, and the requirement of unforeseen changes; or threat to their self-esteem as a group of good workers; or the threat might lie in the unknown, newness, and strangeness of the situation. The children acted as if the group was a source of security in the face of frustration and external threat. The group accepted and acted in accord with a completely solidified and unified group action.

Both embarrassment and hostility are evident in the following description of a group of sixth graders who were unable to respond to questions put to them by an outside expert. Evidently they felt the questioning was a form of criticism and threat. When attacked by their own teacher, their hostile withdrawal was more evident. They used the group for security and support when they saw the situation as having no ready-made known solution.

THE SILENT CLASS

A sixth grade high "cluster" group was visiting the agriculture–natural science center. A series of experiments had been performed but the various children in the group had considerable difficulty explaining the findings of the experiments.

When the instructor at the science center interpreted their conclusions in a questioning manner, the group seemed to freeze. They could no longer respond to questions about the experiments nor would individuals in the group volunteer further information. It appeared obvious that these children were not secure in their knowledge and findings, or else they were extremely anxious and insecure, and their responses were blocked. At any rate, there was an obvious amount of hesitation and embarrassment.

It was interesting to note the behavior of the group's own teacher. She became very defensive and spoke to her class in a flustered manner. She belabored the group as though their responses, or lack of responses, were an attack upon her and upon her teaching. When she finished the group members would not respond to the agriculture instructor at all, even when he singled them out to answer questions. The class members were completely cold and silent. There were some attempts made to remotivate the class and to get them to respond, but all efforts were completely useless.

Apathy in a high school English class, referred to as an "average level" group, was described by the teacher.

UNPREPARED

Our high school is a large one and while the principal does visit the classes, it is rather infrequent. When he entered the class to observe the activities, the prepared speeches due that day were not given. Each student called upon claimed he was unprepared. This was instigated by the curiosity of the students wondering who the principal was there to observe, as well as the familiar problem of a few children being very self-conscious about their speech. Primarily, these persons started the reaction and a stony silence throughout the room followed. After a few minutes, the principal saw what was happening and spoke very briefly to the class concerning some unrelated matter and left. Incidentally, at a later time the principal, teacher, and students finally saw humor in the situation.

Some classes seem to habitually react to frustration with quiet, apathetic, nonresponsive behavior. When teachers report this kind of behavior as a problem, the class usually is described as one composed of low-ability individuals who have had long histories of failure and defeat in school achievement. However, classes containing the ordinary range of abilities can react with apathy and listlessness and use this means to express hostility. A group that reacts this way is usually discouraged and has the general attitude that it is "no use" to fight the situation. The group sees no hope that things will get better so the members do what they are forced to do, but they see no advantage to doing the work well. They are primarily concerned with avoiding punishment, avoiding increased work assignments, and escaping other discomforts that could increase frustration. There is usually no real communication between the teacher and the group because it is more or less accepted that it is hopeless to try to understand. Teachers who create this condition in groups through use of harsh, punitive, and authoritarian practices are not concerned with the destructive effects since the groups are obedient and do not exhibit active and disturbing patterns of behavior. Teachers who are assigned groups who react in this manner often become very disturbed and frustrated themselves. Dealing with passive hostilities requires much skill and most teachers have not had training in this area. Consequently, the difficulties of coping with this behavior cause teachers to become very discouraged.

Another, often unrecognized, type of group reaction to frustration may be observed in a few classrooms, although it is never reported by teachers themselves. This is a type of dependency or regression that develops under the impact of highly authoritarian teachers who disguise their autocratic tendencies, and who appear sympathetic and considerate of individuals in the group. The group desires approval of this kind of teacher, yet there is an unconscious fear underlying the teacher–group relationship. Under the impact of this fear, the children become highly dependent upon the teacher and constantly seek her approval. Often withdrawal is observed, since the possibility of falling short of the teacher's expectations creates anxiety. To escape, the group withdraws from difficult situations. Groups that sense peril often withdraw in a united fashion to escape overwhelming demands.

The list of ways groups react to frustration is extensive. Some groups show consistency; others may alternate among several types of reaction. Some class groups will react with apathy and listlessness in the classroom but on the playground will show direct, and often intense, hostility. In the classroom, some groups may show consistency when certain situations arise, whereas their reactions to other situations will vary or alternate among a number of reactions.

Imitative or Contagious Behavior

Imitative behavior is one possible reaction to frustration. Contagious or imitative behavior is described by many teachers in reporting behavior incidents that occur in their classrooms. They describe behavior in which the class members as a group jump up and rush to the windows, or all leave their seats at the same moment, or all begin to talk at the same time although no one had been talking previously.

Imitative behavior in a group is seen when one person, or a few persons, act in a way that is quickly joined by the rest of the group. The behavior that is used by the instigator is usually appropriate in some respect. It may be appropriate to the immediate focus of the irritation or to the desired goals of the group or the values of the group, or in some other way. Sometimes its appropriateness may be only in its release of the pressure of unpleasant feelings in the group. When this happens, the action appears to be irrelevant to the situation or incompatible with the usual character and way of behaving of the group.

The behavior that is begun or set off by an initiator may sweep rapidly through the group, but not all imitative behavior has a person or subgroup as an instigator or initiator. The total group may act simultaneously, with no time for communication of intentions or for appraisal of how to respond. In response to some sudden loud noise or other fear-producing stimulus, the entire class may "freeze" and become quiet— not speaking and not moving.

A series of studies by Polansky, Lippitt, and Redl [9] and Lippitt, Polansky, Redl, and Rosen [10] dealt with the phenomenon they labeled "contagion." A purpose of their research was to determine the characteristics of successful initiators and recipients of contagion and some of the conditions under which contagion occurs. The studies were made in summer camps for eleven- to fifteen-year-olds. The typical initiator of contagion was found to be a child who is viewed by others in the group as having high power over his peers and who apparently has sufficient security (gained from a correct perception of his own power position) to act spontaneously. In addition, he is ecologically and socially in a position to communicate with the group and is able and willing to relate himself to the group. An experiment performed in one of the camps suggests further than in a situation of stress where the members of a group have a common need or mood, the most impulsive person—the one who first reacts in a manner representative of the shared feeling—is most likely to evoke a chain of contagion. Under these conditions, power position in the group is of little importance and impulsivity becomes the crucial factor. Recipients of contagion (that is, those from whom behavior similar to that of the initiator is evoked) are characterized by many of the same properties as are initiators.

The power of a well-liked and respected child in the class was related by a teacher.

GARY KNOWS

From time to time since the beginning of school in the fall we have had both disaster drills and fire drills. This is a fifth grade class and they have been having these for years now.

The fire drill signal is a series of short rings on the school bell. The disaster signal is a continuous ring on the same bell.

The procedure in a fire drill is for the students to immediately file out the door and away from the building.

[9] Norman Polansky, Ronald Lippitt, and Fritz Redl, "An Investigation of Behavioral Contagion in Groups," *Human Relations,* 3:319–348, 1950.

[10] Ronald Lippitt, Norman Polansky, Fritz Redl, and Sidney Rosen, "The Dynamics of Power," *Human Relations,* 5:37–64, 1952.

The procedure in a disaster drill is for each student to duck under his desk and cover his face. They remain in this position until the "all clear" is sounded. Then immediately after the all clear sounds, we have a fire drill.

No one is alerted in advance of any of these drills; the fire department simply walks in and rings the bell. Then they check and time the procedure.

This had gone without a hitch on previous practices, even though there is a complicating factor. There are two bells that ring during the day that are set to ring one second longer than others that ring during the day. Early in the year, each time one of these two bells would ring we would all pause, ready to "duck and cover." Finally, we became acquainted with the times that these bells rang and ignored them.

On this particular day, the firemen happened to call a disaster about the time that we were used to the long bell. A boy who is generally very calm and much respected in the class said in an excited voice, "That's the *disaster* bell!" Instead of ducking under his desk, he started for the door. Immediately, even though he had said "disaster," everyone got up and started to file out after him for a fire drill.

When about a third of the class had filed out, I stopped them and they came back in to observe a disaster drill.

In talking it over afterward they said, "Well, we thought Gary would know what he was doing!"

"Good" behavior is as contagious as disruptive behavior. Undoubtedly the frequent instances of constructive and socially desirable behavior that sweep through a class or school in the manner of imitative behavior receive less teacher attention than the more troublesome kinds. The enthusiastic attack on keeping the school premises neat or the rallying of the whole school to support the team or a local charitable drive are examples of situations that have at times called forth widely imitated action from group members. The classroom, too, has examples of contagious behavior in carrying out curricular goals.

Evasive, Indirect, or Escaping Reactions

Many times a class group expresses active hostility, not by direct group reactions but by strong approval of a few individuals in the class who do express the hostility the whole group feels. These members act in a way that helps to relieve the frustration that might otherwise build up in the group and interfere with its general effectiveness. Because individuals express the group's hostility, teachers believe that these individuals are behavior problems and do not recognize that the source of difficulty lies in the group. Many teachers have had experience with class groups that approved and applauded individuals for misbehavior. When for some reason these individuals were removed from the group, the teachers found the situation was not changed; it was not peaceful and quiet as they had expected, for other persons in the group filled the vacated places and the same or similar situations continued.

THE CLOWN. It is very important for teachers to identify group hostility, whatever form it takes. When a class group uses a class clown to express its hostility indirectly, it is not easy for a teacher to determine if the problem lies in the group or wholly in the individual. If a child has a great desire for attention and acclaim, somewhat satisfied by acting as a clown, the problem is more or less an individual one, though the group does play a part. If the class group uses a clown to undermine the teacher, or to escape from pressure or boredom, or to work off resentment, the problem is mainly a group problem. Usually, if a child clowns to gain attention for himself, the group may respond when a diversion is needed, but at other times it will show irritation because the clowning is disruptive. The wit who expresses the group's hostility by his behavior is always highly applauded and approved whether his remarks are funny or not. He is the evasive means by which a group expresses its resentful and aggressive feelings.

THE CLASS CLOWN

This particular class laughs at everything Tom says or does. Sometimes he is funny, but mostly he is not. He usually begins his act about the time I am ready to assign a lesson. Just recently the following incident took place. I had made an assignment and then asked if everyone understood. At that point Tom said, "All clear, sir! Men! Charge!" He then picked up a pencil with an exaggerated motion and pretended to write very fast. The whole class rolled in the aisles laughing. They pounded their desks and some shrieked.

It does not do much good to remove him. Some one else will do the same thing and the class acts even worse.

Laughing unduly at Tom's or some other person's behavior was the method this class used to release aggression. A class does not necessarily use the same response, as this one did, if the clown is removed. It might develop some other means of reacting to frustration. Whatever the cause of the hostile reaction exhibited by this class, it seems that the behavior was more satisfying than cooperative behavior.

To distinguish between the class clown, who serves the group as a release for its frustration, and a child who clowns to gain attention for himself, the following illustration is given. The boy in this example appeared to want attention, or perhaps he wished to hide his ineptness at playing ball. Whatever the cause for his actions, it seems apparent he was not being used by the group to express hostility indirectly.

THE FUNNY BATTER

Jay is the boy in my fifth grade who seems to love saying and doing silly things to get the attention of the class. This occurs both inside and outside the room. This week the class was having a baseball game and everything went along smoothly until his time to bat. When he is up, he has to have about three minutes to look over the situation and goes through antics imitating professional players. After finally deciding, he swings and misses and falls down, which tickles the class tremendously. After a few remarks, everything is fine until his time to bat again.

Sometimes he carries his act too far and the class gets irritated because he takes up time. When children begin to complain, it puts a damper on him for a short period and then he tries again.

The boys in both incidents had some problems rooted in individual psychology. Perhaps if Tom were placed in a class whose needs were being met, he might assume another role. On the other hand, he might continue to attempt to gain applause and approval by clowning, meeting with little success. It could be that a class that uses this indirect method for reacting to frustration does so because there is a child in the class who has a tendency to act the clown. If he is removed for a time, another child acts as a stand-in to satisfy the group's need although it is not his normal role. Should a frustrated class not have a clown, the members find some other way to relieve pressure.

THE REBEL. The rebel serves the same purpose as the clown but instead of seeking approval by acting funny he is aggressive and rebels openly. He behaves in a way most children in the group would not dare to act, but instead of being shocked at his behavior, the group applauds and approves. A happy, contented group will strongly disapprove of a rebel's behavior. Only a discontented, thwarted, frustrated group will commend and encourage him.

A rebel behaves as he does because he, himself, has problems. By acting hostile, aggressive, and defiant, he not only relieves his own frustrations but gains considerable satisfaction from the approval and applause he receives from the group. In time his behavior may become more of an attention-getting device than a way of expressing his individual frustration.

The next account reveals group approval of a rebel's hostile actions against a teacher.

THE BOY WHO KICKED THE TEACHER

Word passed like wildfire when a boy (in another room) kicked the teacher on lunch bench duty. Mr. Samuels (Mr. Sam, as the children call him, and who is certainly not disliked) was making the boy wait for the dismissal bell. When the boy left his seat, Mr. Sam told him to sit down. The boy stood still, hands on hips, defying him. When Mr. Sam walked over to the boy intending to talk to him, the boy whirled and kicked him! It took some time to get this story from my class when it came in at one o'clock, excited and elated. In the uproar many approving remarks were voiced, such as, "Boy, that took a lot of guts," "Good thing teachers can't hit back," and "That rule is a dumb one, anyhow!" (referring to the rule about leaving seats at lunch time).

This class had often expressed resentment over the lunch bench rules, but usually after a few criticisms they have settled down. This day, however, the group remained too excited to work. They continued to exchange admiring remarks concerning the courage of the boy who kicked the teacher.

When group reaction is supportive, as it was in this case, there is usually some underlying cause for group resentment. It appeared, in this instance, that the lunch bench rules were the source of group hostility. Since physical expression of hostility is strongly disapproved, and even forbidden in the school society, a class group would not applaud such behavior unless a deep-seated frustration had been relieved by the physical act of violence. Whatever the punishment the boy received for committing the act probably seemed to him a small price to pay for becoming the school champion and for the approval he received from his peers.

Defiant, disobedient behavior was shown by a rebel in the following account. The teacher was unable to understand the class reaction to the child since she considered him a "behavior problem" and expected the group to view him in the same way. The teacher seemed unaware that the group itself had some problem or it would not approve such defiance.

FREDIE

Fredie is really a problem. Day after day he disrupts the class with his aggressive behavior, but if he is punished for his acts, the group becomes sullen and sympathizes with him—though why they do is hard to know!

His behavior recently is a good example. It was late one morning, in fact only ten minutes before the lunch recess bell. Fredie raised his hand. Without waiting for me to reply to his hand waving, he blurted out, "Miss Smith, I'm thirsty. May I get a drink?"

I said, "No Fredie. It is almost lunch time." At that he hopped out of his seat and went to the display ledge under the windows where there was a bouquet of daisies arranged. He yanked the flowers out of the vase, looked right at me scowling, and drank the water in the vase! The class exploded with laughter. They think Fredie is a card and never seem to believe he is out of line.

The class reaction to Fredie seemed to indicate a secret willingness by the group to challenge and defy the teacher. There was a kind of sadistic humor in the situation, since Fredie maneuvered the teacher into giving an expected refusal and then defied her with a surprise action. However, the class laughter was probably given as approval of Fredie rather than as a response to the humor in the situation.

Only a disturbed, upset class develops norms for behavior that are consistently nonsupportive of the teacher. The next incident, for example, shows a class that reacts to support the teacher.

REBEL WITH PAINT

During a lesson in finger painting it was necessary to speak to Charles because his materials were pushed dangerously close to the edge of his desk. His response to my suggestion was to pick up his paper, which was thickly covered with paint and starch, and hurl it against the wall. At the same time he yelled a few choice, unprintable words.

The class at first was very startled and then embarrassed. A few boys laughed slightly but their faces were red. Most of the children took one glance at the mess and then became very busy with their own work. At the same time several children got up from their seats and without any direction began to clean the floor and wall. They ignored Charles completely. Disapproval was very evident.

Charles usually does not react as violently as this, but he often responds to a suggestion with some outburst. The class ignores his behavior but at the same time they always seem to try and make up for his actions in some way.

Sometimes class groups must adjust to seriously disturbed children. If the class is cohesive and is subject to only the normal conflicts that arise when a number of persons must work together for long periods of time, they are able to make the necessary adjustments. If, on the other hand, they are frustrated most of the time, behavior such as Charles exhibited might serve as an outlet for the group's feelings and his behavior might be approved.

THE SCAPEGOAT. A seriously suppressed class suffering from frustration and anxiety will sometimes displace hostility by making a scapegoat of a member. The scapegoat, who may be in some way a weak or vulnerable person, receives the concentrated projections of group blame. The scapegoat is not always a disliked or rejected individual. He may be picked because he is the most likely target at a moment when the group is under pressure.

The child in the next incident was made the scapegoat because she was the likely person for the group to blame. The immediate cause of frustration was the class's being deprived of its ball. The underlying cause was the rule that seemed to be inflexible and did not take intention into account. Since the group was upset, and the class did not feel adequate to challenge the rule, all the feelings of resentment were directed toward Sue.

THE BLAME

A rule was made recently in our school which said that any ball kicked into the street would be confiscated. If a member of one class kicked a ball of another class into the street, the class of the person who violated the rule would lose its ball.

Right after the rule was issued, a ball from another class came rolling toward Sue. She intended to kick it back where it belonged but it slipped off her toe and went flying over the fence. Sue was crushed, as her intentions were only the best.

When we came in from the playground the group was exceedingly loud in its denunciation of Sue. Little work was accomplished the rest of the day. There were many threats muttered by some pupils who said they would "get her" after school.

A scapegoat is one who bears the blame for the failures, misfortunes, and weaknesses of others. The group member who is "different" from the group and set apart in the social relations of the whole or of a subgroup may draw the concentrated attention of the class. The child with unusual interests or a lack of physical skills, for examples, may be made a scapegoat.

When the scapegoating practices are extremely severe, it must be assumed that the internal tension in the group is very strong. The report of the next incident provides no clues why the group behaved so cruelly toward one of its members, but it appears quite evident that the group, not the girl, was in need of psychological help.

THE UNTOUCHABLE

A girl named Lela, in our sixth grade, is treated as an outcast. The behavior of the group toward her started prior to my taking over the class. The class considers her untouchable. If a person accidently rubs or bumps against her it becomes the cause for immediate scrubbing and washing. If she uses the pencil sharpener someone washes off the handle. The members of the class frequently interrupt some work period and ask to go wash if something is passed, such as a book, which she might have handled.

It is always done quietly but if anyone is refused permission it creates an uproar.

Lela is not attractive and she is taller than the rest. She also seems to want to get attention, and perhaps the group feeling is caused by this. For whatever reasons, it causes a good deal of class disruption, and talking to the group about the unkindness shown to Lela does no good.

A group may dislike attention-getting behavior and reject a member for this reason. Usually the behavior signifying rejection is merely ignoring the person. When a group exhibits such extreme cruelty toward a member there is good reason to suspect that the group is displacing its feelings of hostility upon this member. The group behaving this way is presenting evidence that indicates that it is suffering from a severe form of frustration. Unfortunately, teachers report this behavior more frequently than might be expected. This may not mean that this behavior is more prevalent than some other group disorders; it may mean only that teachers are more alarmed over this behavior because it affects individuals seriously and because it is difficult to handle.

The scapegoat may become so established in that role in the eyes of the group that they attribute all untoward events to him. In the case of Donald, which follows, his teacher also added a scapegoating touch. The group's hilarious reaction implies the use of the scapegoat for the release of some tension or emotion in the group.

THE WHISTLE

I heard someone whistle in the room. I looked up from the reading group I was teaching and, as usual, the whole class pointed at Donald. So I said, "Donald, if you want to whistle, go outside!" At this Donald blew up. He threw his book on the floor and ran outside into the rain. The group reaction was one of wild hilarity. It turned out that Donald had not whistled. Someone else had and the class knew it, but the children all pointed to Donald since he usually was the one blamed for everything.

It is difficult to understand why the teacher fell in so readily with the group plot since she seemed to be aware of the fact that Donald was blamed for everything. Since only a group in a poor emotional climate resorts to scapegoating, the teacher probably acted without thought on many such occasions.

In an attempt to ascertain the extent of teachers' understandings of group behavior, over 200 experienced teachers were asked what was the *best* practice to use if a class reacted in the following way toward a member of the group.[11]

> Tom, a quiet average student, was exceedingly fat. The class ignored him completely except when he moved around the room. That brought on taunts and jeers although many of them were whispered. "Here comes Jumbo!" or "See the biggest show on earth." Tom would get flustered and sit down in the nearest seat.

Only 2 per cent of the teachers responding said that if such behavior occurred in their classrooms they would examine their teaching procedures or their control practices in an effort to determine why the group reacted toward one individual in the manner described. More than 80 per cent of the teachers indicated they would moralize or reproach the group for the behavior. Some said they would approach the problem by saying to the class, "Only he who is blameless may throw the first stone." Most frequently the moralizing practices employed the use of "ugly duckling" stories or used the approach of "how would you feel—etc." Some teachers suggested punitive practices. A few said they would ignore the situation since "life is like this." Others said they would work on making Tom more acceptable to the group.

Teacher practices may not be the only cause for scapegoating. As has been indicated, a number of factors may operate to create frustration in a group. Should scapegoating behavior occur, however, a teacher should look for causes for poor emotional group health before trying directly or indirectly to improve the immediate situation.

Questions for Study and Discussion

1. Describe a group in which you were a member and that met frustration. Tell some of the characteristics of the group, the source or sources of the frustration, and how the group behaved.

2. Give an illustration of group perceptions of frustration that was incomplete or incorrect. Indicate what the facts were that were not perceived by the group.

3. In addition to the behavior cited in anecdotes in the chapter, write or tell of a group's reaction to boredom and monotony. State the ages of the group members, the kind of group, and the boring elements of the situation.

4. Why do observers of groups often report only one type of frustration behavior when there was, in reality, a sequence of behaviors?

[11] Mary Abbie Bany, *Teachers' Understanding of Group Behavior,* unpublished doctoral dissertation, Los Angeles: University of Southern California, 1960, pp. 262–266.

5. Outline a plan showing how you as a teacher would prepare your class to meet severe stress. Indicate the age or grade level you are thinking of and how your plan is suitable for that level.

6. Observe a class—in the classroom, play field, lunch room, or other school location—for indications of frustration or anxiety.

7. How would you increase the frustration tolerance of a class group, assuming the usual curricular, organizational, and administrative conditions?

8. Consider the consequences to the future of a group (a) of the group experiencing the making of a scapegoat of some individual, and (b) of the group's using scapegoating as a repeated way of dealing with situations.

9. Why does the presence of a potential scapegoat (a person who is considered "different," "unattractive," or unpopular) result in his being made a scapegoat by some groups and not by others?

10. What is a possible explanation for the fact that some groups employ clowns and rebels to express existing hostile feelings?

11. What conditions might produce an extremely listless, apathetic group?

12. Consider the advantages and disadvantages of a class group that is highly cohesive.

Suggestions for Further Reading

Barker, Robert G., Tamara Dembo, and K. Lewin. *Frustration and Regression: an Experiment with Young Children.* U. of Iowa Studies in Child Welfare, 1941.

Berkowitz, Leonard. "Some Factors Affecting the Reduction of Overt Hostility," *Journal of Abnormal and Social Psychology,* 60:14–21, January 1960.

Billingslea, Fred Y. and Herbert Bloom. "The Comparative Effect of Frustration and Success on Goal-Directed Behavior in the Classroom," *Journal of Abnormal and Social Psychology,* 45:510–515, July 1950.

Bonner, Hubert. *Group Dynamics, Principles and Applications.* New York: Ronald, 1959, p. 88.

Cartwright, Dorwin (ed.). *Studies in Social Power.* Ann Arbor: U. of Michigan, 1959.

Flanders, Ned A. "Personal-Social Anxiety as a Factor in Experimental Learning Situations," *Journal of Educational Research,* 45:110–120, October 1951.

Grinker, R. R. and J. P. Spiegel. *Men Under Stress.* New York: McGraw, 1945.

Lindgren, Henry Clay. *Effective Leadership in Human Relations.* New York: Hermilage House, 1954, Chapters II, III, IV.

Lindgren, Henry Clay. *Mental Health in Education.* New York: Holt, 1954, Chapter III.

Hamblin, Robert L. "Group Integration During a Crisis," *Human Relations,* 11:67–76, 1958.

Ostlund, Leonard A. "Group Functioning Under Negative Conditions," *Journal of Educational Psychology*, 47:32–40, January 1956.

Redl, Fritz and William W. Wattenberg. *Mental Hygiene in Teaching*. Harcourt, 1951.

Warters, Jane. *Group Guidance, Principles and Practices*. New York: McGraw, 1960.

Waterhouse, Jan K. and Irvin L. Child. "Frustration and the Quality of Performance," *Journal of Personality*, 21:298–311, March 1953.

Wright, Erik M. "The Influence of Frustration upon the Social Relations of Young Children," *Character and Personality*, 12:111–122, December 1943.

Part IV   # Techniques for Changing Group Behavior

Chapter 11

Group Decision
Techniques

THROUGHOUT this text the idea is stressed that much of the behavior of children in classrooms is shaped by the class groups, or by the desire of children to be accepted and assimilated within these class groups. The proposition frequently emphasized is that many of the acts of individual children that are labeled "problem behavior" by teachers are caused by pressures stemming from group membership. Thus, it seems, this group influence upon individual behavior is of vital importance to teachers. If teachers focus all their endeavors upon changing individual behavior, and if they ignore the effect of group influence, they will have considerable difficulty in changing undesirable class group behavior as well as individual behavior. Particularly this is true when a group norm for behaving is involved, or if the problem relates to attitude change.

An analysis of teachers' reports of group behavior that they say creates problems in the classroom shows that there are several types of condition producing these problems. One condition occurs when the

285

group does not adhere to the standards for behavior set by the teacher, seemingly with the concurrence of the class. In these cases, the class establishes a group norm for behavior that conflicts with the standards set in class by the teacher and by the class members, who though they may appear to concur with the suggested behavioral standards actually do not.

A second condition occurs when problems suddenly arise that are disturbing to the group or the teacher or both. The problem may involve a conflict between members of the group. It may involve group resistance to an imposed rule or it may involve an unfavorable reaction to some aspect of school work. In any case, this condition generally requires a change in group perception of the problem before a satisfactory solution can be reached.

A third condition arises when the group becomes frustrated, anxious, or is subjected to situations involving stress.

Each of the above named conditions requires a different method of handling the difficulty. The first condition, which involves norm behavior, requires the use of the group-decision technique. Norm behavior is difficult to change. To change a norm the group members must perceive that the other members in the group desire change. The second condition, which usually arises suddenly and often is not anticipated, requires use of problem-solving techniques. Changing group perception of a problem is less difficult than changing norm behavior, providing that the teacher recognizes the problem and the group's perception of it. The third condition requires preventative measures, or changes in group properties, or changes in teacher practices. Teachers may have the most difficulty dealing with this condition, since the problem may require careful analysis and, too, a set of teacher habits or attitudes may be a factor contributing to the situation, thereby making it necessary for the teacher to alter his behavior.

This chapter discusses techniques for working on the first of the three cited conditions—techniques designed to change a group's established way of behaving to that which is considered more desirable by the teacher. The behavior to be changed involves group norms and should be distinguished from group behavior problems arising from group conflict or some problem that requires a collective solution by the group. Problem-solving techniques are considered in the chapter that follows. This chapter, then, involves ways of changing group norms that a teacher believes are interfering with goal attainment in the classroom.

Studies of Group Decision

An impressive amount of evidence has accumulated to support the idea that a greater change in behavior is produced when members of a group are permitted to participate in decision-making than when a decision is imposed upon the group by a leader. Although the specific mechanisms underlying this phenomenon have not been conclusively determined, studies do indicate that changes in some kinds of behavior can be brought about effectively by using the group as a medium of change. The evidence shows that strong pressure for change is established by creating a shared perception by members of the need for change.

The group itself is used as the medium of change. The pressure comes, then, from the group and not from the group leader. The conditions that induce members to be influenced by group pressure were studied in Chapter 6. The group does act as a source of influence upon member behavior in many situations. Teacher efforts to impose a new way of behaving upon the class members can be blocked by the group, since group pressures cause members to adhere to the norms for behavior already established by the group. The group-decision approach uses this same group pressure to achieve change in member behavior. The decision made by group members is used as a new frame of reference for a new group norm and acts as a binding force for maintaining the new way of behaving.

Early Experiments

A series of experiments devised by Kurt Lewin [1] and coworkers during World War II utilized three interrelated propositions, namely: (1) it is usually easier to change individuals in a group than to change them separately; (2) the effects of change through groups is more permanent than if individuals are changed singly; and (3) change is more readily accepted if individuals participate in the decision to change.

The first experiments were carried out in connection with a campaign to increase food-saving and were conducted in an effort to change the food habits of American housewives. The traditional approach to food-saving had been to make persuasive appeals by lectures, posters,

---

[1] Kurt Lewin, "Group Decision and Social Change," in Eleanor Maccoby, Theodore M. Newcomb, Eugene L. Hartley (eds.), *Readings in Social Psychology*, New York: Henry Holt & Company, 1958, pp. 197–211.

films, and other media. The specific objective in the first experiment was to try to get groups of Red Cross volunteers to include such meat items in the family diet as hearts, sweetbreads, and kidneys. Six groups, of 13 to 17 members each, were formed. A "lecture method" was used for three groups and a "discussion method" was used for the remaining three groups.

Attractive lectures were prepared for the first three groups, exhorting the members to use these meats not usually found desirable by American families. Appeals were made to save the regular meat cuts for the war effort. The vitamin and mineral values of the less desirable meats were elaborated. Both health value and economy were stressed. The groups were told how the meats could be prepared in attractive and tempting ways. Recipes were distributed to the group members.

With the discussion groups, an attempt was made to see if the housewives could be induced to participate in a program of change without using exhortations, appeals, and high-pressure tactics. The problem was presented to the groups and related to the war effort and general health. Following this presentation, the topic was opened for discussion. The group members brought up the general objections to using the meats, such as odor during cooking, taste, and the like. After the members had participated in a general discussion, an expert in nutrition provided these groups with the same ideas for preparing the meats as were given to the lecture groups. At the end of the lecture the group members were asked to reveal by a show of hands if they were willing to try the meats and serve them during the following week.

Later, when the subjects were checked to see if they actually had included the meats in their meals, it was found that there were impressive differences in the two methods. Only 3 per cent of the lecture group were influenced enough to include the food items in their family diets. On the other hand, 32 per cent of the members of the discussion groups tried the new food items. When it was found that the discussion and decision technique was significantly more influential than lectures, requests, appeals, and exhortations, the experiment was used as a model for further studies of behavior change.

In the first experiment, different persons were used as leaders of the lecture and the discussion groups. Since the differences in behavior change could be attributed to the personalities of the leaders, a second experiment was performed using the same leaders for both the lecture and the discussion groups. Again in a controlled experiment, housewives were called together and groups formed. Again both the lecture method and the discussion method were used. It was found that once again the discussion method produced a decisively greater change in the desired direction. Also it was found that the effects were retained after an interval of four weeks.

A third study compared the effectiveness of individual instruction with group decision. The subjects were mothers of newborn babies and the problem was one of getting them to feed their babies proper diets. Mothers had been given advice on the feeding of their babies by a nutritionist who talked with each of them just before they were discharged from the hospital. The mothers also received printed advice on the composition of the formula. They were specifically instructed about the importance of orange juice and cod liver oil. However, the effect of this program had not been satisfactory. The group-decision method was tried, and again the results were favorable to the group-decision method, although the mothers were not acquainted with one another and they had no contacts during the weeks that followed.

These studies attempted to change standard ways, or well-established ways, of behaving. The behavior was that which is very similar to what is called group "norms." When norm behavior was discussed previously, it was shown that when an individual tries to diverge from a group standard for behaving, he will be subjected to group pressure in an attempt to make him adhere to a norm. Such an individual may be ridiculed, threatened, or finally rejected by the group if he does not conform to the group's idea of how persons ought to behave in certain instances. That is, group sanctions will be brought to bear on such an individual in an attempt to bring him back into line with the norm of the group.

Lewin's idea in his research studies was that this pressure exerted by the group upon members to make them conform to established standards was the reason that leader attempts to change such behavior so frequently were ineffective. In particular, he pointed out that attempts to change individuals singly were usually unsuccessful because where such attempts did succeed, the individuals who changed became deviants from the group.

These considerations brought Lewin and his coworkers to the conclusion that it is usually easier to change the behavior of individuals who are adhering to an established way of behaving by changing the group standard (or norm) than by changing each individual one by one. It also brought the experimenters to the view that in order to change the standard of the whole group certain special techniques were needed. The special methods used, then, were discussion plus a group decision to try another way of behaving.

The relatively high success of the discussion and group-decision method of change appeared to be the result of two major factors. The first was that this method did not have to work against group pressures that would attempt to cause an individual to adhere to the established group norm. The second was that group pressures were in fact put to work to create the change desired. The process involved weakening the forces that resisted change; then, by means of discussion, establishing a clear idea of the aimed-for behavior or activity; and finally, asking the group members to indicate their willingness to try the change.

Factors Influencing Group Decision

It must be remembered that in these studies, the changes desired related to *individuals*—that is, the group as an entity was not the focus, but rather the technique attempted to change *individual behavior*. These studies should be clearly differentiated from those that involve collective solutions to group problems. Also, the technique involved behavior that was considered desirable by an outside agent, rather than behavior considered desirable by the group members themselves.

The techniques used were simple. The reasons for the desired change and the importance and need for change were presented as effectively as possible. The discussion procedure attempted to secure high involvement of the group members and was conducted in as objective and unprejudiced a manner as possible. The discussion always ended with the leader's request for individual decisions regarding intended action. Although the procedure was found to be more effective than lecture, appeal, or even individual instruction, it was not entirely clear how various factors affected the results, or why a number of individuals changed their established way of behaving to the manner of behaving requested by the group leader.

To determine the factors that contributed most to Lewin's results on group decision, Bennett [2] assessed the contributions of four variables: group discussion, group decision, group commitment, and the degree of consensus. She found that group discussion, as an influence technique, was no more effective an inducement to action than was a lecture. The factor of public commitment was found not to be an essential element in itself. However, the process of making a decision and the degree to which members perceived that there was consensus regarding the need for change were found to be the important variables that contributed to the success of the experiments. In other words, a high degree of actual or perceived group consensus regarding intention to act was found to raise the probability that individual members of the group would execute the action desired.

[2] Edith Becker Bennett, "Discussion, Decision, Commitment, and Consensus in 'Group Decision,' " *Human Relations*, 8:251–273, 1955.

The literature of elementary education abounds with references to the successful use of discussion procedures to determine courses of action and to provide standards for behavior. Bennett's study showed that discussion, as an influence technique, was no more effective in inducing action than was a lecture. Group discussion, *per se*, did not serve to heighten the probability of action. Nevertheless, when an attempt to influence the group was coupled with a request for a decision or a commitment, and when a large proportion of the group indicated a positive decision, the group members perceived this as consensus. Once the group members perceived a high degree of consensus, there was strong probability that the members would carry out the action they said they would perform.

Horwitz and Lee[3] attempted to show why members of groups changed behavior after engaging in decision-making. They concluded that as a result of the decision-making process, motivational energy tended to be channeled into action. When groups were not guided in decision-making, motivational energy tended to be channeled into wish fulfillment. It appeared that when groups decided to act on the basis of agreement, and when members were allowed to choose from several alternative paths before they engaged in activities that led them toward a goal, the process involved a mechanism for controlling the disposition of motivational energy, and this mechanism directed the energy toward action. In groups where the decision-making step was short-circuited by an authoritarian leader who made choices for the group and who told the members they were obliged to follow a selected course of action, the motivational energies of the group were channeled into wish fulfillment. The psychological environment, or the morale of the group, was affected. The group did not strive toward goals set by someone else for the group to follow.

Group decision and group discussion were studied by Pennington et al.[4] in an effort to determine their differential effects. They found that agreement in groups was increased most of all when discussion and decision were combined in the procedure. They found, however, that discussion did have an effect even though no group decision was announced. The presence or absence of discussion seemed to have slightly more effect upon agreement than did the presence or absence of decision; the groups permitted to make a decision without discussion reached more

[3] Murray Horwitz and F. G. Lee, "Effects of Decision Making by Group Members on Recall of Finished and Unfinished Tasks," *Journal of Abnormal and Social Psychology*, 49:201–210, 1954.

[4] D. F. Pennington, Jr., Francois Haravey, and Bernard M. Bass, "Some Effects of Decision and Discussion on Coalescence, Change, and Effectiveness," *Journal of Applied Psychology*, 41:404–408, 1958.

agreement than groups that had no opportunity to either discuss the issue or make a group decision.

When discussion and decision were used together, the greatest opinion change occurred, but when either discussion or decision alone were permitted, opinions also changed to some degree. The effect was more pronounced, however, with use of group discussion. The experimenters concluded that changes in groups result primarily from interaction among members, and that clarifying the group decision implements the effects.

The study supported earlier findings that showed that change in attitudes, opinions, and behaviors can be brought about by use of the discussion and decision technique. Although it also showed that discussion alone had some effect on whether a group would reach an agreement and whether members would change opinions, the effect was not great. The implications are that if teachers wish to change opinions or group expectancies concerning what is desirable behavior, discussion and decision should be used in combination.

Personal Involvement and Active Participation

Other studies have been conducted whose designs closely parallel the experiments initiated by Lewin and his associates. Although for the most part these researches have been conducted in industry, they deserve the attention of teachers, since they show ways of changing the behaviors of individuals in a group in a direction that initially is not considered important by the individuals concerned but is of importance to the leader or other persons outside the group. These studies show that under some conditions, it is possible to change individual behavior by changing the behavior of the group as a whole.

An experiment by Coch and French [5] demonstrated that group resistance to change in methods of work could be overcome by the use of group meetings in which management communicated the need for change and stimulated group participation in planning changes. The problem concerned the resistance of production workers to necessary changes in methods and jobs.

The first step taken before actual change was attempted was to devise a preliminary theory to account for the resistance to change. In other words, the reason for the problem was sought. Once the problem was analyzed, an experiment was designed employing three degrees of group participation. The first group involved no participation. The

[5] Lester Coch and John R. P. French, Jr., "Overcoming Resistance to Change," *Human Relations*, 1:512–532, 1948.

second group involved participation through representation. The third group involved total participation by members. Total participation in planning changes was found to have the strongest influence upon changing behavior. The experimenters concluded that it was possible for management to modify greatly, or to remove completely, group resistance to change in methods of work.

The procedure of getting individuals personally involved in a problem or an issue and having them actively participate as a means of changing behavior has been utilized in various other experiments. For example, a study that demonstrated how a group was helped to discover new facts which then became the group's facts was reported by Marrow and French.[6] The problem in this case was that the management of an industrial concern refused to accept a report which gave evidence that women over 30 years of age could be trained without difficulty. To achieve a change in beliefs, the members of the management group were asked to conduct their own analysis of the situation. When all the facts were collected and presented to the executive group, these facts then became the management's facts, and the policy concerning the hiring of women over 30 years of age was immediately changed.

Levine and Butler [7] found that the group-decision method was much more effective than the lecture method for producing changes in socially undesirable behavior. They were interested in a method of changing behavior and attitudes, since they noted that education in itself did not change attitudes or behavior significantly. The researchers were concerned with comparing group decision with a formal lecture as a method of producing changes in socially undesirable behavior. Two questions were involved: (1) Was the acquisition of knowledge enough to lead a group of individuals to change a socially undesirable behavior pattern? and (2) Was group decision more effective than a formal lecture in producing a change in behavior.

The experiment was done in an industrial plant. The subjects were supervisors whose jobs were to rate the work done by men under their supervision. The usual tendency of the supervisors was to overrate men in higher-grade jobs and underrate those in lower-grade jobs. This resulted in a biased rating on the part of the supervisors in favor of men in higher-grade jobs. The problem was to change this tendency toward bias.

The study made it clear that group decision was more effective in

[6] Alfred Marrow and John R. P. French, Jr., "Changing a Stereotype in Industry," *Journal of Social Issues,* 7:33–37, August 1945.

[7] Jacob Levine and John Butler, "Lecture vs. Group Decision in Changing Group Behavior," *Journal of Applied Psychology,* 36:29–33, February 1952.

reducing the prejudiced ratings of the supervisors than was formal lecture. The study showed also that lecture had practically no influence on the supervisors. Even though they were informed of their error, and were shown that it was their responsibility to eliminate error, they took no action. The findings showed, then, that the acquisition of knowledge did not lead to a change in behavior. Although the study did not show how the group forces operated, the influence of the group decision was sufficient to overcome a habitual way of thinking and acting and created a decided change in behavior.

A study in group decision was conducted in a college classroom situation to find out if an application of the technique would induce a class group to set higher goals.[8]

A control group and an experimental group were matched in the following respects: all of the subjects were freshmen; all were given the same objective tests for the course; the same lecture material was covered for both classes; and the same instructor taught both groups.

In leading the decision-making process in the experimental group, the same techniques were employed as were used in the Lewin studies. A plan for raising each individual student's grades was discussed. Before deciding on a plan, the members of the group discussed such problems as the attitude of some members who did not wish to get higher grades than their friends in the class. After discussing this point, the class members agreed that they did not care if friends made better marks and this would not be held against them. Other objections to raising individual grades were considered by the group. When it seemed that the class had decided on a plan to raise each member's grade by five points, the experimenter called upon every member of the class to express individual feelings concerning the plan of action. All members expressed approval and agreed to try the plan.

The results of the study showed that the marks of the experimental group went up not five but seven points. The gain in scores for the experimental group was so much greater than the gain in the control group that the difference could not be reasonably attributed to chance. It was concluded that the group-decision technique could be applied effectively in classroom situations, and that one of its uses could be the raising of individual levels of aspiration.

McKeachie[9] used classroom groups to conduct an experiment which contrasted three conditions: group discussion followed by decisions; lec-

[8] Max Martin Kostick, "An Experiment in Group Decision, *The Journal of Teacher Education*, 8:67–72, March 1957.

[9] Wilbert McKeachie, "Individual Conformity to Attitudes of Classroom Groups," *Journal of Abnormal and Social Psychology*, 49:282–289, April 1954.

tures followed by the results of a secret ballot; and lecture with votes not announced. The results indicated that the discussion and decision technique caused individual members to shift their attitudes in the direction they discerned the group as a whole was changing. The experiment showed too, that students in classes where group techniques were used actually conformed to the group norms more closely than did students in classes led by leaders who made decisions for the group. In group-centered classes, when a new way of behaving was discussed and agreed upon by members, it was perceived by members as being a group norm, or a way of behaving expected by the group. In leader-centered classes, a discussion devoted to a new way of behaving did not cause members to view the discussed change as having established a new group norm.

Implications for Classroom Groups

For many reasons, undesirable group standards for behaving are sometimes established in classroom groups. Also, there are many reasons why individuals in class groups occasionally develop obstructive attitudes that negate teaching efforts to a large extent. Some group norms for behavior and some individual attitudes toward school and school work strongly influence the amount and kind of learning that takes place in the classroom. The experiments in group decision and group participation suggest that such techniques may be used in the classroom to change those behavioral norms that hinder or block learning or that decrease the time spent on school tasks. Teachers can use these methods to change pupil attitudes and behavior. Findings from the studies indicate that class group influences, which often contribute to undesirable behavior, may be utilized to solve behavior problems that hamper teaching efforts and frustrate teachers—including the very behavior problems to which these influences contribute.

Research has shown how groups themselves can be used effectively as agents in bringing about desired change by creating a shared perception by members of the need for change. Techniques that create this shared perception of a need for change can be used, then, to increase both teacher effectiveness and group productivity.

The Techniques Involved in Group Decision

Teachers indicate that one of the most baffling problems they face is that of helping the children in their class groups develop self-discipline.

When class groups develop ways of behaving that are not conducive to the best learning situations, most teachers wish to handle these behaviors in ways that create desires for change in the members themselves. The majority of teachers who use authoritarian procedures to control unacceptable classroom behavior do so only because they do not know how to bring about desire on the part of children to change their behaviors. They frequently try group discussion and they frequently try to point out values to be gained by acting in more acceptable ways. When they find these methods ineffective, they are forced into using commands, threats, and other authoritarian methods of control. In most cases, teachers find that the use of authority instead of skill serves only as a temporary way of taking care of a problem. Threat may control one way of acting, but another undesirable behavior usually is substituted in its place.

The use of group-decision techniques may be considered as a discipline method that develops desire for change in the children themselves. It is a way of controlling unacceptable behavior through the use of skill rather than the use of authority.

Teachers employing the group-decision technique must have a genuine respect for individuals in the class group. This method of changing behavior is not a way of manipulating people, nor is it a way of selling a group on an idea. It utilizes a number of generally accepted psychological principles, and its use demands understanding and skill.

The processes involved in change usually are presented in a series of steps or procedures. Lippitt, Watson, and Wesley,[10] for example, outline a set of practices to be followed when change is planned in groups. Although not designed for classroom use, the steps in procedure are essentially the same as those that have been tried in educational situations. The steps include: (1) a clarification of the problem and a presentation of the necessity for change, (2) a development of the need for change, (3) an examination of alternative behaviors, (4) an establishment of goals or intentions of action, and (5) the transformation of intentions into actual change effort. If the change to be made is very great, it is suggested that only small changes be made at one time. After each change is established, the group can be led to the next change, and on to higher and higher levels of desired behavior.

For teacher use, the group-decision technique can be divided into the following general areas: (1) studying the situation, (2) preparing the proposal, (3) presenting the proposal to the group, (4) guiding group discussion, and (5) getting a group decision to act.

[10] Ronald Lippitt, Jeanne Watson, and Bruce Wesley, *Planned Change: A Comparative Study of Principles and Techniques,* New York: Harcourt, Brace & Company, 1958.

Studying the Situation

Before attempting to change class group behavior, the teacher must analyze the situation. The teacher should attempt to answer such questions as the following: (1) Why is change desirable? (2) What can be achieved by changing behavior? (3) What is the precise nature of the behavior needing change? (4) In what direction is change desired? (5) Does the desired change require some action on the part of individuals in the group?

Perhaps the steps in the procedure can be clarified using the following example of a common classroom behavior problem.

NOISY BEHAVIOR

The problem of noisy behavior exists in my fourth grade class. It occurs at the time we are preparing to go to the cafeteria for lunch. Room standards have been set to govern behavior when preparing to leave for the cafeteria, and the children know they are expected to leave the room at a certain designated time. Even though they are reminded daily of their standards, it takes from six to eight minutes every day before they settle down and become quiet so they can be excused for lunch.

Since we are scheduled to be in the cafeteria line at an exact time, this means that the class period that immediately precedes lunch (science) must be shortened by at least five minutes. The fifth grade is not allowed to move into the cafeteria line until the fourth grade is in line, so they often have to wait for us.

This problem of getting the room to settle down and become quiet before being excused for lunch occurs daily and nothing that has been tried has any permanent effect—not even making up time after school.

The above example describes a problem common to many class groups. The teacher states that the problem is "noisy" behavior occurring just before lunch period. In reporting the problem, however, the teacher indicates that the real problem is not "noisy" behavior, but instead is a problem relating to the amount of time the class spends in getting ready for lunch. The teacher must see that the class is ready to enter the cafeteria line at an exact time. Since it takes the class from six to eight minutes to get ready for lunch, the time must be taken from the science period. A teacher who views this behavior as being primarily a problem of "noisy" behavior will have difficulty changing the behavior. The teacher needs to analyze the problem further. Answers to the questions suggested earlier will aid in this analysis. For example, the answer to the question, "Why is change desirable?" is fairly obvious. If the time spent in preparing to go to lunch is lessened by several minutes, more time can be spent on the science lesson. Also, the strain on the teacher will be less severe.

If the behavior can be changed, two objectives may be achieved. One, more time can be given to science. Two, the danger of the class not meeting the cafeteria deadline will be lessened.

The precise nature of the behavior to be changed is *not* change from noisy behavior to quiet behavior. The problem is speeding up the process of getting ready for lunch. At this point, the report of the incident gives no clues as to what this activity entails. Perhaps science equipment must be put away. Perhaps it includes washing hands before lunch. Perhaps furniture must be moved back to its accustomed place. The activities the class must perform before being dismissed for the lunch line should be listed by the teacher as part of the analysis of the problem.

The teacher in the example does not state clearly what changes are desired. Thinking through the problem, however, should make the directional change clear. If the analysis of the problem reveals that about three to four minutes is sufficient time for the group to put away materials and get cleaned up for lunch, then the change needed is to shorten the class preparation time by three to four minutes.

The last question, "Does the desired change require some action on the part of individuals in the group?" is a crucial one. The change asked for by the teacher must involve action. To illustrate, suppose that the teacher does not carefully analyze the problem. The teacher then decides to ask the class to make a decision to be "less noisy" and "more quiet" when getting ready for lunch. What does "becoming more quiet" require in the way of behavior from each individual? Each child might interpret the request to be "more quiet" differently. There are degrees of "quietness." A request to a class group to be "more quiet" is not operational. If this decision is interpreted as meaning "less talking," then the behavior expected is clarified somewhat, but it is still indefinite.

Many times teachers say they have difficulty with class groups because the children do not adhere to established behavior standards. This may be caused, in part, by the fact that the standards are not specific about the actual behaviors expected. Terms such as *quiet, careful, prompt, considerate,* and *kind* are subject to individual interpretation, and they do not specify particular behavior patterns. Group standards for behaving and requests to change behavior must be concrete and must state definitely the types of action individuals are expected to execute.

Preparing the Proposal

If the proposed change is not presented objectively, or if it is stated in such a way that the group members feel they are being pressured, the group may fail to react favorably. Hence it is imperative that considerable thought be given to the proposal that will state the desired change in behavior. Deciding on what to say and how to state it requires study and preparation.

It is assumed that at this point the problem is clearly in focus, and that the teacher has clear answers to the following questions: What change is necessary? Why is it necessary? What are the causes of the problem?

The group may be approached in two ways—directly or indirectly. The direct approach involves stating the proposal, presenting the necessity for change to the group, encouraging the group to discuss any objections, restating the proposal as a plan of action, and asking the group for a decision. The use of the indirect approach requires that the teacher guide the group toward recognizing that change is needed. The suggestion for change comes from the group, with perhaps some directions or suggestions from the teacher.

If the teacher of the "noisy" class decides to use the direct approach, the proposal might be planned to include the following ideas, although the vocabulary and the ways the ideas are stated will be individual with each teacher.

Is it possible to cut the preparation for lunch time by three to five minutes?

If it is possible for us to do this we will have more time for our science lesson and we will not run the risk of being late in the cafeteria line.

Do you think it is possible? How could we do it? What suggestions do you have, etc.?

The teacher should prepare the direct proposal so that the statements are in positive terms instead of in terms that might make the group defensive.

For example, if the proposal were prepared as follows, and if the tone of voice were slightly accusing, consider how a class group might react.

It takes us from six to eight minutes each day to get ready for lunch. This means that each day we must shorten our science period by three to five minutes. Some weeks we lose as much as thirty minutes of science time. There is another problem, also. Some days the science period runs longer and if we are slow getting ready on these days, the fifth grade must wait for us. Now, don't you believe that three or four minutes is enough time to get ready for lunch? What do you think?

It seems quite likely that most class groups would react defensively to the last statement. The children might discuss the situation and some might seem to agree with the proposal, but the majority of the children would perceive that the responses were those expected by the teacher rather than expressions of the true feelings of the group members.

The proposal should be prepared so that it interests and challenges the group. Unless the request for change calls forth true responses and real expressions of feeling, and unless the children actually see merit in the proposal, no change is apt to take place.

An indirect approach may seem advisable. In this case, the teacher would prepare a problem statement such as: "What could we do to shorten the time it takes us to get ready for lunch?"

The indirect approach takes more teacher skill perhaps, since the teacher desires a particular change in the behavior of each individual but wishes the suggestion for change to come from the group. This means that at some point the proposal will be made to cut the preparation time by several minutes if the suggestion is not forthcoming from the group. When this idea should be injected by the teacher is not easily determined in advance, since this will depend upon the course the discussion takes.

Presenting the Proposal to the Group

In analyzing a number of situations in which teachers have tried to use group-decision methods and have failed, it seems that most of the failures were due to the same reason. They failed primarily because they did not introduce the proposal in a way that involved the group members. It has been mentioned previously that children in classrooms and even college students have learned to respond to teacher questions and requests in the way they judge they are expected to respond. When classroom groups are observed, this tendency is noticed quite frequently. The teacher asks a question, and either the learned response is given back promptly or the individual gives a tentative answer in a questioning tone, indicating that he is groping for the answer the teacher wishes. This is particularly true in elementary classrooms when the question involves some aspect of social behavior. Since the children in the group recognize the answers made by various individuals as representing desired teacher responses, the answers or suggestions have no influence upon the group. They are not discerned as responses that represent true feelings or true beliefs of the group members.

If a class group has been accustomed to answering questions according to the way the members believe the teacher wants them answered, it may be difficult for the teacher to find a means of overcoming this reaction. The teacher must watch for these responses. For example, a teacher may plan to introduce a problem involving a desired behavior change by saying, "How can we change to our reading groups without taking so much time and without creating so much disturbance?" Very frequently the class members will respond as follows:

"We shouldn't talk so much."

"We should move quietly."

"We could make the noisy ones stay after school."

Unless the teacher is prepared to question these statements, and is able to break through these mechanical answers, the attempt to change behavior using group influence will fail at this point.

If the group members do recognize that the teacher really desires them to express their honest views—that is, if they apprehend that they are being asked to engage in a free discussion, the next reaction the teacher usually must cope with is a punitive one. When children are asked how to deal with a problem they very often shift from a consideration of the factors involved and seek to solve the problem by placing blame. Again, the teacher must be prepared with statements and questions to direct the member's thinking toward certain aspects of the problem instead of ways of shifting responsibility and blame. In a sense, this tendency of children to turn from a consideration of the various aspects of the problem to devising schemes of punishment is a learned response, but it is also a defense reaction. If the teacher is prepared to state the problem in various ways, and always in terms of the nature of the situation, it will help in avoiding this reaction.

Guiding Group Discussion and Decision

A teacher must guide and direct the group discussion when a change in behavior is the issue being discussed. There is a difference between guiding, directing, and controlling discussion. A teacher who guides and directs group discussion is assisting the group in making decisions. Controlling the discussion means that the teacher is exerting (or attempting to exert) manipulative power over the group.

Unless a teacher can adequately facilitate communication in the group, it is doubtful that established norm behavior can be changed. Adequate communication is fundamental to the group-decision process, since, in order to achieve change, each person in the group must perceive that the majority of group members desire to establish a new norm for behaving. The essence of communication in this process is to open the communication channels so individual members will express their ideas and feelings freely. The group members need to know how others in the group react to the proposal for changing behavior.

Teachers can rightfully ask why, if a group has established an undesirable pattern of behavior, the members are willing to change after discussing the situation. The answer seems to be related to the fact that children seek approval rather than disapproval, and they usually "rise up" to expectations providing that these expectations are reasonable. Certain expected patterns of behavior in the school situation are generally known by children, for they are well established in the school culture and have been for generations.

Though many of these accustomed patterns of behavior are not formally stated, children know what is generally sanctioned and what is not. If children are given the opportunity to accept responsibility for improving their own behavior they often will do so, providing it is a group effort. A single individual in the classroom may have an uneasy feeling that his behavior is not all that it should be, but he recognizes that if he behaves contrary to the group norm he will be ostracized by the group. The group norm most often is more binding than traditional school norms. When a child perceives that others in the group feel that an undesirable norm should be changed, this enables him to behave according to the way he privately believes he should, without having to run counter to group expectations. It is recognized that not all children hold values in accordance with what is usually considered acceptable school conduct, but a sizable number of children do.

The point just discussed may be made clearer by reporting a seventh grade girl's account of an incident that occurred in her classroom. The girl, Sandy, was quite upset when she came home from school one day because her friends in the class were "mean and rude" to a substitute teacher. A number of children switched seats, responded to names that were not their own, gave conflicting reports about assignments, and in other ways acted to confuse the substitute. When Sandy had finished pouring out the story she was asked if she conveyed her feelings to the others in the class, or if she tried to help the teacher in any way. Sandy expressed surprise that such a question should be asked. Her response was, "What would the kids think if I stood up for the teacher, or told them off?"

Since her account of the incident indicated that she thought *all* of the other youngsters had joined in the sport of harassing the substitute, this view was explored further. Sandy was asked if *all* of the other children actually joined in this activity. After some consideration, Sandy replied that she guessed that only six or eight youngsters were involved, but she added defensively, "All the others thought it was funny!" Pressed still further, Sandy retracted and said that probably a considerable number felt as she did but that most likely they thought, too, that everyone else was approving the behavior. Sandy was asked if she believed that the six or eight children who changed seats and who otherwise actively participated in causing difficulty for the substitute would have done so if they had realized that a large number of their classmates disapproved of their behavior. Sandy thought for quite a while before she answered. She finally replied that she did not think they would have acted that way if they had not thought the others were approving because they were "really pretty good kids."

Many children feel somewhat as Sandy did in the above situation when a group behaves in an unacceptable manner. Their privately held attitudes may not be very strong, but if they are given opportunity to change to more approved behavior, they will respond readily in most cases, *providing* they recognize that others in the group feel as they do.

Another reason why most class group members respond positively when they are asked to consider a change in behavior is that the majority of children welcome the chance to assume some responsibility for their behavior. They enjoy being asked to consider such a proposal. Of course, some children will not respond favorably to requests for change, but if the group is cohesive, and if these children desire group approval, group pressure will influence them in most cases. Persons who do not accept the idea that children are innately "good," and those who believe that children must be *made* to conform, of course, will be unsuccessful with this technique, because they will not have faith that children can plan ways of improving behavior. Children can detect such attitudes even when they are unspoken.

When a change in group behavior is desired, the group discussion must be guided and directed so that, so far as possible, each individual has an opportunity to express his viewpoint. The discussion must be guided in such a way that allows group members to express their ideas and yet not seem to be in opposition to the group as a whole. Many children should be invited to contribute, even if they do not volunteer, so group members can become aware of the reactions of the majority.

Classroom group discussions are held for a variety of purposes. Regardless of the type of discussion, the teacher performs several general functions. The teacher sees that the discussion is focused on one point at a time. Action is taken to keep one or a few persons from dominating the discussion. The more retiring individuals are invited to express their opinions. Attention is called to facts that are overlooked, and if necessary, issues are clarified.

Besides these general functions, when the discussion is concerned with behavior change, the teacher must keep careful watch of the situation as it develops. One of the important roles the teacher enacts is to integrate the various contributions and to draw out the relationships or true meanings of what is being said. In children's groups it is not uncommon for an individual child to make a comment that appears to have no bearing on the topic being discussed. If the teacher is able to distinguish the meaning and recognize the connection between this apparently irrelevant comment and the main topic, the intention can then be conveyed by the teacher to the group. In this way every contribution can be linked to the main idea.

A teacher who has skill in guiding discussion is able both to reflect and deflect comments back to the group. The process of reflecting comments back to the group is merely a restatement of what has been said, but in a different form. This serves two purposes. One, it promotes better understanding in the group; and two, it makes clear to the person who contributed the remark that he has been understood.

Deflection means that the teacher restates questions asked and turns them back to the class members for answers, but this is done only when the answers lie in the group itself. If the questions are requests for information that the teacher has, then she should answer. Part of the group-decision process is to give the group as much necessary information about the problem as is available. The often-used teacher technique of responding to a question by saying, "Now that is a good question! Who would like to find the answer?" is not applicable in this situation. The discussion must flow toward the decision-making process, building up a force which will aid members in reaching a decision to change.

Since the major purpose of conducting the discussion is to bring forth individual attitudes regarding the proposed change, the teacher must avoid making judgmental responses to individual contributions to the discussion. The teacher may have a tendency to evaluate a feeling or thought expressed. Such evaluations by the teacher tend to block communication. Not only must the teacher's statements be objective, but his actions, expressions, and tone of voice should not convey an evaluative attitude whether this attitude is one of acceptance or nonacceptance. This is not easy to do, but this rather neutral reaction should be maintained by the teacher so far as possible. This point may be illustrated by an example.

A class group was anticipating a field trip; two previous trips had been marred by some unruly behavior. The teacher was trying to get the group to agree that behavior on the bus should be changed. One youngster who was not really concerned with the problem, although he was one of the offenders, was one of the first to speak, "When kids are just riding along with nothing to do, they are bound to talk and make some noise. Couldn't we get a bus with a T.V.?" Of course, the statement was intended to get a reaction from the group and perhaps from the teacher. The boy was not disappointed. The class laughed and the teacher responded with a reprimand. Even though the teacher recognized full well that the boy did not intend that his comment should be taken seriously, it could have been accepted and considered objectively. The teacher could have reflected the statement back to the group with a statement similar to the following:

> Do you mean that since the bus ride is going to be long, we should plan something or arrange for some activity that will occupy our attention— in the same way that a T.V. would keep us interested, if it were possible to get a bus equipped in this way?"

This type of response reveals acceptance but is not judgmental. Such a response keeps the discussion moving in a positive direction. It may act as a subtle suggestion to the group even though it is not intended to do so. Such a response often discourages further attempts by children to block or hinder the discussion by inappropriate suggestions. It encourages others to say what they think, but keeps the discussion in a serious vein.

A change in tone or pitch of the voice, a facial expression, or an emphasis placed on part of a statement may clearly indicate to the group the teacher's acceptance or rejection of a suggestion. For example, during the same class discussion regarding behavior when riding in the bus, one child commented that part of the trouble was that everyone wanted to sit by a window. He suggested that this problem might be solved if seats were changed during the bus trip. Disapproval of this suggestion was conveyed to the child and to the group by the teacher's tone of voice. "Do you think we could change seats while the bus is moving?"

The statement itself did not imply judgment, but the voice inflection did to the extent that the child to whom the question was addressed simply answered, "No, I guess not." Also, when the teacher continued with the question, "Who has another suggestion?", no child responded. The teacher was forced into making some suggestions to which the group agreed, but by this time communication in the group was completely blocked.

Objectivity on the part of the teacher is essential in conducting a discussion directed toward changing the behavior of individuals in groups. Unless the teacher is objective in manner and in statements made, ideas and feelings cannot be disseminated and evaluated by group members. There will be nothing that can be converted into a basis for decision.

In conducting the discussion, certain techniques can be employed by the teacher to expedite the process and simplify certain aspects of it. Consider that a teacher is going to use the following procedure in guiding the discussion toward a group decision.

1. The group is presented with the problem and the related facts.
2. The members are asked if they will consider the problem and they are invited to present their ideas and suggestions.
3. Following this discussion, the group's cooperation is requested. (Can the behavior be changed? How?)
4. After a decision is reached and agreed upon by the group as a whole, individual members are asked if they accept the decision.

In steps two and three, if the teacher organizes the objections and suggestions on a blackboard as they are presented by members, the teacher will facilitate the whole process in a number of ways. When suggestions are written on the board, the teacher does not have to make a comment in every case. The writing of the suggestion or objection on the board is an act of acceptance and the group usually perceives it as such. When an individual's suggestion is written on the board for all to consider, it seems to stimulate others to make contributions. Perhaps the various suggestions arouse other ideas. Organizing the ideas on the board has another value. The discussion can be guided toward a positive solution by putting the positive contributions on the board as well as the objections, and even objections to ideas often have positive aspects. When all suggestions are on the board, step three (the process of selection and elimination of ideas) is hastened, since repetition of an idea is unnecessary. The discarded ideas can be erased, leaving only those that are to be incorporated in the final decision.

Although assembling and organizing the thoughts and conceptions regarding the change in behavior requires skill, the most difficult aspect of this procedure is condensing the statements into short phrases. While the teacher is writing a phrase on the board, the individual's comment may be repeated by the teacher so that all can see and hear what the phrase represents. Sometimes the teacher may rephrase and say, "You mean—?" Although the phrase often does not summarize the main idea, experience has shown that a phrase or sometimes only one word is sufficient for the group members to recall what was said. Experience has revealed, also, that if the group members are hesitant about expressing their beliefs or their proposals, the simple tactic of placing an individual's initials after his suggestion will evoke suggestions from others in the group.

It is necessary to allot sufficient time for the discussion. Since school time is well regulated, it is important that the discussion is not interrupted by a recess period or some other fixed break that would make necessary an interruption or else cause the discussion to be hurried or terminated before the decision is firmly established.

Since the purpose of the discussion in this situation is to get each individual in the group to make a decision, the final steps the teacher takes are to coordinate, harmonize, and ask the individuals in the group if they accept the final decision. It must be kept in mind that although the decision comes from the group as a whole, each member finally decides *how he is going to act as an individual.* The way of acting is clearly defined and it may involve a plan for behavior. However, the plan usually does not involve group action in the same sense that working toward achieving a task goal involves group action and cooperation. Thus, when coordinating and harmonizing the outcome of the discussion, the teacher must keep in mind that it is desired that *individuals* agree to act in accordance with the new group expectations, and each person must clearly understand what this expectation entails.

In the final steps, the teacher pulls the various ideas together and relates them to one another. All the ideas agreed upon are harmonized into a final statement representing the decision. The group is asked to comment on the final decision. Is it acceptable? Are all the ideas included? Is the class as a whole satisfied? Finally, the various members of the group are asked if they are willing to act according to the agreement. The final statement can be an announcement that all have agreed to the proposal for change and it might include the time and other details of the first scheduled evaluation session.

Group Evaluation

The problem of the group-decision method is to change an individual's behavior from a less desirable way of behaving to a more desirable way of behaving. Or, this process has been expressed as moving from one level to a new level. The group forces that cause the individual to resist change in the first place—namely, the group pressures that encourage him to adhere to a given group norm, are used to move the individual to this new level of behavior. Lewin called this process "unfreezing" and "moving to a new level." However, many times the group cannot be changed to the desired level in one process or step. The first decision may carry the group to one point (improve the behavior to a degree), and the decision may "freeze" the behavior at this level, but many times an even greater change is desirable.

The evaluation procedure may serve to "freeze" or maintain the behavior at the new level, or it may serve to move the behavior further in the desired direction. In either case, the technique is very much the same as that used in this first attempt. The steps in evaluation may proceed somewhat as follows.

1. The group is asked to consider whether the decision to change behavior succeeded.

2. In terms of the total result, was the change effective? Were the desired results achieved? In what ways was the change not effective?

3. In terms of member behavior, was change accomplished? Did each member live up to the agreement? (Individuals can evaluate their own behaviors.)

4. Are further changes desirable? What changes are needed? If further changes are needed, what further is required of each individual? (Any new changes must be clearly stated in terms of actual behavior and understood by all.)

5. Do all agree to the new changes?

In discussing evaluation procedures as related to communicative behavior, Borosage [11] suggests that evaluation is operative on two levels. One level focuses on the extent to which the group achieves what it sets out to do. The second level directs attention to individual performance. Since the group-decision process as defined here is used to change individual behavior, failure to allow individuals to determine how well they did in living up to their agreement would be a gross oversight. A caution is necessary, however. The evaluation should not degenerate into a censuring or fault-finding session. This can be avoided by having various individuals state the obstacles or difficulties that kept them from following through on their agreements. The positive behaviors of individuals can be evaluated also, although in some instances this becomes no more than a series of testimonials. These may have a good effect, but since if one testifies, all must be given the same opportunity, the discussion may become sidetracked. The discussion should proceed directly toward a final agreement that the new change is satisfactory or that other changes are needed.

Evaluation sessions are of utmost importance for several reasons. For one thing, the group may after a period of time slip back to the previous way of behaving. The evaluation session serves to freeze or clinch the decision. It is seldom that the desired change is achieved with one group

[11] Lawrence Borosage, "A Basis For Viewing Communication," *The National Elementary Principal*, 41:6–12, May 1962.

discussion period. If the process is completely successful and the desired change is achieved, the members of the group gain enormous satisfaction from evaluating their success. The total group interaction process is improved by recounting and sharing this success. As will be noted in several examples, the teacher also may share the group's feeling of success, and group solidarity may be heightened by the group's recognition that the teacher is proud and pleased with what the group has accomplished. For all these reasons, the evaluation sessions are equally as important as the first sessions, and they should be planned and conducted with the same care.

Utilizing the Power of the Class Group

To further clarify the uses of the group-decision approach to problems of class group behavior, actual examples of trial experiments are cited in the following pages. A number of teachers have attempted to translate the group-decision method into action in their classrooms. Most of the examples represent efforts by teachers who were inexperienced in the use of the technique, and at times their lack of skill is noticeable. However, in spite of their inexperience and limitations, they achieved better results than they had previously been able to by means of lecture, appeal, discussion, and other commonly used practices.

The examples were selected to illustrate the more common kinds of problem that occur in classroom situations, thus demonstrating the practical uses of the method. Certain examples were selected, also, to further clarify the procedures, and to show how the teachers utilized the techniques at various grade levels. Some examples were included to broaden the variety of situations described and to show that the method has application to many kinds of behavior problem that impair teacher effectiveness or interfere with teaching programs.

CHANGING NOISY, DISORDERLY BEHAVIOR IN THE CLASSROOM TO ORDERLY BEHAVIOR

(Example)

The half-hour preceding the lunch hour, which includes the washing of hands for lunch, has been a noisy one despite my best efforts. The children bang on the soap dispenser, crowd around the sink, pushing, shoving, laughing, and arguing. From a point across the room from the sink, I have been calling the children up to wash, one row at a time. I try to keep one eye on them and one on the reading group. Of course this divides my attention.

I need this half-hour for a reading group, because my room is so located that during the afternoon we are subjected to the noise from the lunch hours and recesses of older class groups.

I wished to change this noisy, disorderly situation to an orderly period—at least quiet enough to hear the reading group, and I wished to help the children to learn to take some responsibility for their own behavior at this time.

I had only to wait two days for what I considered an incident of such proportion that all of the children were involved. I was sitting in the far corner of the room surrounded by the reading group, when I called the children up to wash, row by row. I watched the trouble brew and finally boil over. There had been a general understanding in the class that unless it was *really important* the children were not to interrupt a reading period. However, at this time a little girl indignantly stalked up to me to protest in behalf of her friend who was in angry tears because some dirty, soapy water had splashed on her new dress. She was followed by the guilty boy who defended himself, and then before I knew it, I was completely surrounded by a group of children all talking at once trying to tell just what had happened. I explained that I could not hear anyone when they all talked at once and asked if they would think it over during the noon hour. Following lunch we would discuss the situation during our regular discussion period. They still wanted to tell about it then and there. It was only by pointing out that we had to finish washing or we would be late for lunch that I was able to persuade them to wait.

After lunch the children filed in "ready to burst at the seams." In the meantime I, too, had thought the situation over and decided that in the interest of time, it might be wise to ask them to pick some representatives to present the various viewpoints. But I could see that the incident had grown in proportions, for the postponement had created the same effect as putting a lid on a bottle of bees. I gave up the representative idea and opened the discussion by saying, "Now, what happened?" I called on the girl who had come up to me first. She said, "Well, Vicky wasn't doing anything, just drying her hands, and Ronney splashed dirty, soapy water all over her new dress." Ronney countered with, "Somebody pushed me. It wasn't on purpose. It was somebody in back of me." Then followed a dozen versions of who gave the first push and descriptions of a series of other incidents. One girl sitting near the sink complained that her arithmetic paper was knocked on the floor and walked on. At that point I started writing on the board all the things that had happened, making sure that someone in the reading group reported that we hadn't been able to hear the readers in the reading group.

After the "barrel had been scraped" for additional incidents and the list on the board was really a formidable one, I began to sense that what the class wanted now was to pinpoint the culprits and bring them to trial. I reminded myself that with punishment, we don't change attitudes—just surface behavior—and that this was the point where I should try to get them to agree to another plan of behavior.

To get them to propose another way of behaving I continued with, "Why do you suppose people act this way? Why do people push and shove?" A child answered, "Chuck pushes everyday." And another said, "Dennis always tries to get at the head of the line." This was a new angle to me. I could see why a child might want to be the head of the line to lead the class somewhere, but I couldn't see why a child would want to be at the head of a line to wash. In fact, I had held a secret conviction that the children liked to get away from their work and just visit and make noise— or at least so it looked to me—and if they were at the back of the line they could get away from their work longer. I kept right on pegging away at the reasons why people liked to be first in line to wash, and then it came out. Monty said, "If we are first in line, we don't have to miss so much time just waiting there and we can get more work done." I looked around at the children, making sure not to betray my surprise. As I listened further to them, I could not doubt that this really was a very important reason to them. I went on with my next question, "What do you suppose we might do so all these things (pointing to the list of undesirable things that had resulted from the disorderly behavior) won't happen again?"

Again we listed in a few simple words the suggestions given by the class, discussing each one and trying to decide why it might or might not work. This is about the way it went:

Suggestion:	"Have a monitor at the sink."
Answer:	"Well, the monitor wouldn't get his work done."
Answer:	"People don't do what the line monitor says, and they wouldn't do what a sink monitor says."
Another suggestion:	"Have the children wash up during recess."
Answer:	"Then we wouldn't get to play much during recess."
Answer:	"Our hands would get dirty again before lunch."
Suggestion:	"Have the children come up to wash one at a time."

This plan seemed to meet with quite a bit of approval until one child suggested that it would take too long. This was argued back and forth until someone suggested that two children go up at a time, which would take only half as long. Someone else said there would be no need to push and shove and that if they made a disturbance we could easily see who did it. This seemed to be the consensus of opinion of the group, and though I had my own ideas about whether it would work, it was definitely a step in the right direction and did have some merit.

I asked for the plan to be restated so all would understand the mechanics of the plan—just how and when it was to be started, and the exact time the two children would start to wash. The class reasoned that this plan would take longer than it took a row to wash, so it was decided to start earlier. It was decided also that they would start the next day. The plan would be tried for two days in succession and then, following the second day, the class would discuss it to see how well it had worked and how well it had solved the problems involved. At this point each child was asked if he was willing to try the plan. All agreed.

The next day after recess the whole plan was stated again so all would understand it, and so children who had been absent when the plan was made would understand it.

I watched the situation from the reading group out of a corner of my eye. This proved to be unnecessary, as I could soon hear how it was going. Although the confusion at the sink was somewhat diminished, there was more confusion in the room. Everyone in the room watched every move to and from the sink. The watching was accompanied by comments and gesticulations. There were greetings and farewells. The whole thing was proceeding like a relay race. At this point I could see that I had one goal in mind and somehow or other the children had another. The idea of saving time for their lessons had become supplanted in their minds by a speed race.

The second day was not quite so noisy, but the situation was still far from desirable. After lunch, according to plan, we discussed the procedure again to evaluate it and to determine how it had worked out.

The children were jubilant and could scarcely wait to report the official washing times for both days. I agreed with them that we had washed more quickly, thereby giving people more time for their lessons. I suggested that we go over the problems one by one to see just how well each one had been met by the plan.

No one had been splashed.
The class was not late for the cafeteria.
No one had had his paper knocked to the floor or stepped on.
No one had been pushed or shoved.
The reading group could not hear the reading, and had been disturbed.
People did not get much work done because there had been so much confu-
sion.

When I asked why they thought the plan had not worked in the last two instances, answers came back that there was too much noise, people were watching the time and calling out, reminding people to hurry, etc.

I asked for suggestions about what might be done about these problems. We went through a list of ideas again. Finally one boy said that since there was plenty of time for washing we could have just one child up to wash at a time. That would prevent talking at the sink, and there would be just half as much noise coming and going to the sink. Also, since everyone knew we were going to get through in time, it would not be necessary to watch the clock nor any need to time people at the sink. This time I made sure that everyone understood the real goal of the plan—a quiet orderly washing procedure that would permit the accomplishment of work. There was general agreement that this last plan be tried.

The first day the second plan was tried there were a couple of slip-ups. One person forgot to go up to wash when his neighbor was through and there was a lag in time until several people took it upon themselves to notify the forgetful one in a way that the whole class could hear. The second day, however, was noticeably better.

We again brought the matter up for discussion and evaluation after the second day. All agreed that they had been able to get more work done. The reading group had been able to hear. The suggestion was made that when each child returned to his seat, he quietly tap his neighbor if the neighbor were not aware that it was his turn to wash.

The final results showed that this discussion procedure caused the children to perceive that a noisy, disorderly washing procedure caused many things to happen to them that they did not like. The discussion made them recognize that their behavior was not satisfactory to them and that they wanted to change it. I believe that originally the children wanted to find out who was causing the trouble, and their first idea was to have the culprit or culprits punished.

Through discussion, we were able to analyze the cause of the disorder and to see the problem in another light. They were able to see that the cause of the trouble was not the behavior of several children but a fault of the general procedure. Each child began to see that other children did not want to waste time by waiting in line to wash when they could be getting their work done.

The first trial plan—the one having the two children at a time go up to wash—turned out to be a relay race, possibly because the ultimate goal was not stressed sufficiently. Somehow the idea of speeding through the procedure became uppermost in their minds rather than the goal of having enough order that work could be accomplished.

It was only by going back to the original problems and evaluating them that we were able to get back to the real goal—that of having the room quiet and orderly so work could be accomplished. Then the children began to see the problem in a new light.

At the time of this writing, some ten days later, there is no doubt that we are all immensely pleased with the way that the plan has worked. It still is not perfect, but the improvement is so great that it is hard to believe. The children are very proud of themselves because they require very little supervision during wash-up time, and yet it is a *very orderly* period.

CHANGING DISORDERLY CONDUCT ON THE SCHOOL GROUNDS

(Example)

At lunch dismissal time, 11:50 A.M., the class, a low fifth grade, was loud and noisy on the way out. They crowded the cafeteria. They caused numerous bottle-necks at the school gate, and many individual discipline problems developed.

I was usually involved in a number of small duties that kept me from being on the scene to restore or preserve order. I had to clear the classroom of the last reluctant pupil, give change sometimes for cafeteria money, go back and unlock the door to let in some pupil who had forgotten something, etc.

To lessen this lunch-time dismissal confusion, I had tried lecturing, cajoling, threatening—but to no avail.

The change desired was to have the class group plan a workable method for leaving at dismissal time that would prevent many of the problems that were occurring outside the classroom and that were causing many pupils to be sent to the office for disorderly conduct.

Previously, I had been confused about how to even start creating order. I was a new teacher in the state, and I had inherited a clustered group of roughly 85 per cent "discipline problems." It seemed as though I had every kind of class and pupil problem, from the rebel, the clown, the scapegoat, the hero, the dictator, to the fights on the field terminating in after-school ganging-up on a lone pupil.

I decided to take one little step at a time. I analyzed my class under the question: "Do I have a cohesive group?" as a beginning to the solution of the lunch-time dismissal problem. I decided that the group was not cohesive, so the following steps were taken. I gave the class a sociometric test. I brought in a prestige person (the principal) to tell them of their good points—their lining up, for one thing. I established them as the "best-looking" class in the school and coached them in smiling for their group pictures. I rearranged the seating so that they all looked inward in a horseshoe-shaped group. I established a definite goal for them. (We had been losing rather heavily in softball to the high fifth grade.) I built up their confidence in a series of talks over the prospect of winning a game; we wrote a futuristic news article—as having already beaten the high fifth, 23–0. Whenever I could, I stressed how compatible (getting-along-together) they were as a group. I gave the "cooties" [12] special attention and jobs that improved and heightened their confidence and prestige. I gave the group special public speaking and audio-visual classes that the other fifth grade didn't have.

The development of a better group spirit took several weeks. I then set out to define and analyze the lunch-time dismissal problem. I prepared my opening phraseology—the rightly phrased questions, I trusted. Then the plan was put into operation.

I began as follows: "A bunch of healthy youngsters like you must want to get home and to the cafeteria and back again as soon as possible. Right now we are not able to do that because of the crowding in the areas near the school cafeteria, lunch benches, and gate. My job is to help you get home

---

[12] The "cooties" were a rejected subgroup composed of children from a low economic level and so labeled because they were not clean. Previously, the teacher had worked with these children and had succeeded in his attempts to get them to wash and wear clean clothes to school.

and eat—and back again—as soon as possible. To help you do this, I must ask you a few questions. Is that all right?

"As I understand it, you have been getting into difficulty with the principal, from the overcrowding. Is that right?"

"In other words, everyone wants you to get home, and to eat, and to get back to softball—quickly, but you can't do it comfortably, without being benched. Isn't that right?" [13]

"Now, this may seem like a strange question for a teacher to ask you, but would you mind telling me exactly why we have trouble at lunch-time dismissal?" (I left the one question right there, and waited, curbing my desire to pepper them with a confusion of questions as I sometimes do—a what? where? when? how? who?—all together, one after the other.)

I was surprised at the reasons the class members gave, which came thick and fast. I had been utterly unaware of most of them.

a. They tagged bases at softball to get first "ups," which necessitated the rush.
b. The "home" members frequently were held up in the cafeteria lines by an unreasonable safety monitor.
c. The ball and bat monitors lost control if they didn't finish eating first.
d. Sometimes the ball and bat monitors got caught behind and had to wait so long in line that there were fights over the custodianship of the ball and bat.

(It took quite a while to separate the wheat from the chaff in the complaints about individuals—but it all came out.)

I curbed my eagerness to solve the lunch-time dismissal problem entirely myself, and continued the discussion to see what solutions they might have to offer. I summarized their reasons for the trouble and climaxed the summary with the question, "How can we avoid some of these problems when we go out at lunch time?"

Some of their suggestions were startlingly radical, but upon analysis and reconsideration they certainly did help the solution of the problem from both student and administration points of view. We boiled them down to three steps:

Step I   Let the home line go earlier.
Step II   Form the others into two lines—the lunch-bench line and the cafeteria line.
Step III Let the ball and bat monitors be the leaders in the line.

We tried each step on separate days. Later we found that the three steps could be combined into one step. But now we found other classes adopting the same technique—and some crowded days we were assembling our lines with a neighboring room, which reopened the confusion.

Our next step was to revise our plan. We formed our lines out in the middle of the blacktop away from the other classes. Then another problem

[13] The teacher's constant reiteration of, "Is that right?" was an attempt to develop agreement in the group from the beginning.

turned up. Frequently, cafeteria and lunch-bench pupils would surreptitiously go out early with the home line. Instead of punishing them, we gave them the responsibility of owning a special home line card-permit.

The results of this experiment were very gratifying. They may be summarized as follows:

1. We solved our problem to the satisfaction of pupils and administration.
2. We set a pattern for other classes, which gave prestige to our class and gave us reason to be proud.
3. The success of the project gave the teacher further confidence, and encouraged him to explore further the hidden possibilities for use of group decision in his class.

The behavior of these fifth graders has changed considerably and the great benefits and possibilities of these group-motivational techniques reveal themselves more and more.

REDUCING TARDINESS IN A HIGH SCHOOL CLASS

(Example)

This physical education class begins at 8:00 A.M. The girls are given nine minutes to change into their gym clothes, pick up their tennis rackets from lockers, and be in their squad positions for roll call on the tennis courts one block away. For the first three months of the school year, I had no tardiness problem. However, a district policy was formed recently that requires all students to salute the flag every morning. Last month this policy went into effect. At a department meeting, it was decided that all of our first period physical education classes would assemble outside of our building at the 8 o'clock bell to salute the flag, before changing into their gym clothes.

Since this ruling has been in effect, approximately 75 per cent of my class is tardy every morning. This number varies, sometimes more, seldom less. This is a problem involving the whole group, because although some of the class members make it on time each morning, they are not always the same individuals. Class work cannot begin until the entire class is present, as they are assigned to courts spread over a two-block area and instruction must precede dispersement.

We have a department ruling that six tardies lowers the student's grade one point. This has encouraged faster movement of only those few who have already reached the point where their grades are about to be lowered.

There are a number of factors that influence tardiness.

1. The flag salute takes approximately one minute of the nine minutes allowed.
2. 150 girls must enter the dressing room through one set of double doors. (This takes about two minutes.)
3. The girls are busily talking with their neighbors, while dressing, to catch up on the latest news.

4. The girls must stop in the hall on the way out of our building to pick up their rackets from their tennis lockers.
5. They must pass approximately 150 boys assembled for physical education on the way to the tennis courts located one block away from the dressing room.

I firmly believe that nine minutes is enough time for the girls to dress and get to class, even though the flag salute must take place at 8 o'clock.

Obviously, we cannot delete the flag salute from our program, nor can we change the bell schedule. I decided to meet my class in the lecture room one morning to see if:

a. they, as a group, were aware of the problem of tardiness to class;
b. they had any reasons for the tardiness;
c. they had any suggestions about how we could solve the problem and improve the situation.

Upon meeting the group and stating why we were in the lecture room rather than on the courts, I found the group very much aware of the problem. Some already had had their grades lowered, and notes concerning their excessive tardinesses had been written on their report cards issued the week before. Many others, who did not have notes or lowered grades, were nevertheless concerned about the numbers of tardinesses on their report cards.

The class decided to list on the board the reasons why they were late. Practically all hands went up and there was much discussion. Here is what we listed as a result of this discussion.

1. The flag salute takes time.
2. Too many of the girls talk too much while dressing.
3. Distance to the courts.
4. Since the class is first period, the weather is cold and it takes longer to put on additional clothing (sweat shirt and sweat pants).
5. They must stop by the tennis lockers in the hall to pick up their rackets, and the hall is often crowded because other girls are on the way to their respective classes.
6. The dressing sections are overcrowded and there is not enough room to to dress quickly.
7. They must comb their hair after taking sweaters off over their heads and pulling sweat shirts on, as they have to pass the boys on the way to class.
8. The girls move too slowly into the dressing room after the salute to the flag is over (because of only one set of double doors into the building).

We next decided to look over the list to see if there was anything we could do about any of the items.

Following is a summary of this discussion.

1. It might be better to dress first and then salute the flag. (After discussion, it was decided that this would not improve the situation.)
2. Some time would be saved at the flag salute if all of the girls would

assemble on time. (We always had to wait for the late comers to arrive so the ceremony would not be interrupted by unnecessary movement.)
3. Move as quickly as possible into the building following the flag salute.
4. Dress quickly and then do your visiting.
5. Carry sweat shirts and sweat pants to the courts and put them on during roll call.
6. Run to the courts.
7. Have a three-minute warning given over the loud-speaker system to make the girls realize how fast the allotted time is passing.

As a group, the girls decided to try points 2 through 7 to see if the problem could be solved.

In conclusion I must say that I really wasn't convinced that too much could be done, as I was having anywhere from 14 to 24 girls tardy to squads each day. I was concerned, and was trying to hurry the girls as individuals when the total of their tardies began to accumulate, but it never really occurred to me to approach the group for help.

Even though I have used group discussions many times to clear the air of a problem, in this case I had a tendency to blame the new regulation for this problem—just as the girls were using it as an excuse.

Since our class meeting, the three-minute warning over the loud-speaker has been given each day. I have observed my girls really moving into our building after the flag salute. They run to the courts, and I have had no more than three tardies in any one day. Most days there are less than three.

The attitude of the class is excellent, as they feel that they are accomplishing the impossible, and I am pleased with the result.

Changing Student Attitudes and
Improving Group Morale

In a normal classroom group there are numerous and varying attitudes related to each subject area. One individual is affected one way, while another is affected another way. When there is a core of individuals holding positive attitudes toward a certain learning area, the teacher can use this core to obtain an overall favorable attitude toward the subject or the task. Many of the attitudes of youngsters are formed by imitation and they are influenced by suggestion. When a class group is composed of youngsters all of whom hold negative attitudes toward school and school tasks, the teacher has no solid basis upon which to develop a change in attitude. Attitudes have much in common with interests. Interests represent personal experiences and in a regular classroom the interests of children generally differ to a degree. Strong interest by a few individuals in a subject or area of study can be used by the teacher to build interest in the total group membership, but if there is no interest upon which to build—if there is no motivating force—the task of developing interest may be difficult.

Interest that has resulted in successful school achievement in subject areas usually becomes the basis of a favorable attitude toward school and school work in general. Lack of success in school is usually accompanied by a lack of interest and a destructive, hopeless attitude toward the whole situation. As indicated before, in a normal class group, youngsters will differ in their attitudes and interests. There will be some strong interests and favorable attitudes toward each situation, and these can be used to stimulate others. If, however, the group is organized so that all the children lack interest and have strong negative attitudes toward school, the teacher faces a tremendous task. Change is exceedingly difficult.

The examples that follow illustrate how changes in attitudes toward school or toward specific situations in school were accomplished by teachers who experimented with group-decision techniques. The first example cited involved a class of youngsters who, because of years of lack of success in school, had lost all interest in trying to achieve. The last example illustrates how a pattern of unruly behavior caused by lack of interest and negative attitudes was changed.

IMPROVING BEHAVIOR AND INCREASING INTEREST IN SCHOOL TASKS

(Example)

The class in question consists (at present) of 20 eighth grade social studies students. The class is categorized as "low achievers," or a problem group; it is, however, recognized by the teacher as very nearly a class of the ZZ level—meaning that the reading ability of *all* members is very poor, promptness in turning in assignments is ignored (if they are *ever* submitted!), attendance is very irregular, and tardiness is frequent.

The particular behavior to be changed was to bring about more—a great deal more—attentiveness from this class. At the beginning of this experiment the students were noisy, they showed little or no interest in the subject regardless of the method of presentation, and most of them cared little about grades, wanting merely to pass the course, which is a requirement for graduation.

At the slightest pause, these "students" (and this is a *very loose* application of the word) would begin independent conversations, resulting in a great amount of time having to be spent in trying to restore order.

The teacher had had this class since the beginning of the term, and he had resorted to the use of losses of merits for breaches of conduct, and was, in fact, writing out more citizenship reports on this one class than on all others combined! It had reached a point where other action had to be taken, for the merit losses had something less than the desired effect on these do-nothing students.

Even though the teacher and class were aware that other means of handling would probably work to better advantage, the discipline situation was *fairly* well in hand by the end of the first semester. At that time, however, another class was broken up and its members were distributed among other classes. This teacher received seven, *all* of whom were described as "troublemakers" by the previous teacher.

It was shortly after the beginning of the new semester, with the addition of the new students, that it was decided to try a new approach with the class, suddenly enlarged and acting worse than ever.

The teacher was firmly convinced that the problems with the class in question arose from within the class, and resulted primarily from the specific combination of students in the class plus the fact that the class was at the end of the day, which in itself appears to be a problem for many teachers, regardless of their experience.

The class, usually worse in conduct on assembly days, did not fail the teacher when the first assembly of the new semester was held—they came in to class noisily, took a great deal of time settling down, and when finally as prepared as they would ever be for instruction, still went on talking among themselves from time to time. The situation was so bad on this particular day that the teacher changed his plans and decided to begin work with this class at once. The instruction was halted, and the class was asked just what it was that was "bugging" them even more than usual. It was learned that the assembly had been particularly good, and that a student had been imitating one of the performers while roll was being taken. The student was invited to the front of the room to go through his "act" again, for the benefit of all.

The student was only too happy to do so, and after the laughter was somewhat diminished, the teacher approached the class with questions, open for discussion, about what should be done so the class might get on with instruction every day instead of falling farther and farther behind.

They had some very bright ideas at first, such as, "Let us go home," "Let us talk every day," and "Let's watch films every day." After a while, however, some very small bits of intelligence began to manifest themselves, and there were some suggestions such as "Let us read out loud, taking turns," "Go through the text paragraph by paragraph, because we don't understand the book," and "Give us the study guides you used last semester."

(The study guides they mentioned were merely workbook-type ditto sheets of sentences with words or phrases missing, taken in order from the text. They covered "high points" only, and were to be filled in by the students to help them study for tests. The teacher felt them to be of little value, however, as they did not seem to help bring up test grades, nor did they do much to increase the knowledge of these poor students.)

Willing to try anything within reason that might help, the teacher began preparing study guides once again, but with a difference: the students were encouraged to work together to locate the answers in their textbooks. They usually grouped themselves into threes or fours, and some success was achieved in this area. The study guides were not to be turned in, so no grades were given for the work done on them, which did not seem to bother anyone except the few isolates, who felt they deserved "extra credit" grades for their great efforts.

Spelling tests, given weekly, had been dragging down grades (minor grades, which over a period of time, mounted up) for nearly everyone. The class suggested that they be allowed to take the tests over if they failed to pass the first time, and this was permitted. This change improved their grades either slightly or not at all, depending on the students, but they did feel they had a hand in determining policy, probably something they had long needed. The tests on lists of spelling words have since been discontinued, without fanfare, as it was a losing battle and accomplished little; these students are a good seven grades too late to have their spelling brought up to eighth grade standards in the little time that can be taken out of a social studies class for this activity.

Several other suggestions that came from students were tried. Some of them had heard of the great emphasis the teacher placed on geography in another social studies class, and it was suggested that more map work (there had been only a little) be given this class.

This suggestion was tried, and once good atlases were obtained to supplement the wall maps, results were better than expected. The students again were permitted to work together, and though there was some "goofing off" among the groups ("But we'll do them at home!") as they chattered, the work did get done—more or less. Map tests were given on the same level as those given to seventh grade students, and the results were gratifying. The feeling of having accomplished something made a change in some students.

This change *seems* to have been one of *wanting* to learn—but of this the teacher is not yet sure. Five or six students began to quiet down, became more serious about not only their maps, but other work as well, and (wonder of wonders!) have even listened to attempts at intelligent discussion.

A new situation arose when the tempo of movies suddenly increased when the class entered another phase of study. Many films were scheduled, and the teacher decided to put the question to the class about more films and what they might learn from them. The immediate reaction was one of "entertainment!" Still, some of the better students brought up the point that they might learn from the films if the class discussed each one as soon as it was finished. There was some reluctance on the part of the teacher to try this, as past experience had been that the class merely began talking among themselves about films or anything else as soon as rewinding of the films was begun.

This rewinding period, several minutes in length, is necessary and unavoidable. It affords just enough time for the students to get good conversations under way during a time when the teacher cannot be heard by the entire class, but when the students can hear neighbors. It had been, in the past, difficult to restore order after a film, so it was decided that they would talk until rewinding was completed, at which time they would come to order *at once* so the important points could be mutually discussed.

This proved to be a failure, but since the teacher (and the class) knew they were learning something more from the films than could be obtained from their halting use of the texts, the students decided to begin writing brief (even less than one page was accepted) reviews of the films *as soon* as they were completed. The papers were handed in or were collected within a very few minutes, and discussion of what they had put on their papers (for minor grades) was begun. A failure was reversed, and the only students who are still not participating are those who sleep through the movies. (This is still a very difficult problem to solve, for some of these lower-achieving students are up until all hours of the night, doing heaven-knows-what!)

It would be untrue to say in conclusion that all of the difficulties with this class have been resolved. In fact, the teacher must frankly admit that a great deal of improvement is yet needed. However, the class is now more-or-less attentive. They will sit still for brief discussions; they do "get something" from discussions, movies, and map work; and they are, in general, conducting themselves much better than ever before.

Now that the tensions of both teacher and class have largely disappeared, the teacher has found that there really are some "nice kids" in the class, and that their company can be enjoyed.

All in all, the changes made—including a change in the attitude of the teacher—have resulted in a far better classroom environment. There are fewer truancies, probably because social studies period is no longer dreaded. Most of the students are going to pass the course, though most will get C and D grades, with one or two getting B's.

As a class, we have discussed the change in behavior several times. The class, as a whole, seems proud of having suggested most of the changes. They seem to feel they have a part in the activities and are responsible for the improvement.

It is true that the class has learned less of social studies than they perhaps should have, but by the same token, what they have learned is a great deal more than they would have learned under previous methods! And where social studies has been "skipped" (or term it what you will), there has been other learning, or development of new attitudes, or reinforcement of older beliefs that the teacher believes is going to profit these students in years to come more than history or geography ever would. There is no denying that demerits are still issued from time to time, and there is still some chatter, and conduct is still not quite what one might expect of boys and girls of this age, but within their own group, this class has done exceptionally well—and do they like to be told this! It is something they have done, themselves!

OVERCOMING AN ATTITUDE OF DEFEAT

(Example)

This problem is concerned with a class of 27 listless, expressionless, unproductive, yet average-IQ seventh and eighth grade youngsters (and three sixth graders) who entered my class having had a long history of failure and under-achievement. Defeatism was the prevalent attitude in the group, and these youngsters had long since lost the desire to make an effort to do class work. Furthermore, every surface indication revealed that they "just didn't care."

These students were selected to form a special class in an attempt to improve their reading ability, primarily since their lack of achievement in this area was affecting all the other areas of study. Every kind of approach was tried the first few days, but it seemed impossible to get through this barrier of defeatism and reach them. They just sat! They would not respond. After a few days I was so frustrated by the lethargy and the apathy that was shown that I decided to try the group approach to changing this attitude of hopelessness. I knew that something had to be done to make the group more cohesive, or otherwise the project would not succeed. I set up the following objectives:

To make them aware of the enjoyment that can be obtained by working with others and by sharing and helping others with their problems.

To make them aware of their own strengths and of the fact that they were capable of individual expression of ideas.

To help them recognize that they could plan together and work out mutual problems together.

Upon meeting with the group on Friday of the first week after deciding to use group-decision procedures, I took a new approach. The students were told that a new plan was going to be tried so students having mutual problems could get maximum help in improving their reading skills. They would work together to improve certain skills, etc. Then I asked whether they saw merit in the idea. At first there was the usual apathy, but then I heard some mumblings that this was the class of "dummies." Recognizing that this would be a major handicap if this idea persisted, I worked immediately toward a better understanding and toward establishing some bases for agreement.

The group was assured that the information was false. "You have been *selected* to be in this class because you are the ones who offer the greatest potential for gaining from this particular program." It was explained that their feelings about reading were understood—nobody likes to do that in which he is not confident—and that in this class each person would be competing with himself only; therefore, there could be no failures so long as each made the effort commensurate with his ability.[14]

[14] The last part of the statement was no doubt threatening to many students, for probably they had been told many times that they were not working to capacity or that they were more capable than their work showed them to be.

The class listened, but there was silence. No one even bothered to state again that they were "dummies"—or to say *anything*. Again came that frustrating, hopeless feeling! I recognized with a flash of insight that the approach was all wrong. I could not reach them by telling them that they had ability, etc., but I had to do something, so I said, "You think about a plan for working together. Monday we will discuss it, but right now, I am going to read to you, until it is time for recess." That was the best I could think of at the moment, but at least the last announcement raised a slight stir. A few showed some signs of life when they heard they were not going to be subjected to the usual reading lesson. (It was the reading period.)

I realized after this first miserable attempt that I had made no plan for attacking this problem. I had some objectives but no clear-cut idea of how to reach them. So I tried to plan again. First, however, I analyzed my first attempt. After thinking it over I realized that I had raised a response, even though it was only a remark about being "dummies." Someone had talked! But I had immediately jumped in and lectured, appealed, and moralized, and that had made them crawl back into their shells.

Luckily I had the weekend to plan. There were three objectives I wanted to accomplish: (1) arouse interest, (2) change the attitude toward reading, (3) get them to react to *something*—that is, get them to express themselves orally.

I considered two approaches. The first one involved suggesting several types of grouping where children could work out projects together to improve vocabulary, organization of ideas, etc. The second one was to use a film or other visual material, followed by a group discussion and class group study of reading material related to the topic shown in the film. I felt we should concentrate on reading, since this area presented the major difficulty and was in fact the reason for the formation of the group.

The final decision was to present both ideas and have the group decide. I was certain that they would not come up with any suggestions. The approach was to be a question asking if they had thought of any plans, and when none was forthcoming, I would present my suggestions for the group's consideration.

On Monday the plan was initiated. This is what occurred.

The question was asked, "Did they have a plan . . . etc.?" There was a response! Someone muttered, "What's the use trying to make a 'big deal' in this class of dumb bunnies?" This was not what I had anticipated. Stalling for time I asked, "What exactly do you mean by 'dumb bunnies'?" The boy's answer was, "You know what I mean!" I said I really did not know—that being dumb meant lacking the power to speak and that I knew they *could* speak although I would have to admit they acted as if they were dumb in the vernacular sense of the word. I concluded by saying I really wanted to know what they meant, since I probably had the wrong idea.

Well, that shook them loose! All their feelings poured out with a rush. I wrote their responses on the board. It boiled down to the fact that the other youngsters in the upper grades thought they were dumb (lacking in intelligence). When the question was put to them they agreed that they themselves did not think they were *that* stupid. Some said, "I *can* read," and several nodded in agreement. (Of course I realized that deep inside they had self-doubts.) I agreed with them and said I knew they could read. The problem seemed to be that when it came to reading textbooks in science, etc., they had some difficulty. Again, the whole group responded orally and vigorously in the affirmative. They were beginning to look around at each other and to act like a normal group of youngsters. I followed this up with, "When the brakes on your family car need fixing what is done about it?" They quickly responded. "What do you do when you find you have a cavity in a tooth?" Several such questions were asked. Then it came to mind that a particular television program the night before had featured an interview with a popular young movie star. The class was asked if they had watched the program. Several had. Then these persons were asked what the movie star was doing about the fact that he could not speak English clearly and was lacking in several other accomplishments. The answers came back that he was taking special lessons. "Anything wrong with that?" they were asked. By this time many seemed to get the point. The decision was unanimous that it was only intelligent to repair something that needed fixing or remedy a lack in a certain skill if it was needed. On this the group agreed.

"What is the problem, then?" they were asked. The problem was that others looked at them as "dummies." What could be done about this? But with this question the zip went out of the group. They stared apathetically at me again. A few shoulders shrugged—that was all.

Then these suggestions were made. "Let's tackle this problem together. I have some ideas. See what you think. I think we had better do something that proves to the rest that we are not 'dummies' but just people having an opportunity to remedy a difficulty. Now, we could put on an assembly program, or we might plan an exhibit of our work or publish an annual or a newspaper. What do you think?"

The spark was rekindled in a few (but dimly). Some said they thought a program was a good idea. Others said the newspaper might be O.K., etc. Then out of the blue, the problem was solved. Jack, one of the poorest readers, but personable and a hard worker, announced that his cousin had told him about a project his room had carried out in another school. They had a hobby fair and made an exhibit of all their hobbies and invited the other classes to visit on a certain day and had the parents at night. He had gone to the exhibit and he described it. The group response to this suggestion was electric and immediate; thus, the project was launched.

From this point on there has been little difficulty. We have planned for the exhibit, are reading books related to the hobbies, and have put the original plans into operation. (The class members work together in reading, and we also are using the film idea at times.) In a very short time this class has become very cohesive—in fact, the class has erected a barrier between itself and other groups and acts rather cliquish on the playground. They also appear rather smug and superior because they are having more fun than other classes. This attitude is not the best, I realize, but so far it seems wise to leave things as they are, for their behavior is having a "Tom Sawyer" effect on the other classes. A few children from the regular seventh grade have *asked* if they could be moved into the special class—and have insisted that they have trouble with reading, too. When this class was asked how they would feel about admitting new members to the group, they acted so superior and so important that it was hard to believe that these youngsters once thought they were considered the "dummies" and acted as if they cared about nothing that went on in school. (They were none too enthusiastic about admitting new persons into their inner sanctum, but since an increase is not contemplated until the new semester, this subject was not pushed.)

This has been an amazing discovery. The objectives have been reached and the experiment has succeeded beyond the greatest hopes. The only problem is this attitude of exclusion and even superiority. However, since for years these youngsters have believed they were the underdogs, no attempts will be made to change this for a while. Achievement tests will not be given until spring. It is predicted, though, that many—if not all—will improve if only because they will try their best on the test!

Achieving Change

Group decisions that are arrived at by group members interactively and as a synthesis of their own efforts elicit more solid support and result in changed behavior more frequently than do decisions that are only partially agreed upon by group members. Imposed edicts to change, or the use of force or pressure, only consolidate groups and do not change established ways of behaving.

An important aspect of the technique for achieving change is the group discussion. Although the discussion process alone does not bring about a change in behavior, it is by means of group discussion that members discern that a change is desired by the group as a whole, and a decision is obtained. Whether individual members perceive there is a group concensus to change behavior depends largely upon the teacher's skill in initiating the move to change and the teacher's ability to direct and guide the group discussion so that a desire for change is created. Participation by members in a discussion provides the opportunity for individuals to assess the group's opinion, but following this must come the stated decision which provides the clarity that is needed for promoting individual change.

Informal experiments conducted by teachers inexperienced in the use of the technique reveal that these attempts meet with considerable success at all grade levels. These initial attempts at creating changes in behavior show that group forces can be used to create conditions in classrooms that many teachers have heretofore not been able to attain. Moreover, other consequences favorable to learning occur. For example, the process itself promotes a better feeling in the group, and often enhances learning. The attitudes of the members in the group may produce an atmosphere without life or vitality, an atmosphere that is changed when these individuals become involved in group participation involving decision.

Effective use of the technique requires an understanding of the pressures operating in social interaction. Teachers cannot hope to be successful without some understanding in this area, nor can they successfully guide the group in decision making if they lack faith in the group's ability to make a reasonable decision.

Questions for Study and Discussion

1. What are the steps that lead to a group decision? What factors in the process have been found to be most effective in assuring execution of the decision?

2. List several ways of initiating a proposed behavior change.

3. Class groups must change from one activity to another, go to the auditorium on certain occasions, and otherwise move and change location. Describe what you regard as normal class behavior at such times. Compare your description with those of your classmates. If there are differences, how do you explain them?

4. List as many classroom situations as you can think of where group-decision techniques might be used to change behavior. If group forces could be successfully mobilized in these cases, would individual learning be more likely to increase? Why? If individual learning would not be affected, justify changing the behavior.

5. What is the major function of a discussion designed to change the established behavior of a class group to behavior that is more acceptable? What functions does the teacher perform when leading this discussion?

6. What functions may teacher questions serve in a group discussion involving behavior change?

7. Observe a class group discussion in action. How does the teacher initiate the discussion? Is there wide participation? Do the members of the class express their ideas freely or do they attempt to give back the answer they believe is desired? How is the discussion terminated? List the outcomes.

8. Choose one of the incidents of group behavior described in some previous chapter. Make an outline of statements and questions you would use with the group if you were attempting to change this particular behavior.

9. List the skills a teacher must develop to lead a group discussion effectively.

Suggestions for Further Reading

Bartlett, Claude J. "Dimensions of Leadership Behavior in Classroom Discussion Groups," *Journal of Educational Psychology,* 50:280–284, December 1959.

Bennett, Edith B. "Discussion, Commitment, and Consensus in 'Group Decision,'" *Human Relations,* 8:251–273, August 1955.

Cantor, Nathaniel. *Learning Through Discussion.* Buffalo, N.Y.: Human Relations for Industry, 1951.

Carroll, Anne. "How To Conduct A Classroom Discussion," *Grade Teacher,* 74:47–50, September 1956.

Cartwright, Dorwin. "Power: A Neglected Variable in Social Psychology," in *Studies in Social Power.* Ann Arbor, Michigan: Research Center for Group Dynamics, 1959, pp. 2–14.

Coch, Lester and John R. P. French, Jr. "Overcoming Resistance to Change," *Human Relations,* 1:512–532, 1948.

Crary, Ryland W. (ed.). *Education for Democratic Citizenship.* Twenty-second Yearbook, National Council for the Social Studies, National Education Association, 1951.

Gibbs, J. R., Grace Platts, and Lorraine Miller. *Dynamics of Participation Groups.* St. Louis: J. Swift Co., 1951.

Gordon, Thomas. *Group-Centered Leadership.* Boston: Houghton, 1955.

Hayes, Margaret L. and Mary E. Conklin. "Intergroup Attitudes and Experimental Change," *Journal of Experimental Education,* 22:19–52, September 1953.

Hoffmann, Randall W. and Robert Plutchink. *Small Group Discussion in Orientation and Teaching.* New York: Putnam, 1959.

Horwitz, Murray and Dorwin Cartwright. "A Project Method for the Diagnosis of Group Properties," *Human Relations,* 6:397–410, 1953.

Hunt, Maurice P. "Leading Group Discussion," *Social Education,* 15:71–74, February 1951.

Kelman, Herbert C. "Compliance, Identification, and Internalization: Three Processes of Attitude Change," *Journal of Conflict Resolution,* 1:51–60, March 1959.

Keltner, John W. *Group Discussion Processes.* New York: Longmans, 1957.

Lifton, Walter M. *Working with Groups.* New York: Wiley, 1961.

Loree, M. Ray and Margaret B. Koch. "The Use of Verbal Reinforcement in Developing Group Discussion Skills," *The Journal of Educational Psychology,* 51:164–168, June 1960.

Pepitone, Albert D. "Motivational Effects in Social Perception," *Human Relations*, 3:57–76, 1950.

Pigors, Paul and Faith. "The Incident Process—Learning by Doing," in Warren G. Bennis, Kenneth D. Benne, and Robert Chin (eds.), *The Planning of Change*. New York: Holt, 1961, pp. 710–716.

Raths, Louis. "What Is Teaching?" *Sociatry*, 2:197–206, 1948.

Riecken, Henry W. "Some Problems of Consensus Development," *Rural Sociology*, 17:245–252, September 1952.

Sherif, Muzafer. "A Study of Some Social Factors in Perception," *Archives of Psychology*, 27:1–60, July 1935.

Shull, Russell W. *Techniques of Discussion with Teen-Agers*. Chicago: National Forum, 1951.

Steinzor, Bernard. "The Spatial Factor in Face to Face Discussion Group," *Journal of Abnormal and Social Psychology*, 45:552–555, 1950.

Stendler, Celia. "Climates for Self-Discipline," *Childhood Education*, 27:209–211, January 1951.

Utterback, William E. *Group Thinking and Conference Leadership: Techniques of Discussion*. New York: Rinehart, 1950.

Wagner, Russell H. and Carroll C. Arnold. *Handbook of Group Discussion*. Boston: Houghton, 1950.

Chapter 12   Methods of

Solving Group Problems

ONE of the reasons why it is desirable to have class groups behave in certain ways is so learning will be maximized. Teachers say their most persistent problem is motivating children to behave in ways that are conducive to learning. However, it has been emphasized repeatedly that individual behavior is strongly influenced by the class group, and many behaviors that teachers view as individual "discipline" problems are actually problems stemming from the class group. Sometimes individuals do disrupt the classroom atmosphere. Most often, however, it is the behavior of the class as a whole that teachers find difficult to control or guide. Disruptive group behavior is caused by some group problem— something going on within the group that creates tensions, or some barrier that the group is trying to overcome, or some situation that the group feels is threatening its welfare.

The intent of this chapter is to point out some of the causes of group

behavior that upset the usual systematic learning routine, and to show
how problem-solving procedures can be used to modify such behavior.
Since learning problem-solving skills is an important educational objective, the dual outcomes of behavior-modification and skill-learning are
stressed equally.

The following discussion analyzes some common group problems,
summarizes investigations of problem solving in groups, reviews the
group problem-solving process or method, and gives examples of teachers'
use of problem-solving techniques as means of helping groups solve their
difficulties.

Analysis of Group Problems

All teachers at one time or another have become frustrated by conditions that arise in their classrooms because their classes become deeply
involved with problems that seem unrelated to task goals. These problems have many causes. They may be direct outcomes of playground
conflicts, they may develop as indirect consequences of administrative
edicts, or they may come about for any number of reasons. Whatever
the cause, teachers become concerned because individual pupil involvement with the group problem generally causes a classroom disturbance
that interferes with the daily schedule and the planned work program.
Teachers are unable to proceed with the prepared lessons, because pupil
attention is turned toward the group difficulty and away from the tasks.
Teachers usually have good reason for their concern, since group problems, if not solved, decrease individual productivity, and they often
create that condition in the classroom that is sometimes called "lack of
discipline," or "poor teacher control."

This kind of situation, however, need not lead to a wasted class
period or reduced individual work performance. It need not result in a
disturbance or undesirable patterns of behavior. The appearance of such
group problems does not have to create an atmosphere of teacher–group
tension, nor does it have to result in unsatisfactory group solutions.
When a group is confronted with a problem of importance to the members, the teacher can utilize the potential of the situation to develop
group problem-solving skills. Because members have a need to solve the
group problem, the situation is highly conducive to the learning of
problem-solving techniques. If instead of trying to impose a solution
upon the group or attempting to force the group to ignore the problem,
the teacher capitalizes upon the situation to develop group problem-

solving skills, a disruptive, disturbing condition can be changed to one that is satisfactory to the group and the teacher.[1]

Diagnosing Group Problems

When children in the class group misbehave, this behavior is *caused*. When the group as a whole channels its energies away from the tasks at hand and engages in undesirable behavior, there is a *cause* for the group members' behavior. Most likely the group has a problem, or problems, that direct the attention of members away from the regular school work and cause them to act in a manner that disrupts the learning atmosphere of the classroom.

Acceptance of the idea that undesirable and unproductive group behavior is caused and is the result of group problems throws the emphasis upon use of techniques that will help solve these problems. This approach is in contrast to an attitude of blame and reproach, and to the use of punishment. Such control techniques as threat or punishment do not change the problem, and the behavior may occur over and over again. Therefore it is important to approach this kind of disturbance with a desire to correct the problem behavior rather than to control it by force. A corrective approach attempts to modify behavior by solving the problem or by making changes in the situation to eliminate the difficulty. Teachers will be more able to change the behavior if they take the view that the undesirable behavior needs modification and change—not punishment.

Before steps can be taken to remedy the group difficulty, the problem must be diagnosed. Correction requires analysis. Unfortunately, this is not an easy task. It is much easier to find fault. Yet if the teacher recognizes that this behavior has some reason, it will not be necessary to emphasize how important it is to make an analysis of the situation. There is, of course, no one set of procedures that will solve all kinds of group problems, so before a change can be brought about, the teacher must determine what is wrong.

The idea that if a school day is filled with stimulating activities there will be little time for the group members to engage in undesirable behavior unfortunately is not true. If the group has a problem, the members usually take action regardless of whether the school tasks are stimulating or interesting. In fact, a cohesive, friendly class that is helped to handle its group problems is much more apt to work contentedly on dull, routine

[1] L. Richard Hoffman, Ernest Harburg, and Norman R. F. Maier, "Differences and Disagreements as Factors in Creative Group Problem Solving," *Journal of Abnormal and Social Psychology*, 64:206–214, March 1962.

tasks than a group with difficulties which is given interesting, stimulating lessons. Any attempt to ignore the difficulty or to divert the attention of group members is apt to be wasted effort. Logic, argument, appeal, and moralizing do not affect the cause of the behavior. Efforts must be directed toward analyzing the problem, and then steps must be taken to help the group overcome the difficulty.

In some cases the problem situation may arise suddenly, and the teacher may not have all the knowledge necessary to diagnose the group difficulty. Teacher and class together need to analyze the situation. Bradford et al.[2] suggest that when the group is attempting to reach an agreement about doing things differently, the group as a whole should assume some responsibility for analyzing its difficulties.

Some of the problems that class groups meet as the members work and play together in the school situation are easy to analyze and are easy to deal with. Some problems, however, represent disturbances that are hard to identify and difficult to handle. The next section reviews a few of the more common problems that occur in classroom groups.

Some Causes of Group Problems

One of the most common class group problems occurs because the class group is composed of youngsters who hold different values and have different ideas about what is right or fair. Once a group is formed, it attempts to establish a commonality of expectations and values among its members. This defining of what is expected provides the group with the means to evaluate individual behavior, and it enables individuals to predict the group reaction to their behavior. Members feel more secure once these expectations are established. A consequence of this attempt by the group to create changes in values and reach a common agreement is argument and discussion until concensus is obtained. Therefore, the class group often comes in from the playground discussing an issue. The discussion may be heated, since the youngsters do not see the situation in the same light and since they are attempting to reach a common ground. Some teachers say, "the children come in with a fight on their minds." This is not a fight in the sense that there is a feeling of strong dislike among members. There is disagreement, certainly, and argumentation, but the real purpose of the discussion is to reach agreement about what is right, fair, and to be expected. Hence, teachers frequently report incidents such as the following.

[2] Leland P. Bradford, Dorothy Stock, and Murray Horwitz, "How to Diagnose Group Problems," in *Group Development*, Washington, D.C.: National Training Laboratories, National Education Association, 1961, pp. 37–50.

UNFAIR PRACTICES

Most incidents that cause trouble for me in the classroom start during free play time. These fourth graders storm into the classroom arguing about unfair practices, or who was right or who cheated in a particular instance. No matter how many times rules are given or reviewed, this behavior occurs. Some days the whole class becomes disorderly on first entering the room and the youngsters will not begin work until the whole affair is settled—or unless they are threatened that they will have to make up the lost time the next play period.

In most cases, class groups, because of their size, need considerable help in working out suitable and satisfactory play arrangements. If a class group is not helped to organize its play periods, the group may devote much time and effort to establishing some satisfactory plan. Although the behavior appears to be disorganized and disruptive, the class in the following example is engaged in a type of problem-solving process in an attempt to improve conditions in their play groups.

PLAY EQUIPMENT DISPUTES

The children wait on the terrace in the morning before school starts. When a bell rings they can come into the room to get balls and equipment to play with until the 9 o'clock bell rings. Every day it's the same thing. They have difficulty deciding who should sign up for the equipment for their respective play groups. (This is not an organized play period.) To give a specific example, yesterday a number of children decided to play soccer. This particular group did not usually play this game. Bill had been signing for the soccer ball every day. This meant others did not get a chance to play with it in their particular groups. When the children came in at 9 o'clock, they were bursting with grievances. The girls entered in the argument too, since they felt the boys always got the ball to play with in their groups. Some time was spent settling this dispute over what was fair practice, who should sign for the equipment, and whether girls had equal rights to such equipment as the soccer ball. It seems that happenings of this sort occur more often than they should, and settling these constant disputes uses up valuable school time.

Another source of group problems is lack of group solidarity. When there is a sharp cleavage in the group, the atmosphere may be tense and there may be actual quarreling and fighting between members in the group or between subgroups. Usually members take sides. Lack of cohesiveness, poor human relations, interpersonal disputes—all these are causes of group conflict.

What appears to be conflict in the next incident is more an example of a class group attempting to induce pressure upon one member to obtain conformity in opinion. We noted previously that a group has a strong tendency to communicate to members who deviate from the group's expectations of "good" or correct behavior. The group pressure, in this instance, appears to be desirable, although the teacher reporting this situation considered it to be an example of a "discipline" problem.

THE NASTY CRACK

There are two Italian children in this sixth grade class. One of them, a girl, seemed to be having trouble with peer relations from the first day.

One day, after lunch, there was an excited and troubled overtone among the girls as they came in. Maria, the Italian girl, was both belligerent and defensive. When I reprimanded her for pulling Christine's hair, she started to cry and sobbed that Christine had called her a "dirty Dago tramp."

The boys and most of the girls were shocked at this and rallied to Maria's defense. The "dirty tramp" didn't bother them. The "Dago" did. The first opinion they seemed to consider Christine's business, but dragging nationality into it outraged their sense of fair play. Before the group settled down to work, Christine had to be told in no uncertain terms just what they thought about her remark.

Numerous internal and external factors tend to cause a group to be unable to make adaptive changes. Many of these internal factors have been discussed in previous chapters. For example, well-integrated groups are better able to adjust to changes and repel external aggression than poorly integrated groups. Until stability is established, groups may be highly sensitive to influences that disrupt the usual routine. Immediate, spontaneous behavior, the quick rise of emotional tone, unusual or extreme forms of behavior, may indicate that the group is not well integrated.

Rumors, for example, may cause a class group to behave in a highly excited way. This group reaction is often symptomatic of internal group disorder. Sherif and Sherif [3] suggest that when the group structure is still fluid, rumors are accepted and passed on very quickly. A highly suggestible class group may react to rumor by becoming excited and talkative. This repeating of rumor may disrupt class activities for a time, as it did in the next example.

[3] Muzafer Sherif and Carolyn W. Sherif, *An Outline of Social Psychology*, New York: Harper & Brothers, 1956, p. 358.

THE RUMOR

The morning bus had just arrived. Although the pupils had been trained to come in quietly, I could hear their voices as they piled off the bus a good one-half block away. I went to the door to learn the cause of all this excitement. A large number of children had hurried to be first to relay the news. They trooped in the room full of excitement and importance, shouting the news—"Levi spit in the bus!" The rest came in breathless, all carrying the same tale. I managed to ask one child if he saw Levi do this. He said, "No, but everyone says so." Levi did not come in with the others. A few stragglers entered, and sure enough they reported the same story. Finally everyone was seated but no one was quiet. Everyone was speculating on the punishment. Some were embellishing the story—Levi tried to spit on his neighbor but he missed and only spit on the floor.

Attempts were being made to quiet the group—unsuccessfully, I afraid—when in straggled Levi.

"What happened?" was the general question asked from all parts of the room.

"Nothing," Levi answered. "My mother is coming."

"Are you going to be kicked out of school?" and "Did you get put off the bus?" were the questions flying from all parts of the room.

Levi looked puzzled. "Why would I? What are you talking about?"

Well, after half of the first morning class was wasted by all this excitement and talk, it turned out that Levi's brother had become sick on the bus. Levi had taken him to the office and his mother was coming to get him. The whole thing was a rumor.

One kind of group problem that is very difficult for teachers to handle occurs when an administrative rule is resisted by the group. The class may object to the rule and become very hostile to those enforcing the rule, whether it is their own teacher or another member of the school faculty. Questions and remarks that are critical of other teachers, the administrator, or other school personnel are very difficult for the teacher to handle. Often a group will ask a question or make a statement that contains a challenge directed at another teacher or at the institution of which their teacher is a part. Avoiding such a statement or question is successful only temporarily. If the teacher avoids answering the question, the group often becomes more hostile. Diversion never settles a group problem. If the question or comment is answered, the teacher may seem to be siding with the administration against the group or he may seem to be critical of the administration or other fellow teachers. In the next incident, consider whether you believe the teacher should have refuted the comments made about the principal. Should he have moralized, ignored the remarks, or told the children that such statements would not be allowed in the classroom?

My sixth grade class returned to the classroom after lunch, upset and very sullen. At first the room was too quiet. Everyone just sat. Then someone remarked in a loud voice, "Mr. B. (the principal) is mean and unfair. He's always sniffing around to see who he can get into trouble!" Then the story came out. Quite a few of the boys in our class were playing marbles on a corner of the grounds with most of the other boys and girls in the class standing around as an audience. He had caught them "playing for keeps" and had confiscated the marbles and told them there would be no more marbles at school.

After the story was told there were some very explosive remarks. Not long before, because of some additional building on the school grounds, the sixth grade play space had been cut to a very small area. The situation was temporary, as the space was being used to pile lumber; however, there was not much the children could do on the playground at the time. One youngster angrily remarked that the principal was always unjust. First their place to play was taken away and now they couldn't even play marbles. Even the children who did not play the game thought the judgment was very unfair and had some very derogatory remarks to make about the principal and his intolerance.

Sometimes a school rule will arouse psychological forces that affect the group adversely. Particularly this is true if a section of the group believes that the enforcement of the rule works a hardship on them and not on others. Sometimes the rule is difficult to administer and a class group or part of a group may rebel against what they consider is injustice. Sometimes the teacher is the object of the group's resentment, and sometimes it is the rule. The following example shows how one class group became resentful over what was believed to be unfair treatment in the enforcement of a school rule.

WALKING TO THE CROSS STREET

It was the second month of school. Since the beginning of the school year, all the children had lined up at the door at dismissal time. They walked with the teacher down the long corridor and along the sidewalk in front of the school, to be dismissed at the corner crosswalk.

This rule had been agreed to by the school staff before the opening of school. It was incorporated into the list of school rules and standards.

As the second month of school started, 12 new youngsters were placed in this third grade class. They all happened to live in a different direction and had to walk to an opposite crosswalk from the rest of the class. This posed a problem, as the teacher could not walk in two directions at once. So these 12 were dismissed outside the building to walk by themselves, while the larger group was escorted to the crosswalk at the end of the block.

The larger group began to show signs of being unhappy with this rule. They complained that the teacher let the other ones go by themselves. Why couldn't *they*? They began walking in an irregular pattern, pushing and shoving one another to be first in line and generally causing confusion in the line. They felt they should not have to follow the rule of walking in a line to the dismissal point, and have a teacher escort, if the other group did not.

Poor communication between the persons setting the rules and the classes affected by the rules will arouse hostility. Sometimes dissatisfaction with rules and conditions creates a whole series of behavior problems on the playground and in the classroom. The next example describes a number of events that led to disturbing behavior in the classroom.

THE BICYCLE RACKS

I have been on early morning duty in the area where the fourth, fifth, and sixth grade bicycle riders arrive with their bikes.

Originally, we were told (by the administration) to hold the children outside the gate until the first bus arrived and discharged its passengers. Of course, the cyclers got used to avalanching in at that time, but when the bells were finally established, we were told to hold them until the first bell. That meant they all waited until long after the bus was unloaded. Much wrangling, juggling for position, and general noise resulted when the bus arrived and the gate was not opened for the bicyclers. After this policy was explained to the bicycle riders, it was accepted with much grumbling and bickering and a few disparaging remarks about the person making the rules.

Now a new edict has been issued. After two weeks of being allowed to enter with the bell, we have been told to allow the horde to advance five minutes earlier than they had originally. Once again, we have questions, grumbling, general misunderstanding, and criticism.

Another situation crops up at the bike racks because we do not have enough stalls for all to park. Lines have been painted on the blacktop to show where to park the bikes on their own stands, but it is like pulling eye-teeth to get the children to use the stalls and spaces farthest away from the entrance. Everyone wants in first and out first.

Because of all this wrangling over the bicycle stalls, the following happened recently. During recess or some other time when they were on the grounds, some boys tipped over the bicycle rack nearest the entrance. A few of the bicycles were damaged. Some belonged to the youngsters in my fifth grade. I did not know who the guilty parties were, but it was obvious that most of the class members did. However, although the feeling was running pretty high, the class members refused to say a word or tell what they knew about the incident. It was not long before I was aware that the word had been passed around the room that the "culprits" would be "taken care of after school."

Now situations like this really create a whole raft of difficult situations. Parents will complain about the bicycle damage. The pending after-school fight presents a serious problem plus the fact that these youngsters think it is right for them to take the law into their own hands and distribute justice themselves.

Moralizing will not help in these cases—in fact the whole affair presents the teacher with a series of headaches. For example, how can you teach when everyone in the group is considering how best to conduct a lynching party?

Youngsters often become involved emotionally when situations occur that they believe to be unfair. The expression of hostile feelings often provides relief and permits the usual task-motivated behavior to come to the fore. Sometimes, however, even though they verbalize hostility about a problem, group members may not be able to take their minds off the situation and pay attention to class work unless something is done about the problem.

If allowing a group's hostile feelings to be expressed means allowing another teacher's behavior to be criticized, the group's teacher is placed in an extremely awkward position. The teacher in the next incident had to face just such a problem.

THE VOLLEY BALL GAME

Another eighth grade class, having three teams, challenged my eighth grade class of three teams to play volley ball. We were delighted as a class, accepted the challenge, and set a day for the games to be played during the physical education period.

When the challenge was made, they asked us to place our best team on Court 1, second best on Court 2, etc. Our class discussed how we would determine which teams would be 1, 2, and 3. My class decided that court position would be determined by team standings in our own class tournament on the day we were to play the other class. This is the usual procedure for keeping the competitors even in skill.

The other teacher decided that he would place an "all-star" team on the first court, so he selected the best players and placed them all on one team. He left his other teams without their best players. We were unaware of this arrangement the day we played.

The result was that our opponents won the game on the first court, but we won the other two games.

During the progress of the games, my class found out what this teacher had done, as two of the opposing teams were really grumbling because they were losing heavily, since they had lost their best players to the first team. At the end of the period, when it was announced to the groups that the challenging class won one game and lost two, both classes were really upset. The challenging class did not have a part in the idea of stacking one team, and they just couldn't see any advantage to winning one and losing two, thinking it was an injustice to them for not having their regular players on their teams. My class was terribly upset in loyalty to the team that was placed in the position of playing the hand-picked team of all-stars of the other class. The class feeling was very strong and had an upsetting effect in the classroom for several days.

Lack of motivation or interest, or an attitude of dislike, for a particular area of the curriculum is catching, and class members may unify to resist assigned tasks in the area. It requires considerable teacher skill to stimulate interest if it is lacking. In the last chapter we saw how teachers attempted to do this by use of group-decision procedures. However, when the subject is taught by an outside person, the problem has a number of facets and the cause of the group difficulty may be obscure and complex.

For example, what might account for the behavior of the following class group?

LEARNING BY TELEVISION

The fifth grades have two programs that they watch over television. They are a part of our regular curriculum.

Every day the same situations crop up just before the Spanish program comes on. There is a general switching of chairs, comments of all kinds are made, and even after the class has started inattentiveness is quite apparent. A few of the children stare out the windows, others look out the doors, and still others just sit. Those nearest the T. V. set seem to pay better attention than those in the back of the room. As examples of the behavior exhibited: one boy shot rubber bands and was promptly removed from the room; some draw pictures; some read; others fiddle with things in their desks. Perhaps the biggest contributor to ignoring the program is the workbook, which is part of the required material. The children leaf through them, drop them on the floor, and play with them. They are supposed to leave them in their desks until the T. V. teacher asks that they start working in them, but they do not.

Much of the lesson is to be done orally. The T. V. teacher requires that answers be given back to her. The response from our classroom is very poor indeed.

When the children were asked during discussion time about their lack of interest in this particular program, their answers were pretty much the same. "I can't understand what she says," or "It's baby stuff!" or "It's not interesting."

Checking with other teachers I find they have the same difficulty. Since the program is required and we must watch it, it presents a very difficult behavior problem. No one seems to have an answer.

Although the specific causes for disruptive group behavior and problem situations are almost endless, the chief causes spring from internal conditions within the group, or from external conditions that the group views as harmful or not important to its welfare. Groups may show strong resistance to imposed conditions that seem unjust, or they may look for detours around obstacles that keep them from achieving something that is desired. In most cases, undesirable behavior should be viewed as the group's way of overcoming certain problems.

Effects of Group Problems
Upon Member Behavior

The effects of group problems upon members of class groups have been noted by a number of investigators. Studies of groups in classroom situations show that tensions caused by conflicts or various other problems block the learning of individuals in the group. Perkins [4] found that stresses and strains in the group limited the extent of learning in subject fields. The incidents of group behavior problems that teachers report indicate this also. When the group has a problem that affects it deeply, individual members are not able to concentrate on school tasks. Bovard [5] reported that the kind of interpersonal relations that existed in the classroom strongly influence the learning that took place. Jenkins [6] proposed that when group members' socio-emotional needs were not satisfied, pupil energies were not free for other kinds of problem solving. After observation of classroom group behavior, Thelen [7] concluded that class members sometimes directed most of their energies to solving problems of relationships instead of concentrating their energies upon lessons.

An experiment conducted by Schutz [8] emphasized the importance of

[4] Hugh V. Perkins, "Climate Influences Group Learning," *Journal of Educational Research*, 45:115–119, October 1951.

[5] Everett W. Bovard, Jr., "Psychology of Classroom Interaction," *Journal of Educational Research*, 45:215–224, November 1951.

[6] David H. Jenkins, "Interdependence in the Classroom," *Journal of Educational Research*, 45:137–144, October 1951.

[7] Herbert A. Thelen, *Dynamics of Groups at Work*, Chicago: University of Chicago Press, 1954.

[8] William C. Schutz, "What Makes Groups Productive?" *Human Relations*, 8:429–465, 1955.

using practices that aid groups in resolving conflicts and settling difficulties. The study showed that when groups became involved with interpersonal hostilities, they were low in productivity. The more energy group members spent on interpersonal problems, the less energy they spent on tasks to be completed. Although cohesive groups exhibited many different behavior patterns, all assimilated low-status members and members helped one another with their work; non-cohesive groups did not accept any member suggestions at first, and wasted much time. Some of these latter groups rejected members and eliminated them from contributing to the group's projects; schisms developed, creating factions and nonproductive interaction, characterized by alternating periods of fighting, cooperating, and withdrawing. These and other studies seemed to indicate that in classroom situations, attempts to teach lesson content when individuals were concerned with group problems were wasted efforts.

Lindgren [9] suggested that the group situation should be used to further educational goals by releasing the power that lay within the group, rather than attempting to fight the group's power, to dam it up, or to ignore it.

Studies seem to indicate that in some cases at least, tension in groups is eased by a group analysis of the troublesome situation. It appears that groups receive emotional support when the members engage in a process of analyzing the cause of the difficulty and attempting to find a solution. Even though problems are not solved completely, the group process reduces feelings of anxiety and hostility. At times, members' perceptions of a problem change. Thus, even though some problems cannot be eliminated or solved entirely, group analysis of the problem often enables members to return to their regular tasks, relieved of some of the pressures that were interfering with subject learning.

Group Problem Solving in the Classroom

Problem solving used as an attack upon an immediate group difficulty can be considered a means for eliciting conforming behavior or disciplined behavior, if conforming or disciplined behavior is viewed as a condition in which youngsters are using their time in educationally desirable ways. At the same time, problem solving employed in this manner can in itself meet some of the goals of the educational program. Many class group problems are not unlike some of the problems faced by other groups in society. Also, when solutions to group difficulties are sought by use of a group problem-solving process, facts are gathered and key atti-

[9] Henry Clay Lindgren, "The Effect of the Group on the Behavior of the Individual," *Education*, 73:383–387, February 1953.

tudes are developed as youngsters practice skills of critical thinking on problems real to them. In other words, problem-solving techniques can improve conditions in the classroom and at the same time permit children to develop certain concepts, understandings, and skills.

A Point of View

A survey of the educational literature concerning group problem solving in the classroom reveals that a number of differing suggestions are made as to the kinds of problems that class groups should solve by means of the problems approach. Some educators suggest that subject matter be presented in the form of topics or questions, or that the approach should be used to accomplish certain school tasks, such as planning projects, producing reports, and the like. Many times it is suggested that problem solving be used to study the important problems that beset society, even though these problems affect children's lives only indirectly. There are those, also, who maintain that problem-solving skills are best taught when the approach is used to solve a group difficulty; then, it is said, that not only are skills developed, but understanding of group problems in society is increased. For the most part, the literature of education places greatest stress upon developing skills and developing understanding of the process itself, and less emphasis upon the results that may be obtained, such as improved behavior in classrooms.

Problems occurring in classroom groups may at times be very like those occurring in some groups in adult society. City councils, parent-teacher associations, school boards, and other groups often have to settle group member disagreements and resolve group member conflicts before proceeding to the tasks at hand. The disagreements and conflicts that occur in classrooms among group members, and which prevent normal class work from continuing, are not unlike the ones arising in the kinds of groups mentioned, nor are they unlike problems that occur in many types of work-groups in business and industry. The problems that arise in classrooms as results of unwanted rules or desired changes are not unlike the problems faced by many adult groups that seek the repeal of unwanted legislation or the establishment of new legislation. When children object to rules or try to change imposed standards, their objections are often expressed by exhibitions of undesirable behavior because they do not know acceptable processes for attempting to bring about change. Or it may be that the norm system of the group defines acceptable conduct that is in conflict with that expected by the school.[10]

There are groups in society that at times defy social standards or inter-

[10] Ralph M. Stogdill, *Individual Behavior and Group Achievement*, New York: Oxford University Press, 1959, pp. 146–150.

pret legislation to suit their own wishes. Sometimes they inflict punishment upon individuals whom they view as deviants instead of relying upon agencies and regulations set up by society. In other instances, groups submit passively to certain leader dictates even though the members privately express dissenting views. Classroom groups at times exhibit similar behaviors, which disrupt the learning situation. When these behaviors occur, the problems can be indentified and analyzed, and attempts can be made to reach satisfactory solutions, thereby making the problems themselves objects for learning.

It is advocated that when class groups become upset and exhibit undesirable behaviors because the members object to rules or imposed standards, these conditions provide excellent opportunities for teachers to use problem-solving procedures to develop understanding of acceptable ways of objecting to unwanted legislation. The idea that children should be taught to conform to all imposed rules and standards and never express their objections is not consistent with the philosophy of a free society. So that this point of view is not misinterpreted, it is emphasized that this does not mean that children are to be encouraged in any way to disobey rules or to flaunt generally accepted school norms for behaving. Rather it is proposed that if these behaviors occur, children are to be encouraged by the use of problem-solving techniques to examine alternatives. If the attitudes of defiance or resentment still persist, then it is suggested that children be encouraged to take stands against the rules for behaving, and be taught acceptable ways of objecting. In short, it is proposed that children be taught legitimate ways of protesting against rules or conditions that they find unsatisfactory.

An example is used to make this point clear. An incident was reported which involved an imposed rule. If a ball was kicked over a fence by a member of a class, the class had to forfeit its ball. A child accidentally kicked a ball over the fence. The result was that the class did not express resentment against the rule, but the child who kicked the ball became the object of hostility. It is advocated that when such situations occur, teachers employ problem-solving processes not only to improve the behavior pattern but to teach children ways of objecting that are socially acceptable. In this case, the children could assemble all the facts relating to the necessity for the rule, and if their perceptions were not changed after examining the need for the rule, they could then be led to consider the various ways they could legitimately protest the rule. For example, a committee could be sent to the administrator to present objections and new proposals; a letter could be written; or the administrator could be invited to the room to hear the group's comments. It seems that only by the use of such procedures can the concept be developed that authority in a democratic society rests in the hands of the members of the society. Children can learn, too, that such processes do not necessarily bring about change in rules and regulations, because those persons assigned to positions of leadership may have different viewpoints; for example, the school administrator must consider the welfare of the total school. However, this learning itself is very important.

The apathy of citizens as manifested in their failure to exercise their rights frequently is deplored in the current literature. A number of educators, and others as well, have expressed concern from time to time over the fact that a rigid adult-rule pattern in the school situation is very apt to develop an apathetic attitude in the population and thereby weaken the strength of democratic processes. Erikson [11] remarks, for example, that a democracy cannot afford to let matters develop to a point where youngsters must always leave matters of legislation and general policy to those in authority.

Although this is not intended to imply that children should be consulted regarding the establishment of most school policies (they have neither the understanding nor experience to do this), it is suggested that they be consulted in matters that directly concern them. For example, a class group was described as rebellious and antagonistic when requested by the principal to clean the school yard. Had these same children been asked to solve the problem of the littered school grounds, it is likely that they would have devised a plan acceptable to all concerned. The process of analyzing the problem and planning a course of action undoubtedly would have led to different opinions from those demonstrated. In this case, the children were rebelling against imposed authority, thereby creating a poor learning situation in the classroom and a problem for the teacher. The teacher could have handled the problem by asking the children to study the situation and to propose a plan that was acceptable to them. The new plan could have been presented to the administrator with a request that it be considered. The evidence strongly indicates that dissatisfaction and noncooperative attitudes change when the group is asked to participate in a problem-solving process. Studies show also that free expression of dissatisfaction tends to lessen the feelings of discontent, although after discontent is communicated it should be followed by a positive attack upon the problem.

Whether there is acceptance of this point of view, or whether it is believed that social learnings are not the responsibility of the school, few will object to methods that change unacceptable behavior patterns to ones that promote learning in the classroom. A number of studies have

[11] Eric H. Erikson, *Childhood and Society*, New York: W. W. Norton and Company, 1950, p. 238.

found that individual opinions, attitudes, and behaviors are modified in the problem-solving situation. Timmons'[12] investigation of a parole-group problem showed that individual judgments changed after the use of problem-solving procedures. Festinger and Thibaut[13] assembled small groups to discuss assigned problems and found that the communication process that was part of the problem-solving approach changed opinions of group members, particularly in strongly cohesive groups. Other group studies yield evidence that suggests that a group agreement to act in a certain way is more effective in changing behavior than is a lecture or discussion. The problem-solving process includes a consensus on lines of action that the group will follow. So far, the differences between the problem-solving technique and the group-decision technique are not clearly delineated in the research. However, problem solving generally is conceived as a group effort to find ways to complete a task or solve a difficulty of importance to the group, whereas group decision, using similar processes, is viewed as a means of changing an established standard of behaving to a standard considered more desirable by someone outside the group.

Experimental Research in Problem Solving

Much of the experimental research on problem solving in small groups is focused upon the planning process. Problem solving usually consists of planning operations involving the collection of information, proposals, acts of reasoning and critical thinking, and development of plans for action. When the patterns of interaction in problem-solving groups are analyzed it is found that early interactions are concerned with asking for, giving, repeating, and clarifying information. The next stage involves emphasis upon seeking and giving opinions, analyses, and expressions of feeling. The final or control stage consists of asking for and giving suggestions or directions and agreeing upon a possible course of action.[14]

Considerable research in group problem-solving centers upon determining whether observed steps can be refined to make problem solving in groups more effective. Many investigators have based their analyses

[12] William Murray Timmons, *Decisions and Attitudes as Outcomes of the Discussion of a Social Problem,* Contributions to Education No. 777, New York: Teachers College, Columbia University, 1939.

[13] Leon Festinger and John Thibaut, "Interpersonal Communications in Small Groups," *Journal of Abnormal and Social Psychology,* 46:92–99, January 1951.

[14] Robert F. Bales and Fred L. Strodtbeck, "Phases in Group Problem Solving," *Journal of Abnormal and Social Psychology,* 46:485–495, October 1951.

upon Dewey's five steps of effective thinking.[15] Some investigators have concluded that such analyses are more prescriptive than descriptive.[16] Others have said that there is no empirical order.

Leadership skills and the group problem-solving process have been described by the National Training Laboratory in Group Development.[17] From studies made of groups in problem situations, it has been determined that certain steps in the problem-solving process can be identified, though they do not always occur in the same order. The process is considered one in which the leader functions as a "change-agent" in group development, and the description concludes that the leader must first help members become aware of the problem and the need for diagnosing the difficulty. The leader and group together thus diagnose the situation, the behavior, and the causes for the behavior. During this process, the leader has to know how to deal wisely with group members' stereotypes, traditions, and values. The next phase involves planning and practicing group action. After a course of action has been tried, an evaluation is made.

The process, which was developed after experimentation with group procedures, varies little from Dewey's five steps. The differences appear to lie in the emphasis upon leader skill in creating awareness and understanding in the group of the factors involved in the problem. The group, not the leader, defines the problem, discovers the factors involved, and decides upon a plan of action. The leader, by involving all group members, uses the process to change group members' perceptions of the problem and of their own behaviors.

Emphasis is placed also upon leader skill in recognizing that some group behavior problems satisfy a need to relieve tension. As has been shown previously, some groups employ patterns of behavior that help them to avoid difficult tasks or unpleasant situations. The problem-solving technique in such situations helps group members to gain understandings of their own behaviors. In some cases the technique serves to change situations so that tensions are lessened; in other cases it helps groups to adopt more acceptable and desirable ways of behaving even though the situations remain unchanged.

The process by which changes in opinions are brought about by means of group problem solving has been examined by a number of re-

[15] John Dewey, *How We Think*, Boston: D. C. Heath & Company, 1933.

[16] Hugh Philp, and Dexter Dunphy, "Developmental Trends in Small Groups," *Sociometry*, Vol. 22, June 1959.

[17] National Training Laboratory in Group Development. *Report on the Second Summer Laboratory Session*. Bethel, Maine: National Education Association and Research Center for Group Dynamics, University of Michigan, 1948.

searchers. Since these studies have been cited previously, let us summarize briefly here.

When a problem is ambiguous, individuals tend to seek support for their views through agreement with other members of the group. Unless effective communication takes place, group members are not aware of the opinions and views of others. The act of communicating is an influence in changing opinions, for good communication practices lead to more accurate perceptions of the views of group members. It has been noted that in a problem-solving group, the formulation of an opinion or idea for communication leads to a sharpening or refining of the idea. Also, the use of the group problem-solving process helps the less popular members of the group (who many times do not have clear perceptions of group opinion) to acquire clearer ideas of how other members view the situation.

Factors Affecting the Problem-Solving Process

The effects of leadership on group problem solving have been mentioned indirectly in studies investigating leadership influences upon climate, interaction, and behavior. The studies by Lewin, Lippitt, and White; [18] Preston and Heintz; [19] and others showed that democratic or participatory leadership practices produced greater changes in privately held attitudes than did authoritarian practices. Experiments by Bovard [20] showed that when the group leader was endowed with understanding and used cooperative procedures to guide the group, the members were better able to define the problem, were more productive, and were better able to analyze situations and plan action than when leaders were dominative and used pressure tactics.

Studies show, too, that when leadership behavior violates the expectations of group members, dissatisfaction and uncertainty result in the group. Also, leader behavior which violates group expectation of how a leader should behave creates uncertainty in the group. Groups with highly urgent problems want direction from their leaders. As we said earlier in the book, studies indicate that at least initially, leadership style should be consistent with the expectations of group members.

[18] Kurt Lewin, Ronald Lippitt, and Ralph K. White, "Patterns of Aggressive Behavior in Experimentally Created 'Social Climates,' " *Journal of Social Psychology,* 10:271–299, May 1939.

[19] Malcom G. Preston and Roy K. Heintz, "Effects of Participatory vs. Supervisory Leadership on Group Judgment," *Journal of Abnormal and Social Psychology,* 44:345–355, July 1949.

[20] Everett W. Bovard, Jr., "Psychology of Classroom Interaction," *Journal of Abnormal and Social Psychology,* 46:398–405, July 1951.

An indication that leaders should take immediate steps when group problems arise comes from an experiment by Sherif,[21] who investigated group influence upon individual norms. He concluded that although a group's norms might reflect the leader's judgment, after the group has established its norms the leader has little influence in changing them. The implications for group problem solving are apparent: if leaders are to be influential in helping groups establish desirable standards, their influence must be exerted before groups' patterns of behavior are established. In other words, when a group reacts to a problem in undesirable ways, the necessity for solving the problem is immediate; otherwise, the reaction pattern can well become a crystallized behavior pattern of the group. If this happens, change can then be brought about only through group decision and not through problem solving.

Investigations show that in large-size groups there is less satisfaction with group discussion than in small groups and that leadership skill is more important in larger groups than in small ones.[22] These findings are significant to the concept of problem solving. Groups as large as classroom groups seem to require more guidance and direction during problem-solving processes. Considerable ability is required of the leader to help the group define the problem; skill is needed to create wide participation; and knowledge of the procedures is essential.

The finding that individuals in groups are more likely to interact if they can both see and hear one another indicates that in problemsolving situations greater participation is obtained if attention is given to seating arrangements. Studies of feedback show that in problemsolving situations, if groups are not made aware of progress, the members become more aggressive or try to escape through apathy and boredom.

A number of other factors that affect the problem-solving process have been identified. For example, a high degree of cohesiveness in groups causes members to be more influenced by discussion than are members of low-cohesiveness groups. When groups are cooperative rather than competitive, more ideas are verbalized, and members are more attentive to one another and more acceptant of and affected by one another's ideas. When a group is structured with a status hierarchy, the communication process within the group is affected. The problem-solving process can be seriously sidetracked or delayed by the tendency of low-status persons to discuss irrelevant matter. In such situations, the feelings of friendliness between subgroups high and low in status deteriorate. In brief, such

[21] Muzafer Sherif, "An Experimental Approach to the Study of Attitudes," *Sociometry*, 1:90–98, July 1937.

[22] A. Paul Hare, "A Study of Interaction and Consensus in Different-Sized Groups," *American Sociological Review*, 17:261–267, June 1952.

a status hierarchy can interfere with the effectiveness of communication and influence processes; it can affect good internal relations adversely; and it can divert considerable energy from the problem-solving process.

Certain practices or principles have been suggested for those who wish to effect changes in groups by means of problem-solving practices. Thelen [23] derived a number of principles from an integration of general psychological theory and from researches in group dynamics. Some of the suggestions made are: (1) there must be good communication; (2) agreement must be reached concerning common norms or standards; (3) the group must make a reappraisal of the situation as it is; (4) the group must maintain a cohesive state so individual suggestions for action will be influential.

Problem-Solving Methods

The process called group problem solving is a method of analyzing a situation, defining the problem, finding solutions, accepting a solution, and agreeing upon a plan of action. Personal problems may be solved in the same way. So may intellectual problems, such as the formulating of a scientific theory. Genuine group problems, however, are those that affect groups as wholes and that require group solutions because all group members are affected. A class group may be given an assignment and the members told they are to work it out together. If each person is to be graded individually, this assignment is usually not perceived by members as a group problem. It is an individual problem. Even if the group members are given the same grade, the actual group problem usually becomes something other than the one assigned; often the problem becomes one of how to satisfy the teacher and complete the assignment.

Thorndike [24] suggests that problems can be divided into two main categories: (1) practical problems, or the need to get something done, and (2) intellectual problems, involving the need to understand. The group problems we are concerned with are of the practical kind, although in the process of getting something done individuals in the group may solve intellectual problems and may increase their understanding. The problems class groups face arise from factors in the environment that cause dissatisfaction, or they may develop from internal conditions within

[23] Herbert A. Thelen, "Experimental Research Toward a Theory of Instruction," *Journal of Educational Research*, 45:89–136, October 1951.

[24] Robert L. Thorndike, "How Children Learn the Principles and Techniques of Problem Solving," in *Learning and Instruction*, Forty-ninth Yearbook of the National Society for the Study of Education, Chicago: University of Chicago Press, 1950, pp. 192–216.

the group. Whatever the source, there is a need for change, or a need to take action of some sort. Since the whole group is involved, the whole group needs to work out the solution.

A problem such as, "What qualifications are needed to become a professional ball player?" is not a group problem, although if all of the members of the class are interested they may pool their ideas and make a single list of qualifications. This question however, does not *require* a group solution.

This point has been emphasized because unless the problem to be solved is one that concerns *all* group members as group members, attempts to use the group problem-solving method to reach a solution may be ineffective and perhaps another approach should be used.

Steps in Group Problem Solving

The nature of the problem that a class group faces determines somewhat the steps that must be taken in the problem-solving process. If, for example, the group as a whole is restless, irritable, and makes little effort to concentrate on school tasks, the teacher may recognize that something is wrong but have no clue to the nature of the difficulty. Then again, the group may react in somewhat the same way as the class that came into the room after the lunch period vigorously approving the behavior of a youngster who kicked a teacher. The class would not settle down to work, and the teacher was alarmed because of the group reaction plus the fact that the group was too excited to begin work. The reaction of the class was a response to this incident that happened on the playground, but the underlying problem was a resentment of a school lunch-bench rule; this could be determined by the comments made.

When a class group is divided in conflict, the immediate cause of the quarrel may be determined quite easily, but the real source of the difficulty may be quite deep-seated. Before solutions to the problem can be agreed upon by the group, the problem must be identified and stated. Defining and stating the problem may be the most difficult part of the whole process.

The problem-solving method has been described by Utterback [25] as consisting of the following steps:

1. statement and definition of the problem,
2. examination of facts out of which the problem arises,
3. consideration of the criteria to be used in evaluating solutions,

[25] William Utterback, *Group Thinking and Conference Leadership*, New York: Rinehart & Company, 1950, p. 34.

4. examination and appraisals of solutions,

5. consideration of the steps to be taken in carrying out the solution adopted.

When the difficulty is easily identified, the teacher can say to the class, "We seem to have a problem." The group can be encouraged to define the problem and state it and follow this with an examination of all the facts. It is during this process that a change in perception or opinion may come about. However, if the situation involves group conflict or an unknown problem, a slightly different procedure has been found to be effective with class groups.

1. Explore the issue. Have each child briefly state his views and indicate why he thinks as he does.

2. As various children express their views, note points of agreement. Write these on the chalkboard.

3. List the points of disagreement. State these clearly and get agreement that these are the points of conflict.

4. Summarize the disagreements and explore further with the class to determine the real source of the difficulty.

5. Help the group define the problem and state it. Ask group members if the problem is stated correctly.

6. Ask for solutions and list them. Compare solutions with disagreements.

7. Decide upon the solutions considered best.

8. Get agreement upon the steps needed to carry out the action.

If conflict between members is the problem, or if the group is in an emotional state and the teacher does not know the cause of the trouble, the teacher begins by attempting to get agreement in as many areas as possible. The process is one of clarifying the areas of agreement and isolating the areas of disagreement until they are reduced to the smallest number possible. During this process of clarifying the area of dispute, the teacher may discover the source of the problem. Questions can be asked that direct thinking along these lines.

In situations of this kind, it is agreement that is needed. Voting upon a plan of action can split the group. Usually youngsters will agree to go along with a group on a trial plan. Voting may be suggested by those who feel the majority is on their side, but it should be discouraged if possible.

Classroom Illustrations

Because so many different kinds of problem situations arise in groups, and because the process of limiting the problem and analyzing the situation requires flexibility and usually cannot be reduced to steps in a procedure, examples are presented here. In most of the examples, the teachers who attempted the use of problem-solving methods to modify class group behavior were unskilled in the procedure. However, their attempts show various applications of the process to group problems, and reading of these attempts can further clarify the group problem-solving process.

ACHIEVING UNITY IN A CLASS GROUP

(Example)

My sixth grade class this year has consisted of two separate cohesive groups. There has been a clear-cut division between boys and girls, which has been much greater than one would normally expect.

My problem from the beginning has been to try and reduce the conflict and bring about some degree of group unity.

Because of a change in the school district boundaries I found myself confronted with a group of rebellious boys and another group of cooperative girls. All but six members of the class appeared to have fallen into one of these major groups, which were poles apart in norms and goals. To get unified action seemed impossible. Standards that were set up in class meetings and apparently accepted were rejected in practice by many of the children. Reviewing these standards changed nothing. Class elections and attempts at setting up common goals were either fiascos or miserable failures.

Then something occurred that made it possible to try problem solving with the group and thereby get the two factions working together on a common problem. Two of my girls and one of the more dependable boys stayed in after school one day to assist me in preparing for "Open House." While we were working, one of our custodians came in to clean the room. Soon after his arrival, I was called to the office for a short time. I returned to my room to find the custodian gone and the three children in a minor state of shock. They informed me that, while I was gone, the custodian had said in very positive terms that we had "the messiest classroom in the building!"

When school was resumed the next morning, I called upon the threesome to report the incident to the class. The report was met with immediate hostile comments such as, "What does he expect? That's his job," and "What does he think he's getting paid for?"

The discussion continued until some of the hostility seemed to have spent itself. We began to get comments such as "Maybe we aren't careful about picking up papers," and "Perhaps our desks aren't clean and things fall out when he moves them."

At this point I entered the picture saying, "It appears that we do have a problem here. What do we want to do about it?"

Diverging ideas came forth, with three predominating. Some children were sincerely concerned and wanted to prove that we really aren't "messy."

Others, still somewhat indignant, wanted to show him how wrong he was. A few couldn't have cared less!

At this time it appeared that a substantial majority was ready for constructive action toward changing the custodian's mind. I called for oral acceptance of a project. A leader among the boys asked me what would happen if some of them didn't want to do anything about it. I assured him, in my most matter-of-fact tone, that nothing at all would happen—they simply wouldn't be taking part in the project. (I confess his question gave me a feeling of being on thin ice.)

We proceeded with the oral acceptance, achieving total class agreement minus eight. Giving no attention to "minus eight," we launched into a discussion of what we could do to leave our classroom in a neater condition. The suggestions were listed on the chalkboard and recorded by the secretary.

Finally, a child suggested that we send a committee to see the custodian to get his ideas on how we could improve. This having been approved, the class next decided that the committee should be the three children who had been told we were "messy."

The committee met with the custodian later in the day and reported back to the class. There was little to add to our list, as the children had already thought of the things he mentioned. The fact, however, that the committee had accomplished its purpose seemed to be significant. A little side remark by another custodian gave us all a laugh and lightened the situation. The remark was to the effect that the best way to help would be to stay out of the room at all times.

The day ended with a very careful check of desks and floors by most of the children and extra effort on the part of room monitors in straightening bookshelves, paper supplies, and so on. Even one of the "minus eight" entered into the tidying up, though rather obviously making sure that other "holder-outers" weren't watching.

After the class had left, I noticed that Robert, another member of the "minus eight," was still in the room. As I turned to him, he asked me how his desk looked. From a distance, I replied that it looked fine. He pursued the matter further. "How did it look inside?" I went to his desk, checked it, and assured him that I thought it was very neat and tidy. Then, with obvious self-consciousness, he said he guessed he wanted to help with the project. I told him that this was fine, for the more who helped, the more successful would be the result. Robert then left the room. Now, I thought, we have arrived at "minus seven."

The next day brought one new development. Many of the children were showing a greater awareness of things that fell on the floor. One of their corrective measures, of course, had been to keep things tidy throughout the day. The day closed with a quick evaluation and a tidy classroom.

In evaluating our third day, two things of importance occurred. First, the class decided that the committee should see the custodian again for a progress report. Secondly, Randy, one of the "minus seven," suggested that we might put our chairs on top of the desks. Some rooms did this, he continued, to make cleaning easier. The class adopted his suggestion. The surprising thing was that no one gave any indication of remembering that he had been a dissenter! We apparently had arrived at "minus six."

On the fourth day, the committee met again with the custodian. The report brought back was a glowing one of a great improvement and also a challenge in that he wondered how long it would last!

On the fifth day, our evaluation and cleanup were both hurried. The room was left somewhat more untidy than it had been at any time since the project started. This was mentioned by some of the children in our discussion on the sixth day. I assumed part of the responsibility for this occurrence, saying that I had rushed them because of a meeting I had scheduled immediately after school. One child brought out the fact that we shouldn't need much discussing any more, because we all knew what to do.

At the close of the seventh day, today, the children decided that "tomorrow or the next day" the committee should ask the custodian if he still thinks we are the "messiest class in the school."

At intervals I have complimented the class on the good job they have been doing, and for other things when praise has been warranted.

After only seven days, the results are inconclusive, of course. It is too soon to know if the change is permanent. What is very evident is that at the present time the class is working together in harmony. The six nonparticipants do not interfere in any way. They simply will not agree orally to work with the others. They seem to feel the spirit of the project, since they do not attempt to block the group.

Now that some degree of unity is achieved, other small unifying projects will be planned with the group. I shall not be discouraged if future efforts are somewhat less successful. The important thing is that by using techniques heretofore unknown to me, I have seen that what I considered the impossible can become possible, at least for a time. I conclude from this experience that had I understood the use of these techniques and used them consistently from the beginning of the year, my class would undoubtedly have developed a greater degree of cohesiveness and fewer problems.

REDUCING FEELINGS OF RESENTMENT

(Example)

It was softball season and all the children wanted to play ball. Part of the playground was under construction, thus limiting the area. Since the fifth grade did not have a field, they asked the principal about a place to play. She said she would do something about it. Meanwhile, they made their own diamond between two other diamonds.

On Thursday, the principal came in to talk to the class. She said, "I've just come from the sixth grade and it has been agreed that the fifth and the sixth grades will share the field. Both classes will number off, and 'odds' will play against the 'evens.' The sixth will select captains the first week, the fifth will select captains the next week. This seems to be the best solution to our problem of lack of playground space."

Immediately several boys groaned. With a startled look the principal said, "Well, I am surprised to hear this from the fifth grade. I expected the sixth grade to complain because it is their field; instead, they were perfectly willing to let you play with them. However, since the sixth grade children are so cooperative I am sure that you will have a good time. Monday we will start the new plan. Have the class divide into teams."

The attitude of resentment seemed to mount up after the principal left. This class did not want to play with the sixth graders. They did not like the principal's plan, and besides, who agreed to the plan? They were told what to do!

It was decided to try and change this reaction of resentment to a more positive one by using the problem-solving approach. This is the plan I decided to follow.

1. Explore the reasons for the strong feeling of resentment,
2. Define the problem,
3. Decide what could be done about it,
4. Agree on a plan of action.

If the children continued to feel resentful about playing with the sixth graders, I planned to help them make a protest to the principal, since she would cooperate. It was not her regular practice to dictate, but conditions were difficult because of all of the building going on during school time.

The first question to the group was: "Why don't you want to share the playground space with the sixth grade?"

Paul: "It's O.K. to share, but we don't have anything to share."

Teacher: "Why do you think the sixth grade accepted the request that they share? The principal said that the sixth graders were very pleasant and cooperative."

Debbie: "They knew they were going to be big shots—just boss us around and slaughter us."

Ken: "It would be different if they had to play with the seventh grade."

James: "All the good ones in the sixth grade will be on one team."

Tal: "Fifth will just sit on the bench (the boys chimed in with, "yeah"!) or else be put in the field."

Elaine: "Since the sixth will be captains, their friends will be chosen and the fifth will be left out."

David: "The fifth can't play ball as well as the sixth."

Mike: "The fifth needs practice for playing. The sixth will take the good positions, so the fifth won't get much practice standing out in the field."

Cathy: "You are crabbing about the captains and positions. How do you know all these things? You haven't played them yet!"

Someone answered this very quickly. "When we played kickball with them, they dropped the atom bomb when we made a mistake. Also another time when we tried playing with them the first thing we knew the sixth had the positions and the fifth graders were out of the game."

Jack: "It's like playing Civil War—we are the slaves and they are the plantation owners."

David: "They'll put us in the field."

Sue: "It will crowd the field too much with both grades playing."

Alan: "Of course the sixth grade didn't grumble! They will boss us and get the best positions. Fifth graders would be at the bottom of the list."

Cathy: "The principal was only trying to help!"

Chorus: "Bossing you mean! She asked the sixth graders, not us!"

At this point it seemed the attitudes were clear and so was the problem.

Teacher: "What is the real problem that is bothering us?"

(Finally it was stated to everyone's satisfaction.) The problem was the group did not want to play with the sixth grade. They wanted a place of their own to play. (They agreed they were upset because they had not been consulted by the principal.)

After much discussion a plan was agreed upon by the class. It was agreed that a committee of three would go to talk to the principal. Appointments were made. The three children wrote down what they wanted to say. They wanted to present the plan that the class had agreed upon. They returned with this note from the principal:

> Dear Fifth Grade,
>   The committee has suggested a good solution for use of the playground space. They believe it would be a good idea if the sixth grade met with you to discuss the plan.
>   Could we meet in Room 2 at 11:00 on Monday? Please let me know.
>
>   Mrs. X

We had the meeting. Dick presented the plan of alternating days that would permit each class to have its own game. After discussion, a vote was taken. Both fifth and sixth grades were in favor of the new plan.

This plan has been in effect for two weeks, and no problems have arisen between the fifth and sixth grade children. This worked out so well it seems to prove that if children see the problem and are given an opportunity to work it out, their plan will be more successful than an imposed plan.

IMPROVING PLAYGROUND CONDITIONS

(Example)

My third graders entered the room very noisily following lunch. Many crowded around my desk and all tried to talk at once. They were very upset about lunch and recess playground rules. I finally got them settled in their seats with the promise that we would discuss the problem and try to solve it. When I asked for a volunteer to state the problem, every hand went up. We carried on a rather disorderly discussion because the children found it impossible to wait turns to share opinions.

As a little background, third graders have recess with the fourth, fifth, and sixth grades. They have lunch with the kindergarten, first, and second grades. The people who take our noon duty are mothers, not teachers.

The children were upset because of unfairness on the playground. They are not allowed to play kickball or basketball at recess because there are no diamonds or courts available—these facilities are assigned to the upper grades. The older students keep the third graders off the rings, swings, and jungle gyms at recess by sheer size. At lunch the third graders aren't allowed to play on these equipments because they are supposedly "too big" and may hurt the little ones. Hence, my class was "up in the air" about being "picked on" by the whole rest of the school.

The girls and boys all agreed with one another. They *all* backed one another up and stuck together on the whole issue. Even though the discussion was disorderly, the problem was clear enough. It seemed that there was no use trying to change their feelings. The conditions were just as stated. This had been going on for the first few weeks of school, and now the children had all at once rebelled at the situation. I told them that the first thing the following morning we would hold a meeting to plan ways to solve the problem. They were to think of suggestions. When we came up with a good plan we would ask the principal if he would make a change.

This is the basic plan I followed:

1. The problem was clearly stated and all the reasons for the dissatisfaction listed.
2. All the suggestions for improving the condition were listed on the board.
3. The class agreed on the two best suggestions. All angles were considered to see if they could be accomplished.
4. The class then considered the best way to present the proposal.

The class agreed that the two best plans were:

1. To set aside one block of swings and either the rings or the jungle gym for third grade use *only,* during both recess and lunch.
2. To assign one day a week to each grade for use of the equipment. Because of a double first grade and a double fifth grade, it happened that this plan would work out evenly.

Considerable time was spent deciding on the best way to present the plan. It was finally agreed to ask the principal to come to our room to hear the third grade proposals.

Mr. C. came and the children handled the whole meeting themselves. They explained the problem and described their solutions. Mr. C. was very impressed. He praised them highly for their constructive attitude while they wiggled with pleasure. They were so pleased over the whole thing that they really did not stress how discontented they were over the whole situation.

Mr. C. promised he would take the matter up with the other teachers and would let them know the outcome by the end of the week. In the meantime, he asked if they could put up with the conditions until something was done. Of course they said they could.

The second plan was selected and the trouble is over. This experience, however, changed these third graders. They act very adult and important. At the slightest sign of a "problem," they ask if they can discuss it.

Preventive Programs

Situations can arise in any class group that act as barriers to learning. Certain procedures can be used to change interpersonal and intergroup relations. Group processes can be used to lessen group dissatisfactions or change opinions about existing conditions. However, fewer problems will occur if teachers have adequate knowledge about the forces that operate in classroom groups, and if they have skill in recognizing these forces as they occur. Also, when conditions do arise that disrupt the learning program, teachers cannot assume that they can always be handled effectively simply by applying a technique. Whenever possible, it is the best practice to note the psychological forces that are affecting the group and apply preventive measures before serious problems arise. Many group problems of the kind described throughout this book can be avoided if teachers develop skill in observing and perceiving group reactions and take steps to prevent certain problems from occurring or from developing to serious proportions. It is possible for the teacher to formulate problems so that constructive behavior is stimulated.

A teacher who takes preventive measures reduces some of the conditions that commonly disturb the classroom atmosphere. A teacher who involves the group in planning and solving problems rarely has a group that reacts with hostility and defensiveness, nor is such a class likely to approve rebel or clown behavior, or to make a scapegoat of a member.

The ultimate aim of discipline for individuals is to help them develop capacity for self-direction and self-management. This is true for groups also. It is not only desirable, but extremely important that groups develop capacities for self-management and self-direction. If this is to occur, the group must have some opportunity to practice. Since adult groups have difficulty in this respect, it cannot be expected that a class group will accomplish this without skillful guidance and direction by the teacher.

Questions for Study and Discussion

1. Can you recall being a member of a group that had a problem that caused some or all of the members to behave in a disruptive or undesirable way? What was the nature of the problem? Describe your feelings in this situation. Could the problem have been solved by a problem-solving process?

2. It is generally stated in one form or another that democratic freedom is not freedom to do as one pleases, and that social controls are therefore necessary. How can children be taught to respect law and order?

3. If youngsters object to a long-standing school practice because they seem to feel a need to assert independence, what actions do you believe should be taken? Why?

4. Some teachers feel that groups should be encouraged to adhere to a code of honor such as "never squeal on a fellow member." Can you justify this position? Why or why not?

5. If a child made an accurate but uncomplimentary remark about the actions of an administrator, what would you do?

6. What emotional sets may operate to make some groups more suggestible than others? How can children be taught to be critical of hearsay evidence? Could the situation in the incident entitled "The Rumor" be used to develop certain concepts and increase social understanding? How might this be done?

7. Every time an upper grade teacher tried to show a film in the room, there was confusion and a number of disgruntled individuals, because the physical setting of the room was inadequate. Chairs, tables, etc. had to be moved and even then some individuals had to sit in disadvantageous positions. Plan statements you would use to start the problem-solving process moving.

8. A strong feeling of resentment developed in a class group against the safety committee officers in charge of behavior in the corridors going to and coming from the playground. The safety committee officers also complained to the teacher that children in this class were "answering back" when reprimanded. The teacher talked with the class to show the need for the committee. What would you do? Describe in detail.

Suggestions for Further Reading

Ambrose, Edna and Alice Miel. *Children's Social Learning: Implications of Research and Expert Study.* Washington, D.C.: Association for Supervision and Curriculum Development, National Education Association, 1958.

Benne, Kenneth D., Leland B. Bradford, and Ronald Lippitt. *Group Dynamics and Social Action.* New York: Anti-Defamation League of B'nai B'rith, 1950.

Bennett, Margaret E. *Guidance in Groups.* New York: McGraw, 1955.

Bradford, Leland P. "Developing Potentialities through Class Groups," *Teachers' College Record,* 61:443–450, May 1960.

Bradford, Leland P., Dorothy Stock, and Murray Horwitz. *How to Diagnose Group Problems.* Washington, D.C.: National Training Laboratories, National Education Association, 1961, pp. 37–50.

Corey, Stephen M., Paul M. Halverson, and Elizabeth Lowe. *Teachers Prepare for Discussion Group Leadership.* New York: Teachers College, Columbia U., 1953.

Exline, Ralph V. and Robert C. Ziller. "Status Congruency and Interpersonal Conflict in Decision-making Groups," *Human Relations,* 12:147–162, 1959.

Grossack, Martin M. "Some Effects of Cooperation and Competition upon Small-Group Behavior," *Journal of Abnormal and Social Psychology,* 49:3, July 1954.

Hammond, Leo Keith and Morton Goldman. "Competition and Non-Competition and Its Relationship to Individual and Group Productivity," *Sociometry,* 24:46–60, March 1961.

Hoffman, L. Richard. "Homogeneity of Member Personality and its Effect on Group Problem-Solving," *Journal of Abnormal and Social Psychology,* 58:27–32, January 1959.

Hoffman, L. Richard, Ernest Harburg, and Norman Maier. "Differences and Disagreement as Factors in Creative Group Problem Solving," *Journal of Abnormal and Social Psychology,* 64:206–214, March 1962.

Hudgins, Bryce B. "Effects of Group Experience on Individual Problem Solving," *Journal of Educational Psychology,* 51:37–42, February 1960.

Jenkins, David. "Interdependence in the Classroom," *Journal of Educational Research,* 45:137–144, October 1951.

Kelley, Harold H. and John W. Thibaut. "Experimental Studies of Group Problem Solving and Process," in G. Lindzey (ed.), *Handbook of Social Psychology,* Vol. 2. Cambridge, Mass.: Addison-Wesley, 1954, pp. 735–785.

Krech, David and Richard S. Crutchfield. *Theory and Problems of Social Psychology.* New York: McGraw, 1948.

Lippitt, Gordon L. "Improving Decision-Making with Groups," in *Group Development.* Washington, D.C.: National Training Laboratories, National Education Association, 1961, pp. 90–93.

Lippitt, Gordon L. "How to get Results From a Group," in *Group Development.* Washington, D.C.: National Training Laboratories, National Education Association, 1961, pp. 31–36.

Maier, Norman R. F. and L. Richard Hoffman. "Quality of First and Second Solutions in Group Problem Solving," *Journal of Applied Psychology,* 44:278–283, August 1960.

Smith, Ewart E. and Stanford S. Kight. "Effects of Feedback on Insight and Problem Solving Efficiency in Training Groups," *Journal of Applied Psychology,* 43:209–211, 1959.

Stanley, Julian C. and Herbert J. Klausmeier. "Opinion Constancy After Formal Role Playing," *Journal of Social Psychology,* 46:11–18, August 1957.

Utterback, William E. *Decision Through Discussion, A Manual for Group Leaders.* New York: Rinehart, 1960.

Vroom, Victor H. "Some Personality Determinants of the Effects of Participation," *Journal of Abnormal and Social Psychology,* 59:322–327, November 1959.

Whyte, William H., Jr. *The Organization Man.* New York: S. and S., 1956.

Zander, Alvin. "Group Membership and Individual Security," *Human Relations,* 11:99–111, 1958.

Ziller, Robert C. "Communication Restraints, Group Flexibility, and Group Confidence," *Journal of Applied Psychology,* 42:346–352, October 1958.

Chapter 13   Study of
                              Classroom Groups

TEACHERS and school administrators who want to understand children's group behavior need a complete picture of the group in general. In some studies, one or two properties of the group may be pre-eminent in the mind of an observer and be the focus of his attention. Study usually reveals that these obvious properties relate to other aspects of the group life and functioning, and are best understood in that context. The research worker's interest in limited aspects of groups is as typical of him as is the practical school person's interest in the broad complex of behavior that he observes in the classroom and school and works to improve. This chapter is designed to give techniques of evaluating a broad and typical range of group properties and characteristics.

The amount of research on children's groups has been relatively small in recent years. The neglect of group studies at the childhood years of the elementary school and the early adolescent years of the high school is apparent when the research of the past 10 or 20 years is examined. A brief look at the history of the period is explanatory of the trend. The scientific study of children's groups received considerable attention and impetus before World War II from the work of Lewin and his associates. The shift of emphasis to adult studies, such as those in the area of leadership, was in response to the nation's requirements. Congressional appropriations supported research by the armed services in their studies of adult groups, while private funds supported the large number of group studies that were, and continue to be, made in business and industry. The research with educational groups has most frequently been at the college level with young adults, and it often shows the interest of an individual research worker in some fragmentary part of a larger rationale. However, a few researchers have pursued their interests in children's groups, though the psychology of the individual child has continued to receive the primary attention and efforts of psychologists and educational practitioners.

For those primarily concerned with the younger age groups, the years of research with adult groups are far from being wasted or unproductive. From this body of research have come many advances in theory and methodology, some of which have promise for study of children's groups. There are hypotheses whose occurrence and applicability at successive developmental levels need investigation. There are research designs and techniques that may or may not be productive in studies of children's groups.

There is some evidence of growing awareness of the study of children's groups, a general climate of interest, and promise of financial assistance for research. Whether this somewhat auspicious milieu will result in experimenters being drawn to the study of children's groups is yet to be seen.

The research in child development has produced much *normative* information, based on frequencies and averages—for example, the average times of walking, talking, etc. A body of such norms is useful to teachers, pediatricians, and others who work with children, although it has limitations. Normative information for classroom groups at different ages would be an important first addition to our knowledge. These norms for groups might be averages, or given frequencies of specified kinds of behavior, or they might be descriptive. Norms could be compiled that describe types of conditions that exist in school groups.

Normative information, while not useful for explanatory purposes or for prediction of future behavior of a specific group, would give a picture of *what is* (status), or of existing conditions and relationships. Norms would serve, of course, as a base point for the more advanced steps of understanding, explaining, helping, guiding, and changing groups.

The classroom group may be studied in its natural condition or setting. An observational study of the group in the halls, on the playground, or in the classroom is a naturalistic study. A study of the structure of the group as that structure exists in the usual activities illustrates the naturalistic approach. It does not explain how or why the present structure is what it is. Neither does it provide a basis for predicting trends or future development of the group. It is the kind of status study that is made by the fairly common sociometric techniques. It provides the teacher with one test of the accuracy of his perceptions of the structure of his class. There is much to recommend the naturalistic approach.

Manipulation of the group—or, more accurately, manipulation of some aspect or aspects of the group's functioning—is the equivalent of laboratory research in which the experimenter exerts controls. The interjection into the group of a leader to act in a predetermined or trained manner, for example, is used with adults and is intended to manipulate the group or to have weighted effects. Such training of peers for use in younger groups is more difficult, or even impossible. Other types of manipulation are possible. The sequential changes in the adult leadership in the classic studies of boys' clubs by Lewin and associates is one kind of manipulation. The studies that change or manipulate group characteristics or factors are considered superior in precision to those made in natural conditions. However, the difficulties involved in ordering group characteristics are not to be minimized. It would appear that both the natural and planned manipulative approaches to the study of groups have places and can be profitably utilized.

Techniques for Studying Groups

The development of techniques for the study of groups is a challenging and complex problem. It has produced some unique approaches and clever devices, and it is an area in which further resourceful solutions may be expected. A variety of techniques are reported in the literature of group research. School personnel who are interested in understanding and promoting better group living can make little progress until they possess practical techniques and skill in their use.

Knowledge of techniques of teaching and of how to evaluate and achieve change is especially important in this field, where there are few refined and accepted instruments available. For testing intelligence and achievement, school personnel may choose from tests developed over the years for specified uses. Lacking such an array of tests and evaluative instruments for the study of groups, acquaintance with techniques that have proved useful assumes new importance.

Knowledge of techniques is, of course, not synonymous with skill in their use. One may have read and achieved rather advanced understanding of a technique but lack an equal level of skill.

The studies of children's groups, when examined for the research methodology, impress the student with the adaptations to a research problem and to a special situation that the investigators of children have made. Faced with an absence of proven instruments, they have frequently devised their own [1] or adapted from those used with older groups or for different purposes. The lack of standardized tests has further accentuated the noninstrumental approach, which places greater than usual emphasis on techniques.

Observation

Observation is a continuous daily process for everyone, but it has special uses for teachers in their professional capacity as they gather data about children and classes in the school setting. Observational methods serve educational purposes in that they aid in describing and understanding behavior as it occurs, rather than in retrospect. It is a primary tool of scientific inquiry in several disciplines. Teachers do constantly observe. Often, however, they simply accumulate observed facts, impressions, and interpretations without recording or systematically dealing with either their observations or the results.

Direct observation, although it is a primary means of getting information, is not the only way to obtain data. In studies of groups, other methods and tools—questionnaires, interviews, sociometric and available records—have their own values and uses. They are, as well as methods in themselves, supplements and adjuncts to observational methods. Observation as a method has both advantages and disadvantages. Advantages are that it is possible to record behavior as it occurs and in its natural setting. There can be simultaneous recording of on-going, spontaneous occurrences. Disadvantages are that behavior already defined experimentally and that the observer may be interested in studying may not occur or it may occur infrequently, and the observer therefore spends much time at other than his intended pursuit. Also, there are interruptions, changes, and physical conditions—such as weather and lighting—that are unpredictable and uncontrollable and make observation difficult.

---

[1] Albert F. de Groat and George G. Thompson, "A Study of the Distribution of Teacher Approval and Disapproval Among Sixth-Grade Pupils," *The Journal of Experimental Education*, 18:57–75, September 1949.

Observation has the advantage of yielding data independently of the subjects' willingness or unwillingness to report. A related limitation is that observed behavior does not give, or gives indirectly, evidence of feelings, motives, attitudes, desires and perceptions.

Although everyone is constantly observing, it cannot be assumed that observation is correct and adequate. No one sees everything that is occurring. Rather, everyone sees selectively, even in informal, daily observation. Teachers, then, who do of course use observation extensively, use it selectively and in accord with their personal interests and predispositions. Training has been shown repeatedly to improve observation, with the result that training of observers is an expected preliminary to any study in which they are to produce essential data.

There are several ways to improve observation. Establishing some of the requirements of a situation to be observed is one of the ways. It is possible to obtain better observations than would normally occur if the purpose of the observation is clear, if the setting in which it is to occur is decided, and if the behavior is selected, delineated, and described. What, when, and how—that is, in what form and in what arrangement recordings of observations are to be made—are important preliminary decisions.

Treatment of Observational Data

The record of observations may be read and studied as a whole and (a) frequency of occurrence of different kinds of behavior may be recorded (just counting or tallying, such as the number of verbal remarks or minutes when changing activities, interaction in planning or discussion, etc.), (b) ratings may be made on the common or frequent kinds of behavior (scale values may be assigned and totaled), (c) for particular kinds of behavior, durations or continuing recurrences on successive days or in successive situations may be recorded.

The record may use a *unit* of observation, the unit being a natural beginning-to-end interval. This would mean observing and studying a behavior act itself without regard to the length of time or exact personnel involved. An example might be the choice process, and the act observed might be the choosing of team captains or room chairmen. The psychological and emotional content of such acts—cooperation or hostility—are content and not the basis of the units of observation and not units themselves.

Observation is the basic way to study children groups, just as it is the basic and most common way for teachers to study individual children. Observation is more than just seeing—it is an active process of taking notice of many parts of the situation, paying close attention to what the group does and how it does it, and selecting, ordering, and relating what is seen. Observation, to say it another way, involves the attaching of meaning or cognition to that which is seen. Then, still part of the observation process, the observer seeks an explanation of the "why" of the group behavior that he has observed. He brings to bear on the explanation his previous experience with this or with other groups. ("The class is always excited and slow to settle down after an assembly.") He may use theory to aid him in finding a suitable explanation. ("Groups become hostile when they are threatened. Perhaps this class feels threatened.")

No teacher is a complete observer. He cannot take in everything that happens in a group during a class period or during a school day. Since he cannot observe everything that each child does, it is not to be expected that his observation of the interaction of the group can be total. The teacher–observer has duties and responsibilities that preclude his continued attention to the group, even if he wished to give it his sustained attention and to relatively ignore or eliminate other demands of the situation. The teacher is concerned with and gives much time and observation to individual children, although some of these observations may be of the child in his relations to others—that is, the child's relation to the group or subgroups. The observer focuses his observations on certain situations and on certain parts of the group, or on certain kinds of behavior of the group. What and when he observes will partially depend upon his concerns. The kind of information or data he gains from observing will vary with his perception of the problem and the solution that he seeks.

Teachers who use observation will do so for many different reasons. When meeting a new class, a teacher will want to find out what the group is like and what its state of development is as a group. After such an appraisal of group status, he may become interested in helping the group change and progress, and the focus of his observation will then change. Sometimes the observation will suggest further questions, such as new questions about the structure of the group or the effectiveness of certain teaching methods. Continuing observation also results in a new perspective on problems that were formerly considered irrelevant or unimportant. It may also clarify problems that previously have been hazily recognized and ill-defined.

The dynamic and on-going interaction of a school group cannot be seen in its entirety by one person. It has too many dimensions—time, person-and-group relations, direction, relation to nonpresent goals and allegiances, and many more—to be encompassed by even a most diligent and sensitive observer. An added aspect is that the members see the happenings and dimensions of the group life from their contacts with it at given times and from the changing vantage points of their roles and their maturity levels. The teacher who seeks to observe the group whole in all its changing relationships will soon be aware that this is not completely possible. The attempt to study through observational methods the complete continuum of group life is patently impossible, and particularly so for the observer who also has the busy and demanding role of teacher. However, the understanding of a complex group can be approached by selecting and arranging content into observable units.

ANECDOTAL RECORDS. Many teachers have been educated to study individual children with a broad, encompassing approach. They use cumulative records from previous years, observe the child in as many situations as possible, write anecdotal records, and compile other data. In a well-known volume of the American Council on Education, the skill in writing the anecdotal records was given an important part of the child study plan.[2] To help teachers to write the records, they were encouraged to think of behavior as supplying clues to understanding, to learn to notice exactly what a child says and does and to note carefully the situation in which he so behaved, and to learn to hold personal judgments in abeyance until they had adequate data upon which to formulate tentative hypotheses. In response to the question of what to write, the teachers who participated in the plan had difficulty at first, but learned to select incidents for the records that were significant or relevant to the child's development.

Diary or log recording, which is a promising method for the study and understanding of group behavior, has some elements in common with the above-mentioned child-study plan. Since teachers cannot observe group behavior totally, selection and recording are points that require decisions. The problem of recognizing significant group behavior is as difficult as that of recognizing significant individual behavior. The work of Prescott [3] on the anecdotal record has many suggestions that may be, in part, used by the student of group behavior.

The anecdotes of the child-study plan, which are brief word vignettes of behavior written at fairly close intervals by the teacher, accumulate into a body of material. Teachers do, of course, vary in their recording habits. They may, for example, write long or short and many or few reports. The reports differ, too, in content, with some teachers writing anecdotes emphasizing constructive, positive behavior, and others

[2] *Helping Teachers Understand Children,* by the Staff of the Division on Child Development and Teacher Personnel, Prepared for the Commission on Teacher Education, Washington, D.C.: American Council on Education, 1945.

[3] Daniel A. Prescott, *The Child in the Educative Process,* New York: McGraw-Hill Book Company, 1957.

emphasizing negative behavior and tending to be critically destructive. A balanced report that is an approximation of reality is the desired product.

The accumulated anecdotes reflecting several years' observations become a "behavior journal" or "log." Olson [4] succinctly gives practical recommendations for form, and content, and discusses the significance and use of the log.

TIME SAMPLING. Time sampling is a procedure that fixes the attention of the observer upon selected aspects of behavior as they occur within uniform and short time intervals. The number, length, and spacing of the intervals are planned to obtain time samples of certain behavior. The categories of behavior are defined in advance and are coded so the observer can make quick and precise records during the observation. The data may later be scored or treated in accord with the purposes of the study.

As a method, time sampling has been used in numerous studies of child development for 30 years. Often the observer rotates his attention from child to child in a group for the specified time limit and in a predetermined order, coding his observations on prepared forms. However, time samplings of entire groups have many possible uses. It is one important way for teachers or other observers of groups to improve their observations. The use of time sampling objectifies what may be either correct or erroneous general impressions and reduces the "horn" and "halo" interpretations that may be attached to the reputation of a group.

RATINGS AND SCALES. Ratings based on observation are a familiar device. The procedure is to use rating scales after the observer has made a number of observations, which probably have been made on many occasions and over a period of several weeks or months. The scales, then, serve to sum up what the observer has noted. The results may be examined for consistency by other raters or for behavior of the subjects or the group in different situations. Also changes in behavior may be studied by repeated use of the same scale at later times.

A comparison of the effects of different conditions or settings within the school environment upon group behavior may be made through ratings. This may be a promising approach and is one that has been little used for group study.

The use of scales or questionnaires for rating purposes differs as a method from other observational procedures in which actions and conditions are not anticipated but are described and recorded as they occur during the time of observation. In contrast to the latter, ratings are made

[4] Williard C. Olson, *Child Development*, Boston: D. C. Heath & Company, 1959, Appendix D.

on pre-established ways of behaving and are recorded after the observation is concluded. Frequently the teacher or observer takes the precaution of completing the questionnaire or rating instrument immediately after the observation or before there has been a considerable lapse of time. The ratings can be considered as a summary statement of cumulative direct observation.

Sociometric Techniques

Sociometric tests and devices are methods of revealing interpersonal choices and group association patterns or structures. More properly, they are termed *sociometric techniques* because they are not tests in the usual meaning of the term. Another way of describing sociometry is that it is a means of assessing the attractions, or attractions and repulsions, within a group. Each person privately specifies other persons in the group with whom he would like, or would not like, to associate in some particular activity.

Each group member is given an opportunity to name others in a private way, from a given population, and on a specific criterion that has meaning for him, for the purpose of restructuring the group. The question should be suited to the level of understanding of the members of the group. With young children the questions may be given orally and the answers recorded, while the anonymity of each child's response is maintained.

The resulting diagram is a sociogram. The sociogram shows in graphic form the choices of the members for one particular situation. If more than one question is asked, each with its own criterion—"work," "play," or "go to a party with"—then there is a separate sociogram for each question.

Sociometric techniques have been used in many studies of children's groups and they have gained a place as a useful tool for classroom teachers. Since the sociometric test is an informal evaluative instrument which must be fitted to a particular group, it is important that the user have understanding and skill. Its flexibility and suitability to varying situations are advantages, but because it is unstructured, the part of the teacher is important. The requirements for the sociometric test are given by Moreno[5] and thoroughly discussed by other writers.

Each class group has its own structure. The development of a structure, or pattern of relationships, is a normal and inevitable result of interaction in a group. Structure is not a state or condition that is achieved

[5] J. L. Moreno, *Who Shall Survive?* New York: Beacon House, 1953.

once and for all. Rather, it has relative stability, depending on the length of time the group has been a group, the changes in personnel, and changes in task and nontask goals and their related behaviors.

Structure depends, in part, upon the way the members feel about, perceive, and relate to one another. There is in every class group an unseen but existing pattern of relationships, and it affects the teacher's work as well as the children's learning and behavior. For example, a class that has two leaders who show mutual liking and respect and around whom the class is integrated and unified will function quite differently from a class that has several independent subgroups that are competing for influence and status in the class as a whole.

The structure is a pervasive influence in determining the kind of experiences a teacher will have with a class. Some groups are considered "easy to work with" while others are unusually "difficult." The teacher needs to know the structure as one important element in the dynamic interaction in the group.

The sociometric "test," originated by Moreno, has come into rather common use in recent years as it has proved to be a useful and informative technique. As modern education has placed greater emphasis on mental health and on the personal and social adjustments of pupils, the sociometric test has proved to be a popular and practical instrument. It has fitted a need in an area that has come to be recognized as part of the total educative process.

Sociometric devices have been used for varied research purposes. The studies of small group functioning, of group leadership, of the effects of group climate on the learning and behavior of individuals are among the many kinds of research that have used some type of sociometric instrument.

Sociometry cannot furnish answers on *why* the group structure is what it is, as it cannot explain why particular children are or are not chosen. It can only show what the group condition is in relation to the criteria in the sociometric question. This can lead to analysis and to the framing of pertinent questions. The value of the questions that come from analysis of the sociometric test lies in their directing the teacher's attention to further points for observation in the group. The new observation may be of dynamics that had not previously been noticed, or it may be more careful observation of some known factors. The observations may result in further action by the teacher to help the class or individuals. In this sense, the sociometric test and its results are like many other tests. They give information on *what is,* or they define status at a given time and in given conditions. Sociometric tests, because they measure *what is,* are not predictive. Predictions that the structure will remain the same for a semester, for example, are based on other factors, such as the ages of the members. By confirming, changing, or extending the teacher's perceptions, sociometric devices lay a basis for improving the group.

Class groups and schools have both formal and informal structures, and it is sometimes useful to differentiate between them. The formal structure is usually more visible. For example, it is easy to see the team captain, the "star" player, the team members, the "B" squad, or the "subs." This is observable in the president of the student council, other officers, members, and nonmembers. The informal structure is less visible. The "best friend," "best worker" and other positively ranked members can be identified through the use of sociometric tests as can group members who are disliked or who have negative statuses.

Structure may be inferred from observing behavioral clues, such as frequency of association, children meeting to leave school together, or children sitting together at lunch.

Some investigators interpret the group structure, whether it is formal or informal, as if it were a single hierarchy or ordering of members. Other investigators conceive of group structure being composed of several hierarchies. Individuals would, according to the latter view, be at one position in a hierarchy based on a work or task criterion and at another position in a hierarchy based on a criterion of social or personality attributes. A group member might, then, have a high rating in one hierarchy and a low or lesser one in others.

Sociometric data frequently show the presence of subgroups within the larger class group. It is not common to find an integrated pattern for the whole class, because of the tendency for the group to split into subgroups as the group size increases. A series of interlocking subgroups is a usual finding when a sociogram is analyzed.

The sociogram may show a pattern of separated subgroups or a condition of cleavage. At the middle grade years, this may be the time of extreme drawing apart of boys and girls on some test criteria. At other times, the separated subgroups may indicate that the class members are not sufficiently acquainted to choose throughout the total group, or it may reflect teaching practices. It may also be a reflection of community life that separates on ethnic, religious, or nationality grounds.

SOCIODRAMA AND ROLE PLAYING. Sociodrama, like the sociometric techniques already discussed, is an unstructured method whose successful use depends upon the understanding of the theory and skill in its use. Teachers are using it at all levels of the public schools to help students understand themselves and group problems.[6]

---

[6] Psychodrama is not included here, because it is individual-centered and treats individual problems.

It is a method in which pupils act out—or live through—experiences of importance to the group. Sociodrama is always done in a whole group, because the whole group participates in discussion and analysis. Group members who are "observers" add their ideas of what the students playing the roles might do or what their actions mean. So, too, they contribute their perceptions of the problem and they suggest possible solutions.

Sociodrama is problem-centered. Current problems in school life or in the community furnish the contents for sociodrama. An example of a current and upsetting problem to an elementary class was complaints from homeowners that children were taking short-cuts across newly seeded lawns. A high school class, upset about the behavior of visiting spectators at an athletic event, used sociodrama to develop an understanding of the problem as seen from different roles. The student who plays the role of a person whose views are opposed to his own often makes modifications in his attitudes.

Sociodrama is not a technique to be used frequently, but when well directed it can be very effective. The teacher who uses it must be alert to using problems that are real to the group and that are representative of their problems. The class and the teacher should be willing and interested in trying the method. Since there are no set rules, the teacher needs acquaintance with the literature on the topic, which is descriptive and helpful. Our concern here is not with the details of the method, but to recognize its place in the study of groups. It may be particularly revealing of group norms and goals as well as group structure.

Questionnaires

The questionnaire, like sociometric techniques, places reliance on subjects' verbal reports. While the child has a stake in answering sociometric questions honestly because he is active in putting into effect something he desires, this is not a built-in characteristic of the questionnaire. It is, of course, possible to attach such motivation to the use of questionnaires in classrooms. Pupils, for example, may complete with more care the questionnaire that follows a work or discussion period when their answers will result in changed conditions in future class periods.

In a questionnaire the information is obtained by written responses to predetermined questions. With the early primary grades, when the pupils have insufficient reading and writing skill, a series of interviews may be arranged. Interviewing was successful with kindergarten and primary children when it involved 10 relatively structured questions requiring extensive replies by the children and 10 additional questions that could be answered yes or no. The results indicated that young children were able to report reasonably well.[7] This procedure of interviewing is sometimes used with older children when additional information or explanations are not possible with written questionnaires. The time factor is a serious hindrance to systematic interviewing by classroom teachers, who accordingly make little use of this technique for data gathering.

The questionnaire is economical of administration time and its results can be easily tabulated by the teacher. The anonymity of the questionnaire encourages some students to respond more freely than they would in a public situation. Because it lacks the pressure of time limits, children answer at their own rates and give consideration to the points involved in the questions.

Questions may deal with task or nontask aspects of group life, or both. The question content may be about the designated curricular work—task goals, with a wide range of possibilities, including subject content and skills. Questioning is well suited to tapping perceptions, feelings, desires, intentions, and other nontask elements. The teacher studying his group may, at times, want to know not what are facts but what the group members *believe* to be facts; In this category are studies of the values held by group members and their perceptions of what they believe are the group values.

The form of questionnaires varies widely and may appear as an inventory or a scale. The question form ranges from the structured one, in which the respondent is permitted only a choice of alternative responses, to the unstructured or free-type response.

The structured or closed-answer questions may provide for a yes or no response, or for indicating varying degrees of approval or disapproval. The following are examples of structured questions with fixed-alternative answers.

> Did the class stay on the topic for discussion?
>
> Yes _____   No _____
>
> How well did the class stay on the topic for discussion?
>
> _____ very well
>
> _____ most of the time
>
> _____ well enough (about average)
>
> _____ some of the time
>
> _____ not at all

[7] Lee B. Sechrest, "The Motivation in School of Young Children: Some Interview Data," *Journal of Experimental Education*, 30:327–335, June 1962.

The unstructured, or "open-end" question, is designed to allow the pupil to make a free response rather than one within supplied alternatives. Open-end questions raise points or issues without giving suggestions about the answers. Here are two examples of open-end questions.

When our class has a discussion, _____

In our class discussions, I think it is best _____

There are advantages and disadvantages to both open and closed questions. The closed or structured questions are more efficient in gaining clear-cut, well-defined responses. They are most usable when facts are wanted, when all the alternatives are known, and when the students or subjects have arrived at positions or opinions. Open-end or unstructured questions are appropriate when all the alternatives are not known and when the problem or point at issue is not simple. There are times when combinations of closed and open questions are desirable.

Cumulative Records

Examination of the cumulative records of every child in a class group for over-all trends upon which to base an estimate of the whole group is a productive preparation for beginning school. Some teachers study each item that is available or in which they are interested on the cumulative records. They may note the general distribution—highs, lows, and the apparent midpoints or averages for this group of students on whatever point they are studying. Adapting a recommended method of reading essay test answers, they may take one item—for example, home background—and read the information on every record for that item only, ignoring other information for the time being. This procedure is especially well adapted to material that is descriptive and anecdotal, compared with the more exact scores and grades that are also part of cumulative records.

Group Characteristics and Related Techniques

The study of the characteristics of groups, and their interrelationships, is a logical approach to understanding groups. Some techniques appear particularly suited and more promising than others for the investigation of certain characteristics, and other techniques seem to have more general applicability. Relationships of techniques of study to group characteristics are discussed in this section. In some cases, adaptations of techniques are described. This discussion is not, however, intended as final nor as the only suitable combinations of techniques and characteristics.

Cohesiveness

Teachers who want to understand their groups are interested in cohesiveness, which they note varies widely from group to group. The "groupness," or the adhering phenomenon within a group, is one of its distinguishing marks. The question is not whether a group is or is not cohesive, but to what degree it is so. A "yes" or "no" answer to the question of cohesiveness is, of necessity, limited to a certain aspect of the group's performance and is misleading if offered as a complete answer. The investigation of cohesiveness of a group is rather an investigation into the special qualities of the group and into the causes of those qualities. There is limited evidence to draw on for some of the answers, but there are some research findings that are of help.

Cohesiveness may be approached in two ways: first, by studying how the members perceive the group and its characteristics, such as goals, interaction, structure, etc.; and second, by studying the needs of members that may be met or satisfied by the group. The rating scale may be used in either approach.

RATING SCALES. The following items are not comprehensive but are suggestive of possible content and form. They are grouped by headings that are a consequence of, or are related to, group cohesiveness—headings that would not be included in the finished scale.

The wording should be suited to the maturity level of the students who are to reply. Their maturity also indicates whether a three-point, a five-point, or more complex scale should be used as the answering stimulus that follows each question. Using the same point scale on the teacher's form might be desirable, as it would simplify the scoring.

TEACHER RATING SCALE: GROUP COHESIVENESS

1. Does the group appear to like working together?

no	sometimes	yes
1.	2.	3.

2. Do they work well in a group?

no	sometimes	yes
1.	2.	3.

3. Do they show pride in class work, activities, and achievements?

no	sometimes	yes
1.	2.	3.

4. Do they stick up for the group?

no	sometimes	yes
1.	2.	3.

5. Are they ready to defend actions of the class?

no	sometimes	yes
1.	2.	3.

6. Do they stick together against outside influences and opinions?

no	sometimes	yes
1.	2.	3.

7. Do they consider the group's goals important (whether it be spelling achievement or winning a game or a contest)?

no	sometimes	yes
1.	2.	3.

8. Does the group take responsibility for seeing that class routines and other organizational matters are accomplished, that class officers do their duties, etc.?

no	sometimes	yes
1.	2.	3.

Research findings and theory are important sources of question content in a scale or a questionnaire. Adaptations from the literature were made in constructing the items in the foregoing questionnaire. Items 1 to 3 deal with attractiveness of the group; items 4 to 6 deal with external threats; 7 with similarity of values; and 8 with responsible activity.

A pupil response to questions on cohesiveness can take either of two directions. One is the student's report of what he would do or how he would behave in situations involving cohesion; the other is the student's perception of the group's feeling and behavior in situations involving cohesiveness. The second approach is used in the following example of a student rating scale on cohesiveness. It is especially helpful to have teacher responses and pupil responses to the same items. This provides a cross-check. The following questions designed for a pupil rating sheet are numbered to refer to comparable items on the preceding teacher's sheet. The parenthetical headings define the relationships of the questions to cohesiveness; these headings would not appear on an actual form.

STUDENT RATING: GROUP COHESIVENESS

(Attractiveness of the group)
    1. Does the group enjoy working together?
(External threats)
    6. When another class says your class is using a rule wrongly in a game, does your class defend the way it uses the rule?
(Similarity of values)
    11. Does the class think that everyone should go along with what the class decides?
(Responsible activity)
    12. Do pupils in the class talk freely in giving their ideas and plans in group discussion?

The results of the rating scale have the advantage of being structured; all responses are the same kind, and they can be treated statistically.

COMPLETION SENTENCES. Sentence completion is a technique that uses selected content in partial sentences. The child completes the sentence with an unstructured conclusion. He may also add to the completed sentence with other ideas or explanations. This is used in written form with older pupils, but a short form with a few partial sentences may be used orally with younger children.

The completion sentence or open question should be worded in such a way that it does not imply an expected answer. Recent or unusual happenings may distort the answers and need to be taken into account in interpreting answers. Some attention to the timing of the exercise can help to prevent this, however. As in the rating scale, the content of the completion question should be the aspects of cohesiveness that the teacher, or other investigator, is interested in.

Some completion sentences that are designed to secure information from pupils about cohesiveness are included in the following:

COMPLETION SENTENCES: GROUP COHESIVENESS

1. Everyone thinks our class _____
2. If most of the class agrees, _____
3. The class treats everyone _____
4. My class always _____
5. When everyone else agrees, I _____
6. When working together, our class _____

7. The teacher thinks our class _____

8. If someone disagrees, they should _____

9. Whenever we discuss something in class, _____

10. When anyone says something about our class, _____

There is no agreed-upon or prescribed way to analyze the responses to completion sentences or other open, unstructured responses. The following is a procedure that is useful for some teachers.

1. Quickly read through the papers to get a survey of the responses and to get a general idea of the answers in relation to the purpose you had in mind.

2. Reread carefully, marking or underlining key words or phrases.

3. Decide on one question that you will tabulate.

4. Set up a tabulation sheet as you prefer it. Use predetermined categories or develop them from the answers.

5. Tabulate the data.

6. Interpret the results from your background with the class.

7. Select another question, possibly one that is related to the one you have analyzed, and prepare a tabulation for it, using the same process.

Structure, Communication, and Interaction

Techniques for studying structure, communication, and interaction include observation, sociometry, and interaction charts or graphs. The following suggestions are designed to aid in the analysis of the choice structure of a group as shown in a sociogram.

GUIDE TO TEACHER ANALYSIS
OF GROUP STRUCTURE IN SOCIOGRAMS

Look at the *total pattern* of the sociogram, *not* at individuals that are represented in it and do not trace relationships between individuals.

Describe the *pattern* to yourself and in your own words. This will help you to concentrate upon the group pattern. Examples of questions that will occur as you describe the pattern are the following: Is the pattern compact and integrated? Is it scattered and tentatively linked? Is it composed of tight subgroupings? Is it composed of loosely linked subgroupings? Are there completely separated subgroups? Are there closed, exclusive cliques? Are the subgroups of equal or unequal size? Do they show an equal or unequal degree of integration as shown by the amount of choosing within the subgroups?

If the criterion in the sociometric question was related to tasks or work, does the structure accurately reflect task choices? ("Halo" effect may result in choices that are made without regard to the criterion.)

Study of Classroom Groups / 381

If the criterion in the sociometric question was related to tasks or work, does the structure reflect nontask choices——that is, does it primarily meet social-emotional needs?

If the criterion question dealt with nontask or social-emotional behavior and needs, does the structure reflect nontask choices?

If the criterion question dealt with nontask or social-emotional behavior and needs, does the structure reflect task choices?

Are there any closed cliques? What is the status of the cliques? If there are cliques, have any reciprocal and defensive subgroups or cliques arisen?

What is the basis or bases of the clique choices?

academic ability	residential area
special skill	boy—girl
religion	economics
home background	out-of-school activities
national background	etc.
talent	

Are there subgroups? Identify such groupings even if they overlap, as they often do.

What are the relations between subgroups (friendly, antagonistic, competitive, etc.)? What is the relationship between popular members (sometimes termed *overchosen* or *sociometric stars*) of the subgroups? What is the relationship between the most influential members of the subgroups?

What activity, mutual interest, or achievement in the past may have given the subgroup its morale—the good feeling among members toward one another and their subgroup?

What norms are held by each subgroup? (Try to be specific. If possible, make a list for each subgroup. Some norms will appear on more than one list. A norm that is found singly may be a distinguishing mark and the basis for a subgroup. Because norms are often unstated and because direct observation or approach may be misleading, each item on the list of norms may be marked with a symbol indicating the teacher's degree of certainty for the item. A single symbol is a plus (+) when certain and a question mark (?) when uncertain.)

What are the values of the most influential members? What are the values of the popular members? (They often represent the group average, or what the members like in general or consider "good" or "ideal.")

How does the subgroup maintain itself? Are there procedures? (They may be either positive or negative.) Of what kinds? From what individuals or sources?

Communication and interaction must take place for a group to be a group. As a result of communication and interaction, the group develops its structure and other characteristics. The *ordering* of the structure is accomplished through the process of social communication and interaction. In a new class or one with many new members, the process of ordering can especially be seen as the group acquaints itself with the personalities. It is for this reason that it is recommended that sociometric techniques be used after the group has become acquainted.

In early stage, observation is perhaps the teacher's best method. Later, after sociometric data are available, analysis may be made for evidences of communication and structure.

In the ordering of the classroom structure, channels of communication are set up. Communication tends to flow, or at least does so most frequently, in established networks or channels. For example, a clique communicates among its membership also constantly in the classroom and throughout the school. It uses both verbal and nonverbal communication—language, look, gesture, expression, and posture.

A group with a broad and open communication network has members who approach each other and interact freely. Group information, news, and feelings are shared by all. Another group communication structure is one within a well-defined subgroup or clique. In such a situation, a powerful clique might have limited channels that are the primary means of its communication within its confines. It may seldom, or in a limited way, communicate with children outside its limits and whom its members perceive to be in less powerful positions.

There are, of course, other factors than the informal class structure that affect communication and interaction networks and dynamics.

The concentrations of communication channels and ideas to be communicated are shown in the center ring in Figure 6. In succeeding degrees of distance from the center are the group members who have successively less complete communication. They also have successively less access to group information.

The usual oral and nonoral interaction leave no tangible records for study by the classroom teacher. However, the sociogram gives data that may be analyzed for communication and interaction, with the caution that some choices indicate wished-for or desired relationships with other members rather than existing ones. The following is a suggested form.

TEACHER ANALYSIS: COMMUNICATION AND INTERACTION

I. Is the communication network a broad and inclusive one, in which everyone in the group can and does communicate with everyone else?

Does the communication network show differential completeness of information—that is, is all information passed on to some members or some part of the part, while others receive, in decreasing amounts, incomplete, partial, or little information?

Does the communication network show differential accessibility or information—that is, do some have full accessibility to group information while others, in decreasing amounts, have incomplete, partial, or little accessibility to group information?

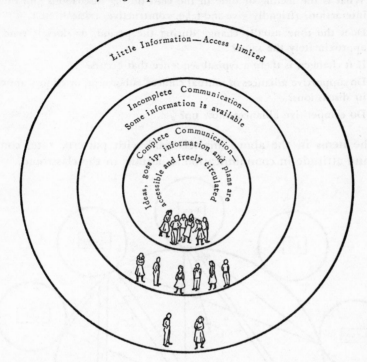

Fig. 6. Communication pattern showing differential completeness and accessibility of information.

   II. How much does the class participate in discussion? (much, some, none, etc.)

How does the class participate? (cautiously, willingly, etc.)

Are there noticeable subgroup or clique alignments in discussions?

Which subgroup, if any, monopolizes or is dominant?

What is the behavior of others?

   III. Does task behavior occupy most of the time and attention of the class?

Does nontask or social-emotional behavior occupy most of the time and attention of the class?

What is the proportion of each on specific occasions?

   IV. What kinds of contribution does the class make in a general discussion period? Recognize problems or issues? Initiate suggestions? Add facts or information? Foresee consequences? Clarify decisions? Identify weaknesses or omissions? Does the class summarize discussions? etc.

What kinds of contribution are typical of certain subgroups, if any?

V. What is the feeling or tone in the class during discussions and other interaction? (friendly give-and-take, constructive, critical, etc.)

Does the tone usually change during the period, or does it remain approximately the same?

If it changes, is there a typical sequence that occurs?

Do supportive alliances of mutual choices, subgroups, or cliques appear in discussions?

Do competitive alliances show up?

The items in the above analysis deal with pattern, rate, content, form, and attitude in communication situations in the classroom.

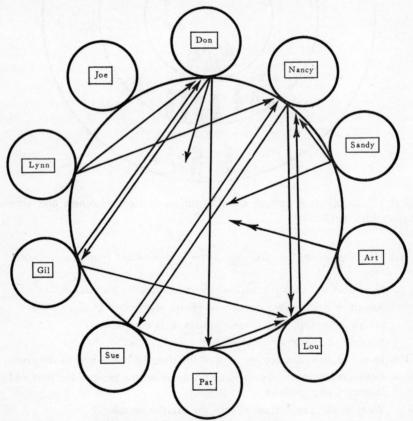

Fig. 7. An interactiongram showing speakers, receivers, and directions of oral speech.

Many of the existing techniques for studying communication and interaction require the use of one or more trained observers. They have proven value in research, but are not practical for use by teachers. One difficulty is that the teacher, as a participant–observer, is usually unable to make continuing records throughout a class period or even shorter periods of time. Some adaptation of some of the instruments is possible, however.

A check list might be made incorporating some ideas from Bales'[8] categories, for example. It could be checked following class discussions to summarize the teacher's general impressions and to direct further observation of the interaction process.

The interactiongram, or "Who Talks to Whom" diagram, is another method that can be used in the classroom. It involves making a record of who speaks, and some users also indicate the order of speaking. An advantage of the interactiongram is that it shows the relative amount of participation. In Figure 7, Nancy, an active participant, is the recipient of oral remarks from several students, and she responds, while Joe neither receives nor initiates oral attention. Art participates by general comments that are not directed to specific persons in the group. Although this apparently simple device has been successfully used, the size of classroom groups often makes its use difficult, especially if discussion is brisk. While the interactiongram shows the amount and pattern of group interaction, its limitations are that it gives no data on speech content, form, or lengths of speeches.

Norms

Groups tend to set and to conform to norms, which are standards for behavior in given situations. When a group accepts the school's values as its own, or when its informally set norms coincide with those of the school, the instructional work of the teacher is easier. The group's informally set norms may be easily observed by the teacher. Fads in dress, speech, and food are among these apparent norms. More difficult for the teacher is to recognize norms that are unstated but appear at unexpected times in behavior that seems to him puzzling and inconsistent.

REACTION STORIES. A reaction story whose plot is based on a norm may reveal to the teacher the attitudes and values of the class. The reaction story may be presented in several ways, and the responses may also be secured in more than one way. One way that has proved effective is for the teacher to read the story aloud to the group. The reading should

[8] Robert F. Bales, *Interaction Process Analysis*, Cambridge, Mass.: Addison-Wesley Press, 1950.

be prepared and delivered in a manner to arouse interest. Then each person is asked to react in writing. The teacher proposes several questions that are involved in interpreting the story and then allows adequate time for the writing. The teacher may then reread the story aloud and lead a discussion of it. The teacher has already secured the private, uninfluenced, written comments, and the oral discussion is a satisfying conclusion for the group. It may also indicate some differences in private individual norms and public, or stated, ones.

The following reaction story is suitable for primary groups and includes suggested questions to guide the writing and/or discussion. The group norm is a positive one, and the newcomer violates it.

PAUL AND THE DRUM

(Reaction Story)

Paul was a new boy in class. During the reading period everyone was working quietly. Some children were reading, others were painting, and some were doing arithmetic. Paul got up, left his seat, and went over to the music center. Suddenly he began to pound the drum. As soon as he did this, the whole class jumped up and yelled at him to sit down! The class was angry about what Paul did.

Why do you think the class was so upset?
What do you think the class should have done?
Do you think the class was upset because Paul made noise?

"The Ball Rule" is a reaction story that is usable at several elementary grade levels. One of the norms involved concerns treatment of violators of school rules.

THE BALL RULE

(Reaction Story)

It was a school rule that all balls were to be placed on the ball rack during lunch, and only monitors were to get the balls. For two days, when Marion went to get her class balls they were gone. When this happened on the third day, the class came into the room after lunch very upset. When the teacher came in, the whole class immediately told her all about the trouble. Everyone wanted the teacher to see what could be done about enforcing the rule. They wanted violators caught and kept after school.

How would you feel about this if you were a member of this class?
Do you think they were right?
What should teacher do?
Should the violators be punished? How?

The restricting of production as an accepted group norm is seen in "How Many Problems?" It is suitable to an upper elementary grade, or, with minor changes, to some high school classes.

HOW MANY PROBLEMS?

(Reaction Story)

The class had spent much of its arithmetic time during the semester on learning new processes and doing examples of them. Near the end of the semester, Mrs. Simpson began one arithmetic period by bringing out a pile of new workbooks, one for each pupil. She said, "We have been doing so much practice on our new processes in arithmetic that we haven't done many word problems. This new book has many new problems. I will give you each a book and you are to work at your own rate, doing as many problems as you can each day. I will come around and help you as you work. I will collect your papers at the end of the period, correct them, and return them to you the next day. You will just continue each day from where you left off the previous day. Word problems are important and I know you will want to do your best. You will get faster and faster and do more problems each day. Are there any questions?"

After the class had been at work for most of the period, Ed got up to sharpen his pencil. On his way he asked his friend Paul how many problems he had completed. Ed then said, "I'll only be able to get *eleven* done." Milton looked over and said, "I'll be doing well to get that many done!" Paul, who was good in arithmetic, relaxed after talking with Ed and spend the rest of the period taking pages out of his notebook and putting them back. Ed took another route from the pencil sharpener to his seat and asked Judy and Linda how many problems they had done and told them how many he expected to finish.

When Mrs. Simpson corrected the papers, she found that the pupils had done their usual careful work and had few errors. Most of the children had completed eleven problems.

The next day Paul looked at Ed during class and mouthed the word "twelve" without speaking aloud. For several days thereafter almost everyone in class handed in twelve problems—no more, although a few students handed in less than twelve.

What did the class agree to do about the number of problems?
Could they have done more had they done their best?
How did they decide what to do? What other ways than the ones in the story might have been used by the class?
What difference did it make that it was Ed and Paul who said how many problems they could do?
What could be done to make the class work more?

The norms of the group and the deviant with her proposed changes are part of the following reaction story.

A NEW PLAN

(Reaction Story)

The class had many members who had been together through elementary and high school years. Everyone went to class meetings, although they were optional. This year the class was giving the Harvest Party for the school, and plans had been underway in committees and in interested informal groups. A class meeting to complete plans was called, and as usual there was a good attendance. The class president, officers, and committees explained the entertainment, decorations, and refreshments, although everyone already knew about them. A new girl, who was majoring in art, asked permission to to speak. Nita wore her hair straight and long, while the other girls wore theirs short and curly. Her skirts were dark colored and tight, while theirs were pastels. Nita told quite simply and well about her plan for stylized decorations, but still using the Harvest theme. The committee was planning on natural decorations, with pumpkins, gourds, and colored leaves. There was polite silence with expressionless faces while Nita spoke. When she finished and sat down, Susie, a popular girl, said, "Nita's new idea is interesting, but since the plans are so far along, perhaps it would be better. . . ." Everyone chimed in, saying it was "too late to change" or that they "liked the old plan." The president considered the matter finished in accord with the majority opinion. While he went onto the next item on the agenda, a decoration committee member leaned over and asked Nita if she would like to work on the committee with them.

What do you think Nita will do?
What was the class trying to do?
How did they try to get Nita to agree with them?

Interpretation of the results of reaction stories may include comparing the group and individual norms, as already suggested. Making categories for the responses is sometimes helpful. One teacher developed the following categories:

> approval of behavior
> disapproval of behavior
> suggested a solution
> made an analysis
> misinterpreted
> made no comment

Goals

Teachers take actions every day that they hope will give their classes better unity of purpose and make them better able to achieve group goals.

The developing of goals that are clear and accepted by the group, together with the organizing and executing of efforts that result in goal achievement, is a complex and inclusive or global concept. It involves several aspects of group development, and it cannot be achieved without effective communication, a workable structure, responsible leadership, and other group characteristics.

Groups have both task and nontask goals, and both kinds are important to global, or broad and complete, achievement. The group finds it difficult to give attention to work when it is worried or anxious about social-emotional problems. The teacher must give at least some attention to the nontask goals while helping the group toward the designated curricular task goals.

RATING FORMS AND SCALES. A procedure that teachers have found valuable in helping them to observe is to develop appropriate scales or categories into which their observations can be fitted. In some schools, scales are used to help teachers record ratings of behavior without writing long reports. The categories for checking behavior on the scales are based on records teachers have made during preliminary observations of the kinds of behavior being studied. Teachers have found that the rating scales give them records adequate for their purposes. The following scale does not treat goal behavior completely, but it gives a number of relevant items for observation and checking by the teacher.

RATING SCALE FOR GROUP GOAL BEHAVIOR

1. Does the class accept task goals that are assigned?

never	seldom	sometimes	usually	always

2. Does the class accept task goals that it helps to plan?

never	seldom	sometimes	usually	always

3. Is the class efficient and effective in determining goals?

never	seldom	sometimes	usually	always

4. Are realistic goals set by the class?

never	seldom	sometimes	usually	always

5. Does the group generally perceive its goals accurately?

never	seldom	sometimes	usually	always

6. Do group goals and their related activities take precedence over conflicting individual desires?

never	seldom	sometimes	usually	always

7. Does the group produce usable, practical ideas that contribute to goal attainment?

never	seldom	sometimes	usually	always

8. Does the group suggest discrete and unrelated ideas?

never	seldom	sometimes	usually	always

9. Does the group evaluate better suggestions and make reasonable choices?

never	seldom	sometimes	usually	always

10. Does the group improve upon the plan it accepts?

never	seldom	sometimes	usually	always

11. Does the group synthesize and integrate several ideas in planning toward a goal?

never	seldom	sometimes	usually	always

12. Does the class use a variety of decision methods?

never	seldom	sometimes	usually	always

13. Does it use active consensus?

never	seldom	sometimes	usually	always

14. Does it use active voting?

never	seldom	sometimes	usually	always

15. Does it use passive consensus?

never	seldom	sometimes	usually	always

16. Does it use passive voting?

never	seldom	sometimes	usually	always

17. Does precedence, or the "usual decision," influence decisions?

never	seldom	sometimes	usually	always

18. Do leaders influence decisions?

never	seldom	sometimes	usually	always

19. Do articulate and verbal members influence decisions?

never	seldom	sometimes	usually	always

20. Do subgroups influence decisions?

never	seldom	sometimes	usually	always

Membership or Group Composition

The group is not the simple sum of the individuals in the group; the presence of other members modifies the function and the behavior of each individual. Detailed research on the personalities of the students in a class is clearly in the province of the research worker and not the classroom teacher. However, awareness of the personalities of the pupils, and some information about their backgrounds, experiences, and abilities, are fundamental to understanding and guiding a group.

INTRAGROUP RATING. Each member of the group perceives the other members' qualities and characteristics in his own way. It is helpful to the teacher to see this peer-perception of the composition of the class. One procedure that has been commonly used to obtain the reactions of a group of people to one another has been referred to as the "Guess Who?" technique. It is a method of obtaining reports from pupils by having them match their peers with a list of behavioral characteristics. The list of personal descriptions ranges from complimentary to unfavorable.

The directions describe its use: "Here are the descriptions of children you might know. See if you can guess who fits each description. You may know more than one child who fits a description, and you may write as many names as you think fit with the description. If you do not know anyone who fits, you may leave that description blank."

A list of names is provided, or the class is told not to worry about spelling but to do the best it can.

"GUESS WHO?" TEST

1. Here is someone who always seems to have a good time and enjoys himself/herself.

   _____
   _____
   _____

2. Here is someone who is always quiet, doesn't talk much, and no one seems to know very well.

———————————
———————————
———————————

3. Here is someone who makes good plans.

———————————
———————————
———————————

4. Here is someone who always works for the good of the class or of his/her team or his/her friends.

———————————
———————————
———————————

5. Here is someone who has ideas of things to do that are interesting and fun.

———————————
———————————
———————————

6. Here is someone who is popular.

———————————
———————————
———————————

7. Here is someone who breaks rules of the school and rules of games.

———————————
———————————
———————————

8. Here is someone who quarrels and gets angry.

———————————
———————————
———————————

9. Here is someone who stays out of games.

———————————
———————————
———————————

10. Here is someone who understands things quickly and easily.

_____

_____

_____

The "Guess Who?" item may be either a statement or a question. It may be:

"This person is a good leader in several things."

or

"Who are the good leaders in several things?"

A combination of "Guess Who?" and an open-end sentence is especially usable with older students. The added information of the individual's reasons for naming another person often shows a teacher some perceptions and values of which he has been unaware. Samples of this combined form are:

Everyone likes _____ because _____.

_____ is popular because _____.

The team chose _____ for captain because _____.

No one voted for _____ because _____.

No one wants to sit next to _____ because _____.

The teacher's estimate based on observations will of course add to an understanding of the group composition. Figure 8 shows an evaluation device to aid in the study of the behavior tendencies of individual

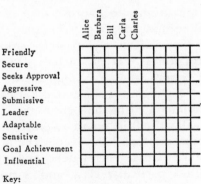

Key:

+ Much evidence of tendency

0 Average or some evidence of tendency

− Little evidence of tendency

Fig. 8. Group composition: tendencies in groups.

students in group situations. The teacher rates each student on each item by a three-point value system. A numerical score can be achieved by using a rating with figures instead of symbols. It is usual in such a comprehensive analysis for a rater to assign a score to every person in the group on one characteristic before going ahead to another characteristic.

Leadership Practices

Teachers are interested in leadership and leadership practices because they are related to group behavior and achievement. Although there is no one-to-one relationship—that is, "good" leaders do not cause "good" groups, the kind and quality of leadership do make differences in group functioning.

Trait analyses of leaders are common in the research literature on groups, and their counterparts in education are studies of teacher characteristics. Although these findings are interesting and valuable to some extent, a more promising approach is to study the leader in action. The situation of a group and its leaders is a totality, or complex, that is difficult to study as a whole, but one must study this complex in action if he is to gain understanding of the dynamics of group functioning. The teacher leadership is best studied, if possible, in such a complete setting rather than in isolation or a collection of traits.

Teachers often estimate the effects of their own leadership practices in teaching. These estimates are informal—usually "mental notes"; seldom are they written. More detailed and objective studies of their performances and of the related actions or reactions of their groups require special efforts.

Teachers who are striving to improve their teaching skills usually concentrate on finding and adopting techniques that produce desired results. Occasionally they deliberately vary their procedures to find which of several procedures seems most productive. Altered schedules, shortened or lengthened periods, and new requirements are naturally occurring changes that may highlight the effects of the changes in their practices for teachers who are interested in these effects.

A few teachers will write brief notations (anecdotal records of a kind) on practices that they have found successful. The perusal of these notes at a later date may indicate a general trend or kind of leader practice that is effective with a particular class, and, incidentally, may reveal some quality of the class.

QUESTIONNAIRES. The teacher's perception of his own leadership performance in relation to the group's behavior, can also be approached through reactions of the group. A direct question about the teacher's leadership that will elicit the "right" answers from the class is useless and a waste of time; a more indirect approach that reflects the ideas and feelings about leadership practices allows the group members to express themselves without undue embarrassment.

A reaction sheet or questionnaire to be completed by each student at the end of a class period can reflect his opinions and indicate what he values and how he perceives the teacher's leadership. The sheet should be brief, with only a few questions. It should be presented as the teacher seeking help in planning, through knowing what the group has accomplished and how the members feel about their accomplishments. It should and can be repeated at intervals to indicate changes.

REACTION SHEET: LEADERSHIP PRACTICES

1. Did you know what the lesson was about and what you were to learn? _____ yes _____ no How did you know (or not know)?
2. Did you know what to do to start your work? _____ yes _____ no How did you know what to do?
3. Did you need help in carrying out your work? _____ yes _____ no How were you helped?
4. How did you feel when you had completed your work? _____ satisfied _____ not satisfied Why did you feel that way?

The students' replies to question 1, telling how they knew what the objectives of the lesson were, can be used to estimate how effective the leader's practices were. Although the teacher may not have given personal assistance (question 3), his provisions for helping students again is an indication of effective practice. Similar questions can be added to fit different classroom situations.

ROLE PLAYING. Role playing of leadership practices will bring out data that are not available by more traditional methods. Role playing will help the students to gain insight into their own and other people's problems relating to leadership situations. Experimenting with real problems in a practice context has the value of the experimenter's not being hurt when mistakes are made. It can be tried in conjunction with other learning.

Role playing problems that could be explored by groups include the following.

Situation 1
  The teacher as leader of a classroom discussion does not provide for all pupils
  to participate—calls on ones with good ideas, the "smart" ones, favorites, etc.
Situation 2
  The teacher brings in and presents the plans made by the group the previous
  day—in changed form. Chart shows plans the group did *not* make. She took the
  class plans but wrote up hers.
Situation 3
  The teacher, in leading a discussion, did not keep on the subject, allowed any
  and all contributions, branched in all directions, did not reach goal of the
  lesson.
Situation 4
  Class had taken test and corrected it, felt very satisfied with themselves and
  their group and with what they had achieved individually and collectively.
  The teacher helped to get and maintain the good feeling.

Other Techniques

In addition to those already suggested, there are other techniques
that are generally useful for the study of group characteristics and factors.

ANECDOTAL RECORDS. Anecdotal records are a flexible way of providing an accurate and continuing record of significant behavior. The teacher
writes anecdotes of group behavior in much the same way one would make
such records about individuals. After choosing an incident that is judged
of significance in revealing something about the group, the teacher writes
the anecdote as a short, clear word picture. It includes the time and situation, the children or groups involved, and exactly what happened, including what was said and done. Descriptions of emotional reactions are included as part of the record.

If a few anecdotes are written each week, a descriptive record of
group behavior soon accumulates. It may be analyzed for a number of
factors: group growth and change, recurring patterns, effects of particular
situations, and group characteristics. Just as "significance" can be used as
the criterion for selection, so can actions that represent a special kind of
behavior. Groups of teachers find it valuable to choose types of group
behavior that are of interest or concern to them and to select and record
incidents in which these types of behavior are manifested. Illustrative
choices are goal behavior, communication, and norm behavior.

TIME SAMPLING. Records that sample naturally occurring behavior at
designated times and for given periods of time are provided by the technique of time sampling. The sample is obtained by the observation of the
teacher or other observer. This technique is practical for teachers, because

the duration of the observation is short. For example, a time sample may be taken for one minute each day at 9:30. The observation may be specifically to see if a certain kind of behavior occurs in that period, or it may be designed to take a free, unstructured record of the period. The former, sampling with a predetermined objective, is usual. A work sheet is usually prepared and a symbol system used for speed in recording. The record is, of course, susceptible to analysis because of its quantitative aspects. Care ought to be taken to observe at different times of the day to get a balance of classroom activities and related behaviors.

GROUP BIOGRAPHY. A common technique used by teachers for gaining understanding of individuals is to have students write autobiographies. This is frequently an assignment in high school English classes, and it is sometimes done for guidance purposes. It is also done at the elementary school level.

The writing of the biography of the group in addition to or instead of the usual individual autobiographies will provide the teacher with added insights into both the group and individuals. At the primary level, the group composition technique will be useful. The children have limited abilities with writing skills and may need the assistance of one another to conceptualize and verbalize their experiences in the school group and the assistance of the teacher to make the written record. The teacher's questions and suggestions may aid recall of ideas and experiences that would otherwise be omitted. The teacher may suggest a beginning sentence by asking, "What kind of group of boys and girls are we?" or "How long have we been together as a class?" etc.

An intermediate grade assignment or project in the writing of a group biography may be started with a group discussion recalling the experiences of the class through the years, the changes, outstanding events, etc. At intermediate grade level, when children have adquate abilities to write individually, they may still profit by some guiding remarks. If the class population has been stable, or relatively so, there will be much shared recall. If there has been an unstable and changing population, the biography will take on more individual than shared experiences. The children can write on the kinds of group experience they have had in different grades and in different schools, on their most pleasant group experiences, etc.

High school groups face a different situation from the more stable and perennial classroom groups in elementary schools. In addition to tracing a variety of classroom group experiences he has had, a high school student is likely to offer analyses of successful and unsuccessful group functioning. His analyses may include his perceptions of his roles and contributions in groups. He will also be able to specify the kinds of group situation in which he achieves best, feels most rewarded, and most enjoys the tasks or activities.

The group biography is a summary technique involving many group characteristics that have been revealed in the unfolding story. Although the teacher may provide some structure through stimulating questions, the device is essentially free and adaptable.

A GUIDE TO INTERRELATED CHARACTERISTICS. The following questionnaire, which includes many facets of group behavior, can be used as a guide to observation. Short descriptive answers can be written, or a scale-type or multiple-response answer can be used. Because the questionnaire directs attention to specifics of group functioning, its repetition at spaced intervals will yield useful data on changes and trends in group development.

OBSERVATION GUIDE TO GROUP BEHAVIOR

1. How does the group react to daily routines?
2. How does the group react to new situations?
3. How does the group react to sudden, unexpected changes?
4. Does the group wait for certain leaders to react before it acts?
5. Does the group wait for the teacher to indicate how to react?
6. Does the group choose the same leaders for many and differing situations?
7. How does the group act when certain leaders are absent?
8. Does the group "use" a member as a scapegoat or to otherwise vent its feelings?
9. How does the group treat a new child?
10. Does the group unite behind a group project?
11. Are there subgroups or cliques that compete with others or that hold aloof from the class?
12. Is the group conduct guided by rules that it makes or helps to make?
13. Is there open communication and sharing of plans and information throughout the whole group?
14. Is there satisfaction throughout the group with group accomplishments?
15. Are there any divisions or coalitions based on sex, race, religion, etc.?
16. How does the group react with different teachers?
17. What kinds of pressure does the group use to encourage or urge conformity?
18. What proportions of time and effort does the group put into task behavior and nontask behavior?

Teachers, administrators, and supervisors, in their close and continuing association with classroom groups, have varied and rich opportunities to study the problems of developing groups. The study of these groups may take the form of observing and making unwritten "mental notes," or it may use the most careful and precise modern research methods. Either approach—or one in between—may yield valuable results in increased understanding and insights on the part of the adults who lead children's groups and in improved conditions of pupils' group lives.

Questions for Study and Discussion

1. Indicate some factors that make it difficult for a teacher to observe objectively and dispassionately.

2. List ways to improve the objectivity and accuracy of observing by a teacher.

3. Some teachers feel that they are influenced by reading other teachers' reports. Should they avoid using the cumulative record folders for preliminary acquaintance with a group?

4. What precautions should be taken in constructing a questionnaire to get as accurate and useful results as possible?

5. If you have used sociometric techniques, describe the situation, procedure, and results.

6. If you have not had experience with sociometric techniques, interview a teacher who has and inquire about her views.

7. Why is it recommended that interviews be used following sociometric tests?

8. Do some teachers find sociometric techniques more valuable in their work than do other teachers? Why?

9. List advantages and disadvantages of sociometric techniques.

10. Select one group characteristic in which you are interested. Plan how you would study a classroom group's changes in that characteristic over a semester or a year.

11. Write a reaction story following these steps:
    (a) Choose the age-grade level.
    (b) Select a problem situation that is appropriate to the level.
    (c) Write the problem using fictitious names and details to add realism; incorporate several clues.
    (d) Try it with a group, if possible, or with individuals if a group is not available.
    (e) Report your results.

12. Why should the role-playing technique not be overused?

13. Is dramatic play in the kindergarten and early primary grades comparable to role playing in older age-groups?

14. From additional reading, prepare a short report on the place of the teacher in guiding role playing.

Suggestions for Further Reading

American Council on Education. *Helping Teachers Understand Children.* Washington, D.C.: American Council on Education, 1945.

Association for Supervision and Curriculum Development. *Fostering Mental Health in Our Schools.* Washington, D.C.: National Education Association (1950 Yearbook).

Bales, Robert F. *Interaction Process Analysis: A Method for the Study of Small Groups.* Cambridge, Mass.: Addison-Wesley, 1950.

Bogen, Isidore. "Pupil–Teacher Rapport and the Teacher's Awareness of Status Structures Within the Group," *The Journal of Educational Sociology,* 28:104–114, November 1954.

Bonney, Merl E. "A Sociometric Study of Some Factors to Mutual Friendships on the Elementary, Secondary, and College Levels," *Sociometry,* 9:21–47, 1946.

Brieland, Donald. "A Variation of the 'Guess Who' Technique for the Study of the Adjustment of Children," *Journal of Educational Research,* 45:385–390, January 1952.

Bronfenbrenner, Urie. "A Constant Frame of Reference for Sociometric Research," *Sociometry,* 6:363–397, 1943.

Bronfenbrenner, Urie. "A Constant Frame of Reference for Sociometric Research: II. Experiment and Inference," *Sociometry,* 7:40–75, 1944.

Byrd, E. "A Study of Validity and Constancy of Choices in a Sociometric Test," *Sociometry,* 14:175–181, 1951.

Cantor, Ralph R., Jr. "The Use of Extended Control-Group Designs in Human Relations Studies," *Psychological Bulletin,* 48:340–347, July 1951.

Carter, Launor F. "Evaluating the Performance of Individuals as Members of Small Groups," *Personnel Psychology,* 7:477–484, Winter 1954.

Cartwright, Dorwin and Alvin Zander (eds.). *Group Dynamics, Research and Theory.* Evanston, Ill.: Row, 1960.

Criswell, Joan H. "Social Structure Revealed in a Sociometric Retest," *Sociometry,* 2:69–75, 1939.

Damrin, Dora E. "The Russell Sage Social Relations Test: A Technique for Measuring Group Problem Solving Skills in Elementary School Children," *Journal of Experimental Education,* 28:85–99, September 1959.

Festinger, Leon and Daniel Katz (eds.). *Research Methods in the Behavioral Sciences.* New York: Dryden, 1953.

Gardner, Eric F. and George G. Thompson. *Social Relations and Morale in Small Groups.* New York: Appleton, 1956.

Gold, Martin. "Power in the Classroom," *Sociometry,* 21:50–59, March 1958.

Gronlund, Norman E. *Sociometry in the Classroom.* New York: Harper, 1959.

Hale, Patricia W. "Proposed Method for Analyzing Sociometric Data," *Research Quarterly of the American Association for Health, Physical Education, and Recreation,* 27:152–161, May 1956.

Hare, A. Paul. *Handbook of Small Group Research.* New York: Free Press, 1962.

Harvey, O. J. and Jeanne Rutherford. "Status in the Informal Group: Influence and Influencibility at Differing Age Levels," *Child Development,* 31:377–385, 1960.

Heber, R. F. and Mary E. Heber. "The Effect of Group Failure and Success on Social Status," *Journal of Educational Psychology,* 48:129–134, 1957.

Hemphill, John K. and Charles M. White. "The Measurement of Group Dimensions," *The Journal of Psychology,* 29:325–342, 1950.

Heyns, R. W. and Ronald Lippitt. "Systematic Observational Techniques," in G. Lindzey (ed.), *Handbook of Social Psychology.* Cambridge, Mass.: Addison-Wesley, 1954.

Jenkins, David H. "Interdependence in the Classroom," *Journal of Educational Research,* 45:137–144, October 1951.

Jennings, Helen Hall and others. *Sociometry in Group Relations.* Washington, D.C.: American Council on Education, 1948.

Jensen, Gale E. "The Social Structure of the Classroom Group: An Observational Framework," *The Journal of Educational Psychology,* 46:362–374, October 1955.

Levit, Grace and Helen H. Jennings. "Learning through Role Playing," in Warren G. Bennis, Kenneth D. Benne, and Robert Chin (eds.), *The Planning of Change; Readings in the Applied Behavioral Sciences.* New York: Holt, 1961.

Lindzey, G. and Edward F. Borgatta. "Sociometric Measurement," in G. Lindzey (ed.), *Handbook of Social Psychology.* Cambridge, Mass.: Addison-Wesley, 1954.

Mitchell, James V. "The Factor Analysis of a 'Guess Who' Questionnaire Designed to Identify Significant Behavior Patterns in Children," *Journal of Personality,* 24:376–386, June 1956.

Moreno, J. L. *Who Shall Survive?* New York: Beacon House, 1953.

Northway, Mary L. *A Primer of Sociometry.* Toronto, Canada: U. of Toronto, 1952.

Sellitz, Claire, Marie Jahoda, Morton Deutsch, and Stuart W. Cook. *Research Methods in Social Relations.* New York: Holt, 1959.

Shaw, Marvin E. "Some Effects of Individually Prominent Behavior upon Group Effectiveness and Member Satisfaction," *The Journal of Abnormal and Social Psychology,* 59:382–386, November 1959.

Smith, M. "Some Factors in the Friendship Selections of High School Students," *Sociometry,* 7:303–310, 1944.

Sokoloff, Myron A. "Socio Drama—Effective Approach to Guidance," *Scholastic Teacher—Senior Scholastic,* 78, No. 15, 4–7, May 17, 1961.

Thompson, George G. "Children's Groups," in Paul H. Mussen (ed.), *Handbook of Research Methods in Child Development.* New York: Wiley, 1960.

Withall, J. "An Objective Measurement of a Teacher's Classroom Interaction," *Journal of Educational Psychology*, 47:203–212, April 1956.

Wright, Herbert F. "Observational Child Study," in Paul H. Mussen (ed.), *Handbook of Research Methods in Child Development*. New York: Wiley, 1960.

Wrightstone, J. Wayne. "Teacher-Made Tests and Techniques," *Educational Leadership*, 19:170–172, 199–200, December 1961.

Zeleny, Leslie D. "Sociometry of Morale," *American Sociological Review*, 4:799–808, 1939.

Index

Index

Ability grouping
  effects, 61–62, 88–91
  reading, 87–88
Acceptance
  desire for, 179
  goal, 177, 189
Achievement, goal, 37, 92, 174–175
Action research, 12
Activities
  classroom, 65–66
  goal, 171–172
Aggression
  communication of, 90, 98–99
  and hostility, 263–266
  overt acts, 149–150
Anecdotal records, 369
Anxiety, 91–92
Apathy, *see* Passive Reactions

Approval
  group, 123
  individual, 124
Atmosphere, 36, 41, 42, 60, 227, 229, 244
Attitudes
  change of, 23–27, 234, 318–319
  examples of change, 319–336
  expectation, 127, 128
  influence, 37, 121
  revelation of, 112–113
  teacher, 121, 203, 207–213, 232, 241
  toward self, 92
Attraction to group, 36, 53, 61, 64–66, 72–73, 103
Attractiveness
  of activities, 65–66
  experimental investigations, 65

Attractiveness (*cont'd*)
  group, 64–66, 72–74
  verbal interaction and, 59–60
Autokinetic effect, 126

Behavior change
  class group, 119
  discussion and, 303–304
  ethical aspect, 23–27
  examples, 309–318
  and frustration, 254, 286
  resistance to, 292–294
  through decision, 287–290
Behavior problems, 14–15, 42–43, 90,
  132, 265, 297
Belongingness, 36, 39, 52

Classroom groups
  characteristics, 43–45
  cleavage, 60
  communication in, 109–113
  composition, 46–47, 60
  control, 5, 7, 30–31, 47
  definition, 32
  formation, 79, 116
  interaction and, 213–215
  membership, 47
  nature, 45–47
  organization, 79, 85–86
  purpose, 46
Cleavage, group, 60, 197, 203, 373
Climate, 23–25, 227–229
Codes, 119, 124
Cohesiveness
  attraction to activities, 64–66
  attraction to group, 36, 64–66, 85–86
  cohesive force, 12, 57, 175
  consequences, 56–58
  cooperation and competition, 67–70,
    175
  definition, 36, 52–53
  determinants, 54–56, 70
  disruptive forces, 57–58, 79
  factors affecting, 54–56, 102–103
  goals and, 175
  interaction, 59–60
  intergroup hostility, 56–57, 69
  leadership style, 70–71
  measures of, 53–54
  needs of members, 36, 57

pressure and, 12, 37, 57
  prestige hierarchy, 60–62
  productivity, 56–57, 175–176
  study of, 377–380
  threat and, 61–62, 70–71
Common motives, 36–37
Communication
  aggression and, 90–91
  aggression reduction, 149–150
  cohesiveness and, 59, 102–103
  deflection, 59
  factors, 101–109
  frequency, 60
  goals and, 180
  in hierarchy, 90–91
  intergroup, 34, 110–113
  need for, 113
  networks, 81, 94
  nonverbal, 113
  patterns, 81, 106–108
  pressure and, 98–99, 149–150
  size of group and, 104–105
  study of, 380–385
Completion sentences, 379–380
Concepts, group dynamics, 4, 17–18
Conflict, 56–57, 69, 78
Conformity, 25–27, 38, 57, 117, 122,
  148–149
Contagious behavior, 264, 270–272
Control practices, 70–72, 241–244
Cooperation and competition
  effects, 19, 67–68
  example, 69
  investigations of, 67–69, 176, 244–245
Cooperative groups, 109–110
Criticisms, group, 17–21
Cumulative records, 376
Customs, 119

Deviant behavior
  ability lack, 150–151
  causes, 143–153
  conformity and, 140
  consequences, 153
  goals and, 184–186
  high-status member, 145–146
  lack of perception and, 147–148
  nature of, 142–146
  from norms, 141, 243
  patterns, 144–145

subgroup, 143
Deviate
communication to, 148–150
individuals, 143, 145–146, 147, 150–151, 152
punishment, 146–147
rejection, 143
Diary recording, 369
Disapproval
communication of, 123
fear of, 135
illustration, 135–136
Discipline, 4–7, 30–31, 296
Discussion, group
decision and, 178, 290–295, 301–307
disapproval, 123–124
goal achievement, 176–177
leadership and, 102–103, 180, 235–236, 301–307
skills, 133
spatial factors, 107–109
Disruption of group
change and, 80
communication, 98–99
decreased valence, 96–98
disruptive forces, 53, 58, 79
Dynamic group, 18–19

Ethnic origins, 203–204
Evaluation
decision techniques, 307–309
by teacher, 243–244
Expectations
group members, 58–59, 130, 211
shared, 117, 128
teacher, 141–142, 211–212

Factions, girl-boy, 185
Fads, 119
Feedback, 95–101
Formal groups, 39, 41, 44–45
Friendliness, group, 55–56
Frustration
age reaction, 257–260, 267–270
aggression, 72, 254
causes, 94, 101
consequences, 72, 272–279
definition, 253–255
degree of, 206–262
factors involved, 255–257

group reaction, 72, 262, 272–279
tolerance of, 257

Goal, group
acceptance of, 160, 173–178, 180
achievement, 174, 179
characteristics, 164–167
classroom, 31–32
cooperation and competition, 67–69, 175
description, 36–37, 159, 163–164
dimensions, 167–168
effects on individual, 32, 174, 178–179, 187–188
expectations, 159
imposed, 176–177, 186–187
inducing agent, 37, 174, 179
intermediate, 166–168
locomotion, 162
long-range, 165–166
nature, 165, 167–168
nontask, 37, 170–173, 184–186, 187
prescribed, 41, 46
study of, 388–391
task, 46, 167–169, 170–173, 179
varied concepts, 159–164
Goal, individual, 19, 36, 158, 159, 160, 161, 163
Goal-directed behavior, 37, 163, 164
Goal operation, 162–163, 173–174
Goal planning, 182
Group
attributes, 38–39
composition, 46–47
concept, 30–31
definition, 31–33
forces, 12–14, 138–139, 185–186, 198
influence, 127
maintenance, 37
need satisfaction, 32, 37
power, 187–188
processes, 13, 19, 21
relations, 20, 186
size, 36, 60, 104–105, 182
Group biography, 397–398
Group characteristics
cohesiveness, 36, 52–53
dimensions, 39
goals, 36
interaction, 34–35, 59–60

Group characteristics (*cont'd*)
  norms, 36
  patterning, 38
  structure, 35–36
  study of, 376–377
Group decision techniques
  discussion, 290–292, 294–295, 301–307
  evaluation, 307–309
  factors, 290–292
  goals and, 294
  and group power, 309
  lecture, 293
  participatory, 292–293
  processes, 295–307
  studies of, 287–290
Group dynamics
  application, 11
  concepts for analyzing, 8, 18
  criticisms, 20
  description, 18–19
  purpose of research, 7, 17, 22
  research findings, 7, 13
Group influence, 11, 119
Group maintenance, 58
Group planning, 19, 60, 177
Group properties
  dimensions, 33
  nature, 43–45
  see also Group characteristics
Group standards
  classroom, example, 142
  teacher-imposed, 118
Group variables
  dimensions, 4, 33–39
  nature, 33–39
Grouping
  effects, 12–14, 61, 86–87, 89
  formal and informal, 41–42, 85
  heterogeneous, 87
  homogeneous, 87
  for learning, 92–93
  reading for, 87, 93
Guess Who test, 209–210, 391–394

Hidden agenda, 37, 171–172
Hierarchy
  behavioral effects, 84
  communication, 103–104
  in structure, 36, 61, 82, 84, 103–104
Homogeneous grouping, 87

Hostility
  communication, 95
  cooperation and competition, 67–69
  frustration and, 259, 263–266
  intergroup, 60
  interteam, 61–62
  leadership and, 230
  structure, 84
Human relations
  example, 172–173
  factors affecting, 202–213
  problem of, 172
  problem solving, 171–173

Identification, 134–135
Imitiative behavior, 270–272
Incentives, 188
Individual
  goals and, 19, 36
  and group, 13, 15–17
Inducing agents, 117
Informal groups, 41
Integration, 53, 184, 189, 240
Interaction
  analysis of process, 34–35
  attraction to group and, 80
  effects, 32
  elements comprising, 34, 80–81
  example, 34–35, 78, 80
  goal striving and, 178–179
  guides, 120
  meaning, 32, 34, 77–80
  member characteristics and, 196–198,
    213–215
  patterns, 77, 80–81, 198–199
  size of group, 104–106
  social, 32
  structure and, 79, 213–215
  study of, 380–385
  system, 31
  teacher-pupil, 59
Interactiongram, 384
Isolates, 149

Kindergarten
  control practices, 241–242
  and frustration, 257–258, 267–268

Leader
  characteristics, 220, 246–247

pupil, 123, 182
restrictive practices, 70–71, 176–177, 240–241
Leadership
autocratic, 178, 221, 226, 228, 235, 246
climate and, 227–230
cohesiveness and, 236–237
communication and, 101–102, 223–224
definition, 221
democratic, 221, 226, 228
evaluation, 243–244
functions, 85, 220–221
goals, 41, 176
group-centered, 103, 228
influence, 27, 221, 226, 246–248
informal, 41
laissez-faire, 221
leader-centered, 103
morale and, 178, 234, 238
participatory, 101–102, 234–235
shared, 220
situational determinants, 222–226
size of group and, 105–106, 223
structure and, 224
supervisory, 101–102, 234–235
Leadership styles
comparison, 219, 230–237
group-centered, 16, 230–234
teacher-centered, 230–234
Learning
cohesiveness and, 57
competition and, 67–69, 176
skills, 93
Level of aspiration, 182–184
Locomotion, group, 162

Maintenance, group, 184–185
Member characteristics
age differences, 196–197
personality traits, 198–201
sex differences, 197–198
Member satisfaction, 64–66, 73
Membership, group
composition, 195–196
effects, 213–215
study, 391–394
Morale
communication and, 79, 94

group relations and, 42, 57, 178
improving, 318–326
productivity and, 170
structure and, 69
Mores, 116
Motivation
competition and, 67–69
group, 57, 178
leadership and, 240
Motives, group, 36–37

Needs
affiliation, 65
basic, 36, 39
expectations, 165
group, 32, 165
individual, 32, 65, 66
Network, communication, 81, 94
Newcomers, 58–59
Noncohesiveness, 63
example, 64
Nonoperational goals, 169–173
Normative behavior, *see* Norms
Norms
characteristics, 37–38, 120–124
class group, 56
conformity to, 38, 56, 117, 122, 124, 125–127, 133–138
definition, 119–120
deviation from, 139–142
deviations, 142–143
dimensions, 121
evaluative nature, 120
formation and functioning, 123, 128–130
as inducing agents, 117, 118, 122
intensity, 124
nature, 117–119
perception of, 119
sharing, 56
sources, 128–130
study of, 385–388
teacher, 116, 118–119

Observation, 366–367
Observation guide, 398
Operating consensus, 160–161
Operational goals, 169–173
Organization
class group, 39, 80, 85–86

Organization (*cont'd*)
  formal and informal, 41–42
Ostracism, 37–38

Participation
  amount, 180–182
  goal setting and, 179
  group size and, 182
  members and, 26, 180, 186, 200–201
  personal involvement and, 292–295
Participatory leadership, 101–102
Passive reactions, 267–270
Peer group
  influence, 117
  prestige, 89
  standards, 134–135
Personality
  behavior and, 13
  characteristics, 198–200
  conformity and, 25–27
  group, 38–39
  self-acceptance, 202
  traits, 198–201
  variations, 198–201
Planning
  change, 59
  goal achievement, 56, 182, 188
Power of group
  aspiration and, 182–184
  cohesiveness and, 57
  communication and, 98–99
  examples, 309–318
  goal achievement and, 187–189
  pressure, 122, 129, 133, 136–137, 185, 187–188
  productivity and, 187–189
  standards and, 57
  types, 136–137
Prejudice, 39, 204
Pressure
  change and, 246, 327
  cohesiveness and, 64–66
  to communicate, 98–99, 145
  example, 185–186
  hostility and, 149–150
  teacher, 110
Primary group, 40
Problem solving
  activities, 171–172

diagnosis, 332–333
  examples, 111–112, 353–359
  group, 18, 100–101
  processes, 100, 351–352
  research, 346–348
  steps, 351–352
Productivity
  achievement and, 41–42, 44–45, 188–189
  cohesiveness and, 57, 187–188
  competition and, 67–69
  goals and, 176, 187–189
  incentives and, 188
  leadership, 101–102, 176, 189, 234–235
  morale and, 56–57, 170
Properties, group
  cohesiveness, 51–52, 66
  dimensions, 39
  interrelatedness, 33–34
  nature, 36–39

Questionnaires, 374–375

Rating scales, 377–380, 389–391
Reaction stories, 385–388
Rebel, 274–276
Regression, 270
Rejection
  communication and, 90–91
  example, 152–153
Restrictive practices, 70–72, 99–100
Ridicule, 134
Role playing, 373–374
Roles, 53, 82, 83

Sabotage, 42
Sanctions, positive, 133
Scapegoat, 276–279
Seating, classroom group, 108–109
Self-expectation, 91–92
Size of group
  change and, 79–80
  communication, 104–106
  goals and, 182
  leadership, 105–106, 223
  member satisfaction, 105
  structure, 105, 182
  variations, 39

Skill learning, 93
Social acceptability, 181, 201–202
Social behavior, 200
Social class
  background, 86
  differences, 204–206
  grouping, 86
Social relations
  age differences, 196
  range, 34
  member characteristics and, 214
  sex differences, 197–198
Social status, 181
Social stratification, 36
Social systems, 36, 43
Socialization, 25, 196–197
Sociodrama, 373–374
Sociograms, 60, 371, 373, 380
Sociometric techniques, 151, 371–373
Solidarity
  degree, 54
  example, 54–55
Spatial factors, 94, 106–109
Standardization of behavior, 37
Standards, group
  changing, 298
  conformity, 37, 119
  demonstration, 56, 118
  force of, 26
  goals, 161
  group decision, 309–318
  nonconformity and rejection, 98–99,
    118, 286
  performance and, 184
  reactions, 26
Status
  ascribed, 61–62, 91
  cliques and, 60
  effects, 61–62, 103–104, 180
  group conformity and, 138–139
  hierarchy, 103, 266
  individual urge to achieve, 151
  mobility, 61
  rise in, 181
  struggle for, 60
  systems, 210–211
  teacher judgment, 212–213
  terms indicating, 83
Stereotypes, 225–226

Stress, 57, 93
Structure
  adjustment of individual, 91
  communication, 90–91, 153
  creation, experimental, 60–61
  development, 35–36, 85
  effects, 224–225
  example, 84, 90
  formal and informal, 41, 81, 85
  group, 41, 47, 60–62
  interrelated network, 79
  nature, 82–84
  organization, 85, 224
  position in, 60–62, 83, 90–92
  prescribed, 60, 81
  security of individual, 91–93
  status struggle, 61–62
  study of, 380–382
Subgoals, 166–168, 173
Subgroups, 36, 59, 60, 61, 69–70, 84,
    231–232
Supervisory leadership, 101–102
Syntality, 38

Task
  acceptance, 175, 189
  achievement, 187, 189
  behavior, 57
  goal relationships, 161, 167–168,
    170–173
  imposed, 178
  leader, 47, 224
  objectives, 179
  performance, 41, 49, 170, 171–172,
    174, 175, 183
  prescribed, 41, 46, 177–178
Task motivation, 176–177, 187, 228
Teacher, as leader
  control practices, 41
  dependency on, 270
  functions, 237–238, 240
  goals, 174, 238–239
  influence, 179, 180–181, 246–248
  personality, 246–247
  studies of, 240–246
  training, 238–239
  traits, 246–247
Teacher education, 12–15, 22–23

Teaching practices
  communication, 95–96, 109–114
  discussion, 301–307
  effects, 226–234, 278–279
  evaluation, 243–244
  frustrating, 278–279
  goal acceptance, 173–174
  goal setting, 160, 238–239
  group-centered, 103, 236
  leader-centered, 103, 234–237
  punitive, 241
  study of, 240–246, 394–396
Threat, 71, 133, 243
Time sampling, 370–371, 396–397
Traditions, 119
Traits, individual, 198–199
Types of groups
  classroom, 45–47

  primary, 40–41
  work, 41–43

Value system, 137, 139
Values
  change of, 23–24
  effect on behavior, 139
  example, 140–141
  expressed in groups, 37–38, 119, 214
  shift in, 122
  teacher, 121
Verbal interaction, 103

Withdrawal, 267–270
Work groups, 41–42, 45–46
  positions in, 89–90
Work standards, class group, 57